THE JOHN GOULD FLETCHER SERIES
Volume II

Lucas Carpenter, General Editor

John Gould Fletcher

THE AUTOBIOGRAPHY OF JOHN GOULD FLETCHER

ORIGINALLY *LIFE IS MY SONG*

Edited by Lucas Carpenter

Introduction by Ben Kimpel

The University of Arkansas Press
Fayetteville *1988* *London*

Originally published as *Life is My Song*

Manufactured in the United States of America
92 91 90 89 88 5 4 3 2 1

DESIGNER: Chiquita Babb
TYPEFACE: Linotron 202 Baskerville
TYPESETTER: G&S Typesetters, Inc.
PRINTER: Thomson-Shore, Inc.
BINDER: John H. Dekker & Sons, Inc.

The paper used in this publication meets the minimum requirements of the American National Standard for Permanence of Paper for Printed Library Materials Z39.48-1984. ∞

LIBRARY OF CONGRESS CATALOGING-IN-PUBLICATION DATA

Fletcher, John Gould, 1886–1950.
[Life is my song]
The autobiography of John Gould Fletcher: originally Life is my song/edited by Lucas Carpenter with an introduction by Ben Kimpel.
p. cm.—(The John Gould Fletcher series ; v. 2)
Reprint. Originally published: Life is my song. New York: Farrar & Rinehart, c1937.
Includes index.
ISBN 1-55728-031-2 (alk. paper)
1. Fletcher, John Gould, 1886–1950—Biography. 2. Poets, American—20th century—Biography. I. Carpenter, Lucas, II. Title. III. Series: Fletcher, John Gould, 1886–1950. Works. 1988; v. 2.
PS3511.L457 vol. 2
811′.52—dc19 87-34660
[B] CIP

CONTENTS

GENERAL EDITOR'S PREFACE

The Autobiography of John Gould Fletcher originally appeared in 1937 as *Life Is My Song*, a title rendered tragically ironic by Fletcher's subsequent suicide in 1950. As the late Ben Kimpel, a longtime friend of Fletcher, points out in his insightful introduction to this volume, Fletcher had more than his share of personal misfortunes, including a failed marriage, a poetic career that fell victim to the vagaries of literary fame, and increasingly severe bouts with manic depression, but these did not prevent him from writing a remarkably candid and straightforward account of a life lived near the tumultuous center of the modernist movement in both England and America. *The Autobiography of John Gould Fletcher* is therefore noteworthy not only as the intriguing and often moving story of a poet's life but also as a crucial document in charting the history of literary modernism.

Lucas Carpenter
Oxford College of Emory University

INTRODUCTION

Towards the end of his autobiography, Fletcher speaks of having made "the supremely fatal mistake of supposing at twenty-one that I must be a poet." This need not be taken literally as an unconditional regret. He *was* a poet, an ambitious one, and was still writing poetry; for many years he had been serious about finding new ways to express himself. His best known and probably most successful work had been written a quarter of a century earlier—the color symphonies—but that work was only one stage in a varied output. Fletcher was discouraged by his comparative obscurity after a long career which at one time had seemed on the verge of success. But he still hoped that some of his poems would survive—and some probably will.

Aside from the degree of his achievement as a poet, his autobiography is one of a large number of accounts of the troubles of the artist in the modern world, specifically in America (though Fletcher's task was no easier in England). It has a good deal to say about what the people involved thought of the movement (or rather movements) still known as Modernism—particularly, but not only, of Imagism. As one would expect, Fletcher speaks of the people he met, including many of the key figures of twentieth-century literature; he is never gossipy, but he has a knack for thumbnail character sketches. Of all these personalities, the one that comes across most strongly is his own.

It is not easy to find an artist with a good word to say for the modern world (or for the world of any age); Fletcher's complaints are familiar, but not clichés. Even before he met another poet, he was devoted to Beauty (one must capitalize the word, and also Art, in this environment). He was one of a number of writers in his generation who did not think of success in financial terms, though when his modest inheritance proved inadequate to support his family, he had to think about money. Greed and the kind of publicity it encourages were his enemies from the beginning. They offended not only his artistic creed but his Southern gentility. "This age, though it has produced remarkable poets, cannot be said to be an age in any way favorable to poetry." The democratic standard of taste was as hostile to poetry as commercialism. Like all the leading Modernists, Fletcher was forced to think in terms of an intellectual elite.

Initially he appears to be a classic exile. He had never been a part of his birthplace, Little Rock, Arkansas; when he went to school and college in New England, he was not a part of them either. He felt, as many writers have, that he learned little at college, and he left Harvard without a degree. He went to Europe in search of a richer life, of the cultural things his mother had taught him to value, though she was strongly opposed to the search.

It has usually been assumed in America (and in other countries) that the finer things are fine as long as one does not take them seriously. Fletcher took them seriously. Historical imagination is needed to recognize how thoroughly Americans at the beginning of the century were convinced that art and thought were foreign products. Fletcher went first, naturally, to the home of Beauty—Italy—in the footsteps of Ruskin. Loneliness soon drove him to England which was to be his home (with visits to France and longer visits to America) for over two decades. But he often felt like an exile in England, also. He would probably not have stayed so long if that typical late Victorian disease—frustrated sexuality with unwilling innocence—had not gotten him involved with the older woman he eventually married and then felt he had to support. Though not at all pornographic, his account of this strange and miserable affair is quite frank. But in England he also met poets, notably Ezra Pound, who were taking poetry seriously; and after some early conventional verse, Fletcher found his own voice.

He was also typical (I do not, of course, mean average) in foreseeing an end to civilization as he defined it. It is one of the striking phenomena of our century that at the height of the apparent success of western civilization (before the First World War) some people began seeing it as a failure. During the War Fletcher predicted that European culture would not survive. Whether or not it did survive can still be debated. Posterity is always right, since its opposition is dead and can safely be ignored, and for the moment we are posterity. Fletcher's contemporaries cannot question whether we are civilized in a sense recognizable by Ovid or Chaucer or Voltaire or Henry James. Fletcher speculated about whether or not America would take over the role of lightbearer, but after some hope he concluded that it would not; America could not create, it could only absorb a decadent European culture. His book *The Two Frontiers*—never absorbed by the public nor even the critics—left no doubt that he thought the Soviet Union had as little to offer as the United States. It is no wonder that he was impressed by the gloomy view of Spengler's *Decline of the West.*

His personal difficulty was a perennial one: there was no way to turn poetry into a livelihood. His ventures into prose did not sell, possibly because he was determined to say what he believed and was never concerned with—or very conscious of—what the public wanted. He tried lecturing, but he had no faith in the activity or in his ability. His description of the paper on the history and aims of poetry, which he read in Little Rock and in Texas, shows that he lacked the lightness of tone and the concentration of a few simple "controversial" ideas which might have brought success. When through a friend he got a chance to write articles for a popular periodical, he scorned the kind of art it catered to. He accepted under financial pressure, but wanted to introduce America to Unamuno and Santayana; he reluctantly agreed to settle for H. L. Mencken, and then found his article on Mencken unacceptable. At one time he expressed envy for the Vanderbilt poets, who had found safe berths in academia, but he lived too early for this now popular solution.

Like many writers of his generation, he began as an aesthete open to new experiments. Experimentation was in the air. It had already spread from France to Germany, Italy, and Russia, and was about to spread to America (where Whitman had cleared a path) and even to a resistant England. One might hold that the Victorians had only temporarily suspended the experiments of the English Romantic poets, but in any case, Fletcher found an unpopular but vocal group in England (but only English in part) ready for something new. As to what the new would be, there was less agreement.

Fletcher described his aims in 1913, when his first distinctive work was written: a full exploitation of the sounds of the English language, and freedom from all rules to "follow the life spirit, the inner rhythm of my own moods." This subjectivity was not in violation of Pound's rules for Imagists, which left room not only for images from the senses but also for those from the mind ("Direct treatment of the 'thing' whether subjective or objective").

Imagism is almost as difficult to define as Modernism. For T. E. Hulme, often called (but not by the Imagists themselves) the father of the movement, its essence was a hard reaction against romantic gush. Pound echoed Hulme when he held that the new poetry would be "harder and saner," and T. S. Eliot and Wyndham Lewis were even closer to Hulme's aims. Hulme was especially opposed to liberal religious and political sentiments and to the confusion of Art with religion. In at least the latter respect, Fletcher was un-Hulmian. To Ford Maddox Ford (then F. M. Hueffer), adopted by Pound as an honorary Imagist, it was mainly the use of a modern idiom to describe modern subjects. Ford's great service to Pound was to eliminate an early archaic diction and exclusive emphasis on periods before Raphael. To Richard Aldington and H. D., devotion to Greece was an essential component of Imagism. For Amy Lowell, the movement allowed description in free verse unhampered by earlier conventions (freedom from conventions may be the one essential feature of all Modernist theory, as well as of much Romantic theory). Imagism in its purest and most successful form can perhaps best be seen in some of the short poems of William Carlos Williams, concise descriptions in modern language, without comment. The term is Pound's, and the letters he (and F. S. Flint speaking for him) sent to *Poetry* are as close as one can come to an authentic definition. They clearly advocate the abandonment of traditional metrics (which finally Pound had not abandoned) and Pound's own peculiar and distinctive determination to cut as many words as possible. What they do not clearly define is the image itself. "Direct treatment of the 'thing'" presumably meant show, not tell. But need an image be concrete? "An 'Image' is that which presents an intellectual and emotional complex in an instant of time" does not answer the question. Pound seemed to be committed to concrete images when he said that "the natural object is always the *adequate* symbol." But he added, "Don't be descriptive." Clearly, however, he was opposed to abstractions and opinions ("Don't be 'viewy'"). The image, at any rate, often stood for a mental state. Pound soon abandoned the Imagists for Vorticism, a more radical movement at least in its rhetoric—violent rhetoric seems to be a legacy of the Italian Futurists. He contemptuously turned Imagism over to Amy Lowell (a verbose "Amygism"), and Amy eagerly accepted it. The differences between Vorticism and Imagism are far from clear, except that Vorticism included all the arts and was dynamic, not static; the ambience, if not the definition, of the movement can best be found in Pound's *Gaudier-Brzeska.*

Fletcher never followed into Vorticism, partly because, like almost everyone else, he disliked Pound's associate and (for a while) mentor, Wyndham Lewis. He admitted that he could not follow the Poundian precept of rigid filing and pruning which reduced twenty lines to two. He wanted richness, not conciseness. He agreed on adopting free verse and avoiding abstract generalizations. He felt he had achieved Imagism in the strict sense in the connected poems called "The Ghosts of an Old House." There was a "bald, stark directness of statement." "Each was a meditation, a flight of fantasy, provoked by some object." He rejected some of his poems on the Southwest as "didactic and non-imagistic," and later reflected that perhaps it was a fault of Imagism to rely too much on description and not to let the poet "draw clear conclusions about life," "to lead its disciples too often into a barren aestheticism which was, and is, empty of content." Like most of the Modernists, he began with aesthetic criteria which denied, or at least de-emphasized, "content," and had second thoughts. But for a while the movement was congenial. "Things interested me far more than people—things and their relations to me personally, or to each other." He compared this tendency to that of the Chinese and Japanese art he loved so well.

After the War, he considered this phase ended. "Since 1916, I have wanted with all my heart to do nothing but write about humanity—not about landscapes." Both in his acceptance and his rejection of Imagism, then, he saw it (to a greater degree than Pound did) as dealing with physical objects. It is doubtful that he found the right technique for his poetry of humanity, though he (like Pound) saw it as achieved by Hardy. He also wanted to formulate and express a view of life, an aim important in his Blakean *Branches of Adam.* Of his contemporaries, Pound and Eliot at least moved in the same direction; and Stevens later wrote a good deal *about* expressing a view of life. By the end of his autobiography, Fletcher had spoken of the Romantics often; he even cited Shelley's "unacknowledged legislators of mankind."

Fletcher's Modernist sympathies are clearly shown in his long and vivid description of the first performance of Stravinsky's *Le Sacre du Printemps.* After the War, however, they are less apparent. The change may be connected with the fact that he had rejected Pound to throw in his lot with Amy Lowell; he became her leading helper in the American stage of Imagism. But after the early twenties, Pound was also less enthusiastic about the avant-garde; in Paris he had a brief flirtation with Dada, but did not go on to surrealism and turned increasingly to didacticism. Fletcher had no interest in Dada, surrealism, or abstract art; he found little to admire in the habitués of the cafes of the Left Bank. He did not much admire even Picasso. He liked Eliot personally, but found his poetry too intellectual, as he did that of Ransom and Tate. He was openly hostile to the post-War sophisticated New York. His praise of *Ulysses* was temperate; like almost all of its early readers, he saw it primarily as a satire and found the "force of life" only in "the horrible Leopold Bloom." (Even Pound saw Bloom as a satire on what is wrong with modern life; the perception of Bloom's positive qualities is post-Modern).

There are sharp and accurate portraits of such key figures as Lawrence and Eliot and somewhat longer ones of Vachel Lindsay and Edgar Lee Masters. But the two chief characters in his literary life were Pound and Amy Lowell. His break with the first was before the main change in his poetry, though probably not unconnected with it. Pound was changing at the same time, and Fletcher showed no interest in his later and more ambitious work, though after the Second World War there was again a cordial correspondence between them. The reasons for the break were probably personal, not critical. Both Pound and Fletcher were difficult to get along with, and Fletcher was never anyone's disciple. Though he was for a while close to Amy Lowell (he finally broke almost completely with her, too) he recognized that she was more a literary politician than a poet. Almost at once, he saw that her "new" poetry (after meeting the Imagists) was derivative of H. D., of Aldington, and of himself. But impressed by her position and personality, he found a way to praise it. There is a statement about her, and Pound's, admiration for Robert Frost that may show one of Fletcher's limitations; he understood her admiration, since Frost represented a side of New England that she did not know, but not Pound's. It does not seem to have occurred to him that Pound was simply reacting to good poetry, whatever it represented—as Pound, unlike Eliot, later saw the peculiar quality of Lindsay. Not that Fletcher was an extreme example of (or that Pound was free from) the tendency to judge art for what it represents, not for what it is.

Fletcher clashed with most of the people he knew, whereas Pound clashed mainly with people he did not know but imagined and generally remained close to his friends (even to Wyndham Lewis). From childhood through college and during most of his first marriage, Fletcher was, above all else, alone—often lonely, always a loner. Though open to outside influences (the French Symbolists, Hardy, Blake), he was stubbornly independent. He was proud, quick-tempered, and honest. He was also a man of broad interests, well-informed about the past and the thought of his own day.

Fletcher was an example of the favorite Romantic figure, the Seeker, still common in the early twentieth century. He inherited a world in which no beliefs were obvious; he continued to want beliefs; and he did not find any which lasted. The most durable was the cult of the nineties, a religion of Art and Beauty, but it also proved transient. From the middle of the War, he was looking for another belief. His failure to find or to hold onto one may have been partly responsible for the gloom which is obvious in his work of the twenties and early thirties, though his rather unsatisfactory career and definitely unsatisfactory marriage surely contributed. Later Fletcher found Charlie May Simon, his second wife, a writer of fine children's books and a person totally sympathetic to him. Her book *Johnswood* is an excellent sequel to his autobiography, *Life Is My Song,* in the last chapter of which he appears, for the first time, happy and no longer lonely.

The last stage of his career to be described was unexpected. He had been an internationalist; he became a regionalist, devoted to folklore and to his native state. Of course others in the thirties were returning from the corrupt cosmopolitan cities to their "roots." There were writers like Faulkner who never left home and others who tried, with varying success, to go home again. The Fugitives were pointing the way (though when jobs in the North became available, they did not follow it). But Fletcher was only a moderate admirer of the Fugitives, and his roots in Arkansas had not been deep.

Perhaps for Fletcher, as for many, there was no home to go to. At the time there was a heated, if not enlightening, debate about writers in exile, which often overlooked the fact that homes, even in the sense that Dorsetshire was Hardy's home or Normandy Flaubert's or Dublin Joyce's, are not as common as they once were. In any case, Fletcher's good poetry was written during his years of exile, though some of it was written on visits to America. His well-to-do family in Little Rock was hardly representative of the "people" of Arkansas. His dislike of democracy, specifically in its local manifestations, was apparent early in his career. Later he often recognized that his art and his manners were those of a small elite. His hopes, on returning to Arkansas in 1933, of raising the cultural level of the state were, not surprisingly, soon disappointed. He had made a grim assessment, in 1927, of the cultural resources of Arkansas; later he made an equally grim one. He might, of course, have forgotten the cultural level, but he did not seem to forget it. His regionalism seemed to be an outgrowth of his theoretical rejection of industrialism, machinery, mass production, and the city, rather than of love for his region. He quotes Masters on the impossible choice between the small town devoid of intellect (Mencken's boobocracy) and the city. Masters chose the latter and Fletcher the former, probably in both cases because they disliked what they were rejecting even more than they liked what they were accepting.

Ben Kimpel

THE AUTOBIOGRAPHY OF JOHN GOULD FLETCHER

To
Charlie May Fletcher

in homage and adoration

Sweetheart, we only knew the moment when
The love that made us one, united here our souls,
Seeking the highest goal of this earth's goals;
For loving so, we live for more than men.

CHAPTER I

Although I have spent more years of my life abroad than most Americans, I am an American; and my Americanism was rooted in me by circumstances which happened long before my birth. I am the heir of two distinct strains of culture, both of which have contributed much, since the beginning of American history, to the development of American life. Whatever I have given to life or to letters here in America has come to me through one or the other of these two strains. One of them was transmitted to me through my father; while the other came, not less clearly, through my mother's heritage. In order to explain who I am, and why I came to be what I am, I must go back to their lives as the appropriate background for my own.

On my father's side the record is clearly one of physical pioneering in the American wilderness. My paternal grandfather, Henry Lewis Fletcher, was born in Hawkins County, Tennessee, on November 24, 1787—only twelve years after the outbreak of the American Revolution, and in the same year as the adoption of the Constitution of the United States. As a young man, he migrated from northeastern to northwestern Tennessee, settling for a time near Dover, where he met and married Mary Lindsey, whose family had come from across the border in Kentucky. Still later, he crossed with his wife and growing family, sometime about 1825, to Arkansas, living for a time in Lawrence County but moving, soon after, southwest to Saline County. There, on a lonely farm, in the hill country west of Benton, on January 6, 1831, my father was born. My grandfather was then already past forty. Of his earlier life little is recorded, except a vague rumor, current in the family, that he started out with Andrew Jackson to fight the famous battle of New Orleans, grew dissatisfied with his commanding officer, and turned back. The rest of his days were fully spent in plowing, sowing, harvesting, and begetting a large pioneer family.

There were six sons in this family, four of whom I can remember—fine, upstanding, resolute pieces of American timber. All married earlier than my father, with the result that I now have second and third cousins far older than I. Although they owned a few slaves before the Civil War, their life partook more of the character of the mountain people, the hillbillies, rather than the lowland aristocracy. They were farmers, but had learned early to be diversified in their farming. On the rocky, hilly soil of their four-hundred-acre tract, still most of it forest to this day, they raised cattle and sheep, doubtless kept pigs and chickens, grew their own vegetables, and may have spun and woven the wool for the clothes they wore. Only about fifty acres was good bottom land, the sand and mud deposit of the North Fork of the Saline River. On this they grew their money crop, cotton, for the things of which they were in need: hats, shoes, shotguns and powder, a plow or a Bible, salt, coffee, sugar. They hauled their cotton slowly into Benton, twenty miles distant, every year. The home in which my father and his brothers lived was a log cabin; for education, they had nothing better than the backwoods school some distance away and only occasionally served by the itinerant teacher. Religion came to them through the backwoods Baptist camp meeting. Such was their life, and so they lived till past my grandfather's death in 1855, all through the years of my father's youth and young manhood, till the coming of the Civil War.

They were, as were most of the mountain people in that wilderness, which only grew to a state five years after my father's birth, staunchly Whig in their politics. No doubt they believed that the South was entitled to keep its slaves under the American Constitution, but they were not so wedded to that peculiar institution as to be ready to wage a war on behalf of slavery. Pioneering had not died down in them, nor the lure of the West, for one of my father's brothers, some years older than my father, went all the way to California in 1849, and returned with nothing to show for his venture. I have heard my father tell me that when the Civil War broke out he was unalterably opposed to secession; nevertheless, when secession came, on May 6, 1861, he and all his brothers immediately volunteered on the side of the Confederacy. Four years later, having been wounded, captured by the Federals, exchanged, and rejoined to the Confederate forces, my father surrendered with Johnston's army. It was an experience of which he spoke little in later years to any but a few old cronies of the battlefield. It left him, I suspect, profoundly transformed physically and mentally, and under the dire necessity of starting life afresh, at the age of thirty-four, in some other pursuit than that of hillside farming.

He moved to Little Rock, and there, with the aid and partnership of a Confederate comrade in arms, Peter Hotze, a cultured Austrian who had come as a young man to the South, he embarked on the business of cotton buying. The business prospered so well that within a few years the partnership was expanded, not in numbers, but in territory: Peter Hotze, or Uncle Hotze, as we all called him, since he married my mother's sister, moving to New York, while my father remained in Arkansas. There he gradually acquired power and influence in the rapidly growing state, and began to be prominent in postreconstruction political life. It was there that he met and married my mother in the summer of 1877; nine years later I was born, within three days of his own birthday, on January 3, 1886.

From my father's side I inherited a physical frame and constitution that has been adequate to the demands put upon it by more than fifty years of living under not always easy conditions; a love for simple, honest, country folk, and for simple ways of living that has persisted despite all my sophistications; a certain streak of dour obstinacy that will not permit itself to be easily turned aside from any course once embarked upon; a love of travel and roving that is, unquestionably, the heritage of the pioneer; and a frankness in speaking out my mind that is also a marked pioneer trait. My heritage from my mother was quite different. It is from her that I trace all those aesthetic hankerings which have made me into a poet—all that love for pictures, architecture, music, which has sustained me throughout life, and has even led me to the extravagances and excesses that the artist usually has to commit in this world. I do not consider it any derogation to my father's dignity and honor to say that he showed ability on the practical, but was deficient on the aesthetic side. My mother's aesthetic side, on the contrary, was overdeveloped.

Some time during the waning forties, when the West began filling up fast from the hordes that Europe, troubled as it was with wars and revolutions, began pouring out on American soil, my mother's mother came to America, from the region around Hanover, in north-central Germany. Her age was eighteen; and for company across the Atlantic, Adolphine Habermann had only an elder brother. The two of them left Germany, I have been told, owing to some schism in the Lutheran faith; they were lured on by the promise of Texas, which at that time was rapidly filling up with persons of German descent. After arrival in New York, an overland journey to Pittsburgh and perhaps Cincinnati, a descent of the Ohio and the Mississippi by steamboat, a fresh ascent of the shallow, treacherous Arkansas—readers of Dickens's *American Notes* or of early American travelers may get some faint notion of the hardships of that trip—the pair made a halt at Little Rock, where there was already a considerable German settlement. My grandmother's brother thereupon decided to leave her behind, and rode off to Texas by himself. He was killed there, less than a year later, by a fall from his horse.

A young woman, barely turned twenty, with only a few dollars in her purse and alone in a frontier settlement, must have had a hard time of it—but my grandmother was equal to any emergency. I have always regarded her life as a startling success. She obtained land cheaply enough in the Little Rock of those days: a brief string of log huts one street deep, along a riverbank. On her land she built a house which was famous enough in its day, being of brick, two stories high, and with a garden of fruit trees and flowers at the back. There she sold quinine and drugs to the townspeople, her knowledge of the local pharmacopœia having been transmitted to her by her brother, who seems to have been originally trained as a chemist. There, too, she married Johanne Krause, a wanderer from Kentucky, who had naturalized himself as an American citizen (his birthplace being Kiel, then in Denmark); and there, after a few years, her husband died, leaving her with four daughters to support. She managed admirably.

The Krause girls were all given piano and singing lessons; they collected books and subscribed to the current magazines; they conversed fluently in two languages, German and English, from girlhood; and they grew up to know the best society that Little Rock afforded.

My mother was born in September, 1854. Twenty-three years later, she married my father. As she was so much younger than he, it was natural that their tastes somewhat differed. My father was then forty-six, a settled man with an income and a position of his own to maintain. As I have said, he was not, by temperament, aesthetic; though he liked to read books, especially books of travel, history, and, in his later years, science. I do not believe he ever read poetry, nor can I recall his ever quoting, though he had a remarkable memory, more than a few lines of it; his single quotation, I discovered years later, came from Byron's "Don Juan." On the other hand my mother knew many poets, principally the classic German ones. But her chief passion was music: she would play and sing to herself for hours. Her voice was a fine soprano, with considerable dramatic feeling. She could easily tackle Schubert's most difficult airs, and might have done credit to them on the concert platform.

As a child, I was allowed by her to read anything that I chose, except for certain books of fictional adventure—I recall that this class contained both *Monte Cristo* and *Tom Sawyer*—which she considered dangerously exciting for a young boy. The result was that I read chiefly poetry, of which there were several volumes in the home library. At six, I insisted on reading aloud, straight through, Coleridge's "Ancient Mariner" to my younger sister, aged two. At nine, I suffered a slight accident, was laid up, and asked my elder sister, aged twelve, to read me Tennyson's "Ode on the Death of the Duke of Wellington." I cannot recall any moment in those years when my chief delight was not in poetry. Music, which was given to my sisters in large doses, I did not acquire; it was thought effeminate in those days for a boy to learn it.

My rearing in other respects was quite different from the upbringing of most American boys of that day and period. Indeed, it was different from that of almost any other American boy I have ever known. As I was the only son, the fruit of my father's later years, I was carefully brought up, and kept so closely guarded from contact with the outer world that I cannot recall having any playmates and companions except my two sisters. Some three years after my birth, my father purchased the historic old house which Albert Pike—once a poet of renown—had built for his mansion in 1840, in the early days of the state. There we moved, in the summer of 1889. It was from this house, with its ten lofty rooms, its wide hall with great folding doors, its six white columns, its green wooden-shuttered windows, its broad lawn dotted with oaks two hundred years old, vast locust and magnolia trees, that I learned what it was to have been a southerner of the aristocratic sort in the days before the Civil War. The flavor of the old South hung around that house and hangs around it still. By its rooms and by its lawn, my life was circumscribed from the days when we came there; I cannot recall ever going out into the street alone, unaccompanied by an adult, until I was well past ten years old.

The influence of the house, in its magnificence and its decay, the qualities of mind and heart that I inherited from my parents, and my own education all urged me later on to become a poet. Had I not been predisposed by my mother to contemplate life aesthetically rather than take active part in the games played by the boys of the neighborhood; had I not been provided from an early period with an endless subject for romantic meditation in the aspect and appearance of the old house, so rich in memories of the past, and equipped besides with an actual, authentic ghost; had I not been carefully trained to the assimilation of literature from childhood, my story might have been different. My education was entirely supervised by my mother. It was through her that I first learned to read and write. Later on, private teachers were sent for. What I chiefly acquired under them were languages, Latin and German first of all, from the time I was seven years old.

At the age of ten, with enough Latin and German to enter classes where sat boys of sixteen and eighteen, and with the feeblest possible knowledge of mathematics, I was taken from home, my hair was cut (hitherto I had worn it long), and I was unceremoniously bundled off to school, a private academy in the west end of the town. There I promptly became the school laughingstock, owing to my puny appearance and my habit, already well developed, of expressing my own opinions. There, too, I learned to be horrified and shocked by the more than Rabelaisian frankness of the older boys, and to read and recite with facility more poetry than before, and to wonder what it felt like to grow up and become a man. The lives of my sisters, and their interests, now slowly receded into the background; but my younger sister remained my chief playmate, and the companion of my reading and dreaming. Up to the age of twelve I still tried to maintain, with her, my faith in Santa Claus.

The private school lasted for three years; at the turn of the century it was succeeded by a high school which kept me for three years longer in Little Rock, the private school having closed down in the meantime. During all that time, my mind was stuffed with information. I cannot recall that I ever took part in the athletic exercises or the games of the school. Owing to a double fracture of the left arm, suffered during childhood, I was awkward at all games; and I never even learned to throw a baseball successfully. History and the writing of flowery prose compositions I soon added to my other accomplishments; and having discovered in myself a retentive memory for facts and dates, I soon passed among my schoolfellows as a kind of walking encyclopedia. In mathematics I still lagged behind, achieving only miserable failures at both algebra and geometry.

At the age of sixteen I was graduated at last, the youngest of my class; and since my parents had decided on Harvard College for me, to Harvard I was bent on going. In reality the decision lay in my mother's hands, my father merely concurring. He was determined to send me finally to law school; his mind no doubt ran back to the time when lawyers were considered the most learned men in the community, as well as being the best paid. It was necessary, he knew, for me to obtain a college degree before entering any good law school; Harvard was, he felt, an excellent college—and he could easily afford Harvard. He knew nothing of the New England tradition, just then entering on its last phase; if he had, no doubt he would have hesitated before letting me go.

Something had happened to his own life, still pursuing the even tenor of its daily four journeys afoot between his home and the bank of which he was now president, with an occasional weekly excursion driving a sleepy horse into the country near by. This left him finally a disappointed man, though his uniformly placid temper was not easily to be ruffled into disappointment. From this event, I date the beginnings of my own political independence.

As readers of Arkansas history know, in the year 1900 a small-town lawyer from the hill section of my state, who rejoiced in the name of Jeff Davis, succeeded in getting himself elected as attorney general, beating several of the old-guard type of politicians in a contest marked by violent personal diatribe. His success in this campaign was attributed to his powers of backwoods oratory and to his skill in using the Arkansas language, as well as to the virulence of his invective against what he termed the "interests," these being the industrial and financial corporations, the bankers, editors, publicists, and all the leading politicians of Little Rock. He promised that if elected he would tear off his coat and light into these trusts and interests generally, and he was as good as his word. A year later, after much verbal pyrotechnics, he decided to run for governor of the state on a "trust-busting" platform—his object being to promote a bill which would make it illegal for anything so much as an insurance company backed by extrastate capital to do business in Arkansas.

Some friends of my father thereupon took the alarm and in this emergency prevailed upon him to run for governor, in the Democratic primaries, against Davis. The winner of the primaries would be the next governor, as there was no Republican party to speak of in my state. My father, twice before, in the years previous to my birth, had unsuccessfully contested the governorship; he was well known as a liberal conservative, with a sound program of road-building, rural school development, and reform administration. Although he was now seventy years of age, he took the stump against Davis, and immediately drew the concentrated fire of that worthy. Since he was a banker, he was immediately accused as being the "tool of the interests"; since he lived in Little Rock, he was declared to be no friend to the "one-gallus fellers who lived up the fork of the creek," for whose support Davis openly bid; since his eldest brother, just dead at the age of ninety, had been well known in politics as a Populist, Davis now publicly affirmed that my father was openly jockeying for Populist support, by pretending to a friendship with his brother which had not actually existed. The climax came when my father, for once losing his temper, raised the heavy hickory cane he always carried and shook it towards Davis. Davis immediately asserted that his life was being threatened, and refused to debate further unless the platform was crowded with his friends, who traveled about with him, and who, naturally, interrupted all that my father said. Early in 1901, in the midst of a wet, chill Arkansas spring, my father saw that the race was going against him, and that he could not prevail against the demagogue tactics of Davis and of his growing political machine. He withdrew, leaving his political career a total wreck on the field.

This incident of my father's last unsuccessful race for the governorship—for five years later he was dead—need not have affected me so strongly but for the fact that I had now arrived at that impressible age of fifteen, when children, and in particular male children, usually make a clear choice between their mothers and their fathers; and I now saw my father in a new light of hero worship at the very moment when he went down to defeat before a clever but unscrupulous poor white politician. I felt profoundly sorry for the six-foot, robustly built, solid figure in the broadcloth coat, the wide-brimmed soft black hat, with the massive hands and feet and features, the candid open blue eyes, the great flowing beard of gray, who had so overawed my boyhood. Moreover, I not only admired my father: I loathed Davis. I had but barely recovered from the shock of the Spanish War, and the revelations of greed, official incompetence, imperialistic ambition masquerading as humanitarian motive, that had followed. Democracy, it was obvious, only too frequently degenerated into vulgar, naked self-seeking and plunder. And here, under Davis, was another manifestation of the same thing. I was sickened at my own country.

It has recently become the fashion to declare that the whole generation to which I belonged, the generation that grew up in America under the shadow of the Spanish-American War, and who launched forth on a sustained criticism which has gone all the way from the "muckraking" of the early twentieth century down to the avowed communism of the present day, were mistaken in their diagnosis; that they betrayed America in the name of ideals which were not American, and that they ignored the solid and abiding honesty and stability of the common people of the Middle and the Far West. That criticism is, to my mind, largely a case of wishful thinking; to say the least, it is remarkably farfetched. Where, one may ask, did the generation who rose up in indignation and scorn against the shallowness, the falsity, the shams of American living derive their strength if not from the American background itself? Most of them, like myself, sprang from a long experience of American ways of living. It is all very well to say that the ideals they upheld against American post-Civil War cheapness and vulgarity were not American but European, ideals. They were only European because they were human; they were ideals not to be found, except among a small minority, in any European country. If America is to congratulate itself merely because it is different from Europe, if it is to assume that all the criticism which has been leveled against it has been false and un-American at bottom, then not only my generation, but the generation of Emerson, Whitman and Thoreau ultimately wrote and strove in vain.

I, at all events, can testify that I began to loathe the sham and corruption that went on in America in the name of democracy fully seven years before I quit America for good and went abroad.

Once elected to the governorship, Davis proved no better than the most machine-made politician of them all. He made enormous personal profit, allowed various grafts to go on, and struck a bargain with the surviving remnants of the old guard which finally took him to the United States Senate, where he gained an unenviable reputation for backwoods clowning. I cannot say that my father, under the circumstances, would have done much better. But at least he would have fulfilled his promises, meager as these may have been. That was not because he was, as Davis affirmed himself to be, a democrat. It was because the backwoods frontier and the Civil War and the reconstruction struggle alike had put into his soul the tradition of unswerving integrity.

The summer of 1902, preceding my entrance into Harvard, was spent in intensive cramming under a woman teacher who still lives on in Little Rock. To her I owe a debt of gratitude for being the first to tell me that I ought to develop into a writer. She noticed that if the subject interested me I would always prepare more than the lesson assigned, and the subjects I was interested in had always something to do with literature and language. Up to that time I had scarcely given a moment's thought to what I might make of myself, assuming with my parents that I would study to be a lawyer. Despite my mother's determination to give me exceptional advantages, and despite the reputation I had already earned of being a walking encyclopedia of knowledge touched with temperamental queerness, I never supposed myself to have any exceptional talent at anything in particular. The cramming I underwent in the summer of 1902 did not enable me to conquer the Harvard entrance examination in the following fall. I passed only, as I recall, in English, German, Latin, and Roman and American history, achieving one more failure at algebra and geometry, Greek and English history, French, and chemistry.

It was decided to send me for a year to a large New England preparatory school. The year at this preparatory school threw me, an unprotected and hypersensitive southerner, into the midst of a school full of New Englanders, all contemptuously ignorant of the South and secure in their ignorance. Thereby was increased my determination to stand aloof, to hold myself in reserve, to be indifferent to the opinion of others. I entered the school underweight and undernourished; but under the regimen of physical exercises twice a week I soon became tall and wiry. Thus I was more or less prepared, not only physically, but mentally, for entering Harvard. In the following year, I was triumphantly admitted.

The year in prep school definitely broke the last ties that still held me to my boyhood. I still took for granted my father's wish that I should become a lawyer; I still accepted my mother's verdict as to what subjects I should study; but in mind and in physique I had shot up already into young manhood. I had already very definite tendencies and ways of my own in many matters; for example, I disliked democracy, shunned the company of most people, preferred the country with its wild flowers to the city, had indeed a passion for all flowers which I inherited from my mother, loved to cover the pages of my schoolbooks with crude drawings, loved to listen to music, or to lie on my back in the grass, looking up into the sky, loved to look at pictures, preferred, on the whole, the past to the present, and spent hours visiting in imagination all the marvelous countries under the sun. In short, I was beginning to prepare for a later career as a poet—unknown to myself, for I had not as yet written one line of poetry.

The Christian religion had made as yet no mark on me. A reading of the Old Testament had left me horrified by the bloodthirstiness, the crookedness, the bargaining morality of those old Jews; and I was too young and too secure economically and physically, to be moved by the New Testament, that gospel of the poor par excellence. My father was, at bottom, a tolerant agnostic, with no dogmas and no particular creed, and only a sense of awe to take the place of formulated religion; in his latter years his favorite reading was Darwin and Huxley. My mother's somewhat narrow and censorious Episcopalianism did not appeal to me. I scarcely now called myself a Christian. Rather had I already evolved a religion of my own: a stoic paganism of defeat, of which the chief heroes were Napoleon and Hannibal, and better still, Stonewall Jackson and Robert E. Lee. Only the summer before going to Harvard, I had read through the *Iliad* for the first time, in Bryant's translation. It moved me profoundly. To be as Hector was, to die crushed by the injustice of the gods, blindly juggling away the lives of men—to die defeated, defending one's own beloved wife and child and city to the uttermost—that surely for me was sufficient.

CHAPTER II

It was at Harvard that the idea first came to me of becoming a poet. In looking back, now that my fiftieth birthday is passed, it seems to me that this idea came to me gradually, and was more or less forced on me by the circumstances of my life and upbringing. This may imply that no one would willingly be a poet in this troubled twentieth-century world of ours; or it may mean that my life at Harvard merely intensified certain conditions of loneliness, of detachment, of contemplative imagination, that found in poetry their proper medium of expression. Alfred North Whitehead has said that religion is what a man does with his loneliness. In my case, art—the specific art of poetry—took the place of religion. Everything in my early life had predisposed me towards the fine arts. The art impulse existed in me, can exist in others, long before the choice of any particular medium in which to exhibit it. Children at play frequently display the ingenuity, the imagination, the organization of form, and the attention to detail that characterize all fine art. One might indeed describe fine art as being equally compounded of childlike disinterested play, of astonished intense wonder, and of maturing sober judgment.

At all events, I can testify that had I not already familiarized myself somewhat with the technique of poetry by reading an inordinate amount of it, I might easily have chosen now to attempt some other branch of art. At Harvard I developed a passion for painting and for the graphic arts generally that has gone with me all through my life.

My first visit to the Boston Museum of Fine Arts, then on its old site in Copley Square, partook of the nature of a revelation. The intensity of Rembrandt, the sustained fury of Rubens, the apocalyptic vision of Turner, the naked magnificence of Blake, the somber melancholy of Delacroix, the peasant homeliness of Millet, all alike enthralled me. Greek sculpture overwhelmed me with its slender, athletic beauty; Egyptian sculpture awed me with its dense, hieratic immobility. And if I failed to respond to the classic Chinese and Japanese art in which the museum collections were so rich, it was because my mind had not yet been trained sufficiently to respect an art which made such a great virtue out of economy of effort and out of its own limitations.

My response to art was complete and immediate; not so my response to music. The Boston Symphony Orchestra, to whose concerts I soon got a subscription ticket, intimidated me. Bach, Beethoven, Brahms, all were above my head; at the most I learned to like Tchaikovsky, Verdi, and Wagner. The emotional side of music interested me before the intellectual; I had not yet achieved that fusion of the emotional and intellectual which, in default of a better name, men have agreed to call the spiritual.

Had I been given lessons in drawing, or encouraged to experiment with paints early, I might, I believe, have come to be a painter. But my literary knowledge already overbore my knowledge of graphic art. I was even more familiar with all the classic German poets than I was with the English ones: Goethe, Schiller, Uhland were familiar territory. The only gap in my knowledge came with the name of Heine; I read him only later. Perhaps my mother considered that his irony, his blend of the realistic and the romantic, was dangerous. In English and American poetry, I was already familiar with Walter Scott, Tennyson, Longfellow, Lowell, Burns, Coleridge, Poe. To these I soon added for myself Fitzgerald's *Omar Khayyám,* the heady and passing intoxication of Swinburne, Rossetti, and the poets of the nineties. In Latin poetry I had already delved deep into Vergil, and was soon to follow up with Horace and Catullus. In Greek, which I read only in translation, I had encountered Homer. I was soon to tackle Dante, in translation also, and to be equally fascinated and repelled. Two or three of Shakespeare's plays had already been gone through, and my knowledge of Shakespeare's linguistics, at least, was soon to be enormously enhanced by taking Professor Kittredge's famously exacting course. For the literary field, in short, I already had knowledge, as well as inclination, to go on; in the graphic arts, I had only deep and unsatisfied hankerings.

It was not until my third year at college that I furtively disobeyed my mother's injunction to continue studying languages, and took two courses on architecture instead. These left me aware of the organic symmetry inherent in Greek and Gothic architecture, and confronted me for the first time with the then still mighty name of John Ruskin. But already in the summer following my second year at Harvard I had begun to profit by the knowledge I possessed of poetry, by actually writing it. The particular events leading up to my decision have possibly passed so far into the background of my life as to be not altogether clear to me now. But the chief motive that lay behind my decision is still vivid in my memory.

During my freshman year I did not mix with my classmates, and I scarcely knew a soul. I took out a subscription to the Harvard Union, on finding that it had an excellent library in which I could browse at my leisure. My life was spent between the Union and the classrooms, except for the numerous excursions I made into Boston to see my favorite pictures at the Museum of Fine Arts, to visit the theaters there, and to hear music. I went through my classes perfunctorily, with no great interest at heart, and did no better than average. Charles Townsend Copeland undertook to guide me through the mazes of freshman English, and took a faint interest in me when he found that I had absorbed greedily all the early scientific romances of H. G. Wells. He recommended me to read Joseph Conrad, then a name little known, which I did, thrilling at *Youth* and *Heart of Darkness* and remaining slightly puzzled at the oblique technique of *Lord Jim.* But Copeland never gained my confidence, nor did anyone else. My experience at the preparatory school the year before, where I was made the butt of the entire school, was still too fresh in memory. I was, I sensed, somehow different, somehow set apart from these New Englanders.

In my second year, at the outset, I discovered on the top floor of the dormitory in which I lived, a lean close-knit Long Islander, with a great shock of startlingly blond hair and an attitude equally compounded of cool self-confidence and intellectual disdain. Lyman Willets Rogers had entered Harvard as a sophomore, having come from some minor New England college—I think Williams. I recall clearly our first encounter. I roomed alone downstairs, and had already met his roommate, an inoffensive little creature who had come all the way from Stanford University. I was invited to call. The conversation chanced to turn upon literary matters, and upon Edgar Allan Poe in particular, whom I had read and reread with increasing interest only the previous summer.

"What I admire most about Poe," declared Rogers vigorously, "was his refusal to be bound by the so-called moral standards of most people. Why, he even justified crime. Take 'The Cask of Amontillado,' for example. The man who commits the crime in that story is not only satisfied, he glories in it. Poe wanted to get beyond good and evil. He was right in thinking that what people call sin is always fascinating and frequently justifiable."

I said nothing, but Rogers's roommate flushed. "Sin may be fascinating, but it is never justifiable," he commented angrily. "Unless you are prepared to admit that Jesus Christ died to save such sinners as yourself."

"Why should I be prepared to admit it?" retorted Rogers. "All that sort of talk is just what you religionists always use. Jesus Christ won't save you, unless you are prepared to save yourself. You excuse your own cowardice by asking his forgiveness for your sins. I prefer to be responsible for my own sins, as well as for everything else."

"Then you don't believe in Jesus Christ?" I asked, fascinated. I had just recently reread the Gospel of Matthew with some care, and had been moved despite myself.

"Certainly not," retorted Rogers in reply. "Jesus of Nazareth was merely an interesting decadent—an example of slave morality, if there ever was one. He wasn't a god—although his followers may have thought so. All that notion about his saving people by sacrificing himself on the Cross is just Paul's notion anyway. Jesus himself would have rejected it, as he rejected the religionists of his own days."

The argument went on from that point, but neither party was convinced. I bade good night at midnight, but before I went I informed Rogers that I was convinced he was right. It was easier to have no religion at all than to believe in such an absurd one as Christianity. For a long time, it seemed to me, this conviction had been maturing in my soul—now Rogers, my first intellectual friend, merely called it forth. It had been strengthened into utterance by having someone to share it.

Rogers had, as I soon discovered, written verses while at his earlier college, for the college paper, and soon showed these to me. I was moved by them into extravagant admiration. Probably if I saw them now I should consider them feeble imitations of Poe and Coleridge, the sort of thing almost any talented undergraduate could do. But at the time they seemed to me works of genius. Finding that he had but little interest in the fine arts, I began to stop going so frequently to the art museum, and spent more time with him exploring Boston, particularly the picturesque Italian quarter of the North End, the packed markets, and the harbor. Our literary tastes so closely coincided that my desire to become a writer, temporarily almost stifled in my freshman year, now came back by leaps and bounds. During my freshman year I had taken up smoking; now, under Rogers's sane direction—he was one of the few Americans of that day who preferred wine to whisky—I began to sample drink also.

When we parted for that summer, we were sworn friends, and agreed to write to each other. That summer led me far afield. At the end of July my elder sister was invited to attend the wedding of one of her college friends, in San Diego, California. It was decided that I should go along. We traveled, as everyone traveled in those days, by railway—the Southern Pacific through El Paso and the Arizona desert, intensely hot and scorched by relentless sun. For the first time in my life I saw real desert, real mountains. I recall that under that raw sun they looked strangely unreal, like the painted back cloths of a tremendous stage. It was hard to believe them solid, hard to believe that such colors actually existed in nature. I stopped off for a few days in Los Angeles while my sister went to San Diego alone. It was there, after a night at the theater, as I recall, that I wrote my first poem. Then we moved on to the Yosemite, which shook me up so thoroughly that further poems followed. We went on to San Francisco, the San Francisco of pre-earthquake days, with three-masted sailing ships still in its harbor, and the smells of the slums, and old Chinatown. When we came back to Little Rock in the heat of early September, we had also seen Portland, Oregon, Salt Lake City, Denver, Colorado Springs; I was a traveled man, and had perhaps a dozen poems in my pocket for Rogers to read and comment upon.

It was thus, at the age of nineteen, that I first began to write verses. What my first verses were like, I do not know. But I know that they were roused in me by scenes rather than by people, that the Arizona Desert and the Yosemite and old San Francisco had as much to do in making me a poet as had my early reading, or the stimulus of Rogers's friendship. In yet another way, too, I had been spurred to express myself—by the fact that, under Rogers's influence, I had begun openly to doubt and even to despise the dogmas of the Christian religion.

At the preparatory school, chapel attendance had been compulsory; and I had steadily attended, being at times stirred, and at other times frankly bored. But at Harvard, where chapel attendance was not required, I had confined my churchgoing to a few attendances at the most picturesque and ritualistic churches I could find, seeking the music, the stained glass windows, the ceremonies which were all more to my taste than long prayers and tedious sermons. Although I had no specific belief, except a vague desire to live righteously, I did not consider myself either for or against Christianity. Rogers, however, did have a strong feeling against it; a feeling which at first startled me by its vehemence, but with which I soon found myself in complete agreement.

Briefly, he was a Nietzschean; and the name of that philosopher, just then crossing the Atlantic in the excellent early translations of Thomas Common, first flashed across my mind in the year 1904-5, barely five years from Nietzsche's own physical death. Nietzsche had declared that the basis of the Christian religion was slave morality, nay-saying to life; meekness, humility, poverty of spirit. He had affirmed, in the teeth of his own Christian heritage, in the teeth of his own weakness, that the basis for man's real religion—a religion worthy of humanity—should be a master morality, the affirmation of life, even the affirmation of life's endless recurrence; pride, power, audacity, abundance. That "the weak and the ill-constituted shall perish" was the first word of Nietzsche's morality; and he condemned Christianity root and branch for being nothing but a decadent faith, inferior as such to Buddhism; which clever priests and popes had once manipulated to gain their own ends, but which had become an incubus and a nightmare to the world since Luther had made it democratic. Nietzsche therefore would have done with Christianity once and for all and would put in its place the will to power and the religion of the superman. Such was Rogers's own disdainful creed; and all through 1904-5 I absorbed it in large doses, reading Nietzsche day after day at the Harvard Union, and dreaming about the superman at night.

It was, I am convinced, partly because I could no longer find a support for belief in the organized religion of my day and time that I turned to poetry as a means of consolation. T. S. Eliot to the contrary, I cannot hold that the practice of art is compatible with the strictest kind of Christian orthodoxy. Rather I believe that it has been precisely in those days when heresy was the most powerful that Christianity made its highest contribution to art—made it because of, not in spite of, heresy. The cathedral builders and the troubadours and the early Italian poets, and Dante and Giotto to boot, were what they were because they believed the essential heresy, not to be found either in the Gospels or in the Primitive Church itself, that Mary the Virgin was Queen of Heaven and more potent there than the Trinity. They believed this because, as sinners, they had to believe it, not because the Church told them so, but because the Church permitted this belief as a pious opinion. And just as the Medievals were the greater artists for believing anything so undogmatic and unfixed by Church authority as the Virgin's power over heaven and hell, so Nietzsche was a better poet for believing that God—the God of his Evangelical Lutheran childhood—was dead, and that man had better prepare for the superman.

In any case, my becoming a Nietzschean, and my break with the religion of my boyhood, made it certain that I would go on writing poetry. Men must believe in something; if they cannot believe in the accepted religion they will believe in art, or in fate, or in machinery, or in progress, or in communism. For my part, I believed, since severing my alliance with Christianity, all the more completely in art; and the part of Nietzsche's gospel that was most lost on me was his stern mockery of all artists as being mere play actors, and his somewhat puritanic and prudish mistrust of Wagner, winding up in an outburst of furious denunciation. It seemed to me then that Nietzsche's mistrust of art sprang from a fear that art might, after all, be far more powerful than philosophy in revealing man to himself, and that his contempt for Wagner came from little more than long-smoldering jealousy of a rival artist.

During the year that followed—the year of 1905-6, the year of my father's death—I continued to write poetry, and to read it. My delvings into the English nineties brought me at last to Arthur Symons, and through Symons I first learned of Baudelaire and of the French symbolist school.

At that time my knowledge of the French language was confined to an elementary course which I had taken in my freshman year, to remove a condition. I had not gone on with the language, so I knew that if I were to read Baudelaire, Verlaine, or any of the other fascinating people whom Symons talked about I must find translations. Search of the Harvard Union drew blanks, so I transferred my attention to the Boston Public Library. There I found translations of Baudelaire and Gautier and Flaubert—some of them by Lafcadio Hearn—which held me for unforgettable hours.

There must be certain writers whom every literary artist can read and reread for the sake of their perfect craftsmanship alone, their supreme aesthetic delight, rather than for their social value or for any message of importance they may speak to mankind. The function of such writers was perfectly fulfilled for me by Baudelaire, Gautier, and Flaubert, first read in translation, and in later years in the originals. The present vogue for Proust, which flourishes even among the literary left wing, is due to the fact that such men who have eyes purely on the social import of literature are yet sufficiently interested in the problems of literary craft to be able to admire one writer whose social import is nil, but whose documentation is immense, and who has been able to employ it with supreme aesthetic skill to describe his own private and peculiar world. There was equally a world for me, a world of intense aesthetic sensation, in Flaubert's *Trois Contes,* in Gautier's *Emaux et Camées,* in Baudelaire's incomparable *Fleurs du Mal.* It was in my third year at Harvard that this world opened before me, the year when I turned twenty. One of those rare moments of discovery and participation and of overwhelming absorption that mark a writer's life then came to me with my discovery of these writers; perhaps the first of such moments, and certainly not the least important to my later development.

My father's death, on January 30, 1906, came so suddenly and unexpectedly, in this same year, as to interrupt the whole course of my existence. Although he had been suffering from a weak heart for years, he had spent the day before in his usual round afoot between his home and his office. He had spent the evening before quietly reading Darwin, had gone to bed early, and had wakened at about five in the morning, complaining to my mother of difficulty in breathing. She had helped him out of bed and into a chair. His breathing became rapidly worse, and she had hurriedly telephoned for a doctor, who had come and seen the case to be desperate. The doctor was about to give him an injection when he suddenly collapsed and died. It was about nine in the same morning that I received a telegram from my elder sister notifying me of the fact; at eleven I caught the first train from Boston to the South.

Owing to bad rail connections, I arrived in Little Rock only about an hour before the funeral. My father's body lay in its coffin in the large parlor to the left of the hall. While I was still dressing and removing the dust of a weary train journey from my body the Confederate veterans assembled before the house to do it honor, as it was borne down the veranda steps. It was a quiet, open, sunny day, one of those calm winter days of the South that seem to mark an arrest between fall and spring. The coffin was borne out of the house and down the walk, and we followed to the church. My mother and sisters were completely overcome with grief; but during the long train journey I had steeled myself and was now resolved not to let my grief appear on the surface. Although I must have been deadly pale, I managed to control myself, and did not shed one tear throughout the Episcopal service, or the scene at the graveyard, which followed. I entered the church and left it with head erect, feeling that I was paying a better and manlier tribute to my father's spirit by silently enduring my loss, rather than by breaking into the loud sobs of my mother and sisters. I did not feel that I wanted the curious crowd of onlookers to see my sorrow. Yet the scene at the graveside, with the crowd standing around, and the negro gravediggers rapidly shoveling earth on the coffin containing the senseless body of the most magnificent man I had ever known, nearly unnerved me altogether. It was the first funeral, in fact, that I had ever seen.

I did not realize then, nor for many years afterwards, what my father as a man meant to me. It had only been during the previous summer that I had come to realize, from talks we had together, that he sympathized with me and acknowledged me no longer as a boy but as a man. I had not yet had time to thank him for his goodness, to show him that his trust in me was not altogether misplaced. I had not dared to reveal to him the fact that I was already cherishing disturbingly vast and vague literary ambitions. He would not have understood. His first idea had been that I must be a lawyer. Since I had gone to college he had heard something about the prospects open to civil engineers, particularly in Central and South America, and was half disposed to wish that I would take up engineering as a profession. I knew that I had as little aptitude for the one profession as for the other, but I was determined not to disappoint him in any way, if I could avoid it. Yet the fact that I had inherited all my mother's interest in the fine arts, rather than his own robust, practical common sense, would have made him puzzled and appalled, if I had failed. I was left to speculate fruitlessly how we would have got along if he had only lived a few years longer, and to come finally to believe that whatever our differences in temperament may have been, he was after all right in thinking that talent was less important than character, and that man as artist was less important to the world than man as man.

His death revealed the fact, hitherto almost unsuspected by me, that he had been, by the standard of that day and that community, a wealthy man. His faith in the city and state that he had helped to build, from the still primitive backwoods South, crushed by the war and by reconstruction, to an advancing commonwealth of educated citizens, had been at least justified in a material, if not a moral, sense; for only a few knew how much he had labored to aid Arkansas's advancement. I went back to Harvard to finish my third year, dazzled with the thought that when I came of age, a year later, I could pass out of my mother's control and become an independent man of means, thanks to his labors.

During the four months that followed I had ample time to reflect on my new situation. I could now do one of two things: I could either go on with my Harvard career, or I could, in a year's time, break it off and go abroad, living within my own means. It was the latter prospect that attracted me. My Harvard education already seemed to me a thing of shreds and patches. Under the elective system then in vogue I had begun, at my mother's insistence, with languages—German and Latin—and history, and had kept that up for two years. Then I had shifted suddenly to literature and the fine arts, which had interested me from the moment of my entering. It seemed to me now too late to learn anything more of lasting benefit, for my later career, which, as I saw, must be that of letters. My father's death had left the field open. I could go abroad, where the mental atmosphere and climate had proved themselves more favorable to the cultivation of fine arts than in America; and there I could travel, study, develop myself without interference.

My mother, however, had already determined to carry out my father's wishes to the last detail. She was already ailing with the incurable disease which was to kill her, four years later; and she had now no further ambitions in life than to fulfill to the letter my father's previous plans, and to die. To my humble hint that I wanted to take up writing, to my mild suggestion that I preferred to go abroad to see pictures and architecture and study literature, rather than go on being educated at Harvard, she replied that I was acting simply as a spoilt and selfish, disobedient son. My father had wanted me to be a lawyer, and a lawyer I must be. There could be no more argument, no more discussion. Shaken by my failure to convince her in the least, I withdrew from the debate. But to my sisters I secretly confided that I was now sick of college, and that next year, since I was coming of age, I hoped to get some share of my father's estate and go away. I found them unsympathetic to the idea that I should quit college, and determined not to divide the estate, but to hold it together.

Feeling like an outlaw, without a soul who cared either to listen to me or to understand me, I crept back to college. Rogers had already gone, having made a spectacular exit in the previous spring by suddenly running away with a young woman of the neighborhood. Where he had gone, I did not know—we were no longer in touch with each other. Again I was faced with the doubtful prospect of finding and making new friends. The few acquaintances I had—two or three at most—mostly lived in a private dormitory, not on the college grounds, and enjoyed a life comparatively free from irksome college regulations and restrictions. I had been chafing against all discipline myself for over a year past, so I determined to join them. Thus in defiance of my mother's wishes, I took the first step that led me out of college.

In a few months I was inveigled into a game of cards, played for high stakes, by two college men living in that dormitory who were little better than professional gamblers; I lost a sum as great as my entire yearly allowance. The best I could do was to promise to pay these men after I came of age. What was still worse, my work at college again began to fall behind. I felt that I hated it. Yet I had half promised my sisters to make the attempt and go on, and I did not want to withdraw. At the same time, the only new friendship I had formed quickly convinced me afresh that my own education had been utterly mishandled. Silvanus Griswold Morley, a name now high in the field of Mayan archaeology, was, like myself, finishing college in that year—and like myself, he too lived in Bradford Hall. His talks about his future career as archaeologist only made me feel more and more bitter against my parents. Why had I not been allowed to study American archaeology? Here was a field that offered more, it seemed, to a man of my type than any other: it required imagination, courage, linguistic, cultural, and aesthetic knowledge to pursue; its rewards were in the exploration of the remote, the romantic past of the Indian. I began to read, and to absorb, all the archaeology I could, with the result that I still further neglected the dry college courses.

At the midyear, at the close of January, I was feeling ill, harassed, sleepless. The thought suddenly came to me: Why should I go on taking examinations in courses that led me nowhere, when I had never been for a moment consulted as to the life I wanted to lead, or as to my reasons for coming to college at all? Would it not be better to be honest with myself and refuse to go on? My resolve was taken. Within a few days I had refused to take a single examination; and I now followed this up with a letter, boldly resigning from the university and transferring myself to a private boardinghouse near by. The blow of my resignation utterly overwhelmed my mother, who had just had me come home for a miserable Christmas, during which time I had felt persistently that all I wished for was to die. I do not recall how I explained to her my action, nor what I now planned to do. My mother's bitter assurance that if I went abroad during the few years she still had to live, I could not possibly succeed in writing anything of value, made me waver. I decided for the moment to stay on in Cambridge and see what else there was for me to do.

Morley, sensing in me an interest in archaeology almost as great as his own, now came forward with a new suggestion. My situation at the college was this: all the courses which I had taken up to my senior year still stood to my credit, and I could re-enter the college next fall and complete my senior year if I wanted to. In June, Morley was taking his degree, with high honors. At the end of that month he was obtaining his first experience of archaeological field work, through an expedition organized and financed by the Peabody Museum, to the Southwest. I might come along, if I would be ready to pay my own expenses, and I might there decide whether I really wanted to be an archaeologist. At all events, it would give me a wonderful opportunity to see some wild, unspoilt western country. I gladly gave my consent.

During all this year, I had given up my verse writing, and had written no poems since the previous spring. I still spent most of my time at the Harvard Union, smoking and reading, and wondering whether I could ever get up courage enough to ask my family outright for a definite division of the estate and go abroad on the proceeds; or if I did go abroad, which country would I sooner visit, the Italy of Ruskin's adoration, or Ruskin's own England, so rich in literature and legend. While I was thus engaged, idly wasting my time and unable to decide on anything, a man approached me and introduced himself. He proved to be a classmate who was preparing to get his degree and leave college in June. It soon developed that he too intended to take up a career as writer, and that he had written verses which had been printed in the *Harvard Advocate* and which I had already read and admired for their rhythmic vigor. He had only written a few, it developed, since his real field was playwriting—a field which I thought far above me at that moment. I admitted that I had written several poems, including a long composition in four contrasted movements which I called "Impressionistic Symphony." He asked me to show him some of my verses, but I have forgotten whether I did, or what he said. This was the only other poet besides Rogers, who had given up verse writing before he came to Harvard, whom I was to meet during my four years there. In regard to living American poetry, I had heard vaguely the names of Moody, of George Sterling, of Santayana, and of Robinson. Yet I knew that there were still poets living and practicing their art in England, among them the veterans Swinburne and Meredith; and Francis Thompson, whose work I was just beginning to admire and appreciate, had only recently died.

What would I do with the rest of my life? That was now the main question. By living very simply, and as economically as possible, I began slowly to pay off the unfortunate gambling debt that still hung above my head. Although I wrote to my mother steadily and persistently, she had never written me; this rule she did not break, though I wanted and hoped still for her confidence. Except for Morley, I had no one in whom I could confide. I had tentatively promised to follow his advice and go to the West with him that summer and try out archaeology; and I decided to keep my promise. But in the meanwhile I had ample time to reflect on my first and seemingly complete failure: the failure to fit into the college standards and the college routine. If only I could have met someone like that poet who had written for the *Advocate,* in my first year; if only I could have taken more courses in English literature, composition, playwriting, or in the fine arts, instead of all that dreary German and Latin; if only I could have entered college with full liberty to direct myself as I chose; if only the path had not been set for me from the outset! But it was useless to waste time in regrets. I was twenty-one and had achieved nothing that mattered. So I faced the world, in the spring of 1907.

CHAPTER III

At the end of June, accompanied by Morley and Alfred Vincent Kidder, another young archaeologist fresh from Harvard, I embarked on the train which would take us to New York and thence to Chicago and so on to western Colorado. Our destination was Cortez, the terminus of a branch line running westward from Pueblo. Beyond, some twenty-five miles away, lay Mancos, an insignificant town which we could only reach by horseback, in the midst of the Mancos valley, rich in cliff dweller ruins. Still further on, some forty miles from Mancos, lay the lonely ranch house, a one-story adobe structure, close to the Utah border, which was to be our headquarters for the three following weeks. We were to spend these weeks exploring, mapping, and describing the numerous prehistoric ruins that lay at the conjunction of the great maze of sandstone canyons which ran from the meeting of the Mancos and San Juan.

The entire expedition was under the control of Dr. Edgar L. Hewett, a pioneer in the field of southwestern archaeology. Except for the first few days, we saw little of him. After meeting us at Cortez, arranging for our horses, telling us how much we would be expected to pay for our board at the ranch house, and giving us directions as to what we were expected to do, he departed, leaving us to our own devices. We had brought camp equipment—a waterproof collapsible tent, beds and blankets, tin dishes, cups, knives, forks, and spoons, canteens, and the like—as the ranch house had neither extra kitchen equipment nor available sleeping accommodations. A wagon was to follow us with our equipment.

We negotiated the first day's ride fairly easily. I had already had some experience of horseback cross-country riding. The joggling gait of the cow ponies was racking to the bones, but we slept happily that night in Mancos's primitive one-story hotel. The journey of the next day was more exhausting, along a rough dirt road, without bridges across the creeks, and we were in a state of soreness from the previous day. Both Morley and I limped exhaustedly out of our saddles at the end, and onto the camp beds, without bothering about supper. Kidder, who had suffered the most, rolled out of his saddle, and without going to the tent, lay and slept on the ground.

During the three weeks that followed we saw a good deal of the country, exploring and riding in every direction on horseback, and becoming inured to the saddle, hardened and tanned by the open-air living and the desert sun, until we were almost as brown as Indians. The country was wild enough in all reality; in order to find as wild a country within the boundaries of the United States today one would have to go still farther afield, to the little-known region of the Navajo Reservation. It was, except for the coyotes and rattlesnakes and prairie dogs, practically uninhabited. We saw nobody except an occasional bunch of cowboys engaged in rounding up and branding horses and cattle, who came in and made the ranch their temporary headquarters, and a few wandering Utes and Navajos, living off their respective reservations. Sixty-five miles to the east lay the nearest railway station; and from it, three times a week, a pony dispatch rider rode through, carrying the mails ninety miles to Bluff, Utah. Except for the grizzled Mormon ranch keeper and his wife and their numerous brood of children, who were the last white settlers in the valley, we were alone. The chief difficulty that we faced was that our horses repeatedly slipped out of the crudely built ranch corral and roamed off into the desert, presumably to join the bands of wild horses that still roved the unfenced country to the south and west.

The archaeological work was not difficult, but somehow it was monotonous. After a week or two of it I grew weary holding the tape measure while Kidder drew plans of some ruined building and Morley checked off the measurements. I began again furtively scribbling down my impressions, in the form of verses. I was glad enough when Dr. Hewett returned, near the close of July, and when after a single day's hard riding we found ourselves again in Cortez.

The Mesa Verde was our next objective. Visitors to that national park who drive today from Cortez by an easily graded and spectacular motor road, and who stop at the excellent tourist camps the government has provided, may wonder what it was like when not a house stood on it, and when it could only be approached by bridle trails. All that I can say is that about the Mesa Verde hung a quality of remoteness which was quite unlike that of any other place I have ever seen. Here we were, literally out of the world, without letters and without communication. Our provisions for the two weeks we were to stay were brought in with us on pack horses. Our numbers were now increased by taking with us a local cowboy as horse and grub rustler, and—as photographer to the expedition—Jesse L. Nussbaum, newly graduated from the University of Colorado. He is now curator of the Mesa Verde National Park, under the United States Government. I wonder whether, with the thousands of visitors who now come to that park every year, he ever looks back and recalls the day when, as a raw youth of twenty, he rode with three young greenhorns from the East? In that vast upland of twisted piñon and juniper and sagebrush, with the long, absolutely soundless yellow canyons running off to the South, where blue-gray Ship Rock hung and quivered like a mirage in the glare above the Navajo desert, we were seeing country which, except for a few archaeologists and cattle rustlers and horse thieves, no white man had ever seen.

Mesa Verde had been unchanged since the last cliff dwellers, perhaps some time in the eleventh or the twelfth century, had vanished south, leaving their towers and house walls and kivas to peer out at the traveler from almost inaccessible ledges of yellow stone. No one knew or suspected what the story of Mesa Verde had been, since none of the ruins had then been systematically excavated; and no one knew, then, that the Pueblo culture there represented had been preceded by centuries of an earlier Basket-Maker culture. We were still less archaeologists than explorers as we rode here and there, scrambled in and out of ruins, and slept close to the Spruce Tree House Spring, now the main source of water in this waterless region, under the stars at night.

Every morning we woke to the sound of the wind in the stumpy jungle of evergreen, like the rising and subsiding of some far ocean; and the noise of the coyotes, yapping their wild chorus in the pale light of dawn, provided the strange commentary to our waking dreams.

Two weeks of this, without letters, without seeing a soul beyond ourselves, and we rode off the Mesa Verde again. Our horses were sold, and we moved by train south to the upper Rio Grande valley to Puyé, now also a national monument, forty miles south of Santa Fe. Here we were in the heart of the Pueblo country; though I, for one, was not aware of it. With the aid of a gang of Indians from near-by Santa Clara we tackled our next big job: the excavation of the entire South House at Puyé. We had become thoroughly toughened by over a month's roughing it; we wore stubby beards, let our hair grow long, slept in our clothes, and looked on ourselves no longer as greenhorns. But actually the job at Puyé was beyond our powers. The Indians were slow and unwilling workers; and the shifting of thousands of rudely cut pieces of lava rock with splinters in them, which had to be lifted out by hand and which tore our fingers in the process, was the worst part of it.

The rainy season was now in full swing. Almost every afternoon, while we three whites—for Nussbaum had now gone back home—toiled and sweated and cursed over the bleak rock piles, poised on the top of the world, which formed the debris of the great South House of Puyé, the clouds would come driving over from the southwest, the vast stretches of the green Rio Grande valley at our feet would be darkened, and immense folded curtains of cloud would descend upon the blue-black peaks of the Sangre de Cristo in front and the bleak Jemez at the back of us. Then the lightning would flicker, the thunder roar, the wind bellow; and we would race from the smoking downpour, down to the rim of the mesa, where there were rows of artificially excavated caves in which the Puyé people once lived. There we would sit while Dr. Hewett would tell us of the history of this region: of Coronado and his Spaniards; of the legend of the Seven Cities of Cibola; of the wild Navajos and Apaches; of the numberless ruins to be explored in this country; of that strange sect, the Penitentes; and of early adventures of his own. Sometimes, at his bidding, the Indians would sing to us, and their singing was perfectly amazing in its complex savagery. The shower over, we would return to our work, and to the amethyst-purple light on the far-off ranges again.

Slowly during these weeks there was growing up in me an increasing resentment against the toil we were undertaking, and against Dr. Hewett in particular for making us do it. Morley had long since begun to irritate my moody, uncertain temper with his perpetual air of rollicking good humor, his boyish love for jokes of the crudest practical sort, his methodical, precise scholarship, his lack of creative imagination. Kidder was too reserved and distant—too much the New England aristocrat turned archaeologist—to be a friend. But Dr. Hewett fairly exasperated me. Why did he keep us, day after day, working over the same old dreary piles of rock, finding nothing of any interest, when all about us, as our eyes could see, lay a magnificent, a marvelous country where Spaniard and cowboy still lived together, and where the American Indian still carried on the life of his remote forefathers? Here the Mexican had his villages, his fiestas, and his weird Penitente ceremonies. Why could not Dr. Hewett show us something of this country? We had been working for him steadily since the beginning of July, and here it was the end of August. Disgusted, I decided that I had had enough. I straightened my back from bending over the rock pile, dusted off my hands, and walked back to camp. Though Dr. Hewett tried to persuade me to return, by half promising a holiday jaunt soon to the Rio de las Frijoles, near by, I was adamant. The next day I took the train to Santa Fe.

I could now return to Little Rock, or go back to Harvard. Since I did not wish to face my mother's fresh reproaches, I decided to return to Boston. I had no clear idea what I intended to do there. Perhaps I would return to Harvard and take up the old thread of my broken life. But the reopening of Harvard came and went, and found me still defiant. After all, I had failed at archaeology, as Dr. Hewett had seen it. He had chosen to look on my final rebellion against his authority as sheer craziness, and had told me so. Very well, if I were crazy as far as he and Harvard were concerned, I would be crazy to some purpose. One heard frequently enough in those days as to the craziness of great artists, as to the kinship between art and insanity. I would go where such crazy folk as I were tolerated. I would go abroad, and study in Europe.

The next summer, after a long and wearisome quarrel with my family over my allowance, I packed my bags and sailed. In September of the year following my archaeological adventure, I was walking from my hotel into St. Mark's Square in Venice, in the early hours of a brilliant day. It did not occur to me then, nor for many years afterwards, that if I had been given the opportunity to see something at first hand of Europe, before sampling the life and the culture of the American Southwest, I might have made more of my early archaeological experience. The contrast between the seething, swarming life of Venice, still going on in the midst of the maze of canals and alleys which enclosed the vast dead shells of a once magnificent heritage of independence and splendor, now lost forever and of no interest to anyone but the tourist—the contrast between this and the remote, lean, spare, austere American Southwest was too great to be understood or even remembered. Europe—or rather Italy, for I had come direct to Italy—baffled me completely. How did it happen that so much culture, so much more than America had ever known, had once lived here, and now lived here no longer? How had it come about that the Italians, once supreme in the arts, had ceased to be an art-creating people? How did it happen that the history of nineteenth-century Europe was the history of a few great, lonely individuals, from whom the mass, the mob, fell so sharply and absolutely away? I could find no answer to all these questions, or to many others.

During my first months in Europe, and indeed during my first four or five years there, I had to progress by making mistakes, by blundering and groping and failing constantly. I had come abroad to try to acquire an education, to learn something concerning the aesthetic, moral, and spiritual values by which man was made worthy of the world he lived in, and which had created man's highest civilizations. In America no part of my hunger and thirst for knowledge had really been satisfied, though I had fulfilled prodigally the restless roving instinct which had driven me to travel over the face of my country, to and fro. I had discovered little there except the "mediocrity, the optimism, the worldliness" which had also so appalled George Santayana. Were there values in Europe, were there values anywhere in the world, which were living and functioning vitally in sufficient strength, to enable me to build up anything from my own American background, to make anything more of myself than a complete failure of adjustment to the standards of my country and my people? I had come to Europe, at all events, to find out. And I knew from the outset that my exile would be neither a short nor an easy one.

Yet, though I regarded myself, and continued to regard myself until my return in 1914, as a complete rebel against the intellectual, moral, and spiritual standards of the United States, I know now that it was my heritage, no less than my own will, that dictated my expatriation. My mother had been, throughout all her life, an exponent of the old German liberal culture of the nineteenth century, nowhere more effectually strangled now than in the country of its birth. She had never felt at home amid the raucous, pushing, commercial standards of America. All her aspirations towards the aesthetic life in all its ways had only been transmitted to me, given masculine force and impetus, and consciously or unconsciously fostered. In going abroad, I was unconsciously fulfilling her ambitions for me; but while her late and bitter opposition to my plan went on, I was made to feel as if I were a criminal. If only she could have written and told me that she felt that, after all, I was trying to do something with my life in the only way I knew, by educating myself through contact at first hand with European cultures, then my eventual return to America might have been easier. But she could not do this, and so I was left to face Europe alone.

It did not take me long in Venice, or in the six months' stay in Rome that followed, to discover that there had been serious flaws in my root-and-branch rejection of Christianity, my half-baked Nietzscheanism. Europe, as I saw now, owed an immeasurable debt to the Christian religion. The Middle Ages, which we in America, growing up as we were in a new country along with the age of rationalism, were unaware of, had inevitably laid the foundations for the Renaissance and for modern Europe, by transforming Christianity from the religion of the underdog to a religion of aristocratic power. Catholic Christianity had been built up, from Charlemagne to the crusades, into one of the supremely warlike and dominant faiths of the world. Nor had Protestantism lagged behind Catholicism in this respect—how otherwise explain the religious wars of the sixteenth and seventeenth centuries? My stay in Rome, lasting from November, 1908, to May, 1909, so completely imbued me with the supreme importance of the Catholic faith as the basis for all European culture that I came close to becoming a convert, and spent hours in studying all the histories of the papacy I could find, in order to discover how it was that the popes had lost their temporal power. Italy, I soon saw, would not have succeeded in winning unification, nor would the popes have lost, had it not been for two reasons: first, the papacy had backed the Bourbons, who were clearly impossible; and second, English liberal nineteenth-century sentiment—the same sentiment that had refused to back up the South in the Civil War—had been mobilized to support the creation of a united Italy.

England, in short, had so dominated Europe from the close of the Napoleonic Wars onwards as to convert all European countries from conservatism to liberalism. This she had done by changing Christianity itself, from the seventeenth century on, from a creed of feudal land tenure and authoritarian government, to a creed of industrial exploitation and parliamentary institutions: a practical creed of bourgeois imperialistic expansion which had given into her hands all the valuable outlying regions of the world, with the sole exception of the United States, which had alone successfully revolted from her sway. As a result, England had given to the world, despite her own desire to effect compromises, despite her fetish of continuity, the two new creeds that, from the nineteenth century on had become too powerful to be ignored: republicanism and socialism. It was time for me to go to England, and find out the significance of this country for Europe, America, and the future.

When I came to London, in the May of 1909, my mind was already made up that in England, and in England alone, lay the key to the complex modern world that I had sought after since the beginning of my exile. I had spent some nine months in Italy, without friends of any sort, alternately fascinated and repelled by the pomp and majesty of the Catholic ritual, by its complex and intellectual structure, and by the open alliance of this faith with the reactionary forces of Europe. I had come near to becoming a Catholic, without precisely doing so. That which prevented me from doing so was, I felt, my own liberalism, my American respect for the revolutionary tradition. I had spent hours reading the romantic poets, Keats, Shelley, Byron, Heine and the Germans, Victor Hugo and the French, Leopardi and the Italians. In these writers, as I could see, the two forces that had made for revolutionary enlightenment, on the one hand, and for the revived power of the Middle Ages on the other, had met and clashed. Such a poet as Shelley, for example, outwardly an atheist, inwardly an otherworldly mystic, completely fascinated and enthralled me. And it was in Italy, above all, that Ruskin had led me on to William Morris, to Robert Owen; and so I first heard of socialism.

When I came to England, I was already prepared for socialism, though it was less the socialism of the industrial revolutionary sort than the guild socialism of the Middle Ages which interested me. My experience of Italy had already disillusioned me with regard to whatever might be the prospects of the new Italy as a source of modern thought and creation. Unlike the writers of that day and hour, I did not think of myself as a realist, but as a romantic; but the current version of romanticism practiced in Italy seemed to me, if anything, rather inferior to realism. The idol of Italy, I soon discovered, was Gabriele d'Annunzio; and his magniloquent blend of paganism and jingoistic nationalism completely repelled me as not only inferior to Carducci, but as leading less to renewal than to perverse decadence.

As a matter of fact, the moment of my coming to England was not ill-chosen. One of the periodical renovations of literature which are undertaken every dozen years was in progress. Ford Madox Ford—then known as Hueffer—had brought out in January of that year the first number of his *English Review;* and though he remained as editor for only two years, the effect of his standard, and of the writers that he backed, such as Joseph Conrad, W. H. Hudson, D. H. Lawrence, was to remain powerful for at least five years longer. In the field of politics, playing a lone hand against the Fabians and the Independent Labor party alike, A. R. Orage was already editing his *New Age,* a weekly devoted to the ideas of guild socialism, which was soon to arouse discussion all over London, no less by the brilliance of the talent contained in its pages than by the independent editorial attitude it displayed. In poetry, Harold Monro, a Scotsman somewhat older than myself, was returning like me from an Italian exile to London, soon to take up and edit the "Georgian poets," and to run his Poetry Bookshop. The last of the Victorian giants, Swinburne and Meredith, were dying or about to die; and of all that galaxy of great talent, only Thomas Hardy remained, to achieve his belated apotheosis during the years of the Great War.

The move from Italy to London, first undertaken in May, 1909, and by October of that year become permanent, brought to me the realization that if one was to be effective as a writer, one had, after all, not only to reckon with one's age, but to take up some definite stand in relation to it. The sensitive Ruskin, who had moved me as author perhaps more than anyone else during my residence in Italy, had followed up Carlyle's querulous grumblings against the nineteenth century by attempting to go back to the Middle Ages, as if the nineteenth century did not exist. It was a tragic decision, ruinous both to Ruskin's sanity and to the future fortune of his own work. For had he but considered Carlyle more closely he would have seen that this Scotch philosopher turned historian was the authentic voice of the nineteenth century, no less so in its tempestuous railings against the soot, the grime, the vulgarity, the cheapness of industrialism, as in its fiery revolutionary evangelic faith, its mingled admiration for and contempt of the mob, and its blind worship of action and of power. Anyone, I saw now, who, like Ruskin, chose to retreat completely from his own age into another, might indeed be ranked as an original and even vital force, but he could have no standing as one of the age's greatest spokesmen. If I were to succeed at literature, I must not hesitate anywhere, neither in the thirteenth nor in the sixteenth century; I must take up my place among the men and women of my time. And this, it seemed to me, I could do better in London than anywhere else in Europe.

It was for this reason that I already regarded myself as a Socialist on coming to London; and immediately after I came there I threw myself headlong into the Socialist movement. I had already forgotten how deeply and apparently inseparably my own country was wedded to the theories of big business, of laissez-faire capitalism. I had already forgotten how those pioneer writers—Ida Tarbell, Lincoln Steffens, Upton Sinclair—who from 1900 on had shown up the ugly and corrupt side of American capitalism in practice had been hailed by the offensive title of "muckrakers." I had already forgotten how every American of my boyhood, from college presidents to newspaper editors, had done lip service to corporate greed; and how the one American who resisted, William Jennings Bryan, honest representative as he was of the western farmer class, had already become a tedious joke by the time I left America. I had forgotten my own country's puritan mistrust of the arts, its habit of treating all reformers as being either "queer" or "knockers," its perpetual hatred of original thought. I had also forgotten my interest in the old West, the old South, the romantic regions, the heroic saga lands of American history. I had come from sixteenth-century Italy to modern, up-to-date London, the capital of the greatest empire on earth, the symbol of the triumphant bourgeois, the dominant industrialist. I was for the moment overwhelmed by it all, but content with my decision.

CHAPTER IV

The four years that I spent in London, from the fall of 1909 to the spring of 1913, I regard as my second education. During that period I first came into contact with people who were engaged in the business of writing, and during that period I took the first steps which were to transform me from a dilettante into a professional writer. It was also during that period that I came to realize the curious purblindness of the English people in regard to other literatures and traditions than their own—a circumstance which, taken in conjunction with my own tendency to be cosmopolitan rather than insular in my literary tastes, finally decided me in favor, not of England, but of America.

When, in May, 1909, I arrived in London, aboard a train bound direct from Rome—I did not stop off in Paris, but remained in my *wagon-lit* while it was being shunted from one station to another—my first feeling was of relief at being again in a land where my own language, or something resembling it, was spoken, and of delight at being in a city where so much interesting literary work was being done. From the moment of my arrival in the British capital, I felt sure that here, if anywhere in Europe, I could feel at home; and I would have preferred to stay indefinitely, had not a letter from my younger sister come suddenly, informing me that she was sailing for Europe in June, and that she expected to meet me in Naples at the end of the month. This necessitated my temporary return to Italy, where I remained till the middle of September, before settling down definitely to my first winter in London.

I have still vivid memories of my first contact with England. It was on the sixteenth or the seventeenth of May, 1909. The train on which I left Paris finally departed at about half-past ten in the morning; the early afternoon found us approaching the sandy piny French coast between Calais and Boulogne. I had been told by so many travelers and so many newspaper reports of the terrors of the English Channel, that I dreaded the crossing of that narrow sheet of water more than I had dreaded the Atlantic in the summer of the year before; but the Channel turned out to have fewer ripples on its surface than a lake, and was as smooth as the proverbial millpond. The opposite shore, with the white cliffs of Dover, was in full sight from the moment we embarked; and the journey across took place without incident. The two hours by rail up to London, through the rich Weald of Kent, riotous in bluebells and hawthorn, and glowing green in uninterrupted afternoon sunlight, passed like enchantment. I arrived in London with the sunlight still beating down through the smoky air and transforming the Thames, dingy Charing Cross, and the buildings along the Embankment to pale gold. A short ride by hansom cab—for there were still more hansoms than taxis in the London of those days, and even horse busses had not entirely disappeared from the streets—brought me to my Bloomsbury hotel.

For a few days the redoubtable British climate, so capriciously temperamental in contrast to the solid and stolidly unemotional people who lived under it, kept on its best behavior. I explored London in all directions, fascinated alike with its diversity of sights and of life. Then suddenly all changed. The sky became sunless; an icy drizzle filled the streets; people passed buttoned up to their ears in heavy coats and bending under dripping umbrellas; and coal fires were relighted in the fireplaces of the hotel lobby. Beside one of these I was sitting rather disconsolately, wondering whether it would ever clear up, when a handsome, middle-aged man with a chestnut-red beard carefully trimmed to a point and a mass of curly, ruddy hair, came up and spoke to me. It soon appeared that he was an Anglo-Irish journalist, a Socialist and a member of the Fabian society. His name, however, was not Shaw but Hobson.

Thus, through the most casual of contacts, the course was set which was to carry me through London for the next four years. During the month that followed I saw a good deal more of my new acquaintance, and gradually unfolded to him my plans and ambitions. The chief of these was to acquire the ability to write prose with the same fluency and ease as employed by writers for the *Times Literary Supplement* and other English literary periodicals. I also revealed to him my hankerings to become a poet. He readily promised aid; offered, if I should return in the fall, to give me letters of introduction to various editors of his acquaintance; took me around to see Orage, who equally dazzled and confounded me with his conversational facility; even promised to train me as a journalist, by means of a series of lessons. In regard to poetry, he could not help. But he asked me whether I had ever read Walt Whitman, and was amazed to find that I had not. "Why not?" he declared, warmly. "He's the one great American poet."

So for the first time I began to pay close attention to a poet whom, while at Harvard, I had merely picked up and glanced at, flinging his book aside when I came upon such a glorification of the braggart, vulgar, utilitarian Yankee spirit as the "Song of the Exposition." In London, under Hobson's urging, I began to look on Whitman in a new light, finding in the surging, moving mobs of Oxford Street, Piccadilly, the Haymarket, and the Strand a democracy of effort and a spirit that old Walt had been first to capture and to preserve in his loose-jointed rolling verses. The contrasts of wealth and sordid misery which had shocked me on my very first days in the British metropolis had apparently not daunted Whitman in the least; he had steadfastly held to a creed which somehow included the meanest and the highest, and which aimed at the reconciliation of all such differences under the vague but all-embracing term "democracy." Such a creed, however Victorian and optimistic in its faith in the future progress of humanity, appealed to me, as an American, far more strongly than did the creed of Tennyson or of Browning. I was so carried away by Whitman's robust realism, by his masterly grasp of the details and contrasts of life to be found in just such a city as I was now visiting, that I immediately broke with all my former allegiances to Coleridge, Keats, Byron, Shelley, and Poe, and began feverishly to try to describe the life of London in terms strongly reminiscent of his own.

I did not grasp, at the time, how untypical such a man as Hobson was in the British scheme of things; nor did I understand how strong a hold the British crown, the Church of England, and the public schools still exerted upon the British mind. In my revolt against the great American institution of big business, I had come to Europe—only to find, in Italy, an institution of far longer continuance and stronger root, which had at once fascinated and repelled me, in the shape of the Roman Catholic Church. I did not at first realize that the British, for their part, had worked out a whole set of such institutions, emerging from the compromises they had been forced to accept under the Tudors, the Commonwealth, and the Restoration. These compromises came from their long-acquired ability to play off one party of extremists against the other, and always to choose the middle ground. I only began to suspect that the vast edifice of Britain's power was built up on such compromises when, after three months of fresh wanderings in Italy in the company of my sister, I returned to London in the fall of 1909. Thus I witnessed, at first hand, the events centering about the death of Edward VII, and the Lloyd George election of the year 1910, all in the company of Hobson, who now constituted himself my sole guide and my chief mentor, and who shared for a time my first permanent apartment in London.

The result was disconcerting to one who, like myself, and, I suppose, every American who has lived for some time in England, has rashly assumed that he knows all that is to be known about the British people. The House of Lords, with Tory thoroughness, threw out Lloyd George's famous budget, embodying his scheme of old-age pensions. This led the Liberal government to retaliate with the threat of the creation of new peers. And so matters stood when King Edward suddenly died. By a series of skillful compromises between both sides, government was sustained until, after King George V's accession, a new election was held, in which the Liberal party came back triumphantly to power, and proceeded to carry its scheme through, despite all opposition.

During this election campaign I saw a great deal of Hobson. I even accompanied him north, to Rochdale in Lancashire, that typical manufacturing town, and birthplace of the co-operative movement. Hobson was scheduled to make a speech there on behalf of the Labor candidate. My experiences there disillusioned me both in regard to the possible strength of British socialism, to which I had already become sentimentally attached, and in regard to the possibility of taking any part myself in the tangled course of British politics. The inhabitants of Rochdale seemed to mind greatly neither their dirt, their poverty, their smug hypocrisies, nor the hideousnesses of their own surroundings. They complacently accepted all these things. Industrial Lancashire still ruled England, and England led the world. When my friend arose among them, and with fine Irish scorn and hatred of all compromise told them that they were not worthy of becoming Socialists unless, as he, they learned to hate and despise their own sordidness and vulgarity, his speech aroused neither their assent nor their applause. The Labor candidate was defeated at the polls; and I was left to travel back to London in the company of Hobson, still windily talking about a forthcoming revolution, and about combinations of forces, underground conspiracies, agitations, and heaven knows what else, which would bring it about.

I had become disillusioned, thus early, with Hobson and with all his Socialist friends and acquaintances. The election crisis of 1910 was still violently raging when news came from my sister that my mother was worse. I ignored the warning, having been told by the family doctor long ago that her disease—cancer of the breast—might go on for years longer. When I next received word, it was already too late for me to see her. I could not return in time for the funeral. This only made me reflect, with increasing bitterness, on my still unfulfilled vows of becoming an author. Alone in London, I returned to the task of working on my poetry, with only such chance acquaintances for friends as I might make. They were a sufficiently motley crew. All of them were near my own age, and none of them, so far as I know, in later life attained to any sort of distinction. They too, for the most part, claimed to be Socialists; but unlike Hobson's, their socialism was founded on no rigid set of principles, but was merely a habit of mind natural enough to any young aspirant set adrift, at that time, in the stony chaos of London. It was sure to be modified later by even a moderate amount of success. The utmost these young people could do was to bestow their support on the mild, weak-kneed policy of the Independent Labor party. Their too easy tolerance in life, in politics, and in art forced me to despise, while I endured them; and the history of the next three years of my stay in England is the record of a man who has many acquaintances, but no friends, and who feels, among any company, increasingly his own solitariness.

The first visit that I made to Paris was in 1911, at the time of King George V's coronation. Feeling that the noise, the shouting, the parades and celebrations would be but wasted effort in the presence of so insignificant a puppet as the British king, I crossed the Channel and remained away till all was over. The French capital, hurriedly seen in about a week, both disconcerted and impressed me. For one thing, I very soon discovered that, though I could read French easily, I could not speak it, nor understand it when spoken.

This difficulty arose at the start, in the small hotel on the Left Bank, near the Boulevard Mont-Saint-Michel, to which I had been directed. The proprietress and her daughter, both respectable, neatly dressed Frenchwomen of the middle class, knew no English; and both must have laughed heartily within themselves at my ludicrous efforts to pronounce the phrase which means, "I want a room." "Y a-t-il une chambre ici?" I went on repeating. Both shook their heads till, in desperation, my hands lighted upon the phrase book in my pocket, and I pointed out the words. I was equally as bad at the restaurant, in the taxi, and at the museums. At that time not so many people in Paris had acquired English words and phrases as came to be the case after the War. In despair, I finally betook myself to the proprietress, repeating painstakingly, after her, words and phrases that I had heard during the course of the day, and striving to get my unruly tongue fitted to the intricacies of French pronunciation. She was endlessly patient and unexpectedly generous with her awkward pupil. And the glimpses I got of her and her daughter, as both sat sewing in the stuffy little room which lay behind the office of the hotel, convinced me that while the English made an art of their politics, but lived badly, the French made an art of their living, whatever their politics might be.

Another and more intimate reason why I cut short my first stay in Paris was that up to the time of my visit I had remained uncompromisingly a virgin. I have no reason to think that my self-imposed celibacy inflicted any less severe a strain on me, as a young man from one of the southern states, than in hundreds of similar cases. Over and over again I had been forced to admit, despite certain tendencies towards an ascetic puritanism more akin to the fierce crusade against the flesh preached by the later Tolstoy than to the childish and at bottom rather envious antifeminism of Nietzsche, that the intimate possession and enjoyment of a woman was among the most pressing of my own needs. Only I was unwilling to accept the first substitute available: I was unwilling to accept, in place of the honest delights of sex mutually shared, a sordid, commercial transaction carried out between me and any one of the innumerable women who nightly hung about Piccadilly. London had made me both more hesitant and more fastidious.

Paris, on my first visit, nearly upset my hard-won and sustained virtue. During one of the first nights I spent there, I was awakened by noises coming through the flimsy partition which divided my own room from the adjoining one. These, I soon ascertained, came from the transports and endearments of a man and a woman next door, which went on during the entire night. Despite my impulse to feel shocked, I secretly envied the couple next door who were so passionately exploring the delights of their love; and I spent the next few days wondering whether it would be possible, in case I approached one of the numerous unattached women in the cafés, for myself to have an experience of that sort. My inability to master the French accent, no less than the fear that I might, after all, confront an attitude no less mercenary and vulgar than that of the streetwalkers of London, deterred me. I fled precipitately from Paris.

The next year, from the summer of 1911 to the fall of 1912, remains in my mind chiefly because, in it, my own cautious prudence, which told me that it was safer to remain a virgin than to take a prostitute, began now to give way before a power which was growing far stronger than my own stubborn resistance. I played about with the idea of entering a monastery. I even visited one, in the company of a Catholic friend. I was still striving to postpone the hour when I would fall victim to some unknown woman, when I invited my younger sister to join me in Naples again that fall, and to tour Sicily together. She unexpectedly consented, and came; but after a few weeks our paths diverged. When she came I was in a state of profound discouragement about my life and my career. I soon felt she could not help me in either. Her sympathetic attempts to make me feel less lonely and unhappy only exasperated me, with the result that we parted shortly before Christmas, and I was again left to myself.

I returned to Naples, and there, in disgust with such sordid and vulgar opportunities for sex experience as offered themselves, decided that I would be better for putting all such thoughts from my mind, and so concocted a scheme still more impractical. A young artist by the name of Brodzky, with whom I had become casually acquainted in London, and who, I had been told, showed promise, had previously expressed to me a desire to visit the Continent and make a sketching trip there. Since at that time I had more money than I wanted, and since he was desperately poor, why should I not write to him and ask him to come on to Italy and join me?

Actually, I knew nothing about him, except that his manners seemed mild and inoffensive. Without pausing to reflect, I instantly put my design into execution, sent him enough money to come from London to Naples, and received within a few days the notification that he was on his way. Late in January, we found ourselves on board a train, bound for Sicily again, I dreaming of a prose travel book in which to embody our adventures, and Brodzky no doubt carefully arranging his paints and brushes in preparation for the opportunity he saw coming.

The trip, as I might have foreseen, scarcely proved a picnic for either of us. Though we remained together till after Easter, we returned, via Rome and Paris, to London, only nominally friends. Any desire I may have felt to find in this young artist a sharer of my own ideas soon disappeared and was replaced by a contemptuous tolerance. We had been together barely a month when, exasperated by my new comrade, I proposed to him that we part, and offered to pay his fare back to London. To my surprise, he accepted, pointing out, however, with admirable good sense, that he had only come because of my invitation, and that he had expected better treatment. I was shamed by his response into carrying out my part of the bargain. I apologized, and the rest of the trip, which had been previously agreed upon between us to last for three full months, went on without further incident.

When we returned to London I presented him with a small sum, in return for some paintings which he had executed during our stay in Sicily. These, I am sorry to say, I returned to him about six months later, on the eve of my removal to Adelphi Terrace, stating that I had no further need for them. I received in reply a letter which revealed just how hurt he was. As a matter of fact, my remark about having no further need for his paintings had been literally true; the new apartment I had taken was planned to hold not a single picture on its cream-white walls. To his last letter, however, I did not reply. He retained his pictures, while I passed over the incident in silence. We met again, many years later, by accident at an art exhibition in London; neither of us referred once to the past.

Since Brodzky is now, or was up to a few years ago, still practicing as an artist in London, and since a book published in America gives an account of our relationship, stating that it concluded by my saying, "Brodzky, you are a fool, and I am tired of you. Clear out!" while offering simultaneously to the impoverished artist the sum of twenty pounds, it is best to narrate these simple facts.

The summer of 1912, so disastrously wet and stormy, was again spent in scouring the eastern borders of the Continent in the company of an American friend, with whom my relations were even less cordial and more violently explosive than those I had already experienced with Brodzky.

It was only in the late fall of 1912 that I again took the road to Paris. This time my stay lasted a little more than a month. I began to study the French language seriously, bought a host of books dealing with the symbolist movement, interested myself increasingly in the art of Cézanne, Gauguin, Van Gogh, and other postimpressionist painters, and actually had the good fortune to meet an American who, like myself, was then an exile living in Paris.

Some time during this second stay in Paris I was walking along the Boulevard Raspail when the sight of a shopwindow, where two or three pictures, painted in a manner akin to that of Cézanne and Matisse, were displayed, brought me to a halt. When I discovered that this was an art gallery, I went in. A tall, gaunt-looking young man, of about the same age as myself, with blue eyes and dark hair, arose from a desk at the back and addressed me in French. I replied somewhat haltingly, whereupon he instantly laughed, apologized, and went on in English as American as my own. It turned out that he was from one of the prairie states, and had been brought to Paris by his American wife, a clever dress designer who served her large clientele of wealthy Americans there. Having nothing in particular to do, he had opened this small gallery, whose entire stock in trade, so far as I could see, consisted of the works of two exiled Scotsmen and one expatriated American. Horace Holley—this was my new friend's name—had also, like myself, cherished ambitions of becoming a poet, and had published a small volume, *Post-Impressionist Poems,* during that year in London. The gallery he was now running was well stocked with the works of his three painters—J. S. Peploe, whose art for a time enjoyed a considerable vogue in London, Anne Estelle Rice, an American expatriate, one of whose pictures shown in the Independents a few months before my visit had achieved a scandalous success, requiring protection by the police from the threatened assaults of spectators, and, finally, John Duncan Fergusson, who, as I recall, still lives and exhibits occasionally in London.

Holley knew all these painters personally, and offered me a letter of introduction to the one I considered the best—Fergusson—which instantly raised him high in my regard. I formed the habit, during my stay, of calling on him often and hearing him tell anecdotes of his own life in Paris, as well as incidents from the lives of these famous painters. Privately, I had already almost decided to turn away from the unlucrative and thankless task of writing poetry, to what seemed to me the more congenial work of the painter. I had played about with the idea of coming to Paris and taking lessons in the craft. Now the door held open by Holley, though I was not able to peep behind it (Fergusson and Miss Rice had both gone away to the Riviera, and Peploe was now back in Scotland), kindled me with the thought, for the first time fully expressed, that I had after all made a great mistake by living in London, and that I would have done better had I settled from the start in Paris.

Nevertheless, I returned to London, with a standing invitation in my pocket to revisit Holley. I returned for the reason that I had, before leaving London, already crowned my three years' stay there by signing a lease for an apartment in Adelphi Terrace. So in spite of Holley and his generosity, I turned aside, and early in November, 1912, was at last settled in a luxurious third-floor apartment in Adelphi Terrace, on which I had spent a great deal of money in transforming it into a habitation suitable to my own aesthetic notions. Thus I abandoned the cheerless and dark top floor off St. Martin's Lane, where I had lived since 1911. I felt, once again, that I must somehow become a literary force, not in Paris, but in London.

If I had romantically dreamed that by removing to quarters far more commodious in their lighting and heating arrangements, with the somberly magnificent panorama of the Embankment and the Thames that my windows commanded, and all the literary associations of the neighborhood—if I had thought all this might take me further towards literary success, I soon found I was utterly mistaken. Being carried away by the spectacle of the great living room with its two fireplaces, no less than by the view from the windows, I only later realized the inconvenient fact that my new home possessed not even a kitchen, nor a gas ring to heat a kettle, and that no meals whatever could be served on the premises except breakfasts and teas provided at extra cost by the housekeeper, a massive Victorian female with iron-gray hair and severe expression who inhabited the basement. This effectually put a damper on a dream I had cherished of collecting together certain friends in the evening, and of entertaining them with light refreshments. Not that my friends mattered much one way or another, but I had lived in England so long on the merest chance acquaintances that I had arrived at the point where any company was preferable to none. My tenancy of these premises had already been hedged about by the landlords, the trustees for this property, with so many restrictions, I had been obliged to give so many references and to enter into such long negotiations before they would hand over to me this apartment, that I now began to suspect that the housekeeper, if I broke but one jot of the letter of the law, would report the fact to them and hand me over to be summarily dealt with.

As soon as I was safely installed, I carefully collected together such poems as seemed best, from my vast heap of manuscripts, and promptly sent these off to all the various London literary periodicals. One by one they all returned, with polite slips of rejection. I did not then suspect that the path to literary success in London, as elsewhere, lay less in merit than in cleverly handled contacts with the dominant figures of the day. If I had known it I would have bitterly resented it as a born outsider. The fact that my poems had all been rejected made them all seem bad to me. I did not know in what way I could make them any better.

As an interloper upon the charmed circle of London literary life, I still made desperate efforts to penetrate within, frequenting Harold Monro's recently opened Poetry Bookshop, despite Monro's iron gruffness and lack of cordiality, and speculating endlessly on whether I could really seek admission into some of London's exclusively literary clubs. As I recall it, I even sent Monro a laudatory sonnet, entitled "The Bookshop in the Slum," in order, through overmuch flattery of his pioneer effort, to enkindle somehow his interest in my own—only to receive in reply a vaguely noncommittal note that was even more deadly than a flat refusal. I was already past twenty-six years of age, was spending my income recklessly on an apartment that had been difficult to obtain and was overexpensive to keep, and had so far got nowhere with all my plans and ambitions. My own loneliness, combined with the gray bleakness of the winter climate, both sickened and depressed me.

Why, I wondered, as I sat in my Adelphi Terrace apartment amid the raw drizzles, the damps, the fogs, and the cheerless, sunless skies of February and March of the year 1913, had I so readily abandoned the thought of moving to Paris? Why had I insisted on staying in London? Had there ever been the remotest chance for me, an American with all the enthusiasms of a younger people, as well as my own gaucheries and timidities, to overcome the insular disdain of the British people? The fact that their reserve sometimes concealed a certain element of envious curiosity—a fact more manifest after the War than before—never entered into my head for a moment. The attitude of the French seemed to me both franker and nobler. They were more tolerant in matters concerning sex morals; they might prove to be more tolerant in art as well. Here, in the heart of the world's greatest city, I had already wasted four years, and had got nowhere, except as a disillusioned eccentric, starved mentally and emotionally, and only prevented from physical starvation by the fact that, as the son of a well-to-do father, I was still able to pay my way. Even so, I was obliged to put up with a considerable degree of inconvenience, and had to turn out twice a day to dine in a restaurant. I chose, by preference, a French restaurant in Soho, having taken a strong dislike to the tasteless monotony of British food. Since none of my friends were either sufficiently wealthy or un-British in their habits to share this preference with me, I always went by myself, and had long had the habit of sitting alone at the table, usually with a book or paper to divert me as I ate. This habit is deadly and dismal enough in itself when one is still young, eager to live and acquire friends, and only prevented from doing both by the general foreignness of the atmosphere as well as by one's own timidity. In my own case, it was almost fatal, having gone on now for over three years. I had literally no one to talk to except the waiters; and heaven alone knows what restrained me from a plan I frequently cherished of going up and speaking to some perfect stranger who sat, as I, alone and silently at some table.

The restaurant that I usually frequented boasted of no one sufficiently distinguished or intelligent-looking to make it seem worth my effort to approach them. For this reason I had taken occasionally to visiting another, equally French in cuisine, but much less pretentious, where I had heard vaguely that literary society was sometimes to be found. The only literary people I discovered there, whom I could identify immediately from their published portraits, were Hilaire Belloc, G. K. Chesterton, and a red-faced blond-haired man whom I soon discovered to be Chesterton's younger brother. These three intrigued me less by their conversation than by their table manners. As soon as they had seated themselves they immediately began bawling for the waiter. Their appetites once satisfied, they launched out on a conversation in voices so hard and rasping as to be heard in the remotest corner of the room. This conversation, as I recall it, was always about politics: the iniquities of the Asquith government, the silliness of the suffragettes, the corrupt influence of the Jews. I have never heard these men make a purely literary judgment.

In my ignorance of London literary society, I too readily accepted their remarks as typical, and began to wonder whether all London literary society was like that. Perhaps it was for this reason that I never dared approach Bernard Shaw, who lived only six doors away from me in Adelphi Terrace, and whom I frequently saw walking in the streets, or attending the same concerts and art exhibitions that I attended. Perhaps this slim, athletic figure, in his neat brown tweed suit, walking with long strides, head erect and white beard floating to the wind, would prove, if I came close to him, no lion, but mere common clay. Perhaps he too, though the thought seemed incredible, would put himself in the class of those who thought their position entitled them to a display of bad manners—a position already occupied in my mind by the figures of Belloc and the two Chestertons.

CHAPTER V

As I sat in my Adelphi Terrace apartment, in the spring of 1913, aimlessly sorting out, arranging, and rewriting the vast heap of poetical manuscript I had brought with me from my former lodging, the resolve came upon me more strongly than before to abandon London for Paris. There were other Americans there, I knew, besides Holley; and among them I might easily find more stimulus for my mind than London now afforded. There was the possibility, more and more seriously considered since coming abroad, that I might myself alter the bent of my own career, and, in some way, emerge not as an unsuccessful poet, but as a capable painter. There was, above all, the hope that in Paris I might find the physical fulfillment I needed, and which I had already put off too long. The fact that I would have to abandon Adelphi Terrace and give up an apartment already leased for three years, after little more than three months' tenancy, did not particularly matter.

The question, however, arose whether I ought to leave London without publishing anything, or whether I ought now to make some further effort to enable the poems I had already written to see the light of print. I had reason to believe that however bad they might be, they were at least no worse than thousands of others which were annually published. In preparation, I had divided them into five small volumes. These were *Fire and Wine,* a book about purely imaginary loves and about poetry in general; *Fool's Gold,* dealing more directly with personal experiences, and with my increasingly pessimistic and disillusioned attitude towards life in general; *The Book of Nature,* in which I tried to ape the Georgians as closely as I was able; *The Dominant City,* the most ambitious of all, in which I attempted to describe the essence of a modern city, in terms less reminiscent of Whitman than of Baudelaire and Verhaeren; and finally, as by afterthought, *Visions of the Evening,* written almost entirely in the winter of 1912-13, and representing perhaps a closer approach to the absolute poetry of the symbolists than anything I had yet attempted. Ought I to abandon all this amateur scribbling and scratching on the eve of my taking up an entirely new life in Paris, or ought I to make some attempt to save it? It seemed to me that the best solution would be to publish all these books, as a memorial of my misspent years in London, before I departed, and to forget about them afterwards.

I had heard that there were publishers in London who were not averse to publishing small books of verse, if they were paid to do so; and I felt certain that this was now the only way left unexplored by which I could ever reach the public. I could, of course, recombine my already divided manuscripts into a single volume, and publish one bulky book instead of five small ones. But I decided that this would not really serve my purpose so well with the critics and reviewers as the bringing out of five volumes, under five different imprints, might do. The only detail that remained was to find my publishers. Four of the manuscripts were immediately shipped off, in each case with a letter frankly stating that I was prepared to cover in part, at least, the costs. These went to Grant Richards, who was known to have brought out many interesting and unusual books, but who was supposed to be in such desperate need for money as to be practically bankrupt; to Constable, an old firm which had been slowly declining, and which was just now reconstructing its staff and personnel; to Erskine Macdonald, already notorious as being willing to publish any poet who would pay; and to a new firm, about which no one knew anything positively, just entering the field under the name of Max Goschen. The only book which, at the last moment, I decided to exempt from the prospect of paying for, and to send to a firm without any such suggestion on my part, was the one on which I had worked the longest, *The Dominant City;* this went to some big London house (I think John Murray) with a simple request for consideration.

The result was much as I might have foreseen. John Murray, or whatever the name of the firm was, declined *The Dominant City* with thanks. The other firms all suggested interviews, which I promptly accorded. I found Grant Richards to be shrewdly disposed to haggle the last possible penny out of me for the honor of appearing under his imprint, but once his price was accepted, frankly amusing about his own ups and downs as a publisher. Erskine Macdonald, on the other hand, was astonishingly cheap, but so unbusinesslike in detail as to cast a doubt on his probity. Constable was eminently matter-of-fact, though fair; and I might possibly have gone no further with them, well knowing that the manuscript I had submitted, *The Book of Nature,* to be the weakest of the lot, had I not sensed a certain sympathy with my aims in young Michael Sadlier, who had just joined their staff, and who displayed before me an unexpected knowledge of modern French art and poetry.

The most sympathetic treatment came from the new firm of Max Goschen. The actual ownership of this firm, I discovered, lay in the hands of a wealthy woman who, having nothing in particular to do with her money, had been persuaded to undertake the launching of this new enterprise; but the management was now in the hands of Douglas Goldring, a young Cambridge graduate who had but recently published some realistic verses of London slum life, reminiscent of Masefield, which I happened to have read and enjoyed. Goldring was perfectly frank with me about the somewhat doubtful prospects of his firm's continuance, since it appeared that his backer was already losing her enthusiasm. He charged me astonishingly little for printing the manuscript I sent him. He was the only one, so far as I know, who followed up the publication of my books by advertising them, and who seemed genuinely in sympathy with many of my aims. His chief poetical enthusiasm lay, as I remember, in the works of my near namesake, James Elroy Flecker, whom he had known at Cambridge, and whom he was now trying to persuade to abandon his earlier publishers in favor of this new firm. Through him I learned much concerning this poet's aims and ambitions. I also learned that he was already a victim of tuberculosis in Switzerland. So I gradually came to respect one of the few Georgians whose work may be destined to outlast his day. The acquaintance struck up with Goldring was in fact so rewarding that I decided to bring out, not only *Fool's Gold,* but also *The Dominant City,* just rejected by Murray, with his firm; and so it happened that two of my books came out under the same imprint, in uniform style and binding.

All these books came out in a single month, May, 1913. By the end of that month I had already closed my flat, had gone abroad, and was installed in Paris. I have still in my possession a score of notices which recall to me the reception they obtained at the hands of the British reviewers. Most of them fell afoul of the somewhat cheaply imitative Baudelairisms of *Fire and Wine.* Most of them tried to find something to praise in the still weaker pages of *The Book of Nature,* which was normal enough under the circumstances, since no doubt all these reviewers came from the public schools, which had carefully inculcated the notion that the only poetry worth reading was English romantic nature poetry. Several of them commented sardonically on the fact that I had published, not one, but five books, in one month. The *Times Literary Supplement,* which did not choose to dignify my name with more than small notices, came out roundly with the opinion that *The Book of Nature* was the best of them. Only two critics, as I recall, gave me notices that were neither contemptuous nor condescending. One of them was A. R. Orage of the *New Age,* whom I had met long ago in my early days when I was still under the influence of Hobson; the other Edward Thomas, whose work on the *Bookman* I had followed with sympathetic interest and to whom I sent *The Dominant City* along with a personal letter. Thomas not only stated that this book contained my best work, but that I was still "experimenting in technique and in moods, so that his 'dominant city,' London, might be any city in the presence of a solitary, sensitive, questioner. But already his words and his solemn or tortured feelings seem to promise an achievement that would satisfy his readers, if not himself."

He followed this up by writing to me, and even consented to visit me, at least on one occasion, at Adelphi Terrace. I have a vivid memory of his shy, sensitive Celtic face, with its great shock of fiery red hair, poised between the back of a gray upholstered couch, and the warm cream-colored walls of my luxurious lodging. I did not realize then that, under the promptings of Robert Frost, he was already blossoming forth as a poet. I noticed only that he seemed friendly enough, but ill at ease, as if astonished at my affluence. No doubt all this affected him strangely and disagreeably with the thought of his own poverty. We came in reality from worlds too different to be bridged by a single contact; and he departed with my warm good will, but having had, in the end, very little to say. I only met him once again in later years.

As I have said, I was already settled afresh in Paris by the time my books came out in London; not only settled, but taking my first steps towards the literary society that I was later to frequent. Holley had already introduced me to one more American exile, Skipwith Cannéll, a southerner like myself, and a graduate of the University of Virginia, who was living in Paris on some thirty dollars a month provided for him by American relatives. He was, I soon discovered, writing short poems of which he was inordinately vain. These poems had been, in the first instance, as profusely strewn with rhymes as those of my early idol, Edgar Allan Poe. But hearing from me that I had long since changed sides, and that, after publishing five books of such poems, I was now writing other verses that laid no claim to metrical constancy, nor to regularity in rhyme scheme, he promptly tore up the bulk of his own early work and declared that he too was done with academic rhymes and meters. He then proceeded to grace our next meeting with a new poem which was entirely rhymeless, and written in cadences closely resembling those of the Psalms in the King James Bible. So early was I equipped, not with a literary comrade, but with a disciple!

Cannéll soon frankly amused me by his desire to go me one better, and to outdo everybody in violence. He was, or averred himself to be, a revolutionary anarchist, declaring that he envied two of that species who had recently been killed by the bullets of the police, after an all-night siege of their stronghold in Montrouge. He had gone from the Latin Quarter and had witnessed this battle, all the while envying the brave men who were thus expressing their contempt for society, and wishing that he could slip through the police lines and join them in death. France, England, and the whole of Europe were only worn-out, emasculated countries, having long ago lost all their virility; and the whole of their culture and art was worth precisely nothing. For his part, he wished he could be an Indian, or go back to the mountains of Virginia, where he had long ago hunted and had once met, he declared, with a panther, and there live on nothing but what game his rifle provided. All this was said with an air so naïvely frank, and accompanied with so candid a look from his wide blue eyes, as to make me doubtful whether his remarks were only a pose, or whether there lay beneath them some vein of sensitive feeling, deeply concealed. He had, as I learned, read practically no poets, and knew almost nothing but Poe and the Bible—a circumstance which I thought might perhaps bring forth literary work no less interesting than the work I was now doing, which was, as I thought, probably influenced by the reading of too many modern French writers.

Paris in May, as those who have seen it can testify, is extraordinarily beautiful. It certainly never appeared to me more beautiful than that spring. The horse-chestnuts which line the boulevards, and which, in late summer, litter the pavements with their scorched and shriveled leaves, were now in the full bravery of young foliage and blossom. Many an hour I spent in some café with Cannéll or with Holley or with Fergusson—whose acquaintance I soon made—pausing in my conversation to admire the beauty of their leaves "silhouetted against the tall and delicate, patrician-tinged Spring sky." The two official Salons were then open, as well as the Independents, which was both more stimulating and more amusing. I literally reveled in pictures. The theaters were all going full blast, and the opera season was approaching its climax. Above all, the Russian ballet which I had first seen in London in 1911, and the year following at the Châtelet, was now about to reopen in its new home at the ultramodern and gorgeously decorated Théâtre des Champs Elysées.

I had now solved the problem of conversational French sufficiently to make myself tolerably well understood. There was so much for me to see and do, so many impressions crowding into my mind, that I put from me, during the entire time of my stay, all thought of sexual adventure. I was in love now, not with a woman, but with Paris herself, that combination of masculine rationality and of the eternally feminine which the French genius had conceived. If I ever wearied of

Paris I could, I knew, take train for Versailles and there spend a day roving about the vast gardens which had enchanted me before with their combinations of wildness and artifice, their stillness and solemnity. I could also have pushed my explorations as far as Saint-Cloud, Saint-Germain-en-Laye, or even Chartres. But Paris, for the moment, was sufficient.

Before leaving London I had begun a series of new poems, written without respect to fixed metrical standards, which were to be exact transcriptions, not of thought, but of mood, and which, in their combinations of vowel and consonant sounds, were designed to produce the effect of modern music. These poems, conceived under the triple influence of Mallarmé, Gauguin, and Debussy, I decided to call "Irradiations." The third of them, inspired by my Adelphi Terrace windows, had already been set down on paper before I quitted London. In Paris others rapidly followed, at the rate, as I recall, of one a day. In them I found such a release for my pent-up spirits as had never come to me in any poetry that I had yet written.

One night, as I was sitting with Cannéll after supper, on the open-air terrace of the Café Closerie des Lilas, facing the great fountain and the green splendor of the alleys of the Luxemburg Gardens, my table was approached by Fergusson and a stranger, whom the painter introduced to me as Ezra Pound. Fergusson said that the thought had come to him, as they had sat inside the restaurant, seeing me on the terrace, that two Americans who were also poets ought to know each other. So having turned Pound—who had just come from London—over to me, he departed. I introduced Pound to Cannéll, and the three of us sat down.

I must confess that I eyed Pound with considerable interest, having already heard about him while in London, and having read, with attraction and repulsion almost equally balanced, his own early volumes. What I saw was a man of about my own age and height, dressed in a brown velvet coat, a shirt open at the neck and no necktie, and pearl-gray trousers. His fine-chiseled, forward-jutting features were set off by a rounded mass of fiery curly red hair and a beard and mustache similarly red and curly, trimmed to a point. Gray-blue penetrating eyes, shielded by pince-nez, peered at the world behind high-projecting cheekbones; and a high-pitched, shrill, almost feminine voice provided strange contrast to the pugnacious virility of the poet's general aspect. He had, I soon saw, slender feminine hands, which, as he talked, he fluttered to and fro. His body was almost equally mobile, jumping and twisting in its chair, with a backward jerk of the head, as he emphasized each point.

We soon launched out on a discussion of vers libre, which I supposed myself to be practicing. Pound immediately averred that he had been writing vers libre for years, and promptly regaled us with a long account of his own theories. This account, involved as it was, was frequently interrupted by gesticulations and by a slight cough which came between every other word. It involved reference to so many critics and theorists whose works I had not read, from Gustave Kahn down to the Italian futurists, that I decided to keep silence.

Cannéll, however, was not to be quelled so easily, and as soon as the endless flow of talk stopped for an instant, interposed with the blunt retort, "As for me, I don't know much about all these French and Italian theories; but the best vers libre is still that of the King James version of the English Bible." Pound, I could see, was instantly impressed and disconcerted by this sally. He took off his eyeglasses, polished them nervously, and coughed several times before replying. Then he asked Cannéll to show him some of his own poems, whereat I, who knew well how Cannéll had simply followed a lead I had given him, took refuge in stony silence.

I contrived, during my stay in Paris, to see Pound several times again. He learned that I was already the author of five books which I had brought out at my own expense in London, as well as of a sixth, embodying a new revolutionary theory of verbal orchestration, which I was now writing in Paris. He promptly promised me a review of my early volumes in *Poetry,* a Chicago magazine of which he was the foreign correspondent. He was as good as his word.

I discovered him to be as baffling a bundle of contradictions as any man whom I had ever known. Internationally Bohemian in aspect, he yet preserved marked far-western ways of speech and a frank, open democracy of manners. Hating the academicians of England, he yet laid claims to be a great scholar in early Provençal, Italian, and Latin. Keen follower of the *dernier cri* in art and letters, his own poetry was often deliberately archaic to a degree that repelled me. In short, he was a walking paradox, a pioneer in the last great wave of American expatriates who, like myself, had turned from the West to the East and had come abroad before the European War, bent on submitting their own rude and untaught native impulses to the task of assimilating and, if possible, surpassing the traditional achievements of Europe.

The wave that succeeded him, the far too famous "lost generation," learned nothing much from Europe or America, but largely discovered their own petty and neurotic selves—a fact of which we are now being reminded every day. Pound and I, on the other hand, were both pioneers, discoverers, self-educators—and we both inhabited London. That made the chief link between us.

I was so desperately in need of friendship as to be ready to accept anyone who was American, literary, and, like myself, an expatriate. Pound supplied the lack, answered the requirements. I genuinely liked him, was prepared to overlook any faults he may have possessed, and was also prepared to return to London, because it was the place where he lived. Here was an American who, by using his wits, had succeeded in the attempt in which I, a more well-to-do man, had lamentably failed; and he had succeeded, through sheer resourcefulness and courage, in keeping himself before the British public. He soon realized how deep and hard-rooted my own literary ambitions were, and how I affected to despise my own as well as all other literary ambitions the more, as my own failure to achieve anything as a writer became more manifest. Towards my own early books he was scrupulously fair in the review he wrote of them, published in *Poetry*, though I cannot believe that he seriously admired them. He was even more enthusiastic, at least at the outset, about the new manuscript of "Irradiations," and spent hours listening to my description of the attempts I was then making to orchestrate in words.

He seldom or almost never discussed his own poetry, I noticed, except with an apologetic cough and a nervous twitching of his fine, leonine head. But about poetry in general he rapidly became dogmatic. His three chief hatreds were superfluity of adjectives, inversions, and rhetoric, all three being summed up in his special cause for detestation, John Milton. He disliked equally all the Georgians, with the solitary and surprising exceptions of Davies and De la Mare. What he chiefly hated in them was less their sentimental nature worship than the habit, equally derivable from that stupid old ass Wordsworth, of tacking morals onto poems where they did not belong, and of lapsing from concrete statement into woolly abstractions. As the Georgians had long been a thorn in my own flesh, I was disposed to agree; and I even, for a time, shared his dislike of that fountainhead of all evil, John Milton. Yet I never considered myself in any way Pound's disciple, feeling from the outset that his brilliant and vivid display of technical resources often concealed a poverty of emotional depth.

I am, however, perhaps anticipating some of the many meetings and talks I had with him on my return to London. Of this I am quite certain: that it was in Paris that he first broached to me the prospect of supporting a literary review under his editorship. I agreed to this project readily, as I had already entertained similar ideas of my own. Early in 1911, when the *English Review* had passed out of the hands of Ford Madox Hueffer and his original backers, I had tried to buy it, feeling that the proprietorship of so distinguished a periodical would be the best means of establishing my name and reputation among the literary circles of London. By the time I met Pound I had become a published and unsuccessful author, and I now felt my money was of no further use to me except as a means of helping other struggling young authors to find an outlet for their work.

The plan that Pound laid before me was simplicity itself. He was acquainted with two Englishwomen, Harriet Shaw Weaver and Dora Marsden, who were then running a weekly paper of radical feminism, called the *Freewoman.* Miss Weaver was financing the paper solely as a means of publishing the writings of her friend, Miss Marsden. As Miss Marsden's writings consisted only of four or five weekly pages of abstruse philosophical comment on feminist psychology and on the need for liberation from all conventions and traditions, couched in a style that was both involved and heavy, and informed by an attitude which was nothing more or less than individualist anarchism carried to the most extreme lengths, the remainder of the paper, left to Miss Weaver's direction, was filled with such scraps as she could find. Pound had met these ladies, had persuaded them that he knew a good deal about the younger and more radical writers of London, and was already engaged in the task of finding literary contributions for them. He now proposed to me that I should put up a small sum every month, to enable him to pay his contributors, and that he should become literary editor of the paper and print whatever contributions I cared to send in, along with the rest. I agreed to this; but inasmuch as my pride had already been hurt by the fact that I had been obliged to pay for my first publication, I refused to continue with the practice. I insisted that I should not myself contribute any literary work to the paper, that my name should not even be mentioned in its columns, and that Pound should not reveal to his contributors the source of the payments he made. I took up this unbending attitude the more readily, as I had myself already met Miss Weaver and Miss Marsden, and had been obliged lengthily to argue the point before they had consented to accept, without payment, one of my own early poems. Pound's judgment I knew to be superior to theirs; but as long as their names appeared as chief editors, I felt that my dignity demanded that I hold aloof.

The paper had been called under Miss Weaver's and Miss Marsden's editorship the *Freewoman;* it was now rebaptized under the title of the *New Freewoman.* But it was not long before Pound's discontent with the name caused it to be called, with a fine disregard of popular feeling, by the challenging and resounding title of the *Egoist.* The money I gave, to pay for literary contributions, together with Pound's own skill in picking them out, together with the continued subsidizing of the printing by Miss Weaver, soon gave the paper a certain acclaim among the more literate; though I must confess that I never discovered anyone capable of perusing regularly the philosophical essays by Miss Marsden on the front pages. I recall, however, that during the next spring, in 1914, the paper went so far as to have flaming contents bills displayed at Charing Cross and other places in London; and one of these which has come down the years in my possession actually bears my name prominently displayed. To tell the truth, I rapidly weakened in my resolve not to use the paper that I was helping to support, as a means to the circulation of my own work, and I began to send Pound contributions some time after the summer of 1913. As Mr. Foster Damon in his recently published life of Miss Amy Lowell has pointed out, I was still resisting Pound's blandishments to enter the columns of the *New Freewoman* as late as September, 1913; but sometime between then and the year following, I yielded.

I am, however, again anticipating my story, and must return to the conclusion of my six or seven weeks' stay in Paris. The contacts and outlets that Pound had already revealed to me as possible with the advance guard of English literary society—for besides his connection with *Poetry* and with Miss Weaver's paper, he was establishing a connection with the *Smart Set* in New York, was still loosely allied to the *English Review,* and had made moves in the direction of *Poetry and Drama,* then appearing under Monro's editorship—these contacts and outlets finally decided me not to abandon London in favor of Paris, but to stay on in Adelphi Terrace. Though Holley obligingly offered to find me a flat in Paris, and though I actually inspected one or two attractive unfurnished apartments there with him, I soon concluded that, thanks to the lucky stroke of my meeting with Pound, my place was still in the British metropolis. I remained in Paris only to witness the close of the Russian ballet season early in June, and to conclude work on my new series of "Irradiations." These were entirely completed when I returned. As I worked on them at the time, I realized, with increasing exultation, that now for the first time in my literary career I was writing something entirely my own, which was closer to me than anything I had yet done, was nearer to expressing my own inmost essence as man and as poet. These verses, so free, wild, untrammeled by respect for form, had come to me quite easily. I had not, as was the case with earlier ones, felt cramped by any restrictions in writing them. And by following my own moods as they led me, I had achieved work that seemed to me to emerge from an entirely different source from that of any I had yet done, and which surprised me myself, as I read it.

Much had gone to making this brief marvelous moment of my first period of full poetic inspiration possible. In the first place, my previous study of the French symbolists and my earlier tentative experiments in vowel sound, to be found emerging here and there in the pages of my early volumes, had convinced me that a poetry which employed the fullest tonal resources of the language, was intensely rich in the combination of vowel sound, assonance, alliteration, internal rhyme, was more desirable of achievement, and might now more easily be achieved. In the second place, the prodigality of postimpressionist pictures and of modern music that I found in Paris were both working on me to fortify me in my determination to forget every rule and precedent, and to bring out a poetry which would follow the life spirit, the inner rhythm of my own moods, and not some preconceived outer pattern imposed by my mind upon nature. In the third place, I had already become intoxicated with the barbaric color, the rhythmic splendor, of the Russian ballet.

As I have said before, I first saw this organization in London in 1911, and had sat spellbound through the barbaric splendor of *Scheherezade* and the Polovtsian dances from *Prince Igor.* I had been moved by these to make some of my own early experiments, such as the poem "The Vowels," and I had specially come to Paris in the year 1912 in order to see their organization again. There, at the Châtelet, I had been swept away by Nijinsky's magnificent dancing in the *Spectre de la Rose,* by Karsavina's superb *Tamar,* by Nijinsky's daringly original and nakedly pagan conception of *L'Après-midi d'un Faune.* It seemed to me that in such works as these lay the fusion of all the arts of which Wagner had merely dreamed; that here the conflict between Apollonian restraint and Dionysiac ecstasy that had gone on throughout the nineteenth century had been finally resolved into an art that was Apollonian only in that it expressed itself through the plastic relationship of the dancers' bodies, but was fundamentally and overwhelmingly Dionysiac in general effect. Now, for the third time, I was under the spell of this extraordinary art. And this time the miraculous Nijinsky stepped out from his role as *premier danseur* to the position of ballet director, replacing Fokine for the purpose of creating two new ballets: *Jeux,* with music by Claude Debussy, and *Le Sacre de Printemps,* written by the then young Igor Stravinsky, who had already flashed across the pages of musical history with his brilliantly exotic *Firebird* and with his mordantly ironic *Petrouchka.*

Jeux, as I recall it, proved to be angular and athletic, of no particular importance except as a display of technical virtuosity on the part of that incomparable pair, Karsavina and Nijinsky. Its music clearly suggested Debussy's waning powers. But long before *Le Sacre de Printemps* was set for production word went out that it was utterly revolutionary as regards both music and dancing, that it broke with every remaining convention of the old Italian ballet, that it represented a solstice festival and the sacrifice of a virgin in remote pagan Russia, that it went back behind recorded history into the realm of ethnology and primitive religion. All the students of the Latin Quarter were naturally anxious to see what the *Sacre de Printemps* was really going to be like; and on the opening night they jammed the top balcony of the theater, prepared to cheer Stravinsky and Nijinsky to the echo. I had already purchased three seats, in the section just back of the orchestra stalls, and I invited, as my guests, Fergusson and Miss Rice, to accompany me.

Thus it came about that I was privileged to witness, at first hand, the most remarkable demonstration I have ever seen in the theater. It was easy to see, by reading the program that Nijinsky, as the new director of the ballet, had decided to take no part in it. In his place was a group of nondescript youths and elders, and in the place of Karsavina was another group of virgins, the leader of whom, the girl chosen to be the sacrifice, was merely an unimportant ballerina who bore the name of Piltz. The ballet was to be in two scenes. In the first, representing the morning of the opening day in spring, the elders were to come forth and dance around the sacred rock which lay in the open fields beyond the village. Then the youths and the virgins were to assemble, the youths pursuing, the virgins alternately fleeing or inviting their advances; until only one virgin was left, who was to signify, by a gesture of touching the earth, that she chose, instead of a mortal mate, the high and fatal privilege of becoming the bride of the sun. The second scene was to take place on the same spot, after night had fallen. The virgin who had elected to be the sacrifice would stand, festively decked, alone on the stage. She would express, in a long solo dance, her ecstasy at having been chosen to insure the earth's fertility for yet another year. Then the elders would rush forward, clad in the skins of bears, seize her, strangle her, and hold her body aloft to the sky.

It was obvious merely from reading through this program that here was to be something altogether novel, shocking, and unexpected. And a noticeable quickening of pulse ran through the packed audience, as the lights were lowered, the conductor took his place, and the music Stravinsky had created began to be played.

For the first four or five minutes, as I remember, the audience sat quiet, absolutely disconcerted by the extraordinary combinations of barbaric sounds and rhythms that were pouring forth from the orchestra, and by the strangely angular poses, jerks, and leaps which Nijinsky had devised to express the essence of this weirdly discordant music. Then slowly, as I recall, from here and there arose cries of protest: first a catcall from one of the boxes, then a loud whistle from the stalls. Then hissings, groanings, and a shouted remark of objection. This was followed by hand clappings, by the beating of programs on the backs of neighboring seats, by louder and louder whistlings. Throughout the first scene, the noise increased, swelling to a climax as the orchestra leapt forward to the moment of the virgin's choosing. As the curtain fell, pandemonium broke out all over the house, and in the tumult I heard clearly one man's voice screaming, "C'est la musique boche," followed by loud catcalls. The lights remaining lowered restored some measure of calm. The conductor's baton was immediately lifted, and the orchestra now launched out on the muted sinister music of the nocturne leading into the second scene. Fearing that some actual violence might take place, I began to whisper to Fergusson, anxiously asking him what would happen next. He assured me that the Paris crowd had always acted like that in the face of any novelty in art, and that for his part, he was very grateful to me for giving him the opportunity to see this ballet, which he regarded as one of the most interesting works of art he had ever seen in his life. The curtain then went up, to the groans of the goaded audience, revealing the dancer Piltz, standing alone in a spotlight, in the midst of the darkened stage.

How this soloist ever succeeded in getting through the long and exhausting dance that followed, I do not know. Her performance was a tribute to that native heroism that shines in common humanity at hours when we least expect it, as well as a revelation of the superb discipline the ballet had given her. Literally, pandemonium now again broke loose, absolutely drowning out the orchestra. Shrieks, hoots, bangings, whistles were coming from all sides at once, and the gallery packed with students only made matters worse by beginning to yell, "Bravo!" Sergei Diaghilev, his face purple, his whole body tense, was standing visible to half the audience, in the wings, shouting, "Continuez, continuez." Loud altercations, even fist fights, were breaking out in the boxes. Somehow Piltz finished her heartbreaking task, and stood breathless and panting before the yelling mob. But by now the students in the gallery had organized their counterdemonstration, and a loud roar of "Bravo!" resounded throughout the house, to be taken up by Fergusson at my own side, and by all those who were on the side of Nijinsky's dancing and Stravinsky's music. From that time on, the minutes which followed were marked by increasing applause, against which the opposition desperately fought on, but in vain; and when the final curtain was rung down on the group of elders holding up the virgin's limp body, there was almost an ovation. But no dancers came before the curtain; the conductor dropped his baton and disappeared and the orchestra followed him. It later transpired that Nijinsky and Stravinsky had both already quitted the theater along with Diaghilev, fighting back their tears.

This performance of the *Sacre de Printemps* more than anything else that I have ever seen in my life confirmed me in my determination to risk everything in order to become a modern artist. To be a modern artist involved, I saw, a determination to make and accept every kind of experiment, and not to flinch from any novelty, however strange and uncouth it might seem, or however deeply it aroused the hatred of the mob. If one wished to be a modern artist, one must be prepared alike for one's own isolation and for the mob's contempt—as Cézanne and Gauguin and Van Gogh had been prepared, as Nijinsky and Stravinsky were prepared. There was but one lesson the modern artist must learn and ponder: the lesson already proclaimed by the Irish dramatist Synge, who had said that poetry, to be human again, must learn first to be brutal. In revolt against the elaborations of end-of-the-century aestheticism, against the romantic movement faltering in sentimental prettiness, against the genteel tradition in decay, artists everywhere were turning back to the primitively ugly, knowing that in primitiveness alone lay strength. As yet none saw the pitfall, that in a world given over to the worship of naked and raw force, war was inevitable. Only the man who had, in my hearing, cried out on that first night of Stravinsky's ballet, "C'est la musique boche," had, probably unconsciously even to himself, hoisted the danger signal.

In the manuscript of "Irradiations" which I took back with me to London were tributes to Nijinsky, paeans to dancing, glorifications of the color and intoxication of sheer life to put all the grim and monotonous pessimism of my early poems utterly to shame. It seemed to me that after so long a false start, I was just launched out on the yet uncharted sea of literary life, and that by accepting each moment as it came, without undue worry about the future, I was now learning how to live. Nietzsche must have been right after all; only he who could learn how to dance with heart and legs would be able to triumph over the future. Man's greatest victory over adverse circumstance lay in the power to dance over tragedy. Dionysus had vanquished Apollo finally. Had not the Russian ballet revealed this in the astonishing performance I had just witnessed? I too, I thought, would regard my art henceforward as a dance, as a game to be played with life, not as a sermon or as a piece of labored moralizing. What other lesson, after all, remained to be discovered, except that life itself was merely a great ballet, and one which—except to the performers themselves—need not be taken too seriously?

CHAPTER VI

Immediately after my return to London the first person whom I sought was, naturally, Pound. And no doubt I detailed to him in full measure the thrills and excitement that had come to me on witnessing the first public performance, by the Russian ballet, of Stravinsky's *Sacre de Printemps*. He had not witnessed this performance, and I was soon to discover the reason.

At the time of which I am writing, Pound was living in a single room in a large block of buildings bordering on Church Walk, in Kensington. In order to reach his lodging one had to go through a narrow alleyway that ran alongside the Church of St. Mary Abbot's—the ringing of whose bells, he declared with emphasis, was the greatest nuisance of his life—and so walk past the disused old churchyard at the back, crowded with sooty marble gravestones, to the door, which reached, by means of a dark stairway, his second-floor furnished room. This room, large and ill-lit by two windows, was, in contrast to that which I inhabited, notably barren of comfort. As I recall it, a plain white-enameled bedstead stood at the right beside the door through which everyone entered. On the same side, directly underneath one of the windows, and so placed that anyone sitting at it would receive the light from the left—a concession to Pound's own weak eyesight—stood a long oak table, serving as desk, usually littered deep with manuscripts and a typewriter. By the opposite wall, facing the bed, stood a tall wardrobe, while on the opposite side to the desk, underneath the other window, was a plain iron washstand. Between these was the fireplace, disused in summer, and generally kept littered with scraps of rejected manuscripts and letters. A smaller square table, in the center of the room, and two or three chairs completed the ensemble. From the spring of 1914 on, a carved alabaster group by Gaudier-Brzeska, of a man and woman embracing, stood on a stand close by the edge of the worktable, and contrasted, with its fine silhouette and delicate surfaces, with the general shabbiness of the surroundings. When I first saw Pound in Paris I had been struck by his dandified airs, and by the general splendor of his exterior. He perpetually wore pearl-buttoned velvet coats, fawn or pearl-gray trousers, a loose-flowing dark cape, sported a Malacca cane with silver top, and, though usually hatless, sometimes affected a sombrero. Here, however, it was immediately obvious that all this display merely concealed a state of poverty bordering upon indigence. I became more and more convinced that I should act as the patron to the young writers and artists he was now helping to name and fame, in the columns of his *Freewoman.*

His manners, however, which had appeared both friendly and frank to me on our first meetings in Paris, rapidly became disconcerting. The more I studied him, the more I was convinced that he was a queer combination of an international Bohemian and of an American college professor out of a job. No one could tell just which side would be uppermost, on any of our meetings. Thus, for example, he soon gave me sufficient personal encouragement, as a poet, to induce me to show to him the manuscript of my newly written "Irradiations." He kept these by him over a week; then, at our next meeting, carefully went over them all, giving me, for each one, his detailed and adverse criticism. I have still by me, in my papers, a record of what he said, a record which reveals fully the meticulous and obstinate zeal by which he strove to make all poets with whom he came into contact, into followers of his own methods. What he chiefly objected to, in my verses, was their not infrequent descent into what he called the "obvious." For example, where I had originally written, in the second of these poems, "I fear to see the ghosts grotesquely gibbering from the shadows," he insisted that "grotesquely gibbering" was "obvious," and succeeded in getting me to change it into "the ghosts that stare at me." Equally obvious was a phrase in the third poem, "Seamews skirl desolately and flick like bits of paper propelled by the wind." This, however, I refused frankly to change. In the fourth of the series, in the lines,

> The palpitant mosaic of the midday light
> Colliding, sliding, leaping and lingering,

the internal rhyme, "colliding, sliding," also was listed as too obvious, while in the fifth, which I myself have always regarded as one of the most successful, the lines

> Lacquered mandarin moments, palanquins swaying and balancing
> Amid the vermilion pavilions, against the jade balustrades,

were again rated as obvious, and therefore cheap.

He likewise disconcerted me by his only too apparent desire to infuriate people, and to gain notoriety by so doing. In this respect, I think, he had modeled his conduct after that of Whistler, who, a full generation before, had sustained his own fame only by making repeated jabs at the hippopotamus hide of the British public. By the somewhat flamboyant romanticism of his early poems, with their skillful blend of the troubadours and Browning, Pound had already roused in London a sort of vague stupefied curiosity. Now in the full tide of that curiosity, and while he was still in the process of transforming himself from a late romantic to a classic poet, he deliberately chose to antagonize more and more people. When I returned to London I found him, as he declared, busily engaged in a big campaign against the Georgians. As I had no particular love for the Georgians, I asked him what he was doing. It seemed that a critical article had just appeared, in one of London's most influential literary weeklies, under the signature of Lascelles Abercrombie, one of the leading figures of the Georgian group, in which the young poets were all advised to abandon their realism and to study Wordsworth. Thereupon Pound had immediately sat down and had written a letter to Abercrombie as follows:

DEAR MR. ABERCROMBIE:

Stupidity carried beyond a certain point becomes a public menace. I hereby challenge you to a duel, to be fought at the earliest moment that is suited to your convenience. My seconds will wait upon you in due course.

Yours sincerely,
EZRA POUND.

For a moment this letter, recited gleefully to me by its author, seemed a clever thing; but it soon seemed to me that its indignation was far too strenuous. Whistler, under similar circumstances, would have contented himself with a contemptuous gibe. Nor was I mistaken in thinking that, in Pound's case, his zeal far outran his discretion. It later appeared that Abercrombie, a totally inoffensive person, took the challenge quite seriously, and having learned from one of his friends that "Ezra was an expert fencer, felt at first so disconcerted that he did not really know what to do. Then bethinking himself that the challenged party has, after all, the choice of weapons, he sat down and solemnly composed a letter to his opponent, in which he accepted the challenge, but proposed that the parties concerned should mutually bombard each other with unsold copies of their own books. Whereupon the laugh was neatly turned against the indignant Ezra, and he had nothing further to do but to retire in disgust.

This leading trait in Pound's own character, thus early displayed, this inability to fight on without losing his temper and giving his own case completely away, explains—if I may be pardoned a digression—clearly enough the situation in which he now finds himself, as an ardent defender of Mussolini to the English-speaking peoples. Unable to impose directly his own will on the literary society which he has frequented, unable equally to win and hold anyone's allegiance for long, he is obliged, by the force of circumstances, to admire publicly anyone who had been able to make *his* will paramount, and so to impose it upon an entire nation. That Mussolini may be a great statesman is totally beside the point. What motivates Pound's admiration is not Mussolini's statesmanship so much as Mussolini's determination to get on. Pound is, alas, and in despite of himself, still infected deeply with the pragmatic American philosophy that "nothing succeeds like success."

I believe that I resisted Pound's attempts to change me into a poet more suited to his liking, violently, from the outset; and I have reason to hope that I gained his grudging respect thereby. In any case, I was able, by quotation and example, to show him that my favorite French symbolists were using my own devices of internal rhyme, vowel assonance, and the like; and my remarks to that effect seemed to impress him with the thought that there might be something in the symbolists after all, whom he had never actually read. Accordingly, on his next visit to my flat, he borrowed an armful of my French books and departed. When I next saw him, he was already enthusiastic over de Gourmont, Corbière, and the early Francis Jammes. On our very next meeting he told me that he was hoping to do an article for Orage of the *New Age* on these poets. The article soon swelled itself into a series of notes which were duly printed, and which ran for several weeks. They have since been reprinted in one of his essay collections. I must confess that I felt somewhat aggrieved at his taking credit, thus blithely, for introducing these poets to the English public, when I had not only discovered them in the first instance for myself, but had discussed them with him minutely. I felt that he had simply exploited the knowledge I had gained before him, to serve his own ends; and this feeling led to the first rift between us. On his next attempt to criticize me somewhat adversely and to treat my writings as if they were the works of one of his disciples, I accordingly retorted in kind, whereupon he returned to me all the French books he had borrowed, intimated that he expected nothing further from me, but expressed the hope that I would still allow him to send the best of "Irradiations" to the office of *Poetry,* where they would be paid for. I could not help admiring the dignity with which he bore the affront I had chosen to administer, nor the real generosity with which he, a poor man, was ready to help a well-to-do poet like myself to gain a hearing. And so the breach was healed between us.

One day he spoke to me very highly of Robert Frost, an obscure New England farmer who, at the age of forty, had come to live in England, and who had just published his first collection of poems, *A Boy's Will,* in London that spring. I duly went to the office of the publishing house where, as he told me, copies were to be obtained of this book, and having bought it, read it. It seemed to me that there were not inconsiderable echoes both of Wordsworth, whom Pound valiantly despised, and of the still hated Georgians, in Frost's work. But I was curious to learn more about this American who, like myself, but at a still later age, had come abroad before he could find a publisher. My curiosity was rapidly appeased, for at my very next visit to Pound's lodging, as I recall it, he picked up a typewritten manuscript lying on the table and proceeded to read it aloud. The title was "The Death of a Hired Man"; the author was Frost. Pound read it to the last syllable with every mark of admiration. Personally, I felt the poem to be somewhat cold and prosaic, a deliberate exercise in understatement. I remained puzzled by Pound's hearty approval of poetry so stark as this; for in my own "Irradiations," despite disagreements about detail, he had already found much to admire. My own verses, clean contrary to Frost's practice, were not at all stark, bald, and conversational in tone; on the contrary, I had tried to be full, clangorous, unrealistic, metaphorical, and confusedly rhetorical. Was it then that Ezra Pound was simply a chameleon, shifting his opinions from day to day as he shifted his coat; or did he frankly possess some touchstone of superior judgment which enabled him to admire equally poems so diverse as Frost's and my own? The question puzzled me not a little. I decided, then and there, that at all events the world which Frost's creations inhabited could be none of mine; and to this decision I have stuck, whatever it may have cost me. Nevertheless I still admired Pound intensely for his championing of another outcast American.

Throughout the months that followed I continued to see a great deal of Ezra Pound; and I soon found his company so stimulating that I consented to come out of my isolation and to accompany him on visits to some of the literary figures whom he admired, here and there, in London. Thus I first met Ford Madox Ford, or as he then called himself, Ford Madox Hueffer. With him I remained painfully shy and self-conscious, and, in the end, somewhat disposed to believe that his attitude towards all Americans was at bottom rather British and patronizing. With W. B. Yeats, I am sorry to say, I got on no better; he seemed too old and too sure of himself to understand what I was after. But with the younger group whom Pound had already baptized with the title of "Les Imagistes," and was even then collecting with a view to publishing a small anthology of their poems, I fared best. There was, for example, the tall upstanding figure of T. E. Hulme, whose theories of language had actually led to the formation of the imagist school. He was far more interested in modern art and philosophy than in poetry, and introduced me, I think, to Jacob Epstein, with whose works I had grown familiar since my arrival in London.

Hulme was, as I remember, excited over the furore that this sculptor's memorial to Oscar Wilde had recently caused when set up in Père-Lachaise Cemetery in Paris. Because the cemetery authorities had insisted on its removal unless the sculptor would modify a detail of the anatomy of the figure, he wanted to organize an international petition of protest by artists, on Epstein's behalf, and was delighted when I said that I would sign the petition. Soon after I met him he startled me by recalling the fact that years before, on my first coming to London, he had met me in Orage's office, and had then asked me to attend meetings of a poets' club held in a Soho restaurant, meetings out of which the imagist movement had slowly grown. I found his company stimulating. Whether he was altogether serious in his beliefs, or merely having a good time by playing with novel ideas, he succeeded in concealing his aims under a cultivated appearance of playfulness which was, at any rate, greater than Pound's. Once, for example, he amazed me by declaring publicly, before some other people, that his chief pleasure in life lay in reading Immanuel Kant's *Critique of Pure Reason* while lying prone, at full length, in a well-filled, warm bathtub—a remark which I was too much of a novice to regard, at first, as being the good-humored swagger of a young man of high spirits and intellectual capacity. I saw a good deal of Hulme up to the onset of the War, when he immediately volunteered, was sent into the trenches, and soon after was killed.

I noted, however, that he avoided meeting Pound, for reasons which he did not state. To tell the truth, there was bad blood between them, a resentment similar to that which I myself had felt since Ezra had decided to write his series of notes on the French symbolists. Hulme felt that Ezra was simply exploiting ideas which he had originally given him, and was claiming them for his own. Ezra felt that he was making sufficient acknowledgment of his own indebtedness to Hulme by printing the small handful of poems which Hulme had written, as an appendix to his own most recent book. Thus the queerly compounded alliance between the young English student of philosophy and the American expatriate was already at an end, though neither spoke of the fact, and always remained outwardly polite to the other.

There was also Frank Flint, bespectacled, shy, apologetic, whose attitude towards life and poetry afforded an instructive contrast to that of either Pound or Hulme. His dominating characteristic was a pathetic sincerity. Born to circumstances of direst poverty, forced to get an education as best he might, never released from the hard necessity of having to earn his own living, he had interested himself in the symbolist movement to such an extent that when Emile Verhaeren came to London and read some of his poems before an audience at the Poetry Bookshop, Flint had constituted himself companion and guide to the Belgian poet, and had shepherded him—ignorant of English as he was—through London for several days. He was, like myself, fully aware of all the literary currents in Paris. Thus he had heard of, and read, the unanimists, who, following upon Whitman and Verhaeren, were then just beginning to be talked of. Unfortunately his enthusiasm, as I soon discovered, was not balanced by over-much discrimination. Regarding himself as a badly educated man, ashamed of his own Cockney antecedents, he could easily be talked down by Ezra, or by anyone who appeared to be better educated, and who was capable of making flat, dogmatic assertions. In life and in his own poetry he was already suffering from that sense of personal inferiority which has made him a tragically ineffectual figure. And though I liked him, I soon realized that he was doomed perpetually to follow, and never to lead.

As I have already said, Ezra was then actively busy at the task of gathering together all the imagists he could find, for the purposes of bringing out an anthology that would serve as a counterblast to Harold Monro's *Georgian Poetry*. Immediately on my return to London, he asked me to join this group. I hesitated for a moment, and then refused. I had already familiarized myself with the imagistic poems and articles which had been, since that spring, appearing in the pages of Miss Monroe's magazine *Poetry*, and I was unable to find that this group had any particular positive program to offer. They had insisted on the direct treatment of the subject, the avoidance of any words that did not contribute to the presentation, and a mode of composition which followed the sequence of the musical phrase, and not the sequence of fixed metrical usages. It seemed to me that this was scarcely enough. Pound's own views on what the poet should or should not do were, as his criticism of my "Irradiations" had shown, rather negative than positive. It seemed to me that I had, long ago, before my acquaintance with him, striven to put into practice most of the positive tenets of the imagists, and that other poets might also be engaged in doing so. Thereupon Pound, no doubt determined to put pressure on me for the sake of breaking down my obstinacy, asked me to meet the American poetess, H. D., then already engaged to the young Englishman, Richard Aldington. I agreed to do so, and the meeting duly took place that summer.

I recall vividly that it was on a warm and sunny afternoon, I think sometime early in August, that I came to meet H. D. at her flat in Kensington, not far away from Pound's humbler lodging. I had already been prepared for the event by Pound, who had assured me with emphasis that he considered her poetry the best example of what he meant by imagism. I had accordingly read as much of it as had then been published, and had greatly admired its very vivid and keen sense of rhythm. But I had been slightly repelled, despite my admiration, by an archaism in choice of subject that seemed to me to bespeak a limitation of imagination as well as by an occasional harshness in tonal quality that seemed to indicate a deafness in respect to the quality I myself had tried to develop by the use of contrasting consonants and vowels. H. D.'s poetry seemed to me too purely visual—not such a combination of visual imagery and auditory echo as I had recently tried to write. Moreover, whether I willed it or no, I was deeply committed to the task of attempting to deal, as a modern poet, with the life all about me to take much pleasure in H. D.'s Hellenism. Where W. B. Yeats, then the reigning god of Pound's adoration—I recall his attempt to change a line in my "Irradiations" into something "more Yeatsian"—had been able, without doing deadly violence to himself, to become a modern poet, inasmuch as his work stemmed from the folklore and traditions of a country which had not, as mine, long since submitted to the destructive influences of modern industrialism, H. D.'s retreat into the past seemed to me to smack somewhat of an evasion. Nevertheless, I had been already fired by Flint's and Pound's obvious enthusiasm for her poetry, and was genuinely eager to meet her.

It was past teatime when I arrived, and I recall vividly that I was in none too good a mood, having already experienced a difficulty in finding the address. Aldington, who opened the door and greeted me somewhat effusively, explained that they had already given me up, and had started their tea, which only added to my embarrassment and irritation. In the pause that followed, while a teacup and cakes were being handed to me, I had the opportunity to observe my hosts, for I gathered from Aldington's introductory reference to his fellow poet as "Hilda" that they were already fast friends.

They were, it seemed to me, an oddly assorted couple, providing a complete contrast. While H. D. was tall, slim, lithe, with a pale oval face framed in masses of dark hair, and a nervous shyness of manner that only emphasized her fragility, Aldington was bluff, hearty, and robust, with the square shoulders of an athlete, the bullethead of a guardsman, and a general tendency to beefiness which proclaimed his British quality. He was, I judged, extremely young, possibly a few years younger than H. D., and I had read nothing of his except a few poems which, in their somewhat playful and faunlike imagism, were obviously derivable from hers. I thought it best to break the ice between us without further delay, so I launched forth on a eulogy of H. D.'s work, in which I especially praised her way of looking at nature, with its unusually vivid quality of seizing upon the emotional essence of some scene, and setting it down directly before the reader. I concluded that I had also striven for, but had probably not obtained, this quality, possibly because I was too much involved in the besetting sin of being either too rhetorical or too abstractedly didactic for the purpose.

H. D. nervously assured me that, for her part, she was never sure that anything she had ever written had been good. Ezra encouraged her to write and to go on writing. She simply wrote as she felt.

Aldington, however, was not to be daunted. He had obviously listened much to Pound, and was prepared to put his own interpretation on Pound's theories. He began:

"If you feel you are either too rhetorical or too didactic, you must have a tendency to write like old Whitman whom I have just been reading, and who might have been a jolly fine poet if he hadn't been spoilt with the idea that all poets should mouth platitudes in pompous language, and so draw a highly moral lesson from what they saw. Like every American, Whitman had to be cosmic. Bah! What is cosmic?" he went on with a laugh. "It's just as silly as old Tennyson's notion to make his King Arthur as much like Prince Albert as possible, in order to please that fussy old frump of a Victoria. The great American peepul had to be flattered, and told they were going to save the world. So poor old Whitman had to go cosmic in order to flatter them about it."

I was annoyed, less at Aldington's derogation of the Whitmanian cosmic cult, which I had already rejected, than at his obvious belittlement of Whitman as a poet. Whitman had, in fact, long since appealed to me as a poet of an entirely different order from Tennyson.

"I don't want to save the world in the least; but if the modern world is either to be saved or damned I want to be able to say so," I replied.

"But why bother about the modern world? If you are a poet, you either feel something or you don't. If you feel it, why don't you set it down, whether it has anything to do with the modern world or not? You remind me of the futurists, making a great deal of fuss over automobiles and aeroplanes, and writing damned bad poems about them. Why don't you write about something that you really feel?"

I realized that it would be useless to retort that I *was* writing what I felt, and that if it didn't turn out to be imagistic, it was no fault of mine, but I held my peace. H. D., who had been watching me somewhat anxiously, now interposed.

"Ezra has already told us that you don't want to go into the new imagist anthology. Richard and I are very keen on this idea of an anthology of all the writers who don't belong to the Georgians. We think we ought to band together, and show everybody what can be done in these new forms of verse. In fact, Richard is to be the editor of this anthology. Why don't you come in and join us?"

This was rather a facer. A few months before, I had been assured that Ezra was unquestionably the leader in the imagist group. He had spoken to me as if the new anthology were to appear under his sole editorship, and had tried to get me to come in. I had only halfheartedly refused, and wondered at my doing so. But why should I accept now, if the editorship was to be in the hands of this young Englishman, who was capable of making jokes about Walt Whitman?

I took a moment before replying.

"I am sorry, but I don't really feel that I can make my poems fit your ideas."

"Can't you tell us what is the reason, Fletcher?" here interposed Aldington suddenly, his face flushing as he spoke. "We are perfectly ready to help you to find an audience, if you will only co-operate with us. We don't ask that your poems should be entirely like ours. Ezra tells me that you have recently written some very fine vers libre poems. Why can't you let one of them stand as your contribution to our anthology? You can pick out whatever one of them you like, and we will make no objection!"

The naked force of this very British appeal for fair play was having its effect upon me; so I stumbled over my next words.

"The reason why I can't come in with you is just this. You see, H. D.'s poetry and yours is rather like a Greek temple: something remote, refined, and pure, like the Parthenon. My poetry is not like that. It is shambling, grotesque, formless, like a primeval monster. In fact, compared with your poetry, it's like a dinosaur. Well, it occurs to me that you don't want a dinosaur in the Parthenon."

H. D., as I could see by the pained expression on her face, was shocked by this remark. As for Aldington, he simply laughed and threw up his hands.

"That's a very good epigram, Fletcher," he said, without a trace of ill-humor. "You may, of course, be right. But please believe us when we say we only wanted to help you."

I was already regretting the impulse that had prompted my sally. Why was it, I asked myself miserably, that now, though Pound was ready to throw his friends in my way, I could not accept them, could not get along with them any better than I had with my earliest friends in London? I tried hard to divert attention from the painful situation that I had created by asking H. D. as to what she was planning now to write. She replied that she had been thinking about translating an entire Greek play, one of Euripides's, perhaps, in a style entirely different, and closer to the original than that of Gilbert Murray. She was now at work on some of the choruses, which she proposed to translate in meters corresponding to the originals. Since I could not read Greek myself, and knew nothing of Greek meter, this left me at a loss, and the conversation languished miserably. As I rose to go, Aldington took me by the hand.

"Maybe you will reconsider your decision yet, Fletcher," he said earnestly. "If so, please let us know in the next few days. We have to send all the material for the anthology on to America, in order to get it published."

I walked away from the flat, but I did not reconsider my decision. On the contrary, I judged that having once made it, I must stick to it, for the sake of dignity and consistency. Having already in my heart objected to the logrolling and backslapping of the Georgian group, why should I not object when Pound and Aldington tried the same methods? So though I could not help feeling a twinge of regret at my lost opportunity, I still refused to become a member of Pound's band of recruits—and all because I felt a dinosaur more appropriate as a description of my poetry than a Parthenon!

I stayed in London that August, as I had stayed in July and June—a season still blent in my heart with tender memories, since this was the last year that the old peace of Europe, which had remained unbroken since 1870, still largely prevailed and spread its brooding and somnolent calm over the world. The summer before, I had been, for a brief time, in the Austrian Tyrol, and had seen everywhere how even the meanest villages were bedecked and beflagged and illuminated in honor of old Francis Joseph. How remote is that day to us now! And almost equally remote to the present generation is the summer I then passed through. It was the day when the Derby and Ascot still had a meaning to all Englishmen as great social functions; the season of horse coaches, with scarlet-clad footmen and coach horns, running down to the racecourses; the hour when the flower stalls of Piccadilly Circus, now I believe, banished, blossomed forth in new and more incredible colors; the time when Caruso and Melba sang nightly at Covent Garden, and when the Russian ballet followed, stirring phlegmatic London to enthusiasm, but not to the fever heat I had witnessed in Paris; the moment of the Royal Naval and Military Display at Richmond, of the "Trooping of the Color" in St. James's Park, of the Flower Show at Chelsea Hospital. The natural stiffness and correctitude of English deportment then unbent; contrasts of wealth and of squalor were more cunningly blended; the grimiest and the dingiest, the most dignified and the most absurd, the worst-planned and yet the most lovable of Europe's great cities, took on new life and color, as the great clouds, blown by the southwest wind past Land's End and Portland, up the Channel, were tinged with blue smoke and the gold of midsummer sunlight while they soared over the chimney-potted rooftops.

One could walk down Old or New Bond Street, between rows of shops, each the most expensive of its kind: shops in which, it was said, everything could be bought from a house to the furniture and pictures, the silver and glass, the groceries, wines, and cigars necessary to stock it. And one could rub shoulders on the pavement equally with duchesses or with ragged, cringing beggars. One could go into Hyde Park and mark the millionaires cantering along Rotten Row on their pure-blooded horses, between a profusion of tulips or geraniums; or go to the other extreme and, by Marble Arch, listen to a hard-bitten old Socialist telling his audience that what England wanted was red revolution. One could dawdle by the Embankment, and see the factory chimneys of Southwark rising amid smoke above the desecrated Thames, while the bronze sphinxes that guard Cleopatra's Needle kept their enigmatic smiles, seedy beggars drowsed on the seats, and a pavement artist recopied his design in colored chalks at one's feet. Or one could plunge into Whitechapel or Soho at night, in the midst of a sea of chaffering and swarming humanity, gathered like flies about the acetylene flares of the stalls.

All this, and more, was London; and it did not relinquish, but rather held more tightly to its Victorian stolidity and its inexplicable charm. From the heights of Hampstead to the north and Surrey to the south, the city then unrolled itself: an endless vague sea of shifting smoke and stolid stone or brick before the alien sight-seer; parks and trees and chimneys, gas tanks, public houses, suburban streets grimly straggling and coiling, a wisp of pale gray for the far river, the dim phantom dome of St. Paul's; all dappled with light and shadow as the clouds raced over the sky. London is unique; dignified, but without the elegance of Paris; opulent, but without the garish display of New York; grim, but without the hideousness of Berlin; sordid, but without the squalor of Dublin. It is the most masculine, and yet the most reserved of cities; and for that reason there are few who can conquer it. Rather does it mark everyone with respect and awe for its own grimly sustained and secret tradition.

How, I wondered, as I again walked the crowded Strand, could such an alien as I ever hope to conquer London? Could I batter down the walls of the exclusive clubs standing along Pall Mall, clubs behind whose tall, yawning windows were to be seen vaguely rows of domed massive bald heads, each drowsing over some vast achievement of his past? Could I ever aspire to the authoritative anonymity of the *Times Literary Supplement,* which Pound affected to despise each week, while he, as I, probably secretly envied those who wrote for it? Could I admire the tame jokes vended in *Punch,* or sit passively through a long tedious day of cricket at the Oval? I knew I could not. I had abandoned America so long ago that America was scarcely any more than a memory. I had long forgotten the sultry baseball games, the restless, noisy crowds, the surging smoke-maned trains, the smell of summer in the remote woods. Yet this sphinx of a city still remained cruelly aloof, and unsubdued by any spell I could command. Secretly, I began almost to regret again the Paris I had abandoned, the city where I had already seen the poets, Paul Fort at their head, dining and arguing and gesticulating night after night in their own particular café room.

Yet there were in London certain compensations. If I could not go to Paris, some part of Paris might yet possibly come to me. Holley, for instance, came over at the end of June, and revealed to me his own discontent, rankling and pitiful, with his economic and domestic situation. Cannéll came too, on a two weeks' visit, to borrow my money, attempt to cut a swath through London's literary society, and to depart as grimly and ungraciously as he came. Fergusson sent me a letter of introduction to Middleton Murry and Katherine Mansfield, then engaged on the enterprise of editing together a magazine called *Rhythm,* which was devoted to the cause of postimpressionist painting, the Russian ballet, the Russianized short story, and modern French poetry. I duly met them and was the more impressed by Katherine Mansfield's frail simplicity than by Murry's rather superior air of bored arrogance. I thought for long of sending them some of my poems for consideration, but refrained. I also met, early that summer, yet another exile who had recently strayed from Paris to London; an inexpressibly ragged and dirty gamin, aged about twenty, with a wisp of beard and eager piercing eyes, looking like a combination of faun and medieval Christ, who told me that his name was Gaudier-Brzeska. He showed me superb line drawings of animals, talked for an hour about his ambition to go to India, live in the jungle, and carve nothing but tigers and elephants, and asked me to come to his studio under a disused railway arch somewhere in the wilderness of Chelsea. I met painters and poets and stage designers, journalists and simple failures that summer; and yet I did not feel entirely at home in London.

In the midst of all this stir and bustle, there came to me news of the arrival of a visitor from overseas whose career and fortune were later to be so closely linked with mine that it was only after her death, twelve years later, that I realized the full importance of this occasion.

CHAPTER VII

It was, as I recall it, early in July that I happened to meet by chance, in my usual Soho restaurant, young Michael Sadleir, whom I have previously mentioned as having been in contact with through Constable. Since I had first met him, he had displayed to me an unusual interest in modern French art and poetry, and our relations were both warm and cordial. Accordingly, the moment he entered the restaurant I invited him to sit at my table, and I immediately began discussing my somewhat dubious relations with Pound and with the imagist group in general.

"You Americans are certainly a queer lot," remarked Sadleir. "Only the other day, there turned up at our office an enormously fat woman who insisted that she was the author of a book of verse which had been recently published by Houghton Mifflin of Boston, and of which, under the standing agreement we have with that firm, we had taken a few copies for sale in England. She wanted to know where those copies were, and when no one in the office could tell her, declared that she would not leave the place till they were all traced and found. We had to scour the basement for them. It took us two hours, and all the while she sat there, refusing to budge till we found them," he concluded with a laugh.

"What was her name?" I inquired, feeling vaguely curious.

"It was Amy Lowell. Apparently she has a lot of money, as she kept her taxi waiting all that time, until we unearthed the precious book.

Anyway, she chose to regard our neglect of it as a personal affront. The whole office was upset until she went away."

The conversation then passed on to other topics, but what Sadleir had said remained in my mind, for a few days later, when I went to call upon Pound at his lodging, it came back to me. I thereupon retold Pound exactly what Sadleir had already said, in the same form as that given here. To my great surprise, Pound changed color and showed by the expression on his face how deep was his annoyance.

"Sadleir doesn't know in the least what he is talking about," he retorted angrily. "I have already met Miss Lowell, and she is both generous and genuinely interested in modern poetry. I am to meet her again at the Berkeley Hotel, in Piccadilly, tomorrow night. Why don't you come along and see what she is like, for yourself?"

I accepted this invitation, and so it came about that a night later I found myself with Pound outside the door of Miss Lowell's apartment on the top floor of the Berkeley Hotel, facing Green Park and the long lamp-lit vista of Piccadilly. A short, stout figure in a reddish-purple silk dress, with a high choker collar, cut in a style which was old-fashioned at the period of which I write, came forward and greeted us warmly. So this was the redoubtable woman of whom Sadleir had spoken, and by whom Pound had been already impressed! Except for the fact that she was obviously the possessor of considerable wealth, she might have been a New England schoolteacher. Indeed, her round pleasant face, equipped with eyeglasses and brown graying straight hair simply dressed, standing up around her forehead and fastened into a knot at the back, recalled distinctly to my mind an English teacher of my high school days, who used to electrify her class by remarking, apropos of some pointless answer by a student, "That doesn't cut any ice with me at all."

Miss Lowell was obviously far more of a lady than the teacher in question, but she bore the same marks of a resolute and masculine determination. Now she did gallantly the honors of the occasion. While we were sitting in the large bow window, I drinking in avidly the view it afforded, while Pound and she discussed the literary people of the day, two efficiently noiseless waiters brought in a table and served an elaborate six-course dinner. During its progress, I noticed that the conversation, hitherto entirely confined to Pound and herself, had shifted from gossip about personalities to theories of free verse and imagism. But I must confess I scarcely followed it. While the waiters were clearing away, Miss Lowell went to a box standing on her writing table, and opening it, offered us large cigars wrapped in tinfoil. Both Pound and I declined, contenting ourselves only with cigarettes; but not to be daunted, Miss Lowell took out a cigar from the box, carefully unwrapped it, cut off its end with a cigar cutter which lay close to her elbow, and having remarked that she always smoked cigars and that her doctor had said they were good for her nerves, lit it.

The conversation, interrupted by the removal of the dinner things, resumed at the point where Pound, having already discussed at great length Hulme's theories of language and H. D.'s imagism, as well as all the French theories of vers libre imaginable, was about to begin again. But Miss Lowell interposed:

"Just what, precisely, do *you* mean when you speak of imagism? What is your personal theory of free verse, and of imagist poetry? I take it that you came to accept this theory after a period in which you tried composing according to the stricter, old Italian and Provençal forms. What convinced you that this new theory was right?"

Ezra here launched out into an involved explanation, accompanied by many gestures and jerks of the head. The explanation took in Chinese ideograms, the late Professor Ernest Fenollosa's essay on the Chinese written character, which Ezra had recently found among the unpublished papers which Fenellosa had left after his death, and other recondite and abstruse matters. He finally cited, as an example of imagism, his own recently written "In a Station of the Metro":

> The apparition of these faces in the crowd;
> Petals on a wet, black bough.

"I think I see more clearly what imagism really is, by now," said Miss Lowell. "I don't suppose I have written a single poem that could possibly fit your definition, but I would like to try it. But you, too, write poetry," she went on, turning to me. "Tell me, are you an imagist poet too, by any chance?"

I replied that I was not, though I had been recently attracted to Pound's theories, and added that I remained a follower of the French symbolists. I asked Miss Lowell whether she had read them.

"I have read Hugo and Gautier and de Musset and all the romantics. I have recently translated plays by de Musset and Rostand. Oh, yes—and I have read with great enjoyment, José Maria de Heredia, and Leconte de Lisle, the so-called Parnassians. Tell me, who are your symbolist poets?"

I mentioned a brief list.

"You seem to have read an enormous amount of modern French poetry. It really is amazing for me to realize that I have had to come all the way to London, in order to find two young Americans so vitally interested in modern poetry. You know in America people have scarcely begun to think about it."

I acknowledged the compliment with a smile. I felt disarmed by the frankness, the friendliness, the sincerity of this unknown older woman.

"I have just bought all of your books," she went on, here turning to Ezra, and indicating a pile of books that lay on the writing table. "Won't you please read for me something, something that you yourself like?"

Ezra complied, and read his "Seafarer," a poem I myself had recently admired, in a voice of rugged emphasis. He followed this up by reading "Sestina: Altaforte" and one or two other earlier poems.

"I have seen that one before," said Miss Lowell, referring to the "Sestina." "It seems to me a fine vigorous poem, absolutely like François Villon. I can see, too, that you admire Browning, who has always been one of my own admirations." So bent was she, from now on, to make a good impression on Pound, that she confined the conversation solely to him. I felt ignored.

As we arose to go, I held out my hand.

"I would like to come again and talk to you, and read you some of my own poems," I said, astonished at my own temerity.

"Certainly, by all means. I can see you next Tuesday evening, at the same time," she said, glancing at the engagement pad that lay on her writing table.

As we went away, I told Ezra that I absolutely agreed with him in thinking that Sadleir had been mistaken. Whoever this woman was, I felt she would be a valuable ally to him, in his campaign for imagist poetry.

On the Tuesday evening following, I again stood outside the door of Miss Lowell's apartment. From remarks that she had let fall on the first occasion, as well as from my own deductions, I had already gathered that she was not only a person of considerable wealth, but of considerable importance in Boston. One of her brothers was the noted astronomer; the other was an almost equally famous professor at Harvard. Here was another American, I had reflected, who was obviously interested in modern poetry, and who was just launching herself out on the literary world; a person of independent judgment, avidly curious to know what the most up-do-date poetry was going to be like, and one who, unlike the resourceful Pound, seemed honestly indisposed to exploit other people's ideas without allowing due credit. Well, then, I must be one of the people who would tell her what modern poetry was. In preparation for the impression I was determined to make upon her, I had already decided to give her the five books of verse I had published barely two months ago; but I decided frankly to tell her that I considered them unworthy of me, nothing but the juvenile wild oats of every beginner in the art of verse writing. I decided to limit the discussion from the outset solely to the manuscript of my "Irradiations," which lay, already typewritten, in my hands. This, I concluded, I had better read from beginning to end; but I would lead up to it by a full statement of my own theories of orchestrated verse, and of mood rhythm, so that Miss Lowell could see for herself my intentions.

As soon as dinner was finished, I accordingly launched out upon a discussion of my own theories of orchestral color in vowels and consonants, with a few examples taken from my early writings, amid which the poem "The Vowels" stood prominent. This, I carefully explained, though it borrowed its title from Rimbaud, was entirely different from his own poem on the subject. Where he had arbitrarily given to his vowels the colors in which they had been printed, in a schoolbook of his childhood, I had tried to match mine with their appropriate vocal and tonal qualities in English, so that the combination of certain vowel sounds might suggest to the reader a summer landscape merging from blue and green to deep red and violet, while other vowel sounds might represent the light and shadow playing upon the landscape in question. Moreover, I spoke of Verhaeren, Mallarmé, Rimbaud himself, and other symbolist poets as being, like myself, concerned with the correspondences between vocal speech and music. The object of my own poetry, I went on, was, in fact, to restate Rimbaud's theory of the "alchimie du verbe," and to prove that there lay in words themselves, qualities of evocation independent of their meanings. Coleridge, Poe, and other English romantics were mentioned as having first discovered this quality. Thereupon, I turned and read my manuscript, "Irradiations."

As I look back on that moment now, I do not know whether to be astonished more at Miss Lowell's reception of my verses or at my own audacity in reading them. Probably I read my poems on this occasion hurriedly, without sufficient dramatic pauses between the various sections. At any rate, I had not got very far when Miss Lowell interrupted me with a request that I read one particular poem all over again. And she added, when I had finished, "Why, that is extraordinary. I have never heard anything in the least like it." I could not help recalling that Ezra's poems had not called forth such lavish praise. On the contrary, she had merely compared him to Villon and to Browning. I myself had felt, as he read them, that my own work had a vitality and a freshness at least equal to his. And here I was being accorded more than I asked for.

"I myself think these particular poems far better than any that I have ever done," I said, and went on with my reading.

I had not gone much further when I was again interrupted.

"Why, my dear boy, you have genius," she said, suddenly. It was the first time that I had ever heard any woman refer to me as "my dear boy," and the phrase increased my embarrassment. I also felt overpraised at being called a "genius." Why was it, I reflected, that if I had genius I had not succeeded in impressing either Ezra or the other imagists with that fact?

"You will find that if you read Baudelaire, Mallarmé, Verlaine, Rimbaud, and Verhaeren carefully, that I am not so original as you think," I went on defensively. "May I now go on and finish the manuscript?"

"Yes, please do." So I finished the poems in the midst of further admiring exclamations. When I had concluded, Miss Lowell turned to me and said, "You ought to get all those poems published, just as they stand. I think they would make a great sensation. Tell me, have you a publisher?"

I detailed to her how, in despair of finding any, I had brought out the five juvenile books that now lay on her desk, at my own expense. I said that I didn't want to repeat that particular experience all over again.

"Ezra is sending my complete manuscript on to *Poetry* of Chicago, so that Miss Monroe will be able to print some of them," I went on. "But I haven't a book publisher at all."

"No doubt Miss Monroe will print a good many of them, since she listens to everything that Ezra says. If I were her, I would print them all, just as they are. But you simply must find a book publisher later on. If you can't find one here in England, I will try and find you one in America. You spoke of those poems as being finished a month ago. What are you working on now?"

"I am eager to write a long poem, or a series of shorter poems, dealing with aspects of life in a great modern city, like London," I said. "Something like I attempted to do before in *The Dominant City,* but in this case, more free in form, like 'Irradiations,' and less abstract. I simply couldn't get away from being didactic in *The Dominant City,* because of influences upon my work of the Victorians. Now I would like to do the subject all over again as a series of pictures merely; pictures of what the modern city is really like, without any moralizing."

"How would you set about it?" Miss Lowell, I could see, was keenly interested.

We were sitting in the deep bay window of her apartment in the Berkeley Hotel as I spoke these words. The flowered chintz curtains had not been drawn before the long French windows; and the long line of the glittering lights of Piccadilly, running parallel to the Green Park, lay below. Along the roadway a double flood of taxis, vans, cabs, busses, and hansoms was passing, rolling over the smooth polished surface that dully reflected their headlights. To the right lay the massively squat, heavy array of hotels and clubs and town houses stretching to Park Lane and the Wellington Memorial; to the left the great alleys of the park were swallowed up in mysterious darkness, only the trees bordering upon the street lamps displaying their dense green foliage.

"I would sit and look at every object in just such a view as this is," I said, feeling the excitement, as I spoke, of having discovered for myself this new way. "I would try and describe all these objects, without in any way identifying myself with them. I would try and put down their essence, their moods, so to speak, by finding words and color sounds that would orchestrate them, make them speak to the reader by means of such combinations. I would thus try and get at the dominant moods of the city; the moods of early morning, the moods of evening, the moods of midnight. Then I would take in other objects. For example, the banks, the hospitals, the churches, the hotels, the clubs, the theaters, the stores, the street traffic, the railway stations, the restaurants, the parks, the public houses, the street corners. Thus the whole city would become re-created in my mind by grasping the objects in it simply as objects and as nothing more. That seems to me to be the essence of what the imagists are trying to do. The trouble with them is that they cultivate too much the fragment. They haven't tackled yet, in perfectly free form, a whole city full of people. It has always been my ambition to do so."

"You certainly are ambitious, and your method seems to me extraordinary. It is fascinating and perfectly original. No one has ever tried it before. You ought to call it the 'unrelated method,' it seems to me."

"Not quite unrelated," I countered, feeling vaguely uneasy. "I simply want to be able to look at everything frankly as if for the first time. For that reason, I want to feel detached from it, as if it had a life of its own, which it is my business to see and describe."

I was not aware how much Miss Lowell could understand of this; but at any rate, I felt, as I sat there, that she understood and sympathized far more than Pound would have done. I had never mentioned this particular desire of mine to him, nor to any of his friends. In his case, he seemed uninterested in such ideas, and confined himself solely to the discussion of new forms and the correct use of words. Moreover, the idea itself was derivable remotely from Whitman's realistic "catalogue passages" interspersed throughout *Leaves of Grass* and from Blake's "seeing through, not with the eye"—and I already knew what he thought of Blake and Whitman.

"Have you been working on this idea since finishing 'Irradiations'?" Miss Lowell asked.

"Yes, I have been doing a series of short free verse poems, dealing with aspects of London as they present themselves," I replied. "But, to tell the truth, I am dissatisfied with them as they stand."

"You are probably tired. You look pale, and are extremely thin. You ought to give yourself a rest after such a manuscript as 'Irradiations.' It is a work of genius, and such works are very exhausting. I am glad you gave me the opportunity of hearing it, and glad, too, that you told me about your unrelated method. It is all very interesting, and I think, if you don't mind, I will try it myself."

"Of course I don't mind," I said, realizing again that I could scarcely call such a method "unrelated" when I was already suffering tortures because it seemed to me I could not find enough new verbal and rhythmic forms that would cover all the poems I was planning to write under it. I had been staring at objects ever since I returned to London; and my eyes and nerves were positively exhausted. Only that afternoon I had passed a green lamppost in the street that had seemed as if it started to swing out and hit me a blow as I went by it. Could the lamppost and I, detached as we were from each other, be called "unrelated"?

"I am keeping you from bed probably, dear boy," said Miss Lowell, suddenly consulting a gold watch that hung on a thin chain, along with a lot of keys and seals and other paraphernalia, at her waistband. "Why, it's nearly two o'clock! I am used, you see, to turning night into day. I do all my work late at night, and get up only in the afternoon. You really should be going home. But let me know, before you go, when I can see you again."

I gave her my telephone number, suggesting a meeting whenever convenient, at the same hour and place, and went out. In my heart was a riot of emotions, among which this much stood out. I had impressed someone else beside Ezra Pound. This someone was a vivid, dynamic personality. And I had been called by her a "genius."

CHAPTER VIII

During the brief weeks that followed, I was destined to see a good deal more of Miss Lowell. Indeed, I found my time fairly evenly divided between her apartment and Pound's room. At least once, and often twice a week, my telephone bell would ring; and when I went to the instrument, I would hear a familiar voice, with a strong New England accent, inviting me out to dinner. The invitations came now so frequently that I felt that it would be necessary to invite Miss Lowell in return. As the rule against having any meals at my Adelphi Terrace apartment was still absolute, and as Miss Lowell informed me that she never dined out in a public restaurant, I felt that the only time of the day for which I could ask her would be in the afternoon, for tea, which I accordingly did.

It was on a sunny afternoon in August that I met Miss Lowell at the Berkeley Hotel. There we summoned a taxi to bear us to our destination, but it had not gone very far before engine trouble began to develop. The driver, soon after, took advantage of a halt in the traffic to explain to me elaborately that he was unwilling to risk his motor further than the corner where Adam Street intersects the Strand. I urged him to continue, and he somewhat surlily consented. But on swinging around the corner from the Strand to Adam Street the motor very definitely broke down, half blocking the crowded traffic. The driver left his seat and got out to inspect his engine, while a traffic policeman followed by a group of street urchins and solicitous street loafers swarmed about us. These naturally began to stare at the strangely paired couple within; and so, for the first time, I began to be aware of the physical bulk of Miss Lowell, so much in contrast with my own marked leanness. Having already been assured by my companion that she never walked, I felt that nothing would be gained by abandoning the cab at that moment; there was not another cab in sight that we could hail, and only two blocks farther away lay my own apartment. I could only hope that the driver's tinkerings with his engine would lead to restarting it, but the presence of so many passers-by and the amused expressions on their faces increased my embarrassment to the point of veritable torture. As for Miss Lowell, she seemed in no way to share my perturbation. She was utterly oblivious of the stares and the smiles of the onlookers, and, in fact, seemed to be rather enjoying the experience of attracting so much attention. Finally, after a delay of several minutes, the driver restarted his engine, whereupon the cab crawled exactly one block further, and then stopped for good. I explained to my companion that she had only a few steps more to go, so she imperturbably got out, and after I had dismissed and paid the driver, we walked resolutely around the final corner.

It was a stroke of luck, I reflected, that the cab, after all, had been able to convey us a few steps from the crowded bustle of the Strand. I was still abnormally sensitive on the score of my own personal appearance, and had been so, ever since the days when, as an awkward youth of sixteen, I had entered preparatory school. During my Harvard days I had grown taller but not heavier; and I had, for a time, gone to the opposite extreme in the matter of attracting attention, and had worn, in defiance of convention, the floppy hats, the drooping ties, the outlandish clothes of the Bohemian. On coming abroad, I had gradually dropped the habit of wishing to appear different from my fellows; and my appearance was now markedly conventional and ascetic. I habitually wore dark blue or black clothes—indeed, after my mother's death I wore black for a full year, and had grown so used to it that I kept on with the habit—dark ties and somber black hats were commonly favored, and except that I usually carried a cane, there was nothing whatever unusual about my appearance, barring the fact that I was still underweight for a man of my size, and that my legs were abnormally long in proportion to the rest of my body.

Not so Miss Lowell. The old-fashioned cut of her clothes recalled the nineties; the mannish coats and stiff collars she affected emphasized her square-built masculinity; and her figure, to say the least, was constructed on principles entirely different from mine. I did not know, of course, whether she shared any of my own sensitivity on the score of appearance. Apparently she did not; but I had already begun to fear that my carefully planned tea would fail to please her in some way. She had lavishly praised my poems, more lavishly, in fact, than they deserved; had so generously and royally entertained me, that I feared that the simple hospitality which I was able to offer in return would not make any particular impression.

The day was sunny and cloudless, and the three windows, which commanded the panorama of the Thames, from Westminster Abbey to St. Paul's, lay open. "Why, you've got the finest view in all London!" exclaimed Miss Lowell; and I glowed with pleasure, since I myself had taken this apartment just for that reason.

"I understand, now, why you are so interested in modern city life," she went on.

I countered this by observing that she must know something about modern city life herself, since she lived in Boston.

"No, dear boy, I live in Brookline, and was brought up among the trees and the flowers. I traveled, though, a lot as a young girl, but always because of my health, because my parents made me travel. I never thought, then, of turning those experiences into account."

I was silent.

"This view really helps me to understand your poems better, and the methods you use."

I tried to turn aside the compliment.

"I am not sure that I have got all that there is in it," I said, and asked her what she thought of my room.

She now turned her attention to my books, the most precious of which were displayed in a large reproduction mahogany bookcase in the far corner of my living room. She said that she had been an enthusiastic collector since her youth, and asked me whether I collected any author in particular. I believe I pointed out the Doves Press Bible, which I had purchased at the original subscription price, and two Kelmscott Morrises which I had recently acquired at a low figure. I also mentioned the Ellis-Yeats edition of William Blake, then the only one purporting to give Blake's full text, which I owned, and which was one of my proudest possessions. She immediately countered with the remark that she herself had bought one of Blake's color-printed originals of his Prophetic Books.

Here was obviously someone far more capable than I of collecting the rarest things; yet there was no malice in her remark. Indeed, she admired all the details of my apartment with the gleeful avidity of a child. She liked the two Adam mantelpieces, the couch of Adam design that stood between them, the plain cream-white distempered walls, the bronze candle brackets, the mahogany bookcase, the rose-upholstered wing back chair, the flat-topped writing table. She even admired the single picture, a still life by Fergusson, of pink hydrangeas in a pitcher, which stood over the mantel nearest the windows. She declared that she thought its color scheme absolutely in keeping with the walls and the furniture. And she was, as I could see, impressed when I began to talk of its decorative values, its massed design. She averred that she knew nothing whatever about modern painting, having been brought up to regard Whistler and the impressionists as revolutionary, and that my knowledge of more recent art developments was as remarkable as my knowledge of modern poetry. She had, however, recently become interested in modern music, and cited Debussy, Albeniz, and Bartok as among her favorites. Here it was my turn to counter her earlier remark about Blake, by mentioning Stravinsky, whose *Sacre du Printemps*, in case it came to London, in the Russian ballet season, I warmly recommended her to see.

So the conversation ran on and on, past the tea which I had ordered, and which was duly served; past the sunset, and on into the lingering twilight settling down, till the long curve of the Embankment lights was kindled, and the trams rolled and rocked between them, like elephants with gold-spangled howdahs on their backs. London had fully taken on its nocturnal aspect and it was half-past eight ere news came from below that a taxi, which I had summoned over the telephone, was waiting outside. She turned to go, declaring with warmth and sincerity that she had spent a perfectly delightful afternoon. As for me, I had already felt a return of my embarrassment at being unable to ask her to stop and dine. But her obvious pleasure in being the recipient of such hospitality as I could command banished all my qualms. The effort of playing the host had, however, exhausted me, and I went to bed, after ordering the removal of the tea things.

By returning Miss Lowell's hospitality I had at least attempted to equalize our respective positions. From the outset of my relations with Pound I had felt that, despite all displays of erudition on his part, I knew at least as much about modern poetry as he did; and I had already begun to resent and to avoid all his attempts to bestow patronage on myself. In the case of Miss Lowell, I was determined, if I possibly could, to prevent her from becoming only my patron, and to stand with her, as much as I might, on a footing of equality. Her family, I knew, was one of wealth and social importance. So too, was mine, in my own community. And I wished her to feel that if she could play the part of superior, so could I. It is true that I had little inkling of what it meant, in her case, to be a Lowell from Boston. Although only six years had gone by since I passed through the gates of Harvard, I had disliked that institution so much as not to attempt to study the social background from which it had sprung. And so I was as nearly unaware of the circumstances of her birth and upbringing as if she were newly descended not from Boston, but from the moon. Although I realized that she was older than I in physical years—she would often refer to this fact by way of apologizing to me for her habit in calling me "dear boy"—it seemed to me that, in many ways, her mind was actually far younger than mine. It was a mind that seemed to have lain long dormant, and which now, for the first time, was awakening: avid, greedy of sensation, fast becoming aware of its own possibilities.

So much I had already gathered from contrasting her present and vivid interest in such people as Pound and myself, with the pages of her first book, *A Dome of Many-colored Glass,* which had come out in Boston only the autumn before. This was the book of which Sadleir had spoken to me before my first meeting with her. She had presented it to me after our second. The work in this volume, the product she declared, of ten years' writing, seemed uniformly stifled, muffled, conventional, academic, timid, and tame. I gathered that she was, at forty, only beginning to conquer the cramping conventionalities of her girlhood. And her attitude of unabashed eagerness, the entire mental semblance she bore to a mine of unfettered energy ready to explode and go skyward, only intensified the contrasts between her early verses and her present personality, and confirmed my impression. Since I, too, had but recently thrown off my own academic shackles, and had committed myself to the hazardous experiment of "Irradiations," I felt in closer kinship with her, for exactly that reason.

Some time during this summer, after our first meeting, she went away, making a trip of several days to Rochester and Canterbury, and to call upon Henry James at Rye—a fact of which I made little, since I did not, at that time, feel particularly attracted to Henry James. I did not fully realize that she, as a member of the older Bostonian generation, shared more of James's own well-bred cosmopolitanism, as well as his own scrupulous puritanism of outlook, than I did. Indeed, the paradox of Amy Lowell's career lay precisely in the fact that she was one-half a member of Boston's most exclusive intellectual set, and one-half an adventurous, restless, modern experimenter with poetry. I was also out of London for somewhat more than a week that summer. And no doubt her meetings with other literary people took up a good deal of her time. After my experience at playing the host at my flat, it was some time before we had another meeting. I cannot recall seeing her again until just before she sailed, at the close of August.

She opened the evening by declaring that she had never before been so stimulated to write as during that particular summer. She had got along so well with all the imagists that she had finally succeeded in persuading Ezra to admit a specimen of her work into his projected imagist anthology. She was going to be represented by "In a Garden," a poem she had written a short time before coming to London, and which she had not, at the time, suspected of being an imagist poem. Despite certain differences of opinion with Ezra, she had found him quite fair and open-minded as regards all modern and experimental work. I think I replied to this by detailing some of my own differences with him, but she promptly brushed these aside. It was necessary, she felt, at this stage of the game, that all those who were modern and were writing the new, freer type of poetry should band together and not create needless quarrels. The new group should be given the widest sort of publicity. She herself would have been glad to sponsor their forthcoming anthology and to find a better publisher for it, had not Ezra already entered into other arrangements, in which she had no desire to interfere. She wound up by saying that she felt sure that Ezra would not continue to exclude me, unless I chose to exclude myself—he was too eager for new material. Whereupon I decided that it would be better to hold my peace.

What she had really asked me to her apartment for, she went on, was to hear some new poems which she had written that summer, and which marked, she believed, a new stage in her own development. She wished to read these to me, and to submit them to my judgment. She would be grateful for any criticism.

Here I was really at a loss, for not only had no one as yet—with the exception of Cannéll—read to me their own unpublished work, but in respect to my own I felt still a considerable degree of hesitation. The adventure into unknown poetic territory which my "Irradiations" represented, was still too recent for me to know fully what would come of it. Like William James, I felt, "What has been concluded, that we should conclude anything at all concerning it?" In this respect, I stood at the opposite pole to such a theorist as Pound. My work came to me copiously, in such sudden bursts of enthusiasm as had marked "Irradiations," and I had recently been going through a period of depression concerning it. I had, at bottom, none of the meticulous care in phraseology which would keep such a craftsman as Pound filing and pruning, revising and altering, till he reduced twenty lines to two. I believed, on the contrary, that it was better for me to write poetry on exactly the opposite principle, to enrich my mind with as many ideas and word associations as possible, not to dissociate the emotional faculty from the intellectual, but to strive for a fusion of thought and feeling. My own unconscious impulses were already pushing me in the direction of a greater richness of detail, a greater complexity of form. So, though I was eager to see what a person of Miss Lowell's intellectual capacity might make of the new poetry which Pound or I or the imagists generally were writing, I did not feel able to criticize her work in any detail.

In rapid succession she now read to me, as I remember, "The Precinct, Rochester," "The Cyclists," "White and Green," "Aubade," "The

Captured Goddess," and finally "A London Thoroughfare, 2 A.M." Of these the first two instantly appealed to me, as I realized they reflected my own mood—which had also been Pound's and that of many other Americans—of keen disillusionment with the smug self-satisfaction, the rotting inertia, the "emotional anemia" of England. They expressed this mood in a form which was sharper and more personal and more free than any which I commanded at the time. I had written my own early verses of disillusionment concerning England, in *Fool's Gold* and other places; but they were inferior to hers, and I promptly said so. When she had acknowledged this compliment, she passed on to "Aubade" and "White and Green," which I adjudged to owe quite a good deal to the influence of H. D. and of Aldington. She did not dispute this verdict; and began reading "The Captured Goddess" and "A London Thoroughfare." As she read these, I felt forced to acknowledge to myself that the new medium in which they had been written was almost entirely my own.

This discovery caused me considerable embarrassment. Should I, as Poe had attempted to do before me, register some protest against imitation carried to the point of duplication, or should I simply hold my peace and say nothing? My companion admitted freely, after reading "A London Thoroughfare," that the idea for this poem had come to her after hearing me discuss, some weeks previously, my own theories of how poems about a modern city should be written, and after watching intently, late at night, the scene that lay outside her own windows. Although this particular poem of hers did convey a vivid, instantaneous impression, like a lucky snapshot, of London, I was not sure that it was superior to one of my own, written about the same time, which was still now fresh in my mind:

> By day or night this street is not still.
> Omnibuses with red tail-lamps,
> Taxicabs with shining sides,
> Rumble, shunning its ugliness.
> It is corrugated with wheel-ruts,
> It is dented and pockmarked with traffic,
> It has no time for sleep.

> It lifts its old scarred countenance
> Skyward, between the buildings
> And never says a word.
>
> On rainy nights
> It dully gleams
> Like the cold tarnished scales of a snake.
> And over it hang arc-lamps;
> Blue-white death-lilies on black stems,

"I shall have to discuss that poem with you later," was all that I said, when "A London Thoroughfare" was finished. "Please read now the other one." And so Miss Lowell complied, and read me "The Captured Goddess."

But if "A London Thoroughfare" had been an altogether independent and honest attempt to render the quality of a single instant in London's life, what was I to say to "The Captured Goddess"? With amazement and dismay I hearkened, while her voice spoke the lines.

> "Saffrons, rubies, the yellows of beryls,
> And the indigo-blue of quartz;
> Flights of rose, layers of vermilion,
> The spotted gold of tiger-lily petals,
> The loud pink of bursting hydrangeas."

And I had just read to her such lines as

> Amid the vermilion pavilions, against the jade balustrades

And also,

> The gardens of my heart are green;
> The rain drips off the quivering leaves;
> In the green gardens of my soul
> The crimson peonies explode—

lines of which Pound had loudly disapproved, but which I had let stand, despite his disapproval. Now they were already coming back to me, with their "peonies" changed into Fergusson's hydrangeas. I had to say something.

I scrutinized Miss Lowell's face a moment before speaking. It wore an openly and frankly triumphant expression, as if she were sure her last two poems were the best of all. No, I could not tell her. She was older than I, and imitation in this case was the sincerest form of flattery.

"I think those two poems are the finest you have ever done," I said, and was not surprised when she concurred with me in that statement. "You have got hold of something in that London poem that has been worrying me for long, and which I have not yet expressed. And in the other, you carry further an idea which I only sketched out roughly in "Irradiations," but which you now develop. You have already come a tremendously long way from your *Dome of Many-colored Glass,* and your work interests me now much more than that of any poet I know."

Miss Lowell beamed with pleasure.

"Of course I owe it all to you, dear boy," she said, frankly, and I thought, on the whole, generously. "But you can't imagine how proud it makes me feel to hear you say that I have gone much further than you. I am afraid you are mistaken. Still, I am so glad that I came to London; if I hadn't I might never have written these."

So it came about that I took her gesture of imitation rather as a friendly challenge than as something to disapprove of or to distrust. After all, if my idea of the use of orchestral color words, or if my notion that the poet should develop his own qualities of detached and detailed observation at the expense of the generalizing faculty, were in any way correct, what did it matter how many poets borrowed from my own work? And, also, Miss Lowell was an American. It was just beginning to dawn upon me that my work might come in time to add something to American poetry, which had seemed so moribund during all my early years. Perhaps Miss Lowell might even learn, through my example, to influence the still young and vigorously naïve effort to achieve a civilization which was now going on across the Atlantic. If so, I wished her well, for the nonsuccess of the years I had spent in England had disillusioned me as to the possibility of making any impression whatever upon the British.

My verses still seemed to me entirely without precedent—no one having, in those days, either read or heard of Gerald Manley Hopkins—and were merely a hazardous attempt to go the symbolists better in a richer, more markedly onomatopoetic language than their own. If Miss Lowell chose to imitate them, why should I resent that fact? My conviction that my work might, after all, be good was only increased by my finding someone capable of sharing it. Try as I might, I could not trace the parentage of my verses further back than to a combination of Coleridgean or Poesque sound effects with the rhythmic freedoms of Blake and Whitman. Therefore I could see no possible objection to anyone's using my technique, or misusing it. I only knew that I must go still further in the direction to which my discoveries tended. Like Columbus before me, by dreaming of a voyage west to reach Cathay, I had stumbled somehow upon America. Now I must prove that the country I found was really Cathay after all. I might fail in the end; but I did not believe that Miss Lowell, or anyone else, could ever rob me of the credit for my discovery.

So Miss Lowell sailed away from England that summer without any breach in our cordial relations. On the contrary, I felt more and more interested in the fact that here was someone older and in many ways more experienced than myself, who had not only found so much good in my poetry, but who was prepared to profit by what she had learned from it. Neither Pound nor any of the imagists, nor Cannéll, nor any of my earlier friends, had paid me such a tribute. And I must confess, it flattered whatever vanity I may have possessed.

In order to show her that the interest I took in her was genuine, I had questioned her closely about the type of poetry which she herself—apart from imagism—wished to write, and soon discovered that she had long felt a special leaning towards poetic narrative, a leaning intensified by her persistent study of Chaucer, Keats, and Browning. Here, however, I was somewhat at a loss, for I had long since felt that I myself had no aptitude whatever for narrative poetry; and Keats, whom she extolled to the skies, seemed to me then much inferior to Shelley. When, however, I said so, citing Shelley's magnificent use of symbolism in such a work as "Prometheus Unbound," together with his love of wild nature, that made him able to project himself into every mood of a landscape, as well as his white-hot passion for perfection which was no less moral than aesthetic, Miss Lowell simply and sharply replied that Shelley was merely a freak and a cad; while Keats was of the great line of Chaucer and the Elizabethans. I preferred not to argue the matter, realizing that something in her puritanic upbringing had kept her aloof from Shelley's half-mystical and half-pagan pantheism, and that not a grain of this so-called "atheist's" search after God was in her practical New England nature. It was, however, an indication of that lack of sympathy which was later to develop between us, the first real rift in the lute of our concord.

I do not recall that we ever went together to concerts that summer, or to the Russian ballet, which duly came over from Paris, but which failed to put on the sensational *Sacre du Printemps*, contenting itself with the acid *Petrouchka* and the pagan ecstasy of Nijinsky's performance in *L'Après-midi d'un Faune*. The English audience, as I recall it, was disposed to be shocked at Nijinsky's rather too frank interpretation of the faun's physical feelings; but they kindled to enthusiasm over *Petrouchka's* stark and sardonic irony, and Miss Lowell agreed with them. *Petrouchka,* she declared later, had been enough to convince her that Stravinsky had genius. I could not help feeling that she might more easily respond to just such an exercise in sophistication as *Petrouchka* was, than to the starker, more barbaric, more primitively instinctive sense of religious awe that displayed itself in *Le Sacre*. And I began to wonder whether, after all, despite her admiration of their detail, she had really grasped the underlying intention of my "Irradiations."

Her refusal to follow Blake, Shelley, or the Stravinsky of *Le Sacre*, her inability

> to see the world in a grain of sand
> and find heaven in a wild flower,

began to disturb me as early as the eve of her sailing. I questioned her as to her attitude towards religion. She replied that, in this respect, she was a complete agnostic. I recalled that, years before, I too had cut myself adrift from my own early low church Episcopalianism, and had only retained respect for the formal ritual, the magical unity and communion of spirit that prevailed in the high Anglican, the Orthodox Greek, and the Roman Catholic Churches. Miss Lowell somewhat indignantly rejected my feelings for ritual as such, by thinking me given up to gross and heathenish superstition. But I had attempted to build up in my art a spell of which I felt these churches held the secret. I had striven not so much to establish a new feeling for nature, as a new communion between man and nature. I had tried to hold, with Morris, and Dostoevski, that it was not through morals or dogma, but through beauty, that man could come to perfection and the world be saved. Miss Lowell would have none of this. She believed, indeed, that art was superior to the matter-of-fact; she did not doubt that artists had something of value to offer mankind; but she refused to go an inch further, and to assert with me that what art had to offer was exactly, in another form, the same unique value that was offered by religion. A grain of stubborn Yankee practicality and common sense remained in her despite all my attempts to convince her of the holiness of beauty.

On her sailing, about the end of August, she presented me with a new volume of selections from the French "prince des poètes," Paul Fort, urging me to read them, as they seemed to bring out in new form something that she herself was trying to capture in poetry. I had not read Fort before, though I had seen him, along with other poetical lights of the day, in Paris. Now, upon reading his *Ballades,* I realized that, despite their picturesqueness and swing, Fort was essentially the same sort of poet that Masefield in England and the recently discovered Vachel Lindsay in America were: he was a great popularizer, vulgarizer. Instead of trying to rise above the crowd, he preferred to entertain it; and he never stood higher than the level of his audience. In acknowledging her gift, I recall, I wrote her a bitterly unjust letter about Fort. He was, I declared, only a minstrel picking at a guitar with dirty fingers. I did not see, at the time, how far her discovery of Paul Fort's *Ballades Françaises* was destined to affect the later course of her own poetic destiny, as well as mine.

CHAPTER IX

It was during this summer of 1913, as I was making my first important literary contacts, that an experience of another nature came to me, when—at the age of twenty-seven—I began to feel the sensation of falling in love.

Since I had left Harvard, my attitude towards all women had been equally compounded of a vague dissatisfied hankering and an almost unsurmountable timidity. During my third year there, at the age of twenty, I had fallen head over heels in love with a dark-haired, blue-eyed Irish girl who had lived near by in Cambridge. One of my college friends introduced me to her, and I had spent that spring visiting her at her house, taking her out to Blue Hill, accompanying her to concerts and to theaters, and writing juvenile verses to her. I was too timid and too shy to offer to kiss her, never having in my life kissed any woman except my mother and my sisters; but I know that I spoke to her of my desire to marry her, and I hoped that she would consent. It seemed to me that if she would only say that she would marry me, I could summon up enough courage to kiss her; but she did not. We saw a good deal of each other for about three months, and I was becoming more and more deeply involved, to the detriment of my own studies when news suddenly came that she had run away with a man whom I had occasionally seen at her house. The blow was so severe that I did not feel that I would ever get over it, and when I sailed for Europe, two years later, I was still thinking about my loss.

Shortly after my removal to Adelphi Terrace, during the winter of 1912-13, one of my English friends turned up one afternoon with a woman whom I judged to be older than myself, but who was handsome and gay in a sort of flashy fashion. She was an old friend of his, he explained, who was interested in modern art and literature. After I had served tea, he went away, alleging some appointment, and left the two of us there. In the gathering dusk, I moved over to the couch where this woman was sitting, and put my arm about her. She merely smiled, and went on talking, neither encouraging nor repelling my advances. I hesitated, and then asked her if she minded my kissing her. No, she did not mind. So I hurriedly and timidly pressed a kiss upon her unresponding lips, whereat she laughed lightly, as if she were amused by my attentions, but was still unwilling to grant anything in return.

Instantly, a revulsion seized upon me. Here I was forcing myself upon a woman who had been unknown to me before she entered my apartment, an hour before. No doubt she found this tête-a-tête with a stranger highly comic. I removed my arm, began hurriedly to talk about neutral matters, and as soon as I could decently manage it, mentioned that I had friends to meet that evening. She did not seem in the least disturbed, and I never saw her again.

This second incident, coming long after the rebuff I had received at Harvard, confirmed me in a frantic resolve not to force my attentions on anyone who was unwilling to receive them, but to wait until I could perceive some signs of encouragement, before speaking. It was during the summer of 1913 that the encouragement came; but I was blissfully and totally unaware of it, until it arrived. When it did come, it shocked me, and may still shock others. But this is to be an unbiased narrative of my life, and I must set down the truth, for whatever it is worth.

During the summer of 1912 I had met a photographer named Malcolm Arbuthnot, a tall, lean, silent Scotsman who had already made a name for himself by organizing, along with Alfred Langdon Coburn, Steichen, Stieglitz, and others, an organization known as the "Linked Ring," whose aim was to improve the quality of photography until it should rank as an independent art. I had previously become interested in the possibilities of the camera, and indeed it was at an exhibition of photographs that I first met my new acquaintance. He made an initial gesture of friendship by offering to photograph me, which I accepted. I bought several of the resulting pictures.

Sometime in the late summer of 1912 he invited me to take tea at his house, which lay in a London suburb. There I was introduced to his wife, a strikingly handsome woman with masses of warm golden hair and delicately tinted complexion, as well as to two shyly self-conscious British children, a girl aged nine and a boy aged seven. I spent the afternoon discussing with him the leading figures among the postimpressionist painters in France, and I learned that he had ambitions of becoming a painter. I did not see him soon again, for shortly after this, he took a post in Liverpool as general manager of a leading camera company's branch at that place. During the spring of 1913, before my trip to Paris, he called upon me at Adelphi Terrace; and I learned that he, with others in Liverpool, was organizing an exhibition of postimpressionist French painting to be held at that city during the summer. Could I not assist in getting together pictures, and would I come and see the show when it opened, he asked? I readily agreed.

So it happened that, towards the end of June, I was asked to come up to his home and stay there for two weeks, while the exhibition was being held. I consented, and I recall that on the opening day of the show I made a speech—probably my first—in which I lamely and haltingly tried to explain something about modern painting, and felt unutterably silly as I sat down. I also recall getting a certain thrill out of Liverpool, which I had never yet seen, and out of its surroundings. This grimly industrial city, with its magnificent new offices of the Cunard Company, and the *Lusitania* and the *Mauretania* leaving from its landing stage every Saturday night, had about it, I discovered, a spirit of energetic democracy which was remotely akin to that of New York, and at a far remove from London's unconcealed snobbishness. The region of sand hills and estuaries which lay at the mouth of the Mersey, where my friend resided, was remote from the sooty center of the city, and possessed a certain wild charm. I enjoyed tramping about it with him, and meeting, on weekdays, his painter friends from the Sandon Studio Club near his office in the city.

So a week passed, but after the first few days I was thrown more and more on my own resources. I explored the Mersey shore alone afoot, taking long walks every day, and writing a new series of poems about the sea and the ships, which gradually began to weave themselves into a single composition which I judged had better be called a "symphony." For companionship during most of the days, I had only my host's wife, unless I cared to go in and meet my host himself at his office. The two children spent the day in the hands of a governess, and no friends came to the house except in the evenings.

So it came about that a friendship sprang up between the wife of my host and myself. The friendship on my side, and I dare say on hers, was at first entirely innocent. She was, I knew, some years older than myself, and the mother of two children. I judged her to be a few years over thirty. I soon discovered that she was a capable pianist, possessed of an excellent soprano voice, but indisposed to display her talent, since her husband had no aptitude for music. So I used occasionally to ask her to play and sing for me. Perhaps, in this way, I gave her some encouragement for what was to happen later.

One afternoon, the tenth, I think, of my stay, I decided to go out for a walk, and I asked her to accompany me. She agreed, and we went along the sands for a mile or so, talking as two friends. On our return journey, I paused for a moment to admire the sunset, when I suddenly felt her arm stealing around my waist, and her eyes fixing themselves on mine. There was no doubt whatever as to what her look and gesture implied. Startled and trembling, I disengaged her arm, begged her not to do that, but to think rather of her children, and we returned to the house together in a complete silence.

That night, alone in my bedroom, I formulated a plan. Since I dared trust neither my own impulses nor hers, I would stay away from the house all the following day. Her gesture of invitation was already kindling in me desires which I might not be able to vanquish. I decided to spend the next morning rambling about the country, to send a telegram to Holley, then in London, making an appointment with him the following afternoon, to meet my host after lunch in Liverpool, and explain to him that I had to see a friend in London who was soon departing for Paris, and to return with him to his house that night. I put this plan into execution the following morning, and so spent the last day, if not precisely untroubled, at least undisturbed.

Two days after the incident of our walk on the beach, I found myself again in London. My Liverpool host had seemed surprised at my sudden decision not to remain for the close of the exhibition, but we had parted as perfect friends. I had not so much as hinted at the attraction that had surprisingly sprung up between his wife and myself, but I was forced to admit to myself that the attraction was already pulling me strangely. At last I was realizing that someone, possessed of considerable physical charm, could love me for myself; but that someone, I felt, I must also renounce forever.

I returned to London in time to see Miss Lowell depart, to have the unsatisfactory interview with H. D. and Aldington that I have narrated in an earlier chapter, to feel more and more restless and dissatisfied, and to face the fag end of August in a state of exasperation with the world in general and with my own destiny. My friend from Liverpool wrote me that he had gone off to North Wales with his wife and family, and was busy sketching there every day. He wished I could join him there. I knew that I could not, that I dared not. Yet London was insupportable. I began now to avoid Pound, whose logrolling and backslapping politics struck me as more and more childish and futile. All that I had to show for my summer was a half-written sea symphony and a dozen more or less unfinished poems on the same old city themes that I had already tried to handle in *The Dominant City*. I simply must get away somewhere. Where should I go?

Early in September I took the road to Paris, this time again hoping to break with London for good. To my surprise, I found in Paris that Holley was away, having closed his gallery and gone with his wife somewhere to the country. Cannéll had just married a tall, graceful girl who was in Paris studying to become a dancer. He and his new wife were hospitable, but obviously too absorbed in each other's company to devote much time to a lonely American. Marriage, I noted, had considerably softened Cannéll's disposition; he no longer emitted long tirades against civilization, and had practically given up writing poetry. Fergusson, too, was away, and I had no other friends. Paris was intolerably hot and sultry, and seemed almost as lifeless as London. Although I had written to Arbuthnot, declining his invitation to North Wales and notifying him of my intention to wind up my affairs in London and to migrate to Paris for good and all, I again postponed my final decision. I would go away to the French countryside and spend two or three weeks tramping about the cathedral towns of Normandy. Then I would return to Paris, and obtain a new apartment at the end of September. I would then come back to London, pack up my belongings, and depart.

I was still in Paris, mapping out a tour which would take me to as many cathedrals as possible, when I suddenly received a letter from England, in an unfamiliar writing. It came from my friend's wife, in North Wales. She wrote me that her husband had told her about my decision to abandon England. She felt lonely and miserable, without friends, and unable to take an interest even in her own children. I was the only one that she loved and she felt exactly the same as she had on the day we took the walk on the beach together. Would I not write her occasionally, just to let her know how I was getting along? Was there any harm in my writing to her? And more to the same effect.

I thought this over for a day or so, and then sent her a friendly but noncommittal letter. I followed this up by dispatching a few post cards from each cathedral town that I visited. I did not hear from her again, for I began my tour of the cathedral towns immediately afterwards, and my mail was left behind to accumulate at the American Express in Paris.

During the previous summer I had become enraptured with thirteenth-century Gothic architecture, after hurried visits to Chartres, Mont-Saint-Michel, and Bayeux. Now, at Mont-Saint-Michel and Bayeux again, I vainly strove to recapture the sense of fleeting ecstasy I had felt at first seeing the soaring arches, the proud towers and pinnacles, the leaping buttresses, the mingled gloom and exaltation of thirteenth-century architecture. Normandy was hot, dusty, shriveled, and dead. I soon lost all sense of delight, in struggling to walk along featureless and shadeless roads, with the perspiration pouring down my body, and my knapsack grinding at my shoulders. I wished I had undertaken this trip not at the dead end of summer, but in the spring, when the apple blossoms came out, affording with their clouds of pinky-white blossom a lovely contrast to the red-tiled roofs, the gaunt gray towers of the towns. I wished still more that I had someone to talk to, someone to share my insupportable loneliness. Finally after about two weeks of it, I became disgusted at Caen, with a gross overfed Norman landlord, who brutally insisted, because of my knapsack and my foreign accent, that I must be a German; and so went back to Paris.

Holley had now returned, and was, as ever, sympathetic, agreeing readily to help me in finding an apartment. But what was more disturbing, I found two further letters from the lady awaiting me at the American Express. In the first, she thanked me for having written to her, expressed the hope that I would be happy in France, and said that she could not forget me. In the second, she thanked me for the post cards, stated that she was returning to Liverpool the next week, declared that she was feeling more and more miserable, and begged me to grant her an interview on my return to London.

Together with Holley, I explored various other apartments in Paris. Finally, I decided on one which seemed suitable. By making a small deposit, I could secure it from being let to any other tenant for a month. This would give me ample time to return, pack up, and depart. Personally, as I weighed this decision in my own mind, I felt no enthusiasm over making it. I had lost hope that Paris would solve my problem; but London, I felt sure, could not solve it.

Then, with my bridges ready to burn behind me, I sat down and did a foolish thing. I wrote my correspondent that I was returning to London on the eighteenth of September. I would only be there about a week, I added, and would be busy packing up all that time. I could not come to Liverpool and see her. Anyway, I felt that it would do no good for us to meet.

Three or four days later found me again in London, when my telephone bell suddenly rang and a voice at the other end of the wire announced that she had come to London, and was stopping with her mother and sister in a near-by suburb. She was coming into London that very morning. Could I not meet her at the station, and see her just once more before she went back to Liverpool? She mentioned the hour and place of her arrival, and I, feeling ashamed and yet attracted, gave my consent.

So it happened that we met again, and this time the tide of desire that she had stirred in me awoke again so strongly that I was forced to yield to it. I remember that we sat in that London station, my arms about her body, I feeling acutely both glad and miserable, and there we discussed what we should do. The children had been left behind in Liverpool. She had come to London to see her mother and sister, and to buy the children some winter clothes. She had planned to return shortly, but had felt that morning that she could not go without seeing me once again. She loved me, and could not let me leave England without letting me know. She had never loved her husband, and only that summer in Wales had discovered that he had been, for a long time, unfaithful to her. She would go anywhere with me, would even give up her children, though they meant everything in the world to her—if I would but say the word.

I watched the tears in her eyes as she said this, and sat meanwhile stunned and shaken, realizing that I knew nothing whatever about women, and did not know in the least what to do. I felt we could not go on sitting there in that gray grimy station waiting room, with curious eyes of strangers passing to and fro; and so asked her finally whether she knew of some nice park near London where we could spend the day. She suggested Kew Gardens, which I had never taken the trouble to visit. So to Kew we went, I feeling more and more disposed to give myself up, to throw myself into the arms that were waiting to receive me, to put a kiss upon the lips that were trying to press my own.

We returned from Kew late in the afternoon, and I accompanied her back to the station where I had met her that morning. The day had fled like a dream amid the blue haze, the bronze-golden great trees, the purple asters, the solemn vistas and walks of the garden where we had wandered as two truants forgetting alike the past and the future, more and more absorbed in each other. We had never once seriously discussed anything except the beauty of the trees and the flowers, and the dawning passion which I now began to feel for the first time in my life. We had kissed again and again on various benches, and then, embarrassed at our own desires, wandered somewhere else, until in the afternoon a sudden thundercloud that drenched the grass for five minutes sent us scurrying off into the shelter. I had decided upon nothing, being too carried away by my own sensations to think rationally or consecutively. But my companion decided not to go back to Liverpool immediately, but to stay on. We would meet the day after tomorrow and repeat the experience.

It was after our third or fourth meeting, after a week of hectic and increasing love-making, that in desperation at the situation in which I now found myself I decided I must act at once. I had already abandoned the project of packing up instantly and going off to the apartment that was waiting for me in Paris. I felt I could not do this, so long as she remained in London. At the same time the passions suppressed in me since my boyhood were now running in me so strong, that I knew I could not resist them much longer, and she no longer wished me to resist them. We had parted the previous day, after a rainy afternoon spent at my apartment, during which I had struggled desperately against the temptation to possess her physically. It was, as I recall, now Friday, and we were not to meet again till the following Monday. I sent off a telegram to the husband awaiting in Liverpool, making an appointment with him for that evening, hurriedly packed a bag, and stepped aboard a train.

It was about six o'clock when we met in the Lime Street station, and I found myself facing the man I had nearly betrayed. He greeted me with the same warm cordiality that he had always shown, and together we bought tickets to his suburban station. It was a gray, grimy, cheerless evening, with the wind rapidly rising to a gale. It was already dusk when we arrived at his station.

It was during the walk to his house—he had insisted on carrying my Gladstone bag—that I began to tell him. I said that I had fallen in love with his wife during the previous summer, and had been meeting her frequently since my return. She too had become attracted to me, but I had shrunk from betraying him physically. I wanted him now to know of it, before things came to that pass.

As I recall it, he put down my bag before replying. It was very dark, and I could not see his face clearly, but I judged that he was in pain. I stood there miserably, not knowing how deeply I had hurt him, or whether he would ever recover from the blow I had just dealt. I wished that he would hit me or curse me, rather than stand and stare at me as if he were incredulous of what I said, and yet unable to bear the thought that it might be the truth.

"Are you all right?" I said at last.

"I came over feeling funny at what you said, but it was only for a minute. I am all right now," he replied, and again picked up my bag, despite my attempts to take it from him, and so moved forward. "I have often thought that she might, after all, find some other man to care about," he went on. "But I never thought you would be the one."

We arrived, and he duly mixed drinks, and served them. Both our hands were trembling, I noticed, as we lifted our glasses.

"What you have just said explains to me some things that happened this summer, and which I did not understand at the time," he went on.

I did not ask him what my statement explained, because I could not. She had already told me that, during that summer, one day while he was out sketching, she had gone to his room and discovered there a letter from another woman. She had accused him of unfaithfulness, and he had not denied it. I myself had felt then inclined to pity him, for she had assured me, and I felt no reason to doubt it, that she had never felt for him, throughout her married life, anything of the physical attraction that had now drawn us together. I pitied him still more now, as he made that remark.

"I am putting myself absolutely in your hands," I went on, thinking not only of him, but of the two children, peacefully sleeping upstairs. "I will not see her again, nor meet her, if you in any way oppose it."

He considered this for a moment.

"You must give me time to think things over," he said, and his face looked haggard and drawn as he spoke. "Stay over tomorrow, and I will give you my decision. I don't have to go to the office. We can talk things over tomorrow in a friendly fashion. And now, if you don't mind, I think I will go to bed."

The next morning, at the breakfast table, he made neutral remarks to the two children, explaining that I had come on important business, and introduced me also to the neighbor's wife, who was now looking after them during the days while their mother was away. She came in during breakfast and shortly after departed with them to her own home. All during the meal, I marveled at his calm, his composure. Whatever he may have thought or felt, he was adept at concealing his feelings.

"And now, suppose we go out for a walk," he said, lighting his pipe, and buttoning up his coat.

The gale had risen overnight, and was now blowing furious clouds across the sky. The wind was intense, but there was no rain. The sand whipped in strong gusts into our faces, and the wind was so boisterous that we could not have spoken even if we had wished to do so, except in a shout. As we went along, I found it difficult to keep walking in the teeth of the wind, and admired the hardy endurance of his spare athletic body easily striding along. In my mind there were coming the phrases of the as yet unwritten opening of my sea symphony:

> The wind, as it strikes the sand,
> Clutches with rigid hands
> And tears from them
> Thin ribbons of pallid sleet,
> Long, stinging, hissing drift,
> Which it trails up inland.
>
> I lean against the bitter wind:
> My body plunges like a ship.
> Out there I see gray breakers rise
> Their ravelled beards are white
> And foam is in their eyes.
> My heart is blown from me tonight
> To be transfixed by all the stars.

And so on to the close:

> The great gale of the winter flings himself flat upon the earth.
> He hurriedly scribbles on the sand
> His transient tragic destiny.

It was not until we had returned to the house, after an hour's tramping through the wet, saturated, and yielding sand, that he at last spoke.

"I can see no objection at all to your meeting her," he said, as we paused outside his gate to catch our breath and brush the sand off ourselves before going in. "If two people are in love with each other, as you and she apparently are, they ought to meet. And now, let us put all this from our minds, and talk about something else."

I stayed there that afternoon, discussing such neutral topics as painting and photography until my flow of conversation ran out, and

I begged to be excused, alleging the need for sleep. I went up to my room, and there spent the last hours of the brief October daylight setting down on paper the description of the gale which would serve as an opening to my symphony. The wind was still rocking the house, as I wrote, and since I felt I could not sleep, I must distract my mind by writing. It might be that he would still reconsider what he had said; it might be that he would still refuse. I was allowing him plenty of time.

He came up and routed me out for tea. He had never asked me before about my poetry, and expressed no surprise at seeing me writing. The neighbor's wife brought in the children, sat through tea with them and saw them off to bed. As they went upstairs, they each came forward and kissed him on the cheek, as I had kissed my own parents long ago. His face did not change, nor did he make any display of tenderness.

The next morning developed into a fine October day. He asked me whether I could not stop, and go with him on one of our combined walking and sketching excursions as we had during the summer. Somewhat astonished, I replied that I could not, since I had decided already on going on to London that morning. Then I asked him again if he had any objections whatever to my meeting his wife. He assured me that he had not in the least.

A few hours later found me on the train again; and as we went through the bronzed and somber, but now sun-washed and peaceable landscape, my heart exulted foolishly, no doubt, over the coming prospect. I was free, free to do as I liked, and would not injure anyone. All the pent-up desires of my twenty-seven years surged up in me, and demanded fulfillment. Why should I be quixotic and resist them further? It was in a delirium of anticipation that I sat that night in my apartment, furiously scribbling a new series of love poems that were coming into my mind.

On Monday we were again to meet, and to go out to Kew Gardens. The weather still held, and the day was fine and sunny. On the way out to the Gardens I purposely kept the conversation fixed on neutral topics. It was not till we had come again to our favorite seat, a wooden bench surrounding an old oak that overlooked the somnolent, quiet lake, with a great weeping willow near by trailing into the gray water, that I asked her whether she would consider divorcing her husband.

"No, John, I would never do that," she replied, and there were tears in her eyes.

I urged on her what she knew of his unfaithfulness and pointed out also that she might, if she could but prove it, still keep her children. But she again refused. My heart sank. I must risk everything.

"Suppose I told you that I have seen him and told him everything?" I cried out, and babbled out the tale of my going to Liverpool. She turned pale and then flushed.

"Why did you do that?" she exclaimed bitterly. "Why did you not speak to me first, and say you were going? I would have told you not to go. You are so headstrong that you have now gone and spoilt everything."

She dissolved into tears, and I sat dumbfounded and shaken, not knowing what to do or say. It seemed to me that my action had proven that I only desired her, honorably and honestly. She had chosen to misconstrue it. I almost turned away from her now in revulsion.

"You won't divorce your husband and you don't want him to know, and yet you want to stay here with me," I went on bitterly. "How long can I expect you to stay?"

"For as long as you like," she said, and buried her face on my breast.

So it happened that two or three days later we indeed came together, in an intimacy that was terrifying and yet delicious, but with this feeling of shamefaced guilt between us. And for my own part, I was already determined to try and keep her with me on whatever terms. Let her husband write or threaten, let her children be neglected. The longer she stayed, the better.

It was about two weeks later that she finally departed. I had begged her, had besought her, not to go, but to stay. I had frantically insisted on seeing her every day, had called at her house, had taken her and her sister as well to various theaters, had done everything possible to keep her near me. But she refused steadfastly to stop away one more day. Her husband had decided that she needed a rest and a holiday among her friends in London. Now she was going back. That was all.

I became jealous then of the plain-spoken, honest-hearted Scotsman, towards whom she had felt no special affection whatsoever; became jealous even of her two children in whose company I had spent happy hours during the previous summer. The experiences we had had together had but doubly whetted my desires. I spoke brutally, angrily. Yet she did not turn back.

A few days after our parting, on the second day of November, I sat down alone in my flat at Adelphi Terrace, and sent off to her all the love poems I had written during that hectic month, without adding another word.

CHAPTER X

A few days after my sending off the love poems another letter came from Liverpool. She was intensely glad that I had sent them, as they brought back to her mind the many wonderful hours we had spent together. They were very beautiful; she had read them over and over, till she knew them almost by heart. She hoped and prayed that she had not hurt me too much by going away. The children had missed her so terribly that they had been almost mad with joy on her return. She felt that she must never desert them again. As for her husband, he and she were simply strangers living in the same house together. She wondered why they had lived together for so long.

I wrote in reply, telling her that the sentiments expressed in my poems were what I truly felt for her, and that I could not say anything more, beyond what they already said, and therefore I could see no reason for writing further. Then I sought out Pound and all my literary friends in London, and strove by means of all the distractions of their company to forget what had been, and what might have come of it. Letters continued to arrive from Liverpool, letters of solicitude, anxiety, and longing, but were answered only by the briefest notes of acknowledgment. Holley wrote me anxiously from Paris, inquiring about my health, and stating that my cash deposit for the flat had already been forfeited; but I answered him not a word. November slipped into December, and December moved rapidly towards Christmas, but I could do nothing but drift. As Christmas came nearer, I was assailed by an old homesickness and an old loneliness. Why had I ever abandoned America? Why had I given my mother the worst disappointment of her life by giving up college and going abroad? Why had I ever fallen in love? Why did I go on living?

As I looked at my face in the glass before shaving in the morning, it seemed now to resemble more and more the face of a criminal. About a year before this, I had definitely given up using safety razors in favor of the old-fashioned hollow-ground variety, and I wondered now whether my hand would have steadiness and determination enough to sever the jugular vein. I would hold my razor blade poised against my neck for minutes, praying for sufficient determination to drive it home.

A little before Christmas, to add to my distress, my younger sister suddenly wrote me that she was getting married in New Orleans to a man I had never met. This brought the past into strong relief in my mind, and recalled the days when I had last seen her in London, in the early summer of 1912. I had hoped then that she might marry an Englishman, and so settle down in London, in order that I could have at least the benefit of her society. She had not stayed, but had returned to America. Now, perhaps, I would never see her again. Why had I not taken a boat and gone back to my own miserable country that fall?

My Christmas was acutely miserable. A single lonely meal, during which I did not speak a word, in a deserted Soho restaurant. Fog and slime in the streets; misery and bitterness in my heart. The year that had started so hopefully with "Irradiations" was guttering out now in the desperation of failure. I tore up another half-written manuscript of city poems, and burnt them, as a sign that henceforward I renounced the major part of my old ambitions. I preserved only "Irradiations" intact and a few short free verse efforts, together with my unpublished sea symphony. These I locked away in a box, so that I could see them no more. Of the poems I had written that October, I had sent the only copies I possessed to Liverpool, and I tried now to forget that they even existed. Literature, to which I had given so much time and effort, henceforward meant nothing to me.

About the time of the New Year, the correspondence from Liverpool ceased entirely. I had myself practically ceased writing, or had written halfheartedly and under the most painful difficulties, so I felt at first relieved by this sign of release. Henceforward I could concentrate on my own situation. I tied up all the letters I had received, put them away in a box along with the other souvenirs of my checkered past, and strove to forget.

So two weeks passed, then one day I received a letter from Liverpool in an unfamiliar handwriting. It was from her younger sister. Daisy had been desperately ill, she wrote, with influenza developing into pleurisy. She had been nursing her for the past twelve days. The doctor had himself thought that Daisy was going to die, and she had begged to be allowed to see me only once again. She was a little better now, but still too weak to get out of bed. So now the sister was writing me asking whether I could not come. It might do Daisy some good. . . .

Thus it chanced that in the atmosphere of a sickroom I saw again the woman who had stirred in me, for the first time, the passions of full manhood. She was thin, exhausted, pallid, and on her cheeks was the hectic flush of fever. She was too weak to say much, or to do more than silently press my hand. The sister eyed me strangely, and curiously, as if she wondered what manner of man was this exile from overseas who had created all this wreckage in a once happy marriage. Arbuthnot was now blunt and grimly silent, and there was no warmth to his greeting. He too was resentful that I had destroyed his life's pattern. Even the children looked frightened and pale. I stayed two or three days, and then fled back to London.

Shortly before I left, Daisy rallied sufficiently to ask me into her room, for a brief interview. She handed me the poems I had sent her, which she had kept under her pillow all during her illness, and begged me to take them. If she died, she said, she hoped I would keep them in memory of what had been. She knew I could not stay, and she was sorry that she had asked me to come. These poems had meant everything to her and she was only giving them back because she felt she was dying. She hoped I would now forgive her for any injury she might have done.

I told her that I entirely forgave her, and gave her a kiss, full of pity as well as passion, as a sign of my forgiveness. I also took the poems with me. The next day I departed from Liverpool alone, in a seething snowstorm. It was, as I felt, the end.

Alone in my apartment, I untied the parcel that contained the poems. I must read them through once more, only to see what they contained. As I read, there surged up in me all that I had gone through that autumn: the loneliness, the desperation of a young stranger in London, the older woman who had come to him unexpectedly from afar, the walks in the garden, the hurried trip to Liverpool, the mingled ecstasy and suffering, the final parting. I had been through an experience which had completely altered my life. These poems were the monument and memorial of that experience. After this, there was nothing to say.

The next day, the twenty-ninth of January, I went alone to Kew Gardens. The day was gray and overcast, with a red sun peering through the drifting fog. I stayed all day in the Gardens, until sunset and the cries of the keepers, "All out," warned me that I must depart. As I sat on the bench we had shared together, alone in the stark, stripped silence of the afternoon, without a soul near by, looking listlessly at the wet sodden leaves that littered the grass, and the dark pool of water in the walks, a blue heron suddenly arose from the lake and slowly winged its flight up the river towards Richmond, in the light of the setting sun. I went home, exhausted and shivering, and slept.

When I wakened on the morning of the following day, lines of a new poem were already forming themselves in my mind. My eight-o'clock breakfast was scarcely over before I sat down to write.

> The darkness rolls upward.
> The thick darkness carries with it
> Rain and a ravel of cloud;
> The sun comes forth upon earth.
>
> Palely, the dawn
> Leaves me facing timidly
> Old gardens sunken;
> And in the gardens is water.

As I wrote on and on, holding my mind passive, waiting till the lines themselves came and spoke to me, it seemed to me that I was in a trance, and that it was not myself, but another who was writing. I had persuaded the surly housekeeper to leave me alone after the removal of the breakfast things, and not to spend the morning tidying and cleaning. She could return later.

Two o'clock came and went, and I suddenly bethought me that the hour for lunch was long since past, and that I had in my pocket a ticket, bought long ago, for a symphony concert at Queen's Hall that very afternoon. I hurriedly put on my hat and coat, and went out, telling the housekeeper that I would return to the apartment at five. Without making either afterthoughts or revisions, I had written, or rather drawn out from my subconscious, three sections of a long poem. I was in a daze of fatigue now, and afraid to go on with the unfinished work.

The concert proved to be Mahler's *Lied von der Erde,* settings of Chinese lyrics for chorus, soloists, and orchestra. Pound had spoken to me enthusiastically about the beauty of these old poems of the Tang dynasty, and I had already read some of them in French translation. Now they were here in the unfamiliar guise of German, attached to Mahler's elaborate and ambitiously exotic setting. As I listened to them, it seemed to me that the poem I was now writing was the same poem so many of these old Chinese poets had already written. My modern loneliness, exile, despair fled across centuries of time and thousands of miles of space and was joined to theirs.

I returned in the violet-blue dusk of the somber January day. At the top of my poem I now wrote its title, "Blue Symphony." Then I sat down once again to write.

Two more hours came and went, and I had finished.

> And now the lowest pine-branch
> Is drawn across the disk of the sun.
> Old friends who will forget me soon.
> I must go on
> Towards those blue death-mountains
> I have forgot so long.
>
> In the frosty evening
> Toll the old bell for me,
> Once in the sleepy temple.

Perhaps my soul will hear.

Afterglow,
Before the stars peep
I shall creep out into darkness.

By seven o'clock the work lay complete before me. It had been a long, full day. Putting on my hat and coat, I went out to the restaurant.

It was about a week after this that the sister again wrote me from Liverpool. Daisy was now much better, and because of this, she herself was soon returning to London. The correspondence, which had been interrupted since the New Year, resumed. This time it was the correspondence of separated lovers: longing, romantic, passionate. I felt that, whatever wrong I had done, it was now inevitable that we should remain in touch with each other. To desire this woman was as natural now as to breathe.

At the same time, I did not neglect my literary contacts. Pound had suddenly grown more cordial, since I again made moves in his direction, and in the direction of his group. We now often dined together, and indulged in long arguments, never entirely convincing each other but always remaining on a footing of friendly equality. I sent him the "Blue Symphony," saying that I wished him to see a sample of what I was now writing. He replied with an enthusiastic note, saying that I had written a beautiful imagist poem, and, without any further ado, immediately sent it off to *Poetry,* where some of my "Irradiations" had already appeared that winter. Soon after, there arrived for me a check for a hundred dollars—the highest price, as I recall it, that I have ever been paid for my verses. I valued this largesse less for the purchasing power it represented than as a testimonial to my merit. All of it went, as I remember, to paying Pound's own contributors in the *Egoist.*

So February passed, and with the oncoming of the March gales and the stirring of the sap in the trees, I began to feel more and more that I could not live without Daisy. Yet what could I do? I could not write her brutally to abandon her children, and fly with me. She was, as I knew, older than I, and her children had been the great compensation for a loveless marriage. So I resigned myself merely to wait.

Early in March I again heard from the husband. He had talked things over with his wife, and had come to an agreement. Would I come up next week and see him? I agreed.

When I arrived again in Liverpool, he unfolded to me his plan. He began by pointing out the needless cruelty of the English divorce laws. Under these laws, his wife could not divorce him except on the grounds of adultery and desertion; and he had not the least intention of deserting her, since she was dependent on his support. Moreover, she had said that she did not wish to divorce him, because of the possible disgrace to the children. Nor could he divorce her, except on the grounds of adultery, in which case I must stand as the corespondent. All this, because of his friendship with me, he did not altogether wish to do. It seemed to him that there must be some other way out.

He then said that he had long been tired of working for a salary. He had merely continued to do so because of his wife and children. He would like to establish himself as an independent photographer in London and he had recently heard of an opening there. If I would but undertake to support his wife and children for one year, until he could get on his feet, he would not interfere with any arrangements we might make together. I could live with her as long as I wished and he would not interfere. Later on, we might come to some other arrangement.

I told him that I must think over my decision, and then sought her out. To my surprise, she seemed delighted at this prospect. I had often said to her that I regretted taking the flat at Adelphi Terrace, as it was inconvenient to live in and cost me more than I could reasonably afford. The house in the London suburb where I had first met her was entirely her own property, and was still unrented; she had not been able to find a tenant for it. All her friends lived there, and her mother and sister were close by. It would cost me far less to live there with her than in my present establishment. I could throw up my lease, move out there, and still see my friends in London. The children and the neighbors would think of me merely as a tenant. She thought the project excellent.

I weighed the prospect in my mind for some time before replying. At the best, it seemed to me a poor compromise; at the worst, it would land me into a ridiculously undignified position. America, at long last, was now actually becoming interested in my poetry, and I had not seen my own country since 1908. I could not take her back to America except as my wife, though I knew that the prospect that the English divorce laws would ever be made less harsh and cruel was infinitely remote. The arrangement Arbuthnot proposed might be more economical in a monetary sense than the prolonged agony of a divorce; for I knew she was far more careful about spending money than I. But I preferred a clean-cut situation.

She seemed upset at my reference to America, and to my mention of the possibility I might go there again. And so the next day she went off alone to another long conference with her husband in Liverpool. Somewhere, somehow, the two people in whose lives I had let myself become inextricably involved were deciding on my destiny. I felt myself the plaything of fate, the toy of circumstances.

A day or so later he informed me of his final decision. He had no wish to be harsh in making terms; he realized completely that his wife and I were necessary to each other. But, at the same time, he could not countenance further relations between us of any sort unless I was willing to bear my share of the responsibility. I had spoken to her of the possibility that I might return to America. She must, in such a case, be safeguarded. So he proposed that I should sign a deed granting her at least a third of my income. That was the least he could do in this painful situation.

I then asked her whether she was aware that such was his determination. She assured me that she had vainly tried to prevent him from making this new stipulation, but that he had refused to listen. She was still thin and weak from her prolonged illness and if I broke off now, she felt it would kill her. I had hesitated before accepting her proposal to come and live in her house, and this hesitation had finally turned him against me. She knew that I must either sign the deed or abandon her forever.

So it happened that I signed the deed a few days later, in the presence of a silent, uncommunicative lawyer and an equally uncommunicative and grimly impassive acquaintance summoned to witness this transaction. And thereby, the sense that our relationship denoted guilt on my part became deeprooted and persistent in my mind.

A few days later I left Liverpool. It was all arranged now between us. Arbuthnot was to resign his position as manager of the camera company at Easter, and to embark on a new career as an independent photographer in London. I was to give up my flat at Adelphi Terrace, move my furniture and books out to her house, and there take up my new life. There was but a month to wait further, and then the new life, according to the terms set, would begin.

As Easter approached, amid the stir and bustle of workmen packing up my books and dismantling my lodging, my mind went back to the preceding spring. Then I had been an obscure struggler, striving to end my long exile by renouncing London altogether, and attempting to achieve a new life in Paris. Now I was already a known poet, published and sought after, was achieving an audience in America, and might soon achieve one in London. Pound had already informed me that Harold Monro had suddenly become interested in his imagists, and was about to throw open the columns of his newly produced magazine, *Poetry and Drama,* to their contributions. His own *Egoist* was going strong. In a literary sense, my career was now flourishing at last, after so many years of disillusionment and obscurity. Even in a personal sense, I was less lonely than I had formerly been. Someone else was now ready to share my destiny. It might be that I could make this new life flourish, might make it bear fruit for the future, if I could only be patient and wait. I did not know.

At the same time, as the moment drew nearer for my departure, I began to regret that I was not to continue living in the heart of London. After all, I had struggled singlehanded with the octopuslike strength of this city for more than four years, and I had pictured myself many times as one of its chosen poets. I had failed to achieve what I had set out to do, and I had not conquered the recognition I had craved. Fate had offered me instead another gift, and I had been forced to accept it.

A few days before my departure I sat down and bade farewell to the city I was leaving behind, in yet another symphony, which I entitled boldly, "A Symphony in Black and Gold." This one I wrote not in a single sitting, but carefully, for several days and nights. It was less imagistic than the other, and yet more openly personal. Consciously, I tried to write in it a farewell song to my solitude as well as to my former ambition. At least, if I could not conquer London, the world would know how I had long lived in it.

On the eve of Easter, with my books and belongings packed, with my furniture moving rapidly, I took the last look around my empty flat, gave the keys into the hands of the housekeeper, and took finally the road that led to Sydenham, and to my new life.

Urged on by my own desires, I had become a poet and had broken with the conventions of British society. My position was uncertain and precarious, and was soon to be undermined, as by an avalanche. How little I, or anyone else, knew or realized at that moment, in the spring of 1914, that neither my symphonies nor my solitude mattered in the least, that neither my poetry nor my love for Daisy weighed as a feather in the scale against a black storm cloud of war that would soon arise on the horizon and, in less than four months, dominate all of Europe?

CHAPTER XI

This spring of 1914 is also memorable to my mind because in it my friendship with Ezra Pound rose to a climax which was only resolved by the sudden arrival of Miss Lowell on her second visit to England.

The new home and the new life I had acquired at Sydenham did not, in any essential respect, cut me off from any important literary contacts. I was still able to go into London whenever I chose, by bus or by train, in an hour. I could devote my days with equal facility to work or to enjoyment, and I was not hindered in either. The rule whereby I did not entertain any of my literary friends at my place of residence still held in force, but I had long since become accustomed to that mode of existence. I could, and did, meet my literary and artistic friends during the day in London, at restaurants or at their places of residence, and sometimes also in the evenings. Whenever, for any reason, they were not available, or I was weary of their company, I could seek a different kind of happiness with Daisy.

The result was that I lived in two worlds simultaneously, each entirely distinct from the other. My domestic life—for Daisy was now wife to me in all but name—and my public life were actually poles apart. None of my literary friends knew of my new *liaison,* and Daisy knew none of my literary friends. The arrangement operated so well for the brief time it lasted that I was completely lulled by it into a false sense of security.

The new poems which I wrote that spring completely reflected this divergence of my interests. In the "Green Symphony" I hymned ecstatically the delights of the waking season as witnessed from the Downs country that lay to the south of my new abode, within easy bus distance from my own green suburb. In the "Golden Symphony" my thoughts went back to Ezra Pound and to his companions, planning, discussing, creating, and working in London, of whose life I was still, in my own estimation, a part. I also embarked on a new series of love poems, designed to reflect the passions of the preceding autumn, in the higher and more joyous key of spring, and on a set of "London Excursions," which were intended to commemorate my journeyings to and fro, between the domestic half of my existence at Sydenham and the literary half in London, by the use of what had been called by Miss Lowell the "unrelated method."

Life still held much that was new and untried to offer me. I was striving to push my literary explorations yet further, and to reach not America, but my own imaginative Cathay. The only serious threat of storms on the English political and social horizon came from the suffragette agitation which that year reached its culmination, and from the insistent danger of a rebellion in Ulster over the prospect of Irish Home Rule. Both these threats were now remote from my interests. To a poet, a creator, a maker of new forms of beauty, politics seemed unimportant. To serve beauty was sufficient.

My chief outlet with the literary world in London lay through Pound, and he and I had long become fast friends. I now admired, and even began to emulate, his American energy and daredevil recklessness, and his habit of picking up new ideas and playing with them so long as they amused him and served to irritate the public began to have its effect also on me.

During the previous year, Harold Monro had begun to publish his new magazine, *Poetry and Drama,* which was intended to cover, in wider scope and more thorough treatment than his namesake's, Miss Monroe's, periodical in Chicago, the entire field of poetic expression in the English-speaking countries. I had already become irritated by what I took to be a cold and unbending attitude of Scottish reserve on his part. I was now still more annoyed by an article he had printed in one of his early numbers, written by Louis Untermeyer, in which it was stated that the leading roles in the rebirth of American poetry were being played by such devotees of the sentimentally humanitarian and the cosmically rhetorical, as William Ellery Leonard, John G. Neihardt, and James Oppenheim. It seemed to me that the roots of American poetic expression lay possibly deeper than in a vague and socialistic Whitmanism. It was time to exalt the savage, the outlaw, the uncultured pioneer. Though I knew but little of any of these elements of American life, and had let all my American roots lie untended, I would attempt, as far as I could, to supply the defect.

Fired by my reminiscences of the Russian ballet and by its production of *Le Sacre,* and also by what I had learned of the ways of savages from my reading, I wrote a series of so-called "Cherokee Ballads," equipped with a set of learned footnotes and a dedication which indirectly implied that they were genuine translations, and sent them promptly off to Monro. To my surprise, he accepted and printed them, minus the footnotes, but with my original dedication left intact. Thus it happened that I appeared before the London public in the guise of the perpetrator of a literary hoax. I was still too youthful, too full of irrepressible high spirits, to care greatly whether I had deceived Monro, and the public concerned, or not. In fact, I later detailed the facts concerning this hoax in confidence to Ezra himself, when the "Cherokee Ballads" appeared, and we enjoyed many a hearty laugh together over what we supposed to be Monro's discomfiture.

I was also directly fired by my fellow exile's intransigent attitude into yet another folly. Ezra was now acting as general literary scout in London for the New York magazine, the *Smart Set,* then in the first flush of its production and editorship under Willard Huntington Wright. He was insistent that I should provide him with some material; whereupon I sat down and composed a series of squibs on the leading American magazines of the day, gave the whole thing the title "Magazitis Americana," and let him send them in. I am sorry to say they were accepted, and still remain buried in the files of this once famous periodical, for anyone who wishes to read them. They had neither the immature freshness nor the juvenile, wild West tang of the "Cherokee Ballads."

I had thus embarked on a course of emulation, in outlawry, of the one literary American who, like myself, was then an exile in London;

but this troubled me very little. I was still much like a young colt who had been left in the stable for too many years; and now that I had discovered my own proper poetical pasture, in "Irradiations" and the "Symphonies," I was disposed to run abroad and kick up my heels at the world. In this, Ezra abetted me powerfully. I might have gone even further than I did, but for a sudden disconcerting shift in his interests, which left me in doubt as to his intentions, and led directly to the breach between us.

Sometime late in the summer of 1913, he suddenly startled me by announcing loudly and with naïve pride that he had discovered yet another genius, a Franco-Polish sculptor named Gaudier-Brzeska, whose work, he was convinced, would revolutionize the art world. He had been so impressed by this young artist's exhibits at the Allied Artists' show in London that he had sought him out, and was now convinced that here was the man destined to destroy the formless and impressionistic chaos of Rodin, and to restore significance to sculptural form. Inasmuch as I had already met Gaudier for myself, I did not feel that I could greet Ezra's proclamation in this case with any particular enthusiasm. Though I realized that Gaudier had great gifts, it seemed to me that he was still too young, too restlessly experimental, for anyone to be able to predict in just what direction those gifts would develop.

Whether it was through Gaudier that Ezra came into contact with his new group of art associates I do not know; but about the time that I moved my residence from Adelphi Terrace to Sydenham, he began to speak to me of them. It then appeared that their leader was Percy Wyndham Lewis, not to be confused with his namesake, Wyndham Lewis, the biographer of François Villon, nor with the young English painter, Richard Wyndham. This particular Wyndham Lewis, as I shall call him, had already crowned a brilliant career as art student at the Slade School by setting himself up the previous year as an independent painter in London. He had rented two floors of an old dwelling house in Bloomsbury, and had there started an establishment which he called, with portentous gravity, the "London Art Centre." Here exhibitions were to be held and pupils taught; here the latest gospel in art was to be proclaimed in lectures and demonstrations by Lewis and his associates, three painters of a like mind to himself. The latest gospel in their case was the gospel according to cubism and the early Picasso; neither Chirico nor surrealism had then begun their ravages. Gaudier had become loosely attached to this group, and it was probably through his interest that Pound was brought in. Pound had heard Lewis pontificate at a lecture to an audience of the faithful and their Bloomsbury followers, on what he called "the vortex," and he had apparently capitulated at sight.

Their scheme, laid before me by Ezra himself in the spring of 1914, was not lacking in grandiose ambition. Whether Pound, or as I suspect, Lewis, had been chiefly responsible for it, it would be hard to say. The London Art Centre was to branch out in all directions and take all the arts under its control. It was to preach the necessity for the vortex not only in painting and sculpture but in architecture, literature, music, and housefurnishings. It was to have a press, and to do its own publishing. An obscure follower of Pound, John Rodker, had already undertaken to bring out an edition of *Timon of Athens* with elaborately cubist decorations by Lewis, and the *Egoist* had also promised aid in bringing out Lewis's first novel, a book called *Tarr,* which Pound pronounced a masterpiece.

There must be, of course, a magazine devoted entirely to the interests of the new movement. For this Ezra was already getting material. Moreover, there must be a series of public lectures at some place which was more central and which would house a greater number of people than the Bloomsbury dwelling house which was the present headquarters of Lewis and his school. One of the smaller London theaters had already been approached, and was willing to permit matinee performances at a nominal sum if enough lecturers could be obtained to entertain the audience. Ezra was already busy on this task of drumming up the lecturers in question, and he eagerly asked me whether I would not serve as one of them, being disappointed when I returned a noncommittal answer.

On one occasion he and I, together with Lewis, took tea in a London restaurant, and thus I was brought into contact with a man whose name and iconoclastic exploits have since aroused controversy in London's most advanced art circles. Pound, as I remember, did most of the talking, and was markedly polite and deferential. Lewis, a grim-jawed, black-haired, and beetle-browed individual, not then wearing the horn-rimmed spectacles which have been so prominent in his later photographs, was disposed to be surly and noncommunicative. He apparently thought that anyone who was as disposed as I to listen to Ezra's exposition of the new concept of "vorticism"—for so the movement had been baptized—must be, obviously, a recruit and an ally, for on parting he assured me that he would see me again soon, at the Art Centre, and that he appreciated my support. As I had given, neither to Ezra nor to himself, any assurance that such support was to be forthcoming, his assumption that all of Ezra's friends must be also his camp followers affected me disagreeably, and I determined to have nothing more to do with the movement.

Ezra, however, went blithely forward with his new plans. The series of three matinee performances arranged for in the London theater was duly given, some time I think, in May. Since I attended none of them, I am unable to report whether they were a success. Above all, the magazine was scheduled to appear in June. It would, Ezra assured me, produce a sensation that would shake London to its very depths. The title had already been selected by Lewis; it was to be, simply, *Blast.* Copies had been ordered in advance by Margot Asquith, wife of the prime minister, and by other Mayfair celebrities. Ezra was already composing two new poems which would shock everybody with their Gallic outspokenness. At last, England was to be removed by force from out its Georgian and academic rut; the Royal Academy would be upset, the pontifical critics of the *Times Literary Supplement* demolished, the bigwig authorities sent scurrying to cover. A fund would be raised to set up a statue of Vincent Van Gogh facing the London Art Centre. But the statue would not be by Jacob Epstein, who, it transpired, was one of Lewis's inveterate enemies: it would be by Gaudier, or by some other daring modern sculptor who was imbued with the "correct vorticist principles."

What the vorticist principles implied, I never completely discovered. According to Pound, they were only an extension of the old principle of imagism developed to embrace all the arts. The basis for poetry, he declared, in his own and H. D.'s case notably, was not an abstract idea, but a concrete image; this emerged from a radiant node, a cluster of energy from which and into which and through which ideas and associations were constantly moving: therefore it could only be called a VORTEX, in large capitals. Large capitals were, apparently, a monopoly of the new school. How Ezra reconciled this fairly concrete notion with the geometrical abstractions and fragmentary disassociations of Lewis's own cubism, I know not.

Before *Blast* appeared I was already aware that Miss Lowell was planning to return to London that summer. She arrived in July, a short time before the new magazine (which was dated June 20, but was delayed because of difficulties with its printers) appeared in loud magenta covers in the London bookstalls. Miss Lowell was eager, as I knew, to go forward publicly as the sponsor for the entire imagist group. I no longer felt any hesitation in enlisting in their ranks, inasmuch as I now fully considered myself to be an imagist. Since my writing of the "Blue Symphony" and Ezra's note of appreciation of it I felt myself as much entitled to formulate my own application of the imagist creed as anyone in the ranks of the original group. Ezra's recent attitude had indeed been doubtful and disconcerting; but I did not entirely cease to hope that his flirtation with the vorticists would prove to be only a temporary one. It seemed to me altogether possible that he might, in the end, choose to rest his achievement on the more solid ground of his original imagism, which was already becoming discussed and imitated in America. Unfortunately, I underestimated Ezra's reckless temper, his desire to imitate every novelty for its own sake, and his inability to get along with other people. And this led directly to our final severance of relations.

During all the month of June, up to the moment of Miss Lowell's arrival, my thoughts had been very busy with the composition of my "White Symphony." This particular poem took me far longer to write than any of the others, and I put more of my own special kind of imagism into it. What I tried to achieve in it was an original solution of all the poetical problems that engaged me at this point in my development.

Circumstances, no less than my own desire to break away from all academic routine and create new forms to express my own emotions, had conspired for over a year past to make of me an experimentalist, as regards both form and substance. "Irradiations" and the "Sea Symphony" had been chiefly remarkable for their innovations in form; there was nothing particularly novel about their substance. But in the color "symphonies" I had tried to pursue this path still further, and to create deliberately a new substance for poetry out of analogies between my own moods and those of nature. The method had worked surprisingly well in at least the "Blue Symphony," the "Green," and the last section of the "Golden Symphony." How would it work if the range of effects were immensely enlarged, to take in practically everything in nature's repertory, springtime and autumn, summer and winter, mountain and ocean, calm and tempest, moonlight and dawn?

The underlying theme of the "White Symphony" was to be my own—the artist's—unending quest for perfection. White was the royal color, the color that existed only as a blend of every other color of the rainbow, the color of paradise, the color of the supernatural. Although I had not, at the time, read Melville's *Moby Dick,* with its long dissertations on the unearthly quality of this color, I myself felt its unearthliness. The pursuit of the impossible was to be my theme—surely as romantic a theme as could be devised. My business was to make the reader share it, by every means possible.

The chief means would be to bring in, as frequently as could be managed, a series of analogies between the phenomena of nature and the color sensation of white, but these analogies could not be chosen haphazardly. They had to be arranged in a given order, in a sequence that started from some given point and went on to another. The range of possible analogies should, I decided, in this case be enlarged as widely as possible; for in a sense this particular poem was to pose my own, and by implication the entire, problem of all romantic and symbolic creation. Perfection must contain all things, and yet be beyond and above them. It must be inherent in the creative process itself and yet be so deeply hidden as to elude its creator. For this reason I decided to let my poem cover all of the seasons, beginning with midsummer, the point of time where I now was stationed, symbolic of maturity, the point I supposed myself to have already reached in my art.

I had an extraordinary difficulty in starting this particular poem. I felt very strongly that I must clearly set the key at the outset, must select from a great stock of associations and feelings such images as would put concretely before the reader's mind the fact that this particular work dealt with the highest possible range of aesthetic experience. My art, now, if never before, must be autonomous, a creation in and for its own right, a fusion of visual and auditory imagery, of concrete statement and abstract implication, something that aspired, in Pater's phrase, "to the condition of music." As Goethe had said of all art, it must "deal with the ultimates" of my own range of experience. My first idea was to begin with a description of a summer thunderstorm which I had witnessed one day from my Sydenham windows. A vast bank of gleaming white cumulus cloud stood on the eastern horizon one morning. It gradually rose, propelled by an invisible wind, till it covered two-thirds the entire sky. In the afternoon the storm came on, with strong whiplashes of lightning, violent peals of thunder, and great gusts of rain. Clouds had already exercised a strong fascination on my own imagination as being the most suggestively poetical of all subjects, and so I began:

> Slowly climb the clouds
> Covering the entire horizon;
> Snow-pure, glittering summits
> Sparkling in azure; thunder-ravines at their feet.
>
> Form uncoils from form.
> In the immense amphitheatre
> Of the sky, the gods are assembled
> As for a festal day.

The difficulty with this opening, I soon saw (though I worked on it for several days, and wrote many more lines that I have now completely forgotten), was that in it I had stated rather too much at the outset. I could not easily descend from the majestic spectacle of a distant thunderstorm to the near and the familiar. I was attempting to open my symphony with a passage which must lead to a climactic fortissimo almost immediately, instead of preparing the reader to expect the climax by slow and steady degrees. Moreover, was it really possible to link together my own human range of limited emotions with the vast and inhuman range of unlimited elemental forces contained in a thunderstorm? In a passage of the "Golden Symphony" I had already tried to link together my own feelings of exultation with the sense of golden light poured out from the sky—and the passage had not, I judged, been an unqualified success. Could I now, in imagination, transport myself into the heart of the thunderstorm itself, and there take part in the vivid warfare of the lightning, the peals of the thunder, the furious assaults of the rain and the hail? I knew I could not. Moreover, would not this violence of the supernatural powers appear better at the conclusion than at the outset of the poem? I thought it would. So I decided to abandon the long opening already written, and to look about for another, more closely akin to the phenomena of my daily life.

One day, during the first weeks of June, I brought home from a near-by flower stall a large bouquet of magnificent, creamwhite peonies, and arranged these in a bowl on the dining room table. I had been attracted to this species of flower since my boyhood; and only the year before in Paris, while I was writing my "Irradiations," there was a bowl of them—in this case, vividly red—which had held my attention for hours in the *crémerie* where I usually took my breakfast. Their forms, so simple and yet so aristocratic, the nacreous iridescence of their petals, and their delicate scent, alike intrigued me. By burying my nose in them, and by looking closely, I had the sensation of being momentarily caught in the midst of a perfumed snow storm. Why should not the "White Symphony" begin with precisely these flowers, suggestive as they were of midsummer, of the exotic Orient, of the ordered splendor of Chinese art?

While the peonies were yet flourishing, and while the happy moment that had brought lines to me which seemed to describe them was still with me; while, in short, the first section of the poem, as it stands now, was already written, Daisy and I had a serious talk about the future, the first I remember since my coming to live in Sydenham. In about six weeks' time, at the end of July, her children, who lived with us, would finish their year's schooling, and it would be necessary for her to take them to the seaside for the summer. She thought it inadvisable that I should accompany them; and her husband, though working hard as a photographer in London, had consented to come and be with them for two of the four weeks' stay that she had planned. Could I not arrange to go away to the Continent for the month of August, and take a walking trip there in the Swiss Alps, as I had done in previous years? It would do me good physically, and also give the children their accustomed holiday. She felt that she had neglected them, had let them look too much after themselves, had indulged in too many pleasures and distractions in my company, since she and I had come to live together. Now she must redress the balance, and sacrifice herself to them, for a time at least. Later on, in September, we could resume our life together.

This announcement came as a shock to me, and caused me to realize again just how uncertain was my present situation. Although I had lived here since Easter, I had not grown to be on familiar terms with the children, whom I rarely saw except at mealtimes, and on our Sunday walks and excursions into the country. I had already come to look upon them as two reticent, well-behaved strangers, in so far as I had noticed them at all. I had bought them books, but had scarcely given a thought to their upbringing. I had scrupulously refrained from giving them any inkling of the situation that existed between their mother and myself. Since I had come to live here, their father had not infrequently visited us, on week ends. We had often gone out to the country near by, and had picnicked together on fine Sundays. The children did not seem to mind my presence. If they suspected anything, they kept all such suspicions to themselves. On the surface everything was still straightforward and correct. But what sort of life was I to have in the future, if I were to be thrown back on my own resources, whenever the woman I lived with said the word?

Since I had already come to an agreement not to press for a divorce, but to let matters stand as they were, for a year at least, until Arbuthnot could establish himself as a photographer in London, I knew it would be useless to protest. So I accepted her decision, and agreed to abandon England during the month of August. But before I arrived at this decision I recall that on one afternoon, a rainy, hazy day late in June which seemed to bring already a presage of autumn to early midsummer, I climbed alone the tower of the Crystal Palace—that hideous anticipation of modernistic steel and glass architecture, which then stood near by—and there discovered, looking at the vast valley of the Thames and the far heights of Hampstead below, the second section of my poem. The third came by contemplation of some snow scene prints by Hiroshige, which I had presented to Daisy, and which ornamented the walls of her bedroom. Thus the three sections of my poem represented roughly midsummer, autumn, and midwinter. The last two sections, I saw, were deeply infused with the old feelings of loneliness and of exile, already present in strong degree in the "Blue Symphony," and now brought back to my mind at the prospect of departing again, after so brief an intimacy. I had intended the "White Symphony" to symbolize only my restless and ever-dissatisfied search for perfection; but it seemed to me, in the end, rather to restate still more clearly the themes of loneliness and frustration that had been the chief subject of the earlier "Blue Symphony."

So much was this the case that I was unable to decide whether the "White Symphony" as it stood was an unqualified success, or whether it merely served as a monument to my own particular brand of ivory tower aestheticism, beyond which no further advance was really possible. The search for an unearthly and impossible perfection had ended in a cry for earthly imperfection:

> O that the white scroll of heaven might be rolled up,
> And the naked red lightning thrust at the smouldering earth!

I had pushed my art further in the direction of the magic spell, the verbal incantation, dreamed of by Mallarmé and Rimbaud, and had only reached this stopping point. After I returned, in the autumn, I would have again to modify my practice, and attempt to approach more closely to the real world, the world which, in Wordsworth's phrase, was "too much with us." I felt, after the "White Symphony," that I would write no more poems of this particular sort, and indeed I made no attempt to do so for three months following.

It is perhaps for this reason that this particular poem has always remained my own favorite among all the "symphonies." Granting my intellectual premises of the time, that the poetic art deserves to be an autonomous creation in its own right, paralleling life but distinct from and superior to it, I feel that there is less in this particular poem that I would now alter than in any of the other "symphonies." It is the most completely aesthetic in its appeal of all, and also the most completely expatriated in its sentiment. It tries to do for poetry precisely what Whistler had already tried to do for painting: to reduce the complexity of the problem whereby art can only suggest life, only stress certain sides of life, to a neatly formulated equation. The more suggestion, the more art; the more arrangement of rhythm, symbol, analogy, the more poetry. If I could but have combined its self-conscious technique with an equal depth of insight into reality, I might have possibly become a great poet, then and there. I do not know. But in the possibility that I might combine something of the precocious virtuosity of this poetry with a deeper realization of life itself, lies the essence of my later development as a writer.

"London Excursion," written at the same time, and as influential in the development of Miss Lowell's poetry as the "White Symphony" was, about a year later, in Conrad Aiken's case, is a less successful experiment, on the face of it. In it, as in two other "London Excursions" written at the same time, and destroyed later, I chose to regard myself as a foreigner visiting London for the first time. I deliberately let my mind lie passive and receptive, in the mood I had come to know as that of "detachment," of "action without attachment to action," throughout an entire day. Unlike the "White Symphony," this particular poem was written during a single day: in jottings on a bus top, notations during my walks, attendance at an afternoon concert, return to a railroad station, and departure for my suburb. The result is rather a suite of fugitive impressions than a symphony of interlinked moods. Here were also certain concessions to realism, and it was from just such works as this that Miss Lowell culled the essence of her own, later famous, "external method."

The "White Symphony" was complete. "London Excursion" was already written, and had, in fact, been somewhat severely criticized by Pound, who complained—perhaps justly—of its general diffuseness and lack of a central vortex, as well as of its rhetorical flourishes, when I suddenly learned that Miss Lowell had again arrived in England and was now installed in London. This time she brought with her a maroon touring car, a chauffeur, a maid, and a new companion, Ada Russell, who later on became her survivor and devoted executrix.

CHAPTER XII

Had I been wise enough, with that wisdom that comes only to the intellectually mature, I would have seen in Miss Lowell's fresh arrival in England the opening attack in a carefully planned and long-sustained literary campaign; a campaign, in fact, which only ended on the day of her death, and which, I am convinced, she enormously enjoyed. But I was inexpert in the tactics of literary campaigns at that time, having seen at close range only the one already waged by Pound. I did not fully realize how extraordinary a combination of restless energy, thwarted ambition, and practical application to circumstances of the means at hand lay behind Miss Lowell's placid exterior. And if I had, I doubt if I could have found the force to resist it. Between the time of her first trip in 1913 and her second she had become transformed from the obscure amateur of *A Dome of Many-colored Glass* to the professional leader of the new poets. From being a mere student and a pupil of her younger contemporaries, she was already on her way towards becoming their most picturesquely popular defender. From one included in the first imagist anthology only for the sake of filling up space, she had already grown so important as to be able now successfully to dispute the leadership of the group with Ezra Pound.

The influence of Pound's, H. D.'s, and my own poetry—taken together with that of the French symbolists—had already done its work. All that she had to do was to add this influence to her own natural and inalienable talent for vivid dramatic narrative, to find, set in her own hands, a medium of the utmost flexibility for the display of her literary skill. With the uncanny insight of the old merchant princes of just such a city as her own native Boston, she crammed her own poetical shop from cellar to garret with the rarest and most exotic wares. Here was a glowing vase of Ming porcelain, there a piece of Venetian glass, here a gold and ivory fan from Japan, there a damascened sword blade from Toledo, here a narwhal tusk from the Arctic, there an Aztec mask, or a piece of glowing tapestry from Peru. The effect of all this profusion, as set out in the volumes she published during the next dozen years, was to produce a feeling of stupefied admiration on the part of the public. Finally, the person who was chiefly responsible for this extraordinary collection, Amy Lowell herself, died in mid-career. Then with the great cicerone and guide to this poetical museum absent, fewer and fewer people naturally knew what to make of that amazing assemblage.

I myself cannot pretend to say what her poetry is worth. That is for the critics of 1950 to say—if, indeed, at that time, anyone reads poetry at all. What I know is that Amy Lowell herself was an extraordinary personality, an amazing combination of the practical woman of the world and the eager, vividly alert, impulsive, and imaginative child. She might have been, had she been born to a different set of circumstances, any one of a dozen things besides a poet; but in whatever sphere she had exerted her gifts, she would undoubtedly have been a success. The reason is that she was able always to gauge the immediate, concrete, practical effect of whatever she did, though not its general drift and tendency. She had great gifts for organization, great executive capacity; but the creation of the new and unforeseen, the sustained effort for perfection that had led me into the "White Symphony," was beyond her grasp.

When she made her second visit to England she had already determined to make imagism the challenge and the rallying cry that it became under her leadership, during the years 1915 to 1917. I was apprised of her intentions from the moment she landed. In the very first conversation we had together she stated that she was prepared to back the imagists to the extent of several annual anthologies, each one to contain the same group of poets, with every poet allotted the same amount of space, and no editorship. Pound, H. D., Aldington, Flint, myself, and herself were to form the original group. Only those poets were to be added whom all agreed to be imagists. The whole thing was to run for several years, until imagism and free verse poetry generally were both fully established and accepted. She was convinced now that a great poetic renaissance in America was close at hand, and we could lead it if we would but hold together.

I believe that I detailed to her some of my own recent difficulties with Pound, and with his new band of vorticists, of whom she had not yet heard. I told her, as I had often done before, that I admired her energy and her determination, that I was prepared to back her to the utmost; but I warned her against becoming enmeshed in London literary intrigue. The terms she set for my entry into the proposed new and permanent imagist group were entirely accepted, so far as I was concerned. But I wanted to have nothing to do with this new vorticist crowd. She listened intently, told me that she would remember all that I said, and would walk warily with them.

When I next saw her she informed me that Ezra had been making trouble already. He had at first peremptorily refused to allow her to bring out any imagist anthology whatsoever unless he was to be the editor and to pick out all the poems for it. This she declined to grant, inasmuch as she was personally staking the venture, and had a publisher for it already in her pocket. Thereupon, in a huff, he had refused to come into the anthology at all. She hoped he would reconsider this decision. Meanwhile she was going to meet his vorticists on their own ground and attend the dinner they were going to hold, on the night of the fifteenth of July, to celebrate the appearance of *Blast.* And she was going to have a dinner of her own, at the same restaurant, a few nights later, to which the imagist crowd, the contributors to his original anthology, would all be invited. Her wits and resources would be pitted against his. Unless he chose to saw off the branch he was sitting on he would have to capitulate. She had no doubt of the outcome.

Meanwhile, she vented her personal feelings about him in the poem "Astigmatism." She also took the trouble to see H. D., Aldington, and Flint, and to secure their support, in any case, even if Ezra should go on withholding his. With this in her pocket, she would march up to the vorticist dinner and get a line on their plans, if they had any beyond making the London public angry with their ridiculous *Blast.* She felt sure that she would be the winner in this contest of wits. I admired the bravado which she now displayed, and was convinced, from that moment, that my lot lay with hers.

As she had already insisted upon taking the manuscript of "Irradiations" out of my hands, and had pledged herself to find a publisher for it on her return to Boston, I now fully realized that her willingness to help me must be met on my own part with an equal willingness to support her. This I was the more eager to grant, inasmuch as I had already, on at least one previous occasion, become disgusted with Pound's own tactics, and had recently again become dubious of him, on account of his sudden and disconcerting shifts of ground. By backing her up to the hilt, I felt that we would continue to meet as equals, fellow adventurers bound on the same poetic quest. I did not realize that her fame was destined soon to eclipse mine. Her ability to pull wires was unsuspected by me, since all these lay now concealed from my view, three thousand miles across the Atlantic, in the land I had abandoned.

Two nights after the vorticists had their dinner, at the Dieudonné Restaurant, she held hers, presumably in belated celebration of the bringing out of the "Des Imagistes" anthology. The occasion, the seventeenth of July, 1914, is still a memorable one to my mind, as it happens to be almost the only formal dinner in celebration of a literary event that I can recall having attended. I have still two souvenirs of the occasion in the shape of a menu and an autographed copy of the "Des Imagistes" anthology in my possession. The group invited were Aldington and H. D., who had married the previous autumn, Pound and his wife, a pretty and shy young English girl named Dorothy Shakespear, whom he had married that spring, Ford Madox Hueffer and his wife, Miss Lowell and Mrs. Russell, and, as unattached males, Flint, Allen Upward, John Cournos, Henri Gaudier-Brzeska, and myself.

There were thirteen of us present, so two sat at a side table, but I was not one of them. I sat at the main table and regarded my vis-à-vis, John Cournos, whom I do not recall previously meeting, wondering alike at his melancholy, troubled, Russian Jewish face and at the avidity with which he ate his food. Cournos's presence at the table was justified, inasmuch as he had already been admitted by Pound into his original anthology; but why Gaudier was asked to be present, I do not know, unless it was that Amy had seen enough of him to realize his talent, and to seek to wean him from his early association with the vorticists. As I recall it, Miss Lowell sat at one end of the large table, flanked by Hueffer and Upward, and Pound at the other end, flanked by Cournos and myself. The atmosphere from the start was one of embarrassed expectancy. The fact that Amy had definitely flung down a challenge to Ezra was known to most of us. I felt that the dinner might break up in some sort of quarrel, and, like most of the others, knew that I had but little to say.

The dinner progressed through its various courses, and as the coffee was being served I turned to Pound and mentioned that I had brought along a copy of the "Des Imagistes" anthology, which I wished the company to autograph. He informed me that, in that case, I had better ask Hueffer first to put his name down, and that the others would then follow. So I rose from my seat and presented the volume to Hueffer. He duly signed, and the volume then passed around the table, until all those who had appeared in its pages had put down their names.

As if taking the cue from me, Amy then called upon Hueffer to make a speech. Whether he was embarrassed at these honors thrust upon him, I do not know, but—although the hostility between him and Miss Lowell was already rising to a head—he was equal to the occasion. He began by informing us that he did not know in the least what an imagist poet was. Ezra had assured him that he was an imagist poet, but if so, he had been one long before the world had ever heard of imagism. His poems, which Ezra had insisted should be printed in *Poetry* as examples of imagistic poetry, were all derived from Heine and Browning. He personally doubted whether Miss Lowell was an imagist poet, or for that matter, whether Ezra himself was, though he knew him to be interested in imagist poetry. The only imagists he saw present at that table were Aldington and H. D., whose imagism seemed to him entirely devoid of foreign admixture. He sat down, amidst an embarrassed silence.

Ezra, who seemed to be hugely enjoying himself, next called upon Allen Upward to speak. Upward, a short, stocky figure, with ruddy complexion, iron-gray beard, and hair also turning gray, nervously adjusted his pince-nez and rose. I had been intrigued with this obscure barrister turned equally obscure author, and—as such—author of several sociological and anthropological works no one had ever read, as well as a few brilliant Chinese adaptations which I had read and enjoyed in the "Des Imagistes" anthology. Pound had already assured me that he was extremely witty, and a genius. So I, in common with the rest, eagerly hung on his words.

Upward stated that, in common with Mr. Hueffer, he did not really know what an imagist poet was. For his own part, he was neither poet nor imagist. He had merely written, years before, some imitations of old Chinese poems which Ezra, with his uncanny flair for the unusual, had ferreted out, dubbed imagistic, and insisted on printing in his anthology. He thought, for his part, that Miss Lowell too, on occasion, might easily turn out to be as good an imagist as he was, provided Ezra found it in his heart to say so publicly. Apparently, only one person in the world knew anything at all about imagist poetry, and that was Ezra Pound. He sat down, and a general laugh, in which Amy joined, ran around the table. Apparently Ezra's allies were not, after all, so firm in his support.

I had expected Miss Lowell to speak next, but she called upon Aldington to deliver himself as to imagism, since he had been one of the two cited by Hueffer as pure imagists, and since H. D. was too embarrassed to explain herself. Aldington thereupon arose and complained that he too, for his part, could not take this to be an imagist dinner. To him, the essence of imagism resided in the restoration of the Hellenic view of life, the worship of concrete, sensuous, pagan beauty. He agreed with Mr. Upward that Miss Lowell might be an imagist, but he knew of others there present who were not. For example, Gaudier-Brzeska was no imagist, for he despised the Greeks as being the great introducers of naturalism into art. Would Gaudier explain why he hated the Greeks so much?

Gaudier now arose and stated, in fascinatingly broken English, that as a sculptor he wished to think of his work as primarily consisting of the stone block, organized into a form adapted to its own material. The Greeks had, after Phidias, tried to substitute for the stone block, a perfect reproduction of the ideal human body. Neither the Gothic cathedral builders, nor Michelangelo, nor any other great sculptor had ever been able to follow them, for the reason that this was not sculpture, but a superior kind of photography—and unsuited to its material to boot!

Aldington now countered with certain objections, and while these were being stated I looked up to see that Pound had suddenly and noiselessly slipped out of the room. He had apparently gone out at the back, by the waiter's entrance. The wrangle between Gaudier and Aldington went on. Most of us were ceasing to pay attention to it, when there was a sudden scuffle at the back, by the waiters' entrance, and in marched Ezra, flushed and disheveled, bearing upon his head a large tin bathtub, of the old-fashioned round-edged variety, to the amazement and consternation of all present.

Where he had obtained that bathtub, I do not know. Presumably, it had come down from the old hotel upstairs. Several waiters followed him, crowding to the doors to see what next would happen. Ezra carefully deposited the unwieldy object on the floor, swept back the dank, disheveled locks from his forehead, and addressed the gathering.

He wished, he said, to make an important announcement. Since, according to Mr. Hueffer and Mr. Upward, he was an authority on all schools of poetry, he wished to say that henceforward there would be a new school, no longer called the "imagiste," but the "nageiste," school. This bathtub might be taken as their symbol. Miss Lowell had herself inaugurated this new school with her poem "In a Garden," which had been included in the "Des Imagistes" anthology. Her poem had concluded with the lines, "Night, and the water, and you in your whiteness, bathing." Hence this symbol was entirely appropriate to the new group.

Here everybody again laughed, but I, for my part, felt that Pound had considerably overplayed his own intellectual arrogance. I anxiously eyed Miss Lowell. She did not appear in the least disturbed. Ezra, she said, must have his little joke, and she personally was glad of his interruption, as it brought to an end the discussion between Gaudier and Aldington, which seemed to her to have little to do with poetry. As our hostess, she merely wished to thank us all for coming, and for her part, she was sure that, whether as "imagiste" or as Ezra's newly discovered "nageiste," the new movement in poetry would go on.

Ezra's squib had fizzled out, after all. Everyone felt, as I did, that we now owed homage to the gallant spirit of this woman who had brought us together, and who had maintained her position with unruffled dignity under the most difficult circumstances. The tin bathtub was forgotten; two waiters, shortly after, bore it off into a neutral corner. The evening ended in a general display of high spirits, a good deal of it at Ezra's own expense, which he was forced to bear as he best might, his face twitching at every reference to his own wild West upbringing. As Amy had already informed me, Ezra was so spoilt that, on a recent occasion, he had refused to go late at night to a London railroad station to greet his own parents, newly arrived from America, until she had shamed him by offering to go in his stead. I therefore henceforth held him to be irresponsible, and began to share her prediction that he would only end by wrecking his own career. In the handshake I gave her at the conclusion of the dinner there was already the understanding, warmth, and sympathy of a complete alliance. Although her poetry already owed much to mine, she was, I felt, welcome to whatever she had taken.

It is difficult to recall all the crowded events and the emotions of that particular July. In the first place, Sir Joseph Beecham, father of the brilliant conductor, had that summer leased Drury Lane Theater, and in deliberate defiance of the Melba and Caruso nights at near-by Covent Garden, invited over from Paris the combined forces of the Russian opera and the Russian ballet. Though the latter organization was now without its chief star in the person of Nijinsky, Sergei Diaghilev had, it was reported, found another brilliant young male dancer in Leonide Massine, who would now star in the new, specially commissioned ballet entitled *La Légende de Joseph,* which no less a person than Richard Strauss had composed. Moreover, on the opera nights, the audience would see not only Stravinsky's new opera, *Le Rossignol* but also Rimski-Korsakov's *Nuit de Mai,* the same composer's *Ivan le Terrible,* and, most important of all, Moussorgsky's *Boris Godunov,* in the title role of which Feodor Chaliapin, as yet unknown outside of Russia, would produce—it was said—a great sensation. Both the ballet and the opera would combine their forces for the unique presentation of Rimski's *Coq d'Or*—and most important of all, Stravinsky's *Le Sacre du Printemps* would appear in London at last. The season of four or five weeks would unquestionably eclipse anything so far given to England. All London was agog for the event.

I attended these performances at least a dozen times, having spent so lavishly on tickets for myself and for Daisy that three times every week at least, during the whole month of July, we were found together in our seats, usually in the first balcony. The season still remains in my own memory, and perhaps in that of some other people, as a culmination of all the possibilities of the modern theater, great acting, great singing, great dancing, great music, and great stagecraft welded together into complete harmony. Where in Covent Garden, near by, the scenery was tawdry, the costumes cheap, the pieces given were heavy, indigestible Wagner, Verdi's melodic rant, or Puccini's and Gounod's cheap sentimentalities, here everything glittered with the fierce sensuousness, the naïve barbaric rhythm of semi-Asiatic Russia.

Above all, Chaliapin proved the supreme sensation, eclipsing even the ballet—Chaliapin and the perfectly drilled, vividly unified Russian chorus. When the curtain went down on the great coronation scene of *Boris Godunov* the audience literally yelled themselves hoarse. And no wonder. None who ever saw this singer in his prime, in this particular part, can have ever forgotten him. Despite the number of times he must have made up for it, each time that he gave it, he somehow conveyed the impression that he was reliving the mind-tortured czar's existence for the first time. And to do this, on the stage, is genius.

On the part of the ballet, the great and sensational novelty of the season was the presentation of Rimski-Korsakov's fairy tale opera, *Coq d'Or.* This was sung by two groups of singers arranged in ranks on both sides of the stage, and dressed uniformly in stiff scarlet garments, like the figures in a Byzantine fresco, while the action of the piece was mimed in the center of the stage by the ballet troupe itself. This entirely successful combination was set off by Goncharova's amazingly barbaric stage settings, a great sunburst of the most vivid primary colors. The dancing of the lovely Karsavina, who had too long been thought of in the public mind as a mere foil to Nijinsky, was never more suave and seductive than in the part of the Queen of Shemakan; and Adolph Bolm, chief male dancer, revealed unsuspected gifts as a grotesque comedian in the part of the absurd King Dodon. Rimski-Korsakov's music, with its caressingly suave melodic flow, like that of a Russian Mozart, and its wide range of atmospheric effects, from the dreamy and sensuous oriental languor of the scene of the enchantment of the king, to the menacing and barbaric march rhythm of the return to the city at the opening of the last act, seemed an absolute and unquestioned masterpiece. I had read that this particular opera was the composer's swan song, and that he had died disappointed, because the stupidly unimaginative Russian censorship, suspecting in its fairy tale atmosphere some concealed element of political satire, had suppressed it. How his ghost would have rejoiced, I thought, if it could have visited London and been present at this amazing and triumphant production!

In a view of such a work, Stravinsky's new opera of *Le Rossignol* seemed labored, forced, cold, lacking in freshness and life. And even *Le Sacre du Printemps* now failed to move me for the second time as it had the first. It seemed unnecessarily stiff and ungainly, both in its command of musical resources and in its dancing. It was received with none of the frenzied protest or the equally frenzied acclamation that had greeted its first appearance, over a year ago, in Paris. I could see that its atmosphere was one too deliberately calculated to arouse a sensation, that its primitivism was too intellectually forced. Rimski-Korsakov's power of melodic utterance, on the other hand, had been exactly matched by his musical skill. His creative instinct had been neatly balanced by his intellectual capacity, and the fairy tale atmosphere of his opera emerged as much from his musical knowledge as from his own sunnily imaginative temperament. In contrast with *Coq d'Or,* Stravinsky's music in *Rossignol* sounded merely bookish, a derivative from Schoenberg's, as Pound's poetry had been from the French satirists. I suspected him of being a pedant, as indeed he has later largely turned out to be.

But if Stravinsky's music seemed bookish and pedantic, what was I to say of Richard Strauss, and his new ballet, *La Légende de Joseph?* Here were trotted out again, to grace a stage setting and ballet done in the elaborate style of rococo Venice, all the solemn pseudo profundities and the heavy sentimentalities that I had grown long since to despise in Wagner. The work had none of the sparkle, none of the life spirit of the work of the great Russians. It was given in an atmosphere already ringing with those ultimatums between Austria and Serbia which led, two weeks later, to the outbreak of the greatest and most fatally destructive war in history, since the downfall of imperial Rome. Probably not one in a thousand of the packed audience who saw it and greeted it with their applause, from the lovely Lady Diana Manners in her box to the humblest looker-on at the back of the top gallery, realized that its art had anything to do with the existing European situation. But for my part I was disgusted that Strauss should have seen fit to tack his music, so lacking in Dionysiac *élan,* to the vivid dancing of the ballet. At the end of the performance, when all the rest of the London audience were applauding, I hissed loudly, whereupon my hisses were taken up by one or two who stood near me. Others turned round, and frankly stared in amazement, as I stood at the back of the stalls. Thereupon my hisses were repeated. Daisy, who stood at my side, was embarrassed. Three weeks later, half the European countries were echoing with those hisses; but I knew nothing of this at the time.

By spending as much money as I could afford on tickets for this brilliant season of Russian opera and ballet, both for Daisy and myself, I strove to forget the situation in which I now found myself. The woman who was my wife in everything but name was about to depart to the country, as if still attached to her husband; and I was arranging to go to Switzerland immediately, upon the conclusion of the season. What Daisy herself made of this introduction to a world of elaborate and sophisticated art, which I had contrived to give her, I do not know. She had come late in life—later, indeed, than I suspected—through her own and my flouting of convention, to a point where, like me, she was living a double life. Circumstances, inevitable in our case, made it impossible for both of us to continue in this way. I cannot help drawing the contrast with the situation I then had been drawn into with my situation now. I have now achieved a life perfect in its understanding, its comradeship, and its reciprocal mingling of tenderness and passion, so that nothing stands external to it. May that life continue, and not only serve as contrast to the past, but illuminate the future!

July lengthened out to August. The Russian ballet and opera announced its final performances. All London prepared for its annual exodus to moor and seashore. As the curtain fell for the last time on the excited Drury Lane audience, I already had my bags packed, ready to take train the following day to Paris. The chancelleries of Europe, like frantic and purblind gamesters, were now staking note against note, and matching ultimatum with ultimatum; but neither I nor any of the thousands who stood beside me realized that when that curtain next would rise, long years would have passed, millions would have been slain, the world ravaged, and such a complete change in human circumstances have come about, that mankind in general no longer seemed to stand on the same earth.

CHAPTER XIII

On Sunday morning, July 26th, 1914, I left Victoria Station, bound for Paris.

Although, in common with everyone else, I had read in the London newspapers the daily accounts of increasing tension between Austria and Serbia, nothing was further from my mind than the thought of an immediate war between all the countries of Europe. The game of bluff and counter-bluff diplomacy had been played for so long between all the chancelleries, the economic rivalry between Germany and England had so often been publicized by the semisensational press—without anyone in the least being disturbed by it, except a few die-hard old Tories—that no one now heeded the new danger signals which had been publicly hoisted ever since the assassination of the Austrian archduke. True, there was great tension in the Balkans. But there had been tension in the Balkans every summer for as long as anyone remembered. There had even been a war in the Balkans, in 1912-13, and no western European nation had been drawn into it. Serbia was a long way off from France or Germany or England. The whole thing was Austria's own affair. That Russia would intervene, that Germany would back up Austria's impossible demands, that the German armies would be sent across Belgium to strike at France, occurred to no one. The British public was apathetic; it thought far less of the European situation than of the prospect of an imminent revolt in Ulster, over the old subject of Irish Home Rule.

It was not till I arrived in Paris, after a smooth and uneventful Channel crossing, that I observed anything unusual. The Gare du Nord, settling down to a hot and thundery night, was somnolent and deserted. Not so the Gare du Lyon. As the taxi which I had taken to cross Paris deposited me on the steps of the station, I noticed several companies of French infantry, wearing the familiar wide-skirted blue coats and the red baggy trousers which later on marked the early days of the War, crossing the platform. A curious crowd of onlookers, workmen, women, and children, no doubt drawn in from the near-by streets, stood gaping as they filed past in the strong light of the arc lamps that beat down upon the platform. The porter who carried my two heavy suitcases in his strap was unable to cross the platform and reach my waiting train, because of the marching ranks of the soldiers. He put down his load.

"What are those soldiers here for?" I asked. I had never before, in Paris, seen anything like this.

"They are going off to the summer maneuvers," he said, and shrugged his shoulders.

I decided to buy a paper from the near-by kiosk, while we waited for the troops to pass. The news was far less reassuring than I had been led to suppose by the London papers. There was nothing here about the suffragette outrages, or the Ulster troubles. Instead, the European crisis was blazoned across all the main pages. After I had nervously scanned the news for some five or ten minutes, the porter by my side lifted my cases again to his shoulder, and we moved forward to my train. The inspector who examined my ticket at the iron grille which led to the train was smiling and deferentially polite, as befitted a Frenchman.

"Ça fait chaud, ce soir," he remarked, mopping himself as he looked at my ticket. "Pour la Suisse? Très bien! Beaucoup de neige et des montagnes. Magnifique! Maintenant, il arrive un orage."

I wanted to ask him about the troops, but I somehow thought it foolish to do so, in the face of so much good humor. He was right about the thunderstorm. I could hear it distinctly rumbling away in the distance, as I entered my train compartment.

Having arranged my bags to my satisfaction and obtained a pillow from the attendant, I sat down and again unfolded the paper. I had still over half an hour before departure, and I read the news this time more carefully. Perhaps, after all, the fear that Russia might forbid Austria to proceed against Serbia was unfounded. Had not the czar himself recently gone on a pleasure cruise in the Baltic aboard the yacht of no less a person than Kaiser Wilhelm, Emperor of Germany? And it was quite true that the French did hold field maneuvers every summer. The sudden spasm of dread that had gripped me as I stood on the platform and watched the troops file past, a few minutes ago, had been nothing but blind unreasoning panic. I could complete my journey without further worry. I put the paper down, took off my coat, adjusted the pillow to the back of my seat, shaded the lamp overhead so it would not shine in my eyes, and went to sleep to the tune of the train starting and the thunder advancing from the south to meet it.

The next afternoon, at about three or four o'clock, I disembarked at my destination, Coire, a sleepy medieval-looking Swiss village in the valley of the Upper Rhine. Feeling fatigued from the long trip, and knowing that in any case I could not start my walk till the morrow, I took a room in a hotel and went to bed very early, so as to be thoroughly rested before my start. I do not think I even looked at a newspaper, for I was too weary, and Coire was extremely warm.

The next three days were spent in nothing more important than walking, with a knapsack fastened to my shoulders, up the Upper Rhine valley, and across the Oberalp Pass. I had shipped my two suitcases on to Domodossola, where I expected to rejoin them in about a week. The weather was excellent, my shoes fitted me perfectly, and the walking was good. The scenery of the Upper Rhine region was fully up to my expectations, and the inns I stopped at on the way were adequate. I had enjoyed myself in the revivifying Alpine air, which is calculated to banish the fatigue even of the most indifferent pedestrian. I was sunburnt, tired, and happy.

On Thursday evening, July 30, I approached the beautifully situated village of Hospenthal, lying at the foot of the St. Gotthard Pass, which I had planned to cross next. At Andermatt, where I had stopped on the way, I had seen a newspaper, my first for three or possibly four days. The news had taken away my appetite. Austria's ultimatum to Serbia expired tomorrow, Friday, midnight. What did that mean? Russia had mobilized her army on her frontier. What did that mean?

Kaiser Wilhelm had begged the czar to stop the Russian mobilization before it was too late, but the czar had gone on. What did that mean? France was already mobilizing, and would back Russia. Nothing but rumors of war!

Would this crisis pass, as so many others had passed? Or would it end by engulfing the whole of Europe? I could not answer that question. My baggage lay at Domodossola, far away across the Italian frontier. I had nothing with me but a knapsack, some American Express traveler's checks, and, in my knapsack, by the merest chance, an out-of-date American passport, issued in 1908, the year I had come for the first time to Europe. I had lived in Europe too long to think of myself any longer as an American. I thought of myself, rather, as a "good European." But were there any good Europeans? Did Europe, except as a convenient fiction for writers of history books, really exist? Or were there only various European countries, all more or less opposed, even in times of peace, and now getting ready to grab at each other's throats? Even peaceful Switzerland, buried in the very heart of Europe, lying athwart the great mountain barrier that had barred North from South, Latin from Celt and Teuton, since time immemorial, spoke three languages. If a European war should come, Switzerland too might be drawn in, and fall apart.

The landlord of the most picturesque inn at Hospenthal, Die Drei Krone, was unable even to offer me a room, so I judged there were plenty of tourists still in Switzerland. I went near by to a less pretentious *Gasthof,* and having there washed off the dust of my day's walking, changed my shoes and my shirt, I returned to the Drei Krone, and was given supper in a picturesquely medieval dining room with carved wooden paneling along the walls. It was now utterly dark, and the room was half deserted; it was empty before I had finished. I had already drunk my coffee, had paid the waiter, and was sitting smoking a pipe on the terrace outside, feeling drowsy after a long day's walk in the open, when I thought I heard a bell ringing and looked up.

A priest was descending the narrow street that led on to the church, at the upper end of the village. He was flanked by two acolytes, each bearing candles. One of them was ringing, as he walked, the small hand bell whose tinklings I had heard. The priest carried in his hands something under a silken cloth, presumably the Sacrament. He descended the street rapidly, looking neither to right nor to left, went past the terrace where I was sitting, and kept on into the maze of narrow alleys that constituted the lower town. A small group of villagers, men and women, the men with their hats off, followed.

I hurriedly pulled out my pocketbook, put a small tip on the table, and started out after the procession. I caught up with them a few doors lower down, just before they turned up a narrow, steep, and unlit alleyway to the left. Here was a house with light streaming from its open doorway and from two lighted open windows upstairs. The priest went in, and some of the villagers followed. Others began to kneel on the stones of the street, and, pulling out rosaries from their pockets, proceeded to tell their beads. After a moment or so, I thought I could detect the sound of chanting coming from the open lighted windows on the third floor upstairs.

There is something so simple, so dignified, and yet so completely universal about the Catholic ritual as to impress even the most skeptical of unbelievers. Whatever we may say about the dogma of this Church, in her ceremonial and ritual she is equal to any occasion. Here, obviously, the last sacrament was being administered to some simple Swiss villager who lay dying, to comfort and console his spirit in its last moments. And the small group of some nine or ten people who now knelt on the pavement of the cobblestoned alley in the Rembrandt-etched light from the doorway were trying, in their simple, unsophisticated way, to waft this soul safely to heaven, while the last rites of earth were being administered to it upstairs by the priest. I too, though a heretic Protestant, and a skeptic at heart, longed to join them. I too felt that I would like to kneel and pray, not so much that this simple inhabitant of Hospenthal might survive, as that all Europe itself might not perish that evening. I had taken off my hat when I first saw the procession, out of respect for beliefs I neither inherited nor shared, and it was still in my hand; but I did not join the small group by the doorway, and kneel with them. Were there others that night who prayed as I did, standing upright, that the heritage of European culture which Christianity—and the Catholic Church foremost—had saved and re-created from the wreckage of the pagan past, might not perish, and that mankind might be spared the horrors of universal warfare? I do not know, but I suppose there must have been thousands who echoed my prayer. Yet heaven was deaf, and returned another answer to all of us.

After standing for a few minutes, I turned, and went back to the hotel; and after asking the night porter to be sure to rouse me by five-thirty on the following morning, went to my room, where I slept a dreamless sleep.

The next morning, a few minutes after six o'clock already found me on the St. Gotthard road, bound for Airolo. From there, I knew I could get to Domodossola by train, and I was determined to reach my destination before sunset. I actually reached Airolo some time before, having walked harder and covered more mileage than on any of my previous days. The people in the hotel were reassuring. War was unthinkable for them; neither Switzerland nor Italy would ever, under any circumstances, be drawn in. I was safe where I was. So I sat on the terrace of the hotel and watched the swallows circling in the rosy Alpine glow of the great peaks to the north, and thought that I had never seen a more beautiful evening. Tomorrow, the first of August, I could go down to Milan by train, and take another train back to Domodossola. I might, however, have to spend the night in Milan, where the weather was likely to be extremely warm, or else arrive so late at Domodossola as to find the baggage room at the station closed for the night.

By careful study of maps and routes in my guidebook, I discovered there was yet another alternative. I could walk from Airolo up a combined road and old mule track that led to the Tosa Falls, a cataract that was listed in the guidebook as being interesting. And from there I could descend directly into the valley that led to Domodossola. The only difficulty with this plan lay in the fact that I could not possibly walk the entire distance in a single day. My forced march to Airolo had wearied me, and the way up to Tosa valley promised a steep climb. About the only stopping place en route lay at the Tosa Falls itself, where there was a second-class Italian inn—but this was no more than one-third the way. I should have to rely in any case on my feet, as there was no train or conveyance of any sort up this unfrequented valley. Should I make the attempt, and indulge in two days more of my vacation?

Alone in my hotel room, I decided to risk it. After all, I had come abroad to walk; and I had not yet walked for a full week. My muscles were getting into shape now, I had still plenty of money, and the hotel people at Airolo had accepted my American Express check without a murmur. Two days more of fairly easy walking would bring me to the Italian end of the Simplon Tunnel. If war was coming, after all, it would not disorganize the Paris-Simplon-Milan express service, the most famous train in Europe, in the short space of two days. So I reasoned, knowing nothing whatever of modern wars, nor of the fate that overshadowed me, along with the rest of humanity.

The next morning I was again early afoot. I had gone about a mile or so along the road that led to where the mule track for the Tosa valley diverged, when I noticed a good-looking young man sitting by the roadside, his knapsack beside him, holding a bloody handkerchief up to his nose. As I knew something of the ways of nosebleed in the Alps, having occasionally suffered from the same complaint myself, I stopped to speak to him, and advise him to lie flat on his back, with a handkerchief dipped in the adjoining stream on the back of his neck, if he wished the hemorrhage to stop. I spoke to him first in Italian, then in French. He only shook his head.

Finally I tried German. He instantly replied, and was grateful to me for my advice. The cold handkerchief soon stopped the flow of blood. It had only come on, he explained, because he had descended too rapidly from one of the near-by peaks that morning. He had been climbing about for the past week.

"Where are you going?" I asked him, half hoping for a companion on my walk.

"I am going into Airolo, to catch the St. Gotthard Express this morning. I must get back to Germany."

"Why are you cutting short your holiday?" I asked. He seemed so frank, so friendly, so easy to talk to, as he sat there.

"I must rejoin my regiment," he replied. It was exactly as if a dark shadow had fallen across the face of the sun. I suppose I must have turned paler, under my Alpine tan.

"Then war is certain?" I asked.

"I am afraid so," he replied, fatalistically, getting up and putting on his knapsack. "Thanks very much for helping me. Are you English or American?"

"English," I replied, scarcely thinking of what I said, and immediately after I had spoken, wondering whether the country to which I now made claim of allegiance would really be dragged into this senseless war, as her own jingoistic press had predicted long before. Fervently I hoped not, as I rose and gripped his hand.

"Well, good-by and good luck," I said. "Or rather, auf Wiedersehen. We may meet somewhere again."

"Auf Wiedersehen," he said, and smiled for the first time since my eyes had rested on his face. We turned our separate ways.

As I went along, up a road that soon diverged into a track that led sharply upward, paved with large flat stones that had lain undisturbed, I suppose, for centuries, I wondered why I had lied to him, and called myself an Englishman. I had never supposed, before this, that England meant anything more to me than a refuge from the blatancies and the commercial crudities of my own country. Yet I felt now that England meant more. It had, after all, taught me more than America of life and of poetry. Even if the unthinkable could happen, even if a war should spring up between the country where I had lived for close on to five years, and Germany—a war incredibly fantastic in my eyes, since this fine-looking athletic young man and I were at bottom blood relations—I still owed an unconscious homage to England.

I arrived at the hotel which lay at the summit, close by the Tosa Falls, at about three in the afternoon. The way up the old mule track had been steep and sultry, and I was weary, having had nothing to eat since breakfast but a cake of chocolate, washed down by water from a wayside spring. The proprietor of the hotel frankly advised me not to stop, but to go on. In two hours I could descend to a highway where I could catch a bus which would bring me into Domodossola that night. All of his guests had departed a day or so before, and he expected to close the hotel soon and return to Milan.

Nevertheless, I knew I was too weary to go on. All during that day, and throughout that lonely walk up the valley—for except for the young German and a peasant or two, I had not met another soul—what the young German had said to me that morning remained fixed in my mind, and blent with the lush green of the Alpine meadows, the dark woods of spruce, the sunburnt rock, and the sparkling snow of the distant peaks. Was I, after all, English or German or American?

My mother, I knew, had been German. My father had come from pure Scotch and English stock. I had been born in America, but had adopted England as my place of residence. I had even linked my fate to that of an Englishwoman; a post card from her announcing her arrival in Cornwall lay now in my pocket. Where did my country exist? What was my country? I could not answer these questions.

Fagged out, I took a room in the hotel, went into it, took off my clothes, and slept for over two hours. When I wakened, the sun was already going down. I had just time enough to walk over to the waterfall, the roar of which could be heard from the hotel itself, to look at it, and to stroll into the empty whitewashed church, barren of interest except for a carved, gilt German Gothic altarpiece. Then I returned to the hotel, for a simple but satisfying meal. The last bus had gone for Domodossola long ago. I was the sole tourist left. What the morrow would bring forth, I did not know.

Before I went to bed I ascertained from the proprietor that if I arose at six I could catch a bus that would bring me into Domodossola about ten-thirty. The next one would not come along till between one and two in the afternoon. I could only reach the road along which the bus ran by walking for at least two hours. Newspapers and mails and supplies would come up to the hotel by mule transport about eight-thirty in the morning.

I fully determined to catch the early bus, but circumstances willed otherwise. About one or two in the morning I was awakened by the roar of the waterfall, so much louder in the nocturnal silence than it had been by day. Had the armies already started their movements across the map of Europe? I lay awake, tossing uneasily, till dawn showed in the sky. Then I slept, not to waken till past eight o'clock.

Breakfast over, I waited for the muleteer to bring up the mail and newspapers. There was nothing to do but wait. The newspaper, when it came, proved to be the *Corriere della Sera* of the afternoon before, fresh from its presses in Milan. There could be no doubt now what had happened. Austria was at war with France and Russia. It was reported that German troops had already crossed the Belgian frontier. In England, Parliament had been summoned to meet on Monday. No one knew what Italy would do, but it was hoped she would remain neutral.

A little after ten o'clock, being unable to stand my isolation any longer, I left the hotel and descended in the two hours I had allotted to myself into the valley leading on to Domodossola. There I walked for another hour, in increasing heat and sultriness, along a shadeless and dusty road, with traffic flowing continually past me, bound in the direction of Italy. Finally I took refuge in an inn, by the wayside, ate a hurried lunch, and awaited the bus. It duly came, crowded with shirt-sleeved and chattering Italians. At about four o'clock, after a dusty and sweltering ride, I alighted at last at the railroad station which lay at the mouth of the Simplon Tunnel.

I obtained my bags, summoned a taxicab, and drove to the best hotel the town afforded. The lobby was packed with tourists, English, American, German, drifting hither and thither, some with their baggage, some not, all of them unwilling refugees from the War. The babel of their voices was terrific, and the staff of the hotel was being swamped with their demands. I stood irresolute among them, merely another waif of the War, not knowing what to do next. Finally I managed to draw the hall porter, a fine-looking mustached Italian, aside for a moment. He spoke perfect English.

Briefly I detailed to him the situation. I wanted to get back to London, via Paris.

"There are no trains going through to Paris," he said, as if repeating the news for the thousandth time. "You might get as far as Geneva tonight, but after that you won't go further. The best thing for you to do is to stay here. Here you are safe."

"Safe? How?"

"Italy has just officially declared her neutrality. We heard the news only about twenty minutes ago. But she is closing her frontiers at midnight, and will not reopen them again for three days, as a measure of precaution. If you desire to stay here, you will not be able to move till the sixth."

"Have you any rooms?"

"There is not a room available in the hotel, and we have been trying for hours to get cots from the hospital, to take care of this crowd. You might find things less crowded at Geneva. The frontier closes at seven, and the last train goes at six-thirty." He glanced at the clock that hung over the cashier's desk. Its hands pointed to four-thirty.

"Could I find a room here just to wash up and change my clothes in?"

"Certainly." And he led me to his own little cubicle, where I spent the next thirty minutes.

When I emerged I had removed my walking togs and sweaty shirt, and was dressed in my usual civilian costume, in which I had quitted London. I was neatly washed and brushed, had put on light shoes in the place of my heavy walking boots, and no longer bore traces of the grime and sweat of the morning. The crowd was still jabbering and drifting, or sitting helplessly, everywhere about the lobby. The hall porter smiled at me, accepted a generous tip, and summoned a taxicab.

The station clerk readily sold me a ticket as far as Geneva. The train was due in about an hour. I went out on the train platform, and there received another shock. The platform was heaped high with boxes, bags, bundles of bedding. These were the belongings of the Swiss workmen, engaged in the completion of the Simplon Tunnel. They had been ordered out of Italy and were leaving by the final train.

I drifted into the buffet and ate mechanically. At about a quarter to seven, fifteen minutes from the time set for its arrival, the train came in. It was packed and I got aboard, but finding no place to sit, put my bags somewhere in the already overcrowded corridors, and prepared to stand. The train was jammed with English and Americans, all of whom seemed to regard the War, and everything connected with it, as a huge joke. Gales of laughter swept the corridor as one tourist group after another told of their broken holidays, their last-minute escapes, their misadventures with their baggage. We were like a group of irresponsible school children, playing truant for the day and having nowhere in particular to go.

At about nine o'clock the train reached Lausanne, and I, who had been standing for over two hours, finally dropped off. We were now safely within the frontier of Switzerland, and I could complete my trip on the morrow. A near-by hotel offered me a room, and I gratefully accepted. I turned in and slept.

The next morning, Monday, August 3, I went to the American Express office and to Thomas Cook's on the way. Both offices were besieged by stranded tourists. Cook's could sell no tickets and did not know when the next train would go through to Paris. The American Express refused to cash a traveler's check, except in the case of an emergency, if called upon to do so by the American consulate. I still had my unused ticket to Geneva, and some funds. I might therefore have gone into the garden of Gibbon's villa, and meditated with that immortal ghost on the downfall of empires, but I did not. Instead, I took a train to Geneva that afternoon.

The next day, August 4, the only news in Geneva was that England had entered the War. So the inevitable had arrived at last! The American consulate, after viewing my out-of-date passport, stated that the best thing I could do would be to return to the United States via Italy and the Mediterranean. I pointed out to them that all my belongings were in London, and that I had lived there continuously for the past four or more years. Finally, after long and aggravating delays, they yielded. I was granted a new temporary passport, which was valid for three months only, which would take me to England—if I could find a train.

It was not until Monday, August 10, that the train to Paris was put on. It consisted almost entirely of old-fashioned, worn-out, third-class carriages, and those who wished to travel by it had to be in their places early, as a long line of applicants for seats stretched down the Geneva platform. There were no porters, and everyone had to carry his own baggage. I staggered under the weight of mine—two heavy suitcases and my knapsack. At seven-thirty the train was packed up to the doors, and we waited another half-hour till the engine driver decided to pull out his throttle. Finally we departed.

I have only the haziest recollections of the journey. The train took us, at a rate of not more than thirty miles an hour, by a route which penetrated far into the South of France. Where we went, I have no idea; but I suspect we diverged far into the lower valley of the Rhone. The train made frequent halts at the most unimportant places, and the French peasants kept drifting in and out, mostly eyeing me and my German-made knapsack with suspicion. The fifteen or twenty English-speaking tourists aboard who had finally risked the journey were scattered about, here and there, amid a horde of Midi villagers, climbing in and getting out, eating their lunches on the seats—but offering me none—and jabbering Provençal dialect. Most of the English, no doubt, as I, soon regretted their haste in getting away; probably, a few days later, better trains were to be had.

We traveled all day and night, and on Tuesday afternoon, August 11, arrived finally in Paris. For the last two or three hours we kept passing long strings of French freight cars, going up to the front, with the legs and arms of French *poilus* dangling from their doorways, cheering and laughing, and with the words "*à Berlin*" exultantly chalked on their sides. I had been so anxious to depart from Geneva that I had neglected the elementary precaution of buying any eatables before we left. During the whole of the two-day trip we had stopped some four or five times at stations which boasted of buffets. But here nothing whatever was to be had except bread, cheese, sour red wine, and coffee, at prices which were utterly fantastic. My breakfast on the morning of the eleventh had consisted of a roll without butter and a cup of coffee. I had not lunched when we arrived at Paris. Nevertheless I contrived to drag my baggage—there were still no porters—along the length of the platform and into a taxi, which bore me to my usual hotel.

At the hotel the proprietress and her daughter, the same I had seen in 1911, in 1912, and in 1913, were dressed in black crepe, with heavy black-bordered handkerchiefs in their hands, and looked pale and tearful. I did not question them about their loss. They informed me that I could not stop for the night without a permit from a near-by police station. They hoped only that the French armies would soon defeat those wicked Germans, and retake Alsace; whence, it appeared, they had originally come to Paris. I reassured them, curtly, that I saw no reason why the French could not retake Alsace, and went out in search of the police station.

The police officer was disposed to be inquisitive. He wanted to know whether I could speak German. Truly this was a different world I had fallen into, in the short space of two weeks! I cut him short and, armed with a permit for twelve hours, went back to the hotel, changed my clothes, and obtained a square meal at last.

The next morning I quitted Paris, without seeing any of my old friends there. Where was Cannéll, Holley, or Fergusson? I did not know. The train was packed with English, as was the boat, a rickety old Channel steamer, which, thanks to fine weather, made the voyage between Boulogne and Folkestone uneventfully in about two hours. The port of Calais was already closed. As we approached the French coast, the spirits of the crowd gradually rose. I had already seen enough of Paris, with its shops closed and mobilization notices posted across the iron shutters, to realize that I was flying from a dead city, a city already stricken by the economic paralysis, the hectic rumors and alarms, the emotional hysterias of the War. Shops with German-sounding names had already been attacked, looted, and burned by the mob. Juarès had been assassinated, and the Socialists had gone into hiding or into uniform. The newspapers were already full of German atrocity stories and the legends of the heroic defense of Liége. Colmar had fallen—a great victory. England was coming. The only thought was of the advancing shadow of the German armies, extended across Europe.

On Boulogne pier a solitary British sentry in a new khaki uniform, his rifle to his shoulder, was pacing up and down. Beyond, three or four lean British torpedo-boat destroyers were patrolling the Channel. Aboard the steamer I breathed more easily, and soon settled down to a state of quiescence. The long nightmare of my flight across Europe was over. I had come again to the inviolate peace, the sure refuge of seagirt England.

CHAPTER XIV

London, unlike Paris, looked almost entirely unchanged during the first weeks of the War. About the only signs of England's active participation were numerous recruiting posters at various points, and signs above several shops, announcing "Business as Usual." The streets and hotels were still filled with American tourists, many of them unwilling refugees from the Continent, now unable to find a ship to take them home. Had I but known it, Miss Lowell was herself in this class. She was still in London, waiting for an opportunity to depart. I only stayed in London for two days, and did not inquire about her. On the fifteenth of August I left for Cornwall, where were Daisy, her husband, and the children.

By chance I managed to find a room in the Cornish fishing village where they were stopping, near enough to their boardinghouse to enable me to take my meals with them, and there I spent the last week of my holiday. In a way, I was glad that I was, for a time, not under the same roof with the woman whose life had become so entangled with mine. I was aware that her husband had only come in order to make it appear to the boardinghouse proprietor that he and his wife were still a married couple. They did not share rooms; she slept with her daughter, and he shared a room with his son. Their relations were merely that of two strangers, outwardly polite, inwardly aloof, sustained by a hypocritical conformity to a legal fiction. But in any case, they did not and could not help me to a solution of my personal problem. For this I needed to be alone now, and to think.

The problem was, how long would this war go on? If it were long sustained I knew well that I could not remain in England. I had obtained a permit to stay for only three months, which would bring me up to the middle of November. After that, what? What did the British people think would be the duration of the struggle with the magnificent machine which Germany had unloosed? Kitchener was already enrolling his recruits "for three years or duration of the war." But in the excitement of unexampled feelings, none knew how far Kitchener need be taken seriously. Everyone was still taking holiday: London had been full of pleasure seekers, secure in the invincible might of England. And in the Cornish boardinghouse, all, from Daisy's husband down to the humblest bootblack, argued that England would win easily in a few months. They all expected that the small Expeditionary Force which the War Office was now dispatching overseas would eat their Christmas dinners in the Kaiser's palace at Potsdam.

Day by day brought no news except of the irresistible advance of the German armies. England was safe from invasion, thanks to the Channel seas, and her own navy. But what about France? The German armies swept aside the feeble Belgian resistance as a strong man might break a stick in his two hands. Now they were already on the French frontier—and the British Expeditionary Force met them at Mons. The War Office issued a reassuring dispatch. The German advance was halted. Yet the next day, the British had retired ten, fifteen, twenty miles farther back.

It was easy by looking at the map to see which side was advancing and which retreating. But everyone had, by now, heard that Russian troops had been seen passing through London. They had come all the way from St. Petersburg and the Baltic to fight on the soil of France. This was the carefully guarded surprise that Kitchener and the War Office had prepared for the Germans. Even in England they had traveled in trains with blinds drawn, so that news of their coming would not leak out. Yet everyone knew about it: some had even seen them. Day on day passed, and the German advance went on and on. Would anything halt it, short of Paris? That was the sole question facing the world at the hour.

On the ninth of September, with the whole course of the War still hanging in the balance at the Marne, I realized that one month of the three I would be permitted to stay had already gone by. I had no light whatsoever on the situation. Daisy's husband had returned to his work as a photographer, being over age for the army, and was doing well photographing officers who wanted pictures of themselves in fine uniforms to send to their girls. Everybody was writing patriotic poems, and two or three anthologies of them were being hurried through the press. The newspapers were lauding Belgium to the skies. King Albert was already a demigod.

London was more full of recruiting posters than ever; everyone was now doing "his or her bit." The women were getting into uniform. The theaters had ceased to be taken seriously; Charlie Chaplin films and undressed revues were all that anyone cared to see. The new song, "Tipperary," was everywhere. While it was being played the whole audience stood up. There was not the least danger of invasion; but—a new and ominous note—in view of the fact that the zeppelins might raid London, and to save gas and electricity, the streets were going to be darkened by official order.

The Marne came and went, but the German armies still stood on French soil, with the Allies unable to deliver a strong counterstroke. The autumn rains came, the equinoctial gales raged up and down the Channel, the leaves littered the London parks and the streets of my suburb. I had only a month left. It was at this time last year that my resistance had been broken, and that Daisy and I had first come together. Then I still felt young and hopeful about the future. Now I already felt tired, discouraged, and old. To stay was horrible; to return to America was a desperate expedient, and would throw me back into my old loneliness. What should I do?

A new note was now creeping into my poetry. Try as I would, it was impossible to get away from the pervasive influence of the War. Kitchener's recruits were everywhere. Some were billeted even in my suburb, and drilled in the open parklike road that led to the nearest railway station. Marching columns were continually passing here and there through London. They soon became so familiar as to rouse, on the part of spectators, not the faintest sign of interest. Along with the ascendancy of Mars, Venus, too, began to rule the world. The arrests and hunger strikes of the suffragettes, which had made so much history in the London press only the preceding spring, were already an ancient tale. The women were now busy at a different and more obviously biological task: the capture of a male, preferably one in uniform. Young girls of good families were already pinning white feathers to the lapels of their boy friends who were hesitant to join the army. Every evening I witnessed from my suburban home servant girls stealing forth to the embraces of stray soldiers. And the parade of harlots up and down shadowy Piccadilly at night redoubled.

I felt a new mood of revolt against my own ridiculous situation, and against the ridiculous situation of the world, rising up in my blood. Who was to blame for what had happened? Not Germany, nor Russia, nor France, nor England, but only the baseness of human nature. I began writing feverishly on a new poem, which I called with unconscious irony, "Middle-Age." As a matter of fact, my age was exactly twenty-eight years and nine months. But I probably would be killed in the War anyway (enormous casualty lists were already appearing in the papers), and besides, I felt middle-aged. So I began:

> Sombre revolt
> Smoulders in my heart,
> Breezes crackle in the trees, dry artillery,
> Burnt leaves are flung, shell fragments,
> On the hoar withered grass.
>
> The sky is one steel spiderweb
> Of cruel rays.
> Dry laughter of a vagrant bird
> Quivers and trills among them
> Deviously.

This free verse opening contrasted with the meter of the second section (for this poem, too, was a "symphony," a symphony of a new sort):

> It is harvest in our village,
> Now we troop out to the fields;

For the owner has invited us
To gather up the fruit that the earth yields.

Once we harvested gladly;
Now unwillingly we come,
For the violins of life resound no longer,
The tambourines of youth are hushed and dumb.

And there are dark brows over cornstalks,
Dull scytheblades that do not shine;
Blight and rust on the harvest,
Bitter lees in the wine.

The whole poem concluded with violent stanzas, expressing the sense of the entire futility of all revolt, and yet the more desperate sense that my own revolt must go on. I laid the poem aside, judging it to be self-pitying and entirely immature. It was not published for twenty-one years, when the hour of middle age had long since truly sounded in my life. Then I let it appear, unchanged, except for title. As an example of the symphonic treatment of themes drawn from real life—the "symphonies" themselves were not devised to touch on real life except accidentally—this is one of the earliest, in point of time, of my poems. And I had called it "Middle-Age!"

I also wrote war poems, but they were different from the poems of Rupert Brooke and of others who were now vocally thanking God for the War:

Under the soft grey windswept sky,
Between two rows of yellow trees
Soddenly dripping;
The brown backs of an army
Go marching.

Like an enormous snake with undulatory movement,
Past the old church with scarlet creeper hooding its stiff grey walls,
Past the drowsy churchyard
Where wet leaves cling to the stones;
Up the hill and past the village,
Through the curving lines of hedgerows,
Beyond the brow of the hill, lost in brown stubble,

The brown backs of an army
Go writhing in the distance.

Under the flying clouds that hide the eastern sky,
Footfalls, footfalls, repeated clamor of footfalls,
One, two, left, right, the road is full of them;
And the noise rises and strives to cling
To the wet windblown branches,
It penetrates the empty church and echoes up the aisles.

Whirling leaves drift over the endless footfalls,
Striving to hush them to quiet;
O agonized hands!

Truly the ominous prediction which, unconscious of its full import, I had written at the end of the "White Symphony," was coming true at last:

O that the white scroll of heaven might be rolled up,
And the naked red lightning thrust at the smouldering earth!

In a halfhearted fashion I still tried to keep up my literary contacts, hoping against hope that I would soon waken from this nightmare and find the War suddenly come to an end. Pound, however, was no longer available. Soon after my return to London from Cornwall I received a letter from Amy, informing me that she had been forced to stay in England till the twentieth of August, and that she was now already busily engaged in getting together material for the new imagist anthology. Pound was out for good and all. The whole thing would be called simply *Some Imagist Poets.* Aldington would do the introduction. She was going to include D. H. Lawrence, not because he was an imagist, but only to take the place of Pound. Aldington did not object. She was enthusiastic over the prospects of imagism in America, and wished I could come over and see things for myself. As she and I had already had some differences of opinion about the value of Paul Fort's poetry, she wanted me to see a new poem she had recently written in this vein. And she included "The Bombardment."

The news about Pound came as no surprise. I had already realized that Ezra was adamant, and would never acknowledge anything to be imagism that he did not run and control personally. His new vorticist group were following up their first *Blast* with a war number which finally appeared the next year. In this they tried to continue the sensation of their first appearance. It was useless, I knew, to argue further with him, or with them. "The Bombardment," however, did come as a surprise to me. Up to that summer I had resisted all Miss Lowell's attempts to get me converted to her employment of the Paul Fort form, with its mingling of poetry and prose statement. I had disliked her early works written in this form—"The Forsaken," "The Basket," "In a Castle." But "The Bombardment" was somehow different. It seemed to me to possess a form immeasurably superior, more flexible, and dramatic than anything that Paul Fort had written. And it chimed in with my own mood. It drew the complete contrast between the beauty of serene art and the folly and desolation of destruction the armies had unleashed on the world. I had long since been envious of Amy's ability to write poems of dramatic contrast and narrative climax. "The Bombardment" did this in a new and unexpected way, owing nothing to the old, academic models. I was enthusiastic, and realized that I was being outstripped in the race by my competitor.

Still doubtful as to what I ought to do in regard to the War situation, which was growing steadily worse, and wishing to find some literary contacts, I looked up Aldington. Flint was no longer available, being up to his ears in work at one of the most important public buildings in London, the Post Office. Aldington had taken over the position vacated by Pound on the *Egoist,* and was busy with small funds largely obtained, I suspect, from Miss Lowell herself, in keeping the magazine together. He was no longer the gay, insouciant, jaunty, swaggering Aldington I had known. His new post kept him busy at the *Egoist* office every day. Pound and he no longer spoke to each other, and he was scornful of Ezra's efforts to whip up interest in this topic of war. The business of the artist, now more than ever, he was convinced, was to conduct a crusade against all this false patriotism and to uphold the cause of beauty at all hazards. Everything in England was simply reeking with the contest. Everybody was writing patriotic poems. He wished that I, or someone else, would show up the whole thing. He was perfectly willing to join up with the army, had let his name be put down on the list of possible recruits, but he was damned if he was going to feel all steamed up with patriotism over the stupid Germans. The artist had something better to do. He really wished that somebody would let himself go, and make fun of the whole business. He wondered now why I did not go back to America. He wished he could go there, and he would have gone, but for the fact that he was inescapably an Englishman. Neither H. D. nor he had enough money to leave England. His new job of editing the *Egoist* would keep him busy till he could find something better. If the worst came to the worst, he would quit London, bury himself in the country, and wait till he was drafted.

This new phase in Aldington only increased my bewilderment. I knew I must take up some attitude towards it. I was an American, with a literary career of little more than a year to my credit. I was living now in London, had lived in London practically continuously since 1910. The English people, I could see, were convinced that they were fighting in a righteous cause, the cause of small nations, against Germany. The London newspapers were soon full of atrocity stories, as London itself was full of Belgian refugees, and everybody believed them. I did not know what to believe. President Wilson had already proclaimed America to be neutral. Whether he was right or wrong, I could not say. I only knew that as a neutral I could not stay on in London, even if I could obtain an extension to my passport. I had no business of any outstanding importance to keep me there. My business was to write poetry—not patriotic poetry, or antiwar poetry, but poetry. Even in times of peace such a task had often appeared to me as the creation of a pure luxury product. In wartime it was frankly useless.

On the other hand, all I could do to show my attachment to the cause of the Allies—whom, in common with everyone, including Miss Lowell herself, I favored—was, in case I remained in England, to volunteer to help fight England's battles; in much the same spirit as my father, who was not an advocate of secession, had been among the first to enter the service of the Confederacy. I considered that, if I stayed, I should join the British army; but when I mentioned this idea to Daisy, she had simply burst into tears. Why could I not remain where I was, and wait till the whole thing was over. The War would be finished by Christmas, at the outside; England was bound to win in three or four months; better men than I were already fighting for her, and thousands more were joining daily. There was no reason for me to think I could add anything to the force which England was proposing to employ. Besides, if I got myself killed, where would she and the children be? They would be paupers, since she now had no claim on her husband that he need respect, and since my own income lapsed entirely at my death. She thought it selfish that I should even express a desire to go. Frankly, I thought her attitude unreasonable. She hated the Germans to such an extent that she declared that certain neighbors of ours, who happened to bear German names, should be interned; yet she protested bitterly when I offered to go and help England fight her own battles. It was true that my annuity did lapse on my death, and if I were killed she would be left entirely unprovided for. That was not, however, my fault. I resolved that, come what might, I would not be swayed by her attitude.

Aldington's attitude seemed, on consideration, far more reasonable, and more worthy of respect. He recognized that the War existed, and that he must himself take up an attitude towards it. Yet his attitude differed from that of the conscientious objectors—already they were being discussed—who, brave and sincere men as they were, simply refused to have anything to do with the War at all. His attitude was that of an artist. It was not unworthy of such a figure as that of Leonardo da Vinci, who had entered Cesare Borgia's service, striven to serve his patron as he best might, and then when all the Borgia schemes collapsed, wrote calmly in his journal, "The Duke has lost all his lands, and all his projects have come to nothing," and returned to his work in Milan. He recognized that his task lay not in serving the blood lust of mankind, but in helping them towards a finer perception of beauty. Beauty, to his mind, was a thing of a higher order than the mere sentimental gush over one's own country. It was universal, and the business of the artist was to find it and to serve it. It seemed to me that his attitude was dignified, and worthy of my regard. Daisy's was not; it was merely a sentimental prejudice common to her class, and selfish to boot.

September had slipped away into October, and the news from all the fronts had become more and more discouraging. The first Russian advance had been completely smashed at Tannenberg. The "miracle of the Marne," as the press hailed it, had temporarily saved Paris, but the Allies were in no position to deliver a counterstroke. They might save Paris, but they probably would lose Calais. And, after Calais, what? There was a determination to win the War on the part of the Germans which was greater than Napoleon's determination had been. He had merely assembled that flotilla of his at Boulogne, but had not dared to cross, in the face of the prestige and courage of Nelson. But where among the English admirals was a Nelson now to be found? Perhaps the Germans might even produce a Nelson now of their own to match their old hero of Tannenberg, Field Marshal von Hindenburg. The Germans had built up a fleet fully equal to England's. It lay at the mouth of the Kiel Canal, protected by the invincible defences of Heligoland. German naval officers were already drinking toasts to "The Day." They were rapturously singing Ernest Lissauer's "Hymn of Hate"—"We have one foe, and one alone: England!" They were all praying, "Gott strafe England!" Or so the English press declared. How soon, then, would "The Day" arrive for them? My day, at all events, must soon end. In a month at the outside I must either join the British ranks or be branded as a coward—or quit England and return to my own country.

Meantime, Miss Lowell was writing long, optimistic letters, advising me to return and see for myself how well the "new poetry" which she had sponsored was flourishing. She was bringing out, that October, her *Sword Blades and Poppy Seed,* which would score, she was sure, an initial success for the cause she was championing, and she would follow this up with the publication of *Some Imagist Poets* in the next spring. Ezra's refusal to go on with her, together with the War, had killed England's last chance to make anything out of imagism. She already had interested a publisher in the project of printing my "Irradiations," but she wished I could come over and follow this up for myself. America was on the eve of an artistic and poetic renaissance. I had an opportunity, now, to score the success which England had so long denied me. I ought not to let it go by. Such letters still further upset my equilibrium, already disturbed by Aldington's expressed wish to quit England. It seemed to me that Amy was right—that indeed, in my own interests, I ought to return.

At the end of October, almost a year to the day when, after our first yielding to passion, Daisy had gone back to her husband and children, I finally made up my mind. We had a long and serious talk together. I told her that I had definitely decided to go back to my own country. I said that I could not do England any service by continuing to remain as I was, and that, as she herself had pointed out, if I joined the British army, I would probably be killed and leave her and her children in poverty. I would continue to support her, according to the agreement I had already entered into with her husband, but only on condition that I remained in my own country as long as this War lasted. I would return to her only when it was finished, or if I could return as her husband. Personally, I wished now that I had insisted on her obtaining a divorce from the outset. I had only accepted this alternative arrangement because of her serious illness, and in order to spare her further suffering. But I had not, at that time, foreseen the coming of the War. The War had changed everything, and made it impossible for me to continue as I was. I knew that the arrangement I had entered into that spring would no longer work. Therefore I was returning.

She listened this time quietly, her cheeks paling. Then she said that she recognized that there was much in what I had just said. Ever since I had returned from the Continent, ever since I had resumed the old life with her, I had seemed miserable and distracted, and had held aloof from any demonstrations of affection. She hoped that the War was responsible, and she did not want me to stay if that was the reason for my present state. For her part, she had tried to do everything that was in her power to make me happy; but she knew that whenever I took an idea into my head that I had to do something, there was no way to persuade me to the contrary. Had I not, last year, gone secretly to her husband and informed him of what was going on, without asking her advice? Now it was the same with this new notion that I must go back to America. Perhaps, therefore, it would be better for me to go. She only hoped that I would not forget her.

A day after this I went into London and bought a steamer ticket. The first ship available would not depart till the sixteenth of November, some days after my passport ran out; but I found, by inquiry at the American consulate, that neither the British nor the Americans would object to this, so long as I signified my immediate intentions of leaving the country which had harbored me for so many years. The rest of the time remaining was spent in packing, in making ready, in last sentimental visits on the part of Daisy and myself to the garden which had witnessed the first full avowal of our emotions. Winter was at hand and the remnants of the first British Expeditionary force—French's "contemptible little army," the "mercenaries" of A. E. Housman's immortal epitaph—were dying like flies that Ypres might be held. The battleship *Audacious* was sunk in the Irish Sea by a daring German submarine, but the Admiralty, fearing the effect of this news on the British people themselves, tried to make it appear as an accident. As I had already written in my "Orange Symphony," "My time is up—I must go." and to tell the truth, I breathed now more easily. Somewhere beyond the black seas and the November gales of the Atlantic lay a new and undiscovered America: a country I had abandoned long ago, now perhaps awaking for the first time to its destiny as a great power. I was prepared to face it, to make what I could of it.

So, and in such a spirit, I confronted the most important decision that had yet come to me in my life. The decision had been arrived at through Aldington's clear view, through Amy Lowell's encouragement, through Daisy's own unreasoning and purely emotional attitude of protest. The fact that, despite my determination to regain my own country, I was leaving behind me a still unclarified situation in respect to a woman and myself, was largely lost sight of, in the hurry of my preparations. I had asserted myself at last and taken the only course left open to me. Not knowing what sort of future beckoned to me, and realizing only that I must struggle onward to meet it, I ventured forth into the unknown.

CHAPTER XV

After an eight-day voyage, the roughest of my entire experience as a sea-traveler, the unladen ship accomplished its task of battling through the November gales, and drew towards the American shore. We dropped anchor in New York Harbor on the Tuesday before Thanksgiving—a magnificent day of vivid sunlight, sparkling coldness, and clear horizons. Fresh snow lay sprinkled on the russet-red soil of Staten Island. We waited in the Narrows from twelve o'clock till four, in full view of the city in the distance, while, one after one, thousands of mail sacks were discharged from the sides of the ship into two waiting tugs. I had come home at last, having already projected my emotions during the voyage into the violent storm images of the "Red Symphony."

As we went slowly up the harbor, in the waning glory of a late autumn afternoon, I was given ample opportunity to study again the aspects of the land from which I had sprung, and which I had neglected and ignored for over six years. The Woolworth Building, then newly finished, dominated the lower end of Manhattan Island, no other skyscrapers, except the far inferior Singer Building, having as yet been built near to it. It seemed, as its gilt Gothic crockets and finials glittered in the descending light, to represent the spirit of my land in a new and more victorious affirmation. Reims and Louvain and the town hall at Ypres might fall, but their spirit lived on in this cathedral of commerce, minted out of the nickels and dimes of the American people. Alas, I did not see—and few then did see—how shabby and sordid a reality of greed these same finials and Gothic spires concealed.

I spent a dozen days in New York, and then, in the midst of a whirlwind of new thoughts and impressions, moved on to Boston. Amy Lowell had sent me a message of warm welcome to my ship. I dined with her one evening at the St. Regis, and knew that her hospitality and generosity were open to at least one wayfarer. I felt I was not utterly lost in this new America, so recklessly piercing the clouds in one final effort, as long as I had one such friend. For New York was new to me—though at that time not all the landmarks I had known in my youth had been swept away, as they later were, under the furious overbuilding of the boom years.

One of the first poems I wrote after my arrival was, in its way, an unconscious tribute to Miss Lowell. The sight of the Woolworth tower rising amid the gaunt steel frames, the traveling cranes, the rat-tat-tat of riveters at work on newer skyscrapers all about it, had caused my impressions to take shape in the new Paul Fort manner, which she had used so successfully in "The Bombardment":

> Out of the black granite she is rising, surprising as sunrise over the head of the Sphinx; glittering towers coated in linked scales that seem as if they might melt away, they are so pale . . .

It seemed to me that this new form, a form far more free than Paul Fort's semi-Alexandrine jingle, solved at a blow the old problem that so long had tortured my mind: the problem of describing the essence of a great modern city in words. It used every resource of the poetic orchestra—rhyme, assonance, refrain, rhythm freely resolved and resumed in a single sustained composition of dithyrambic intent and emotional diversity. In its spontaneity, its unexpectedness, this new form was absolutely American: a linking together of Whitmanian energy and of Poesque music. It was the one form needed to release all my pent-up feelings about modern great-city civilization. America and Miss Lowell, each in their own way, had now set it in my hands.

Unlike New York, Boston, seen again after an interval of more than six years, seemed to have changed little outwardly. About the only change on the surface was that the old Museum of Fine Arts which had faced the Library and Trinity Church across Copley Square was now gone, and a new museum had been built out on Huntington Avenue. I had never supposed that I could enjoy the new museum as much as the old, but I did. The entire wing dedicated to housing the superb collection of Chinese and Japanese art especially held me; now, for the first time I understood what I—with my eyes still deluded by the triumphs of western naturalism—had missed before: how the Orient, by refusing to proceed along these lines, had achieved an art of such sustained spiritual intensity as the West had but rarely glimpsed in a few such figures as Cimabue, Giotto, Leonardo, Michelangelo, El Greco, and William Blake. The hours I spent then in the Oriental Wing, seeing the Sung or Kamakura masterpieces with new eyes, reeducated me in regard to the purposes of a pictorial art close in spirit to my own poetry, and to the function of the poetic artist in reshaping the world. They rededicated me to the vital instinct, and to the soul of nature. Not from the materialistic Occident, but from the traditional Orient must spring the new life-giving spirit, old and yet new, conservative and yet free, to create in western languages a new rhythm and a new vocabulary, a new form and a new feeling for the interrelation of man and nature. Now more than ever I understood the nature of the task to which I had dedicated myself: to fuse the East and the West, to combine the inner insight of the Chinese sages with the restless, dynamic energy of modern America. It seemed to me that in so far as I might help in accomplishing this task, I would not only be striving to achieve the greatest and most profound necessity of twentieth-century humanity, but that my work might possibly even lead to some advance of the human spirit that would be greater still, to some religion of the future that would combine the calm, detached self-awareness of Buddhism and the dynamic, passionate, world-awareness of Christianity. How little did I think, in those days, of my own inadequacies for such a task, or of the fact that the western world was so little concerned with achieving any spiritual harmony between man and his environment as to be ready to accept as gospel any shoddy substitute offered it by nationalism or by laissez-faire economics!

Not less important than my rediscovery of the treasure house of Oriental art at the Boston Museum of Fine Arts were my renewed talks and meetings with Amy Lowell. I remained, during the week I spent in Boston, a guest in her home. Ere this I had been sometimes a little disconcerted by her attitude of complacent and practical worldliness; now I saw, clearly and inescapably, the reason why this attitude existed. Here for the first time I was brought into contact with a being who knew of no other life than the life of luxury, had never experienced any other kind of life since her earliest years. That she had at least partially escaped from it, had freed herself from it sufficiently to look at the world with the imaginative eyes of a poet, was enormously to her credit; but it was scarcely enough. Before one can speak for humanity, before one can make laws or produce ideas that will rule the humblest as well as the highest, it is necessary to share in imagination the lives of all classes of mankind. Whitman had seen this as the essential task of the poet under democracy. He was right, but he had never come into close contact with such a person as Amy Lowell. Born to the superior station and wealth of her family, and so imbued with its importance in the affairs of the world, she was utterly unable to look at life from any other viewpoint. Here was one person who was doing exactly as she pleased, simply because the opportunity had been given her, and for no other and more profound reason. Surrounded by a dozen devoted servants, with a companion and friend in the warmhearted Ada Russell, who, for her part, was equipped with all the forbearance and tact of one who had lived long in the real world and dealt with real humanity, Amy behaved as an autocrat, simply because that was her real nature and her heritage. I soon saw that I had underestimated what it meant, in her case, to be a Lowell from Boston, and had overestimated her natural and human desire, which nonetheless existed, to be something else on her own account. She simply took her wealth and position for granted, and made the most of it.

All this did not come to me at once. For the first few days I was charmed and overwhelmed by the beauty of her great house, with its magnificent library, its secluded garden, its air of refinement and splendor, its well-ordered ritual of existence. Coming straight from a noisy and uncomfortable hotel room in New York, it seemed to me a haven of rest from the world. But I soon noticed that, whatever her house was, she did not live in it. Somewhere on the top floor, in rooms I never visited, she spent her days, never appearing downstairs until after nightfall. For the business of getting through the day, my hotel bedroom in New York might as easily have served the turn. The rest was for display, for a place to entertain others; and it satisfied her own estimate of herself that she visited it occasionally and realized that she could command its resources. Even her books and her unrivaled Keats collection seemed to be rather for appearance than for use, though all luxury is unnecessary unless it is used and enjoyed. She objected to others handling the books, and she kept the Keats collection locked away in a steel vault, built in the library wall. Knowing this, I did not even ask to be shown it. I would gladly have spent hours looking over the elephant folios of the original edition of Audubon's *Birds of America* which she possessed, and the possession of which I envied her; but I refrained from pulling them out, fearing a reprimand such as befell me during my very first days, when she discovered me in the act of looking at a rare Keats volume, and told me to put it back on the shelf. So instead of enjoying the books, I contented myself with admiring only her flowers. A profusion of these, always renewed, was kept blooming on the library tables by her English gardener. Realizing the devotion and care these represented, I told her that I thought her gardener a true artist. She was not in the least annoyed by the remark; indeed, she repeated it to him, and no doubt he was grateful for the compliment.

It may have been that my distaste for her worldliness affected me disagreeably. It may have been that I was simply exhausted with being kept up by her at all hours of the night, and having to meet face to face her lack of realization of the demands she made upon others. But I did not leave Boston without an outburst of my own peculiar bad temper. She invited me to meet Emile Gebhard and Carl Engel, two of her oldest and most valued friends, and there was a delightful evening of music which they gave at her home. Shortly before I left for Chicago and the West, these two excellent musicians also asked me to dine with them at the Adams House in Boston. Their gesture, I knew, was motivated by nothing but their kindliness, and a desire to recognize in me a fellow artist; but as the time drew near when I must fulfill my part as their guest, I began to have the strangest misgivings. I knew nothing of them, nor they of me, I reflected. Miss Lowell had already shown herself to be far different in many ways from anything I had expected. How would they turn out?

The day duly dawned, and I wakened with a dull headache and a sore throat, the sure signs of an oncoming cold. I should have telephoned Engel, whose party this was, to put him off, but I did not. Instead, I tried to feel better by remaining in bed all the morning. At lunch time I got up, put on my clothes, and joined Ada Russell at the table. She did not realize what was the matter with me, nor indeed did I fully realize it myself. At that time, and for many years later, whenever my body began to fail to respond to the demands made on it, I invariably tried to revenge myself on it by driving myself far beyond the limits of my own physical strength. It is only gradually that I have learned the least wisdom in this respect.

In the afternoon I took a lonely walk—and returned, with head burning, to lie down, fully dressed, for over an hour. Then I took the streetcar into Boston.

Engel was awaiting me, but Gebhard did not arrive for ten minutes. To Engel I explained that I was feeling ill and exhausted. He suggested a drink, and we had a cocktail. This made my head only worse, in the midst of the noise and heat of the crowded barroom. Finally Gebhard, an older, more staid and graying German with a foreign accent, turned up, and we moved off together to the dining room.

With the very first course I discovered that I could not eat anything. This dinner in my honor was certainly turning out differently from what I had hoped. Engel suggested milk toast, or something light, but I rebelled against being treated as an invalid. I made a show of eating the oysters and the soup. Gebhard, whose culture in the literary sense was far less than Engel's, began asking me questions about myself, my work, my career. I am afraid that I cut him short, being far too weary to explain. He was soon reduced to talking only about music with Engel.

With the fish course, I felt I could not swallow another mouthful. I could not eat, could not talk, could do nothing but sit and wish miserably that I had never come. I suddenly asked to be excused. If I had added that I felt too ill to go on I might perhaps have been forgiven. But I was annoyed at myself for feeling ill, and did not want to admit it. So I said merely that I felt I did not want any more company that night. Gebhard, quite naturally, chose to regard this as a personal affront.

"You have been acting strangely ever since you came," he retorted caustically. "Now you want to go. Did you come here only to insult us?"

I flared up. It is always so in such cases. I had restrained myself as long as I was able—had said nothing to Amy herself of the demands on my time and patience which had led to this stage of utter exhaustion—and now I was losing my temper with someone else, for no particular reason, simply because I could not keep it. Poor Engel had looked acutely miserable as I failed to answer the questions with which Gebhard had plied me. No matter. This was the last straw. Gebhard had said that I was insulting him. Very well. I would show him what a real insult meant.

"Since you chose to think that I am tired of your company, you are quite right. I never asked for your company. I don't want to sit here seeing you making gluttons of yourselves any longer."

I rushed out of the restaurant. One moment later, too late, I realized the full enormity of what I had just said. I had deliberately cut myself off from two friends whom I might have had, and these friends had been given me by Miss Lowell. Now I was going back to her house, already an outcast, a pariah from society. If only I had not gone—if only I had not lost my temper!

At half-past eight or a little later I descended wearily from the streetcar and made way again up Heath Street to Miss Lowell's front door. She was sitting quietly in the library, and came to the door at my ring. I must have looked acutely miserable, though the cold air was making me, in fact, feel less ill physically. She lost no time in asking the inevitable question, "What on earth has happened?"

I detailed carefully the circumstances and the causes of my affront. I literally threw myself on her mercy. She was furious, and began berating me as if I were a schoolboy. I suddenly burst into tears—I did not want to stand there weeping before her and yet I could not stop myself.

"I will go—I will go," I kept on saying, thinking that I had lost my last friend on earth.

Seeing that I was really suffering, her manner changed to solicitude. She offered to telephone both Gebhard and Engel, and say that she had insisted on my going, and that I had not wanted to go—as, in fact, I had not—but had merely gone to please her. She even offered to procure me a doctor, which I refused. And she let me go to bed, after I had promised to write Gebhard and apologize in the morning.

After all, I had not lost her as a friend, I reflected; whether Gebhard or Engel liked me or not mattered far less. I inwardly resolved, however, not to let her, under any circumstances, cut into my hours of sleep and keep me up long past midnight, as she had done on every night I spent under her roof. I took off my clothes and slept a long sleep of exhaustion for nearly twelve hours. The next day I felt much better, and, on the following evening, I was already on my way to Chicago. Engel, who undoubtedly knew her habits, since he had been a frequent visitor at her house for years before her first trip to England, and who had persuaded her to read the French poets before our friendship came about, remained friendly to me personally, and actually helped me later on financially by persuading me to translate the French texts for some songs by Gabriel Fauré. Gebhard I only saw distantly, as he continued to come and play at her house the following spring.

On my way to Chicago I stopped off at Buffalo and took a side trip to Niagara Falls, which I had never before seen. It looked savage and Scandinavian, with its banks beautiful in deep snow, and the leaden sky brewing another blizzard overhead. I recalled how Lowes Dickinson, already then a name among English intelligentsia, had said that Niagara Falls was the true symbol of America, since it displayed power carried to inhuman lengths, energy perpetually going to waste, the dramatic intensity of epic effort running on to the whirlpool rapids of death and destruction. I wondered, as I saw it, whether it were indeed so. Certainly it would be more difficult for me or for anyone to control the abysmal energy of America in the future than it was for man to harness the falls, though it was claimed that it had already been done successfully.

I arrived at Chicago, after an all-night train journey, in a temperature some degrees below zero. The sun was shining brilliantly overhead, but there was a biting wind from the northwest. The contrast between the overheated train and the intense cold of out-of-doors was so great that, on my way down State Street, I had to pause frequently and seek the shelter of doorways. I had never before stopped overnight in this city, and the contrast to New York and Boston was tremendous. Here was another America, the America of the great plains and the great Northwest, with its fierce scrambling animal energy, its vast stores of iron, copper, nickel, wheat, corn, cattle, hogs—a city of naïve boastful greed, of childlike exaltation over its own prowess, won by the blind toil of millions of ignorant immigrants, a city where the hard old New England idealism had grown soft and sentimental, an excuse alike for evangelic missionaries and for civic corruption, a predatory city, carried along, since the great Exposition of 1893, by its own naïve faith in the superiority of outward mechanical effort over inward harmony. It was so ferociously, intensely young and yet so hard and obstinate. It fascinated me to watch it, and yet it terrified me; for under the grim black shadows of its skyscrapers I learned what Niagara Falls had already shown me: that the struggle to establish the supreme imaginative art of poetry in America could be neither a short nor an easy one.

Miss Harriet Monroe, just celebrating the second anniversary of her editorship of the magazine which was already making literary history, seemed cold, somewhat dry and unemotional, and aloof. I scarcely realized what a degree of crusading ardor lay beneath her exterior, which was much like that of the schoolteachers I had known in my boyhood. She afforded a complete contrast, both in age and in manners, to the young, ardent, and far less emotionally stable Margaret Anderson, to whom Miss Lowell had given me a letter of introduction, and who had already embarked, with no funds, and no prospects except those procured by her own undiscriminating enthusiasm, on her spectacular career as editor of the *Little Review.*

Miss Monroe seemed frankly disconcerted and bewildered by the explosions of modernistic literary frankness her magazine was already provoking. Especially she seemed to be in awe of Pound. And I recall that she showed me, either now or on my later visit of a week in February, a poem that Pound had just sent in from London, written, as he said, by a young American who was the most intelligent American he had ever met in London, T. S. Eliot. She did not know what to make of the poem, which was entitled "The Love Song of J. Alfred Prufrock," and so she asked me for my frank opinion. I read it, and advised her to print it. As I recall, almost the only ultramodern "discovery" about whom she was deeply enthusiastic was Wallace Stevens, a poet concerning whom no one then—or since—has been able to unearth or discover any particular personal history. It may be that Stevens, with his peculiar romanticism of understatement, appealed to her because of certain affinities he showed with Chinese art, about which she was glowingly enthusiastic. Her sister, Mrs. Calhoun, then living in Chicago with her husband, was the wife of an American minister to China, and through her Miss Monroe had enjoyed the advantage of contact with China itself, which she had actually seen and visited. I suspected that it was her own perception of the Chinese echoes in my "Blue Symphony" which had led to her acceptance of it.

For the rest, Miss Monroe's chief ambition seemed to be the desire, in which all Chicago apparently shared, to uphold Chicago and the Middle West at all hazards. Her account of the founding of her own paper, and the struggles she had gone through to get the Chicago millionaires to support it, was epic; and her chief intellectual interest lay now in the discovery of new mid-western poets. Of the three outstanding figures who already answered to that category, I did not meet Vachel Lindsay, who was not in Chicago, but at Springfield. And had I met him, I doubt if we would have agreed on any point, as I had already taken a strong and possibly unreasoning dislike to his "General William Booth Enters Into Heaven," with its tone of a backwoods revival meeting. Carl Sandburg I did meet for a brief moment, as he sat in her office, his feet on the desk, a derby that sloped forward over his eyes, and a stogie cocked up between his lips. He was busy correcting some proofs, and did not look up or utter a word of greeting as I entered. The sight of him so disconcerted me that I could not utter a word. The most interesting and generally illuminating encounter I had with the mid-western group was with Edgar Lee Masters, whose *Spoon River Anthology,* supposedly rejected by Miss Monroe for her magazine, was already appearing in William Marion Reedy's obscure *Mirror* and causing a sensation which grew and increased in volume as each new installment saw the light.

There was not much that proclaimed the poet in Masters, or, if there was, it was such a poet as Henrik Ibsen had been before him, in mid-century Norway. There was indeed, I thought, more than a hint of Ibsen himself about Master's own physical appearance: the rounded, resolute face, with its fine forehead and keen eyes scrutinizing the world behind their glasses, the firm-set, determined mouth, the slow, deliberate, dignified manner. Here was one whose long and hard experience as a lawyer had given him a unique and devastating insight into the corruptions that followed fast upon the acquiring of great wealth in the Middle West. He had turned aside from the vices and scandals of modern Chicago to trace in a typical frontier community, such as that in which he had spent his boyhood, the ideals, the tragedies, and the failures that had made the frontier significant, and the later great city life possible. The value of his *Spoon River* lay not so much in its poetical power as in the fact that it was a document of firsthand importance as history—history as lived and not as written in textbooks! These epitaphs summed up, in unforgettable precision, the kind of lives out of which the great westward migration, the American dream of free men in a free continent, the Civil War, the development of industrialism, the shameless scramble for pelf and profit, had sprung. I felt an immediate sympathy with Masters's poetry, despite all its realism; but in many respects the man himself baffled me. He seemed to be largely a bundle of contradictions: so much the pushing, ambitious, self-made middle-westerner, so much the aristocratic, disdainful, unaccountable genius.

I remember a luncheon meeting at some Chicago club when he pushed across the table a typewritten copy of one of the "Spoon River" epitaphs and asked me to read it. It was the one about the sculptor who goes abroad, does not return, and spends his life carving Apollos—but is nevertheless a failure, because, about all the Greek gods whom he fashions, there is the remote suggestion of Abraham Lincoln. I wondered, as I read it, whether this was Masters's deliberate retort to Ezra Pound, to myself, and to all other Americans who had gone abroad and striven to adjust the American literary craft to its appropriate background of world tradition, so that American literary art might cease to be incoherent, such a thing of fits and starts as Poe, Whitman, or even Emerson had made it—so that American literary art might take its place in the rightly ordered continuity of the great tradition. I did not, however, feel in the mood to contradict Masters on this occasion, and to say to him that his sculptor, though an expatriate and a failure, had possibly striven for a more valuable kind of success than came to those inhabitants of Spoon River who stayed behind and glorified the exploits of their bank presidents, meat packers, and the jingo imperialists of the Spanish American War. I merely kept my peace, and handed the epitaph back to him without comment.

Besides Miss Monroe and Masters, I had the pleasure on this visit to Chicago of meeting Alice Corbin Henderson, the indefatigable assistant to Miss Monroe on her magazine and a poet in her own right, as well as the wife of a hard-working artist and the mother of a charming young daughter. She proved to be a southerner, with all the easygoing individualism that is so natural to the southerner, and with none of the angularity which was manifest in such notable middlewesterners as Miss Monroe and Masters. Her chief trait was a wholehearted generosity, which she has never lost. I found her more sympathetic to my poetry and its aim of fusing melody and vision, dream and reality, than I could have even remotely hoped for; and she was also an ardent convert to imagism. Without her influence Miss Monroe's paper might have been, I felt, narrower in its scope and less epoch-making in its effect. Although, only two years later, she was obliged to abandon her post as Miss Monroe's chief assistant and go to Santa Fe in New Mexico to repair her shattered health, the influence she had on the early course of *Poetry* was decisive.

New York, Boston, and now Chicago had alike checked my own drift towards a too narrowly personal and too abstractly aesthetic poetic art in the "symphonies." I was consumed by a fresh wave of objective curiosity concerning the manifestations of real life in this strange and fascinating country. Whether those manifestations could take shape as the great imaginative myths and legendary sagas which were the substance of poetry, or must seek rather the lesser art of prose fiction, Edgar Lee Masters had himself brought sharply into question. Now I was again thrown back on myself, and on my own personal antecedents. After a stay of only two days in Chicago, I returned to my native town of Little Rock, still wearing most of the aspects which I had known in my boyhood, though American life, here as elsewhere, was being transformed by the noiseless and complete revolution in all American habits which had been so successfully engineered by Henry Ford.

My elder sister, who had shared in my early education, but who had grown up to a life totally different from mine since the years I had spent at Harvard, was still living, as she has always lived, in the house associated in memory with my own boyhood. She was now married, and had already a family. It seemed strange to me to be called "Uncle John" by the youngest members of the household. There, freed entirely from the distractions of literary society, and left largely to my own devices, I spent hours in reading Nuttall's *Travels Into Arkansas Territory,* published in 1822, a book which helped me to the quasi-Indian poems called "Songs of the Arkansas" which continued the vein of my "Cherokee Ballads." I also spent further hours poking about the old house, absorbed in the rich collection of souvenirs of my boyhood, which its rooms, and, even more, its fascinatingly full attic, still displayed. Now I began to go back to my personal life again. But it was no longer the personal life of my manhood, but that of my remote boyhood; of a shy, sensitive, possibly spoilt only son, much given to reading and dreaming, whom two adoring parents had given every advantage except that of rough, direct, practical contact with the external world, and who had been turned loose, to become quite different, possibly, from what either of them hoped or expected. Now I already stood at an immense "aesthetic distance" from this, my own past, and, frankly, it haunted me. Had I been a success or a failure in regard to it? I did not know.

Christmas went past, and New Year's Day—the New Year of 1915. The War, which had already scarred my spirit, as the latest "symphonies" and the war poems I had already written could testify, seemed far away in this sleepy Arkansas town, slowly losing the last links of its pre-Civil War heritage of old southern culture, and becoming rapidly a little more "progressive," advanced, and middle-western. But now I felt that what I had already seen of the European War at close range had modified my own early attitude to the Civil War. During my boyhood the stories of the Civil War that I had heard from members of my father's generation, so much older than I, but living still on their memories of the great contest, had seemed to me at best only tedious legends. During my college years, Lincoln and Stephen Douglas, Jefferson Davis and Robert E. Lee and Stonewall Jackson, had all been less real to me as human beings than Whistler, Rossetti, Oscar Wilde, Baudelaire, Swinburne, and William Morris. I had gone abroad because I was already tired of American history, and wished to learn something of art, which seemed to me both better and more important than history. There are still people who look on religion with precisely this attitude, and to me art had become a religion. The War had already taught me that there was no escape from history. Had the people of France been conquered by the Germans, their culture destroyed, their homes despoiled, they would have looked on their lost heritage no differently than the folk of my father's generation. It would have become, to them, something so uniquely precious that nothing in it needed modification, and they would have lived solely on its memory, without making any further effort. So my father's generation had largely lived; but I had been too young, too restless, and too aesthetically sophisticated to realize that fact. Now I saw that the Civil War had actually been fought, and what it had done to my people. The European conflict brought it all back.

So, after a January visit to New Orleans to meet my younger sister and her soldier husband, a visit which brought the old South still more vividly into the foreground of my own thoughts, I found myself in the first two weeks of February at Little Rock, writing a new series of poems entitled "The Ghosts of an Old House." These poems, twenty-four in number, were written on themes supplied me by my own boyhood. They were far more imagistic, in the narrowest and strictest sense—the sense of H. D. and Pound—than anything I had yet written. Each was a meditation, a flight of fantasy, provoked by some object that had definitely reminded me of the past. Their poignancy resided, not in any rhetorical elaboration of detail nor in the working up of analogy between the object and myself—as in the case of the "symphonies"—but in bald, stark directness of statement. Thus I may claim for them that they are the only imagistic poems which are also purely southern poems. The later southern school of the Nashville "Fugitives," appearing on the American literary landscape seven years later, would have treated these themes, no doubt, far differently than I. But at the time when I was writing them no one had so much as heard of the Fugitives, nor of the more modern "proletarians," nor of the still more modern surrealists, about whom we may all be hearing tomorrow. I had to do the best I could with my subject—a subject that had suddenly revealed to me its significance.

Of minutes dragging slowly
And repeating
Some worn out story of broken effort and desire,

according to the technical ability that now lay in my grasp. And it is for that reason that I may claim for "The Ghosts of an Old House," not indeed that they anticipated the later "literary renaissance" of the South, which can now apparently drag almost any novel about the Civil War, written from the southern standpoint, into the lists of the best sellers, but only that they were southern and imagistic, at a time when there were no southerners who were ready to restate the thesis of the South, in any new form, at all. They covered the old ground—the ground of a vanished past, of unforgettable losses, of a tradition so long overlooked that to recall it in this new way was for me, too, poignant torture—in an unfamiliar way. And they aroused Amy Lowell to such admiration as nothing in all my work hitherto had yet done. It was soon after hearing me read them, later on in this spring of 1915, that she wrote her poem "The Mirror" and dedicated it to me. I had held the mirror up to my own past successfully, and had shown her thereby, unconsciously, what she could do with hers.

My stay in the South had lasted from December to St. Valentine's Day. I had obtained out of it my polyphonic prose, "The Old South," inspired by the aspects of New Orleans, my "Songs of the Arkansas," and now my "Ghosts of an Old House." I was content with this literary booty. Had I been able to discover more then, or had I been granted any inkling of the fact that, in ten or twelve years' time, a real literary revival would take place in the fields of Dixie, rather than in the North, I might have stayed on indefinitely. I might also have unlearned thereby some of the lessons of courage, of independence of thought and action, of the need for experiment in new and daring forms of imaginative expression, which my exile from the South had already thoroughly taught me. But now I decided not to regret that I had ceased to belong wholly to the South, nor to regret that, at twenty-nine, the South had not, as yet, even heard of my name. There was another spot on the map of America to which I could and should go; this place was Boston. Amy's indefatigable persistence had already persuaded Houghton Mifflin there to take the plunge. They were bringing out, that spring, a "New Poetry Series" in which my own *Irradiations* no less than her *Some Imagist Poets* were to figure prominently. I knew that I must be there, on the spot, to make the most of my opportunity. I must meet and stand and live, so far as I could, with Miss Lowell, on equal terms. She herself had hoped that I would decide to settle in Boston. Her presence there was both a stimulus and a challenge to me—and I must meet both. So, with my trunks repacked, and with plenty of new work accomplished, I turned my back anew on Arkansas. I was not to see my native state again for twelve years.

CHAPTER XVI

On my way back to Boston I dropped off again at Chicago, where I remained for a week. I found that the chief literary topic in Chicago was only the increased sensation which Masters's *Spoon River* epitaphs were now causing. William Marion Reedy's obscure magazine had become almost a leading organ of American literary opinion on the strength of this one feature alone. The fierce sincerity, the detailed power of character drawing, the knowledge of American types which Masters increasingly displayed, were stirring all literary circles to their very depths. It may be that this, almost the first outstanding success which the new poetry was having, influenced me subconsciously; indeed, I think it must have been so, in view of what followed.

Masters's *Comédie Humaine* owed its renown chiefly to his power to draw credible American characters and to generalize about life. So far my own poetry had been largely a poetry, not of human beings, but of objects. Things still interested me far more than people—things and their relations to me personally, or to each other. My poetry was, as I know now, akin in spirit to the pictorial presentation of natural atmosphere and life rhythm which had been the secret of Chinese and Japanese art. Like that art, the landscape had been more important to me than the human beings. Not only Masters, but Robert Frost, who had but recently returned from England to score a sensational success with his *North of Boston,* seemed to concentrate their art less on the landscape than on the human figure. I wondered, frankly, whether it would be ever possible for me to do so.

As it happened, Chicago's Art Institute was holding an important exhibition at the time of my return. A great collector of Japanese prints had left his entire collection to the Institute, and these were now being exhibited in the galleries. I had already been aware of the power of oriental art, in all its phases, to furnish subjects and to govern their treatment, for all my poems, without exception, since my writing of *Irradiations*. Now, as I visited this large collection of beautiful prints, produced by the "ukiyoye" or "passing-world" school of painters, who were despised by the superior taste of the art aristocracy of their time, because they concentrated their skill on the depiction of daily life and on the human figure, I was stirred to make a new experiment. Why should I not use these prints as a pretext to express my own views of human life and destiny, in the shape of brief, epigrammatic poems, much as Masters had already done?

During the week I spent in Chicago I visited the Art Institute repeatedly. There, in the galleries facing the actual prints themselves, I wrote no less than fifty epigrams. I concentrated exclusively on the earlier specimens of this ukiyoye art; I left out of my survey the later masterpieces of both Hokusai and Hiroshige, who had carried this print-designing triumphantly into yet another field of oriental genius, the field of landscape. As I have said, I wrote fifty of these epigrams during the brief week I spent in Chicago; I might have written more, had my stay lasted longer. Later on, these were assembled with some sixteen earlier epigrams dating from bygone years, extracted from my notebooks, and were finally published, as late as 1918, as *Japanese Prints*.

What I intended by *Japanese Prints* was a brief commentary on life and on manners, a kind of *Spoon River à la Japonaise*, more compressed indeed, and more decorative, but not less valid and direct. I was by no means convinced that Masters's own brand of meticulous American realism had anything in particular to do with the practice of the poetic art or with his commentary on life which ran side by side with it. If poetry was to be taken, not only as an arrangement of emotions, which my own poetry had largely been, but as "a criticism of life," to employ the phrase of Matthew Arnold, then there was no reason, as far as I could see, why one should not achieve just as valid a criticism of life by generalizing as by particularizing. Poetry of this sort should be concentrated, suggestive, brief, much as the Japanese poetry itself had been. There was no need of all this proliferation of sprawling and prosaic detail. A few lines, a few details sufficed, as in the Japanese prints that stood before me as I wrote. On the other hand, the concentration of the Japanese on the Yoshiwara and on the popular theater was a limitation; there were whole sides of life they told me nothing about, whole commentaries they did not make. One could not help admiring among them such a solitary and, at bottom, such a shockingly nonoriental figure as Sharaku, who had revolted against conventionalized and expressionless faces in the direction of savage caricature. Still, it seemed to me that when I had concluded my week's task in weariness, and had written fifty epigrams, that I need not—despite its faults—feel ashamed of *Japanese Prints*. If any imagist wished to comment on life, this was the way, I felt, the comment should be made.

Boston had now become my center, intellectually and physically; except for the four months between June 25 and October 21, I did not quit it. The friendship established between Amy Lowell and myself not only persisted, but was now actually stronger than ever. I had myself set this friendship on an equal footing, beyond all cavil as to which one of us was borrowing ideas or technique from the other, by following her into the domain of rhymed prose poems. I had already written three in this form before quitting Little Rock, in my "New York," "The Building of Chicago," and "The Old South," all subsequently published in my *Breakers and Granite*. Within a month after my return I was to add another in the shape of my "Clipper Ships," the most genuinely popular of all my achievements in this medium.

We had a long discussion, probably inspired by this particular poem, as to what we should call this new way of writing, which stood midway between verse and prose. Amy now agreed with me that though Paul Fort's far more metricalized *Ballades* may have given her the impetus, the result that she had arrived at was so complex in its use of varying rhythm as to be as unlike Fort as possible. The new form was neither, strictly speaking, prose nor verse. I thereupon remarked that its basis was the elaborately rhythmed prose of Sir

Thomas Browne, De Quincey, or Melville, with this addition: that all the wealth of English rhyme, assonance, verbal onomatopoeia, was deliberately woven into it exactly as the masters of polyphony, such as Bach, had woven over their simple chorales the most elaborate contrapuntal forms. "Then what ought we to call it," she asked, "since it is neither Paul Fort's half-free Alexandrines nor straightforward prose?" "Suppose we call it polyphonic prose," I replied, and she was delighted with my reply.

During this spring, I am happy to think that I may have been of some further assistance to her in the preparation of her lectures on "Six French Poets," all of which I heard delivered at Miss Putnam's house. And now, for the first time, I was impressed with her powers, as a reader of poetry, to sway and to stir her audience. Despite the obvious physical handicap of her figure, whenever she read poetry aloud she became a great dramatic interpreter in her own right. I was personally overwhelmed by her vividly dramatic readings of my favorite Verhaeren, as well as by her reading of Paul Fort. America at that time was already ringing with the acclaim that had followed Vachel Lindsay's first appearances on the reading platform. I did not hear Lindsay then, nor for many years afterwards; but it is possible to doubt whether Lindsay, for all that his own poems, the only ones he ever read, were perfectly adapted to his manner, ever achieved so much in this line as did Miss Lowell. For one thing, Lindsay, in addition to the possession of a fine tenor voice, had an extremely mobile face, a command of physical gesture and of platform effect that might have been disdained by his own hero, William Jennings Bryan.

Miss Lowell had to depend almost purely on her voice alone. As I recall it, it was a full contralto in its speaking quality, and was reinforced by such a sense of emotional conviction and of dramatic fitness as made her audiences entirely forget the heavy body from which it sprang. Moreover, she was equally impressive, whether as reader of her own poems or of those of other poets. I have heard her read not only the French poets, but Robinson, Frost, Sandburg, H. D., myself, and others; and she shone in them all. Truly, the admiration she always felt for Eleonora Duse was neither forced homage nor the weak-kneed tribute of a mere amateur to a great professional. It was the acknowledgment of one who, but for the fact of a physical handicap laid upon her, might have been a rival. She could, and did, as Foster Damon in his *Life* observes, hold an audience spellbound, and reduce them to tears.

So that I would not interfere either with her habits, nor she with mine, I had engaged from the moment of my arrival in Boston two furnished rooms at 9 Walnut Street, on the third floor of an old-fashioned comfortable house just off Beacon Hill, overlooking the Charles River Basin. It was there that I lived and wrote. The Public Library was within easy access across the Common and the Public Gardens. There I did most of my reading, till Miss Lowell furnished me with a ticket to the Athenaeum. Among its shelves I spent many hours, incidentally discovering there some poems by Thomas Holly Chivers—among them, his "Railroad Song," with its curious anticipation of Vachel Lindsay—in the files of moldering American magazines. At the Public Library, I recall, I looked up several points for at least one of Miss Lowell's French lectures, and occupied myself with various other matters. I generally saw Amy herself at her house, twice a week, and then always in the evenings. We would meet, read over to each other what we had written, and comment on events in the poetic world as they came up. Our relationship was thus regulated by the respect in which we held each other; it was warm, frank, and cordial.

That Miss Lowell was rapidly becoming a public figure through her campaign on behalf of free verse and imagism did not trouble me in the least. I had few, if any, ambitions to become such a figure. My business was to write poetry, to push to the utmost my own capacity for creation; and this I did. Whether or not she got the credit for her championship of the new poetry was to me a matter of complete indifference. The files of *Poetry*, the *Egoist*, the *Little Review*, exist to show that I granted her full credit for her achievements. She had found me a publisher, at last, for *Irradiations*, and for this I was more than grateful. Since I no longer now had to pay in order to appear before the American public, I was content with my position.

I realized that a public career of the spectacular sort was almost an essential to her full functioning as a poet, and I was glad that she had undertaken it. I have never seen another person so richly endowed with mental energy and dynamic curiosity about life as she was during the years of which I speak. That she may have made a mistake in backing the imagists, free verse, and the new poetry generally is a question for critics. I cannot pretend to anticipate, nor to dispute, their verdict. But that she did back the advance guard, that she flung down the challenge to the academic pontiffs and to the public and to the sensation mongers of that day, is not a question that can ever be in doubt. She championed me as well as all the other imagists in the group, with every atom of her brains, every ounce of her skill. And thereby she made the new poetry so much a topic for discussion that other poets, not of her group, undoubtedly profited.

Not, however, if they openly attacked her. Her independent position, her unflagging vitality, and, still more, her persistence made of her a formidable fighter. As Foster Damon is at pains to point out, in his biography, she was not of the sort to crumple up under adverse blows. The tales told of her publicly bursting into tears at various critical moments are one and all apocryphal. If they contain any modicum of truth, it must be that they refer to her final years, when, exhausted under the burden of her work on Keats, exhausted with her own prodigal overproductivity, exhausted with an incurable illness, she sometimes gave way. I am glad never to have seen her thus. To me, she was always a champion in her own right; always able to take blows, and to deliver more telling blows in return.

I delighted, as far as a spectator watching a supreme display of skill may delight, in the tale, as it unfolded itself, of her various battles and her many victories. Soon after my return to Boston I met, at her home, Robert Frost, whose poetry she had been the first in America to praise publicly. I understood the causes for this praise better in her case than in the case of Ezra Pound, whose admiration for this poet had so much disconcerted me, nearly two years previously, in London. It was because Frost stood in her mind for unfamiliar New England, not the New England of the cultivated and the affluent, among whom she had always lived, but the remote, shy, hermitlike New England of Thoreau and the backwoods farmer, that his work made such an appeal to her. And Frost himself, as I recall him at that first meeting, seemed to me to have all the qualities to be expected from a man of his type. I was struck by the Celtic dreaminess of his eyes, his quiet unworldliness, his serene detachment of manner. He sat on her sofa and said little, but I realized through and through his genuineness as a human being. Though his life had been carried on through scenes and circumstances as remote from my own as possible, and though his poetry was something from which I could not obtain anything but a clear vision of a world totally unfamiliar, which could never be mine, yet I admired both the poet and the man. We have met since then, and always on the same footing of distant equality. If I continued to admire him, it was entirely because of Amy Lowell's first generous championing of his work.

It was still more interesting than my meeting with Frost to hear from Amy herself her own account of the various battles and skirmishes in which she now engaged on behalf of the new poetry. The imagist anthology was to appear in April, and on March 30 the first of these historic battles took place. She was invited to New York to address the meeting of the Poetry Society of America held there. And she used the five minutes allotted to her—tacked on to the end of an already long program—to proclaim the virtues of imagism and to read her most recent poem in the "polyphonic prose" method, "Spring Day."

The result was a battle of insults and objurgations that went on and on beyond the written rule of the Poetry Society that poems by guests were not to be discussed, and beyond the unwritten laws of common decency and courtesy. Far from quelling the object of their attack, this onslaught of the conservatives simply primed Miss Lowell. Her Yankee blood was up, and she gave as good as she got, now and henceforward. She realized, once and for all, that the type of poetry she was championing must make its way, not through paeans of praise nor through sane and balanced discussion, but despite all the attacks directed against it. And her realization of this fact led her to throw aside all native caution, and to be determined to succeed at all costs—even at the cost of turning the fire of the critics against themselves. Which she accordingly did.

Some Imagist Poets appeared shortly afterwards, and drew such a torrent of denunciation as has never fallen to the lot of any single volume in my lifetime—a denunciation only equaled, I think, in the past by Walt Whitman's *Leaves of Grass.* That is not to say that this small, green-covered, innocent-looking volume, nor the two other imagist annuals which succeeded it, was in any sense equal to Whitman. But it is to say that in the midst of the hullabaloo of hundreds, all setting out like dogs to bait Miss Lowell and her present following, there was seldom heard the voice of reason or of sanity. One need only contrast the reception given by the critics to *North of Boston* or to *Spoon River,* both of which appeared that spring, with the reception given to *Some Imagist Poets* to note the difference. In the two former instances the work done was judged and praised on its merits; in the latter, it was not. It was sufficient that Miss Lowell was championing the imagists to thoroughly damn them. In view of such attacks as emanated from William Ellery Leonard or O. W. Firkins—to name but two cases—it henceforth devolved on the imagists to fight back, to close their ranks, to stick together. They had to praise and, in fact, even overpraise each other in order to succeed at all. They had to become the very thing which Miss Lowell and myself had tried hard to prevent them from becoming: a cult and a clique.

So it happened that the furious onslaught of the critics on imagist poetry in general, and on Amy Lowell in particular as leader of it, had the effect not of killing imagism at all, but rather of intensifying certain of Miss Lowell's own faults as a writer. The arrogant, autocratic side of her nature was henceforward deepened and intensified; and deepened and intensified also was her own technical virtuosity, often at the expense of manifest sincerity of feeling. Her poems became and remained, more and more, "external" attempts to register a certain effect. A great number of them might be listed under the title she gave to one: they might be called "Fireworks," causing an "Ah!" of gratified astonishment in the reader upon his first reading, but later on a feeling of wonder why the astonishment had ever existed.

So it is now, with the poem in polyphonic prose which had produced the first outburst of indignation at the Poetry Society meeting, the once famous "Spring Day." Anyone now reading this particular poem dispassionately, and carefully, will find it rather a simple, straightforward, a pleasantly phrased, even a sentimentally pretty affair. Compared to the hobgoblins of Hart Crane and T. S. Eliot, the general nightmarishness of Conrad Aiken or of many of the Fugitive poets, it is thoroughly innocuous. Yet all the fuss and fume was made over it because the critics and the public thought that Amy Lowell, the monstrously fat Amy Lowell who smoked black cigars, was describing in this poem how she took her morning bath. None of them realized that the mature Amy Lowell who wrote this particular poem was an altogether different being and lived an entirely different life from the person described in it, and that if this person existed at all, it must have been in Amy Lowell's girlhood. None of them could, by comparing the texts, see that this poem derived from my own boyish exultancy as expressed in *Irradiations,* no less than from my own more recent stirring up of childhood memories in "Ghosts of an Old House." Here, as elsewhere, Amy Lowell had merely followed a lead given her by another; if the lead landed her in a difficult position, that was none of her fault.

The violence of the critical outburst over the first anthology of imagist poetry which appeared under her leadership had two very important effects. In the first place, it had the effect of making her the leader of imagism once and for all. Imagism was henceforward her ism, as it had once been Pound's, and she could do with it exactly as she liked—as he had once tried to do. The result was not so disastrous as it might have been, but it did have the effect of reducing all the rest of the imagists to minor figures, and made any revival of imagism impossible as long as she lived, and also after her death. The second effect was on Miss Lowell herself. After the scandalous success of *Some Imagist Poets* she became, of necessity, not only the Bostonian aristocrat of generous impulses which she had always been, but the Bostonian aristocrat promoted to the official leadership of a notoriously eccentric cult. That there was nothing particularly freakish about the members of the cult made no difference. All of the imagists, without exception, were seriously trying to add some new quality to English poetry as written in their time; but this fact did not affect the estimate of the conservatives. Miss Lowell had to appear freakish, and to go on battling for freakishness, henceforward. And the tragedy of her later career was that she so often did what was expected of her, and behaved freakishly.

Such are the reflections that now come to me as I contemplate Amy Lowell's public life and career. But at the time of which I write I had no such advantage of perspective. On the contrary, I was as ardently engaged as anyone in the fight she was now making to establish imagism and to defend the new poetry. More ardently, in fact; for I alone of all the imagists enlisted under her banner, enjoyed the advantages of physical proximity. I lived in the same neighborhood as she did; I was able to study closely her mind at work; I completely backed her career throughout the publication of the three anthologies, and gave no public indication of any change in my feeling until my *Chapbook* of May, 1920, appeared. Therefore I think I am now entitled to point out that her success, great as it was, was not of such a nature as to increase her stature as a writer. She remained a challenging and interesting figure of many and various talents, but not essentially a great writer, if one classifies only those writers as great who are able to extract out of the common and universally human themes of birth, love, loss, death, struggle, achievement, and failure, new meanings of universal import and new notes of perpetual poignancy. She was, and is, a writer well worth reading from every point of technical interest; but it was only towards the very end of her life that she began to use her technique on themes of universally human import. Occasionally, though, even in this early period, she touched on such themes—in her "Patterns," notably, in the very year of which I write; and that she had the capacity to do so is abundantly proven. She did not care to exert it often; and this was not so much her own fault as the fault of the public and the critics, who demanded, only too often, from her a showy brilliance of surface at all costs.

Through her insistent interest on my behalf I now had a publisher in the shape of Houghton Mifflin of Boston; and my *Irradiations* appeared alongside of *Some Imagist Poets,* that spring. In this publishing office I discovered a new friend in R. N. Linscott, a tall, broad-faced, handsome, and vigorous son of backwoods New England who combined a humorous and deprecatory skepticism about life in general with a vivid enthusiasm for all forms of artistic beauty. He became one of the earliest admirers of my own poetry, and sensing in me a feeling for nature not less keen and vivid than his own, we took many long walks and rambles together, through the countryside that lay at the back door of Boston. His special admiration was Thoreau, an admiration I shared despite all Thoreau's abolitionism and his fanatic defense of John Brown. I could accept the rebel and the nonconformist in Thoreau, as well as the shy, sensitive lover of the wilderness. Had I not myself failed to conform to the standard set by the South? Linscott now became my chief male friend, and has remained a friend down to this day. Through him I came to understand more of the real background of New England than Miss Lowell herself could show me.

It was Linscott who introduced me to another poet in Conrad Aiken, three years younger than myself, and about the same period of time removed from his career as a college student. Within a month of our meeting he removed with his wife and young son from Cambridge to 10 Walnut Street, Boston—in order, as he has since said, to be near me, in whom he sensed a poet in many ways maturer and more stimulating to the development of his own talent than any he had met, since his companionship with T. S. Eliot at Harvard. Though he lived next door, we both ate our meals under the same roof, a fact which led to my seeing a good deal of him. He was, in fact, just then emerging from an early career as facile versifier into poetic independence. His first book, which had appeared the year before, was marked by nothing more remarkable than a great facility in rhymed verse, and the combined influences of Keats and Masefield. His second, appearing the following spring, went rather in the direction of Masters. It was not till his third, *The Jig of Forslin,* written directly under my influence, and read by me in manuscript, that he began to develop in the direction of his own peculiar bent towards a combination of keen psychological analysis and romantic disillusion. Something in my own *Irradiations* and "symphonies" set him traveling in this path, so that he was obliged, by sheer force of circumstances, to retract, or at least largely to modify, much of his own early avowed hostility to imagism.

I remained in Boston from the middle of February to past the middle of July. When I left, the battle over the imagists, provoked by Miss Lowell, was still raging violently in all the papers in America. Miss Lowell was already arranging to go to her summer home at Dublin, New Hampshire, and I had, in fact, accompanied her and Ada Russell on an excursion by automobile to this remote village, in order to get her summer home open. It seemed to me now that the time had come for me to get away, to see the world afresh for myself, and to grasp the direction in which I could travel as a poet in the future. My experiments in polyphonic prose had already shown to me that I possessed a special aptitude for poems descriptive of places and natural scenery. Therefore I should travel as widely as possible, in order to develop this special gift. My elder sister had come north from Little Rock to Chicago, and now invited me to join her there for the summer. I decided to go, and, by letting my mind receive the impress of new scenes and environments, develop further towards the more objective kind of writing that I had recently begun to practice. Accordingly, soon after the middle of July, I left. I did not return to Boston till towards the close of October. Long before leaving—in early March, in fact—I had written what I supposed to be a final farewell to my series of "symphonies," in the shape of the "Grey Symphony":

Three lofty pines
At the corners of my heart
Waited apart.

They only see
In the mystery
Of the grey sky,
The jaggled clouds that fly
Endlessly.

I was now about to follow those "jaggled clouds" far to the West, to that part of the country I had not seen since my last years at Harvard. My stay in Chicago with my sister lasted only a few days. At the close of it I went northward to a cottage facing the spruce- and birch-clad shores of northern Lake Michigan, in a country where there were authentic Indians. Here I wrote, as an afterthought and postscript to all my "symphonies," the two poems later on included in their number, under the titles of "Midsummer Dreams" and "Poppies of the Red Year," the former an idealized version of the theme of sexual longing and frustration that had been the chief motif of the original "Blue Symphony," the latter an attempt to pierce to the heart of the passions that were now being unleashed in the European War. Both these poems, in conformity with my original intentions in the "symphonies," were stated in terms of subjective vision, rather than as items of objective fact. They seemed to me to sum up the chief themes of the entire "symphony" series: the themes of loneliness, of wandering, of aspiration, of conflict, of remote sublimation in mysticism, and of quiescence. With these two final fusions of dream and reality I finally put the entire series of "symphonies" behind me, and entered a fresh phase of development.

On August 21 I arrived, after a brief stay of four sweltering days in Chicago, to which I had returned from my retreat in the Michigan woods, at the town of La Salle on the Illinois River, where a steamboat was waiting, ready to take me down the Illinois and down the Mississippi to New Orleans. The trip was to take a week, and was a special summer excursion promoted by an enterprising travel agency. I had seen it advertised in the Chicago newspapers, and the moment I saw it I recalled the fact that to go down the Great River in a steamboat had been one of the earliest of my boyhood ambitions, an ambition held, in fact, ever since I first read the inimitable pages of Mark Twain. This ambition was now about to be realized at last. Two days and nights of the sluggish green Illinois brought us to Cairo in the early morning, and going on from there we arrived at St. Louis late in the afternoon, where other steamboats, now, alas, all vanished, were standing at the wharves, and negro dray drivers urged their mules across the brick-paved water front. We passed Memphis in the dead of night, but on the fourth day stopped for two hours at Helena, where I was back in Arkansas. The fifth day we arrived at Vicksburg, where all went ashore and inspected the battlefield where Grant's reputation was finally established, and the South had sustained a siege that need never have resulted as it did had the southern leaders seen the situation as clearly as Grant did. We passed Natchez again at night, paused at Baton Rouge the next day, and by one o'clock in the morning of the seventh day since we set out were tied to the wharf at New Orleans.

On the trip down I had written the series of poems, "Down the Mississippi," in which I gave my new technique of description derived from natural objects themselves, rather than from my feelings about them, a full chance to show what it could do. And from then on throughout my life I have always felt a special kinship with the Mississippi River itself, a kinship expressed by several of my later poems.

New Orleans was too stiflingly sultry to be endurable. After two or three days of it I moved on to San Antonio, which was hot too, but at least drier. It was there that I met an authentic relic of Texas' heroic past in the shape of an old man reduced to driving a taxicab, who recalled that as a boy he had helped haul Confederate cotton down past the border into Mexico, that he had witnessed the fencing in of the open range, and the great drive of the longhorn herd all the way to feed the train crews who were building the Union Pacific in far-off Wyoming, and that he had personally shot fifteen buffalo in the Panhandle, as late as 1877.

Had I stayed in San Antonio for longer than a day I might have made a poem out of Texas life and history, with just such men as himself as central symbols of it; but the limited state of my financial resources made departure necessary. As it was, I wrote out a brief character sketch of this incident in prose, which later, as I recall, appeared in some of the obscure little magazines to which I was then sending many of my contributions. After a long day's trip from San Antonio we arrived at El Paso about sunset—a furiously western sunset of orange and vermilion against which the peaks of that arid and vast land stood out splendid and appalling. And there we changed from the Southern Pacific to the Santa Fe tracks and were taken up the Rio Grande valley through the night into New Mexico.

The next day found us going through western New Mexico, en route to Arizona. I was by now so accustomed to the movement and perpetual change of travel as to be able to think, and even to write, in comfort on the train. The result was another series of six poems, intended to counterbalance the seven already written during the trip down the Mississippi, and composed generally of what I saw from the train, and of reminiscences crowding back on me more strongly than ever of the unforgettable archaeological trip of three months I had taken after quitting Harvard. This trip had been my first introduction to the unsurpassed magnificence and wildness, the strange, semi-Mexican, semi-Indian life of the Rio Grande region. Its memories had lain absolutely fallow in me for eight years till the magic touch of the selfsame region and landscape caused them to come forth and take shape in words. Mesa-crowned uplands, dotted with yellow arroyos and sprinkled with gray sagebrush, with low, tan-colored, flat-topped Pueblo villages surrounded by irrigated cornfields snatched from the desert, flocks of sheep followed by alert Navajos, riders loping far to some great blue-black peak hull down in the distance—all this repeated itself inexactly and fragmentarily, but vividly, in the poetic sequence I then wrote on the westward rumbling train.

But what was I to call this sequence? Some of it was written in Arizona and some in New Mexico. Some had been inspired by glimpses of the Mexican life I had obtained at San Antonio—the "Mexican Quarter," so much anthologized later, derives from no other source—and some, notably "Rain in the Desert," "Cliff Dwelling" and "The Fuel Vendor" from memories of the summer spent in the upper Rio Grande region, as long ago as 1907. I might call it, then, "New Mexican Memories"—and no doubt this title would have been better than the one I chose. Or I might call it "From the Seven Cities of Cibola," using, for my own purposes, the strange myth first created by that fascinating character, the explorer Cabeza de Vaca.

I judged my readers would not understand so elaborate and far-fetched a title; therefore I called the entire set simply "Arizona Poems," because the train I was on, at the time, was bound for the Grand Canyon in Arizona. This title was inexact, and I have since regretted it. But two of the poems, "Mexican Quarter" and "Rain in the Desert," proved as successful as any I had written up to that time.

The only spot of actual Arizona soil that I was to stand on during this trip, apart from glimpses of it caught through Pullman windows, was the South Rim of the Grand Canyon, where I arrived a day or so later, early in September, and spent three unforgettable days. This too was given its memorial in the shape of another poem, a poem owing everything in method and structure to the lines already laid down in the "symphonies," and like them perhaps more revelatory of my inner life than of the Canyon itself—a subject which, so far as I know, has never been successfully treated in words. I also wrote, during that brief halt, another series of verse visions, inspired by the plateau-and-canyon architecture of just such scenes as I was then witnessing. This at last was called, in defiance of all convention and geography, "The Seven Cities of Cibola." Judging this series to be unsuccessful, I gave them no place, finally, in my later *Breakers and Granite*, which was to deal altogether with my American impressions. They still remain buried somewhere in the files of the early *Southwestern Review*. I judged them to be didactic and nonimagistic, as in fact they were. But it was the fault of imagism never to let its devotees draw clear conclusions about life and to force the poet to state too much and to deduce rather too little—to lead its disciples too often into a barren aestheticism which was, and is, empty of content. I was already beginning to realize that fact there by the rim of the Grand Canyon. Poetry merely descriptive of nature as such, however vivid, no longer seemed to me enough; there had to be added to it the human judgment, the human evaluation.

The next stop on my journey was San Francisco, and there I stayed for nearly a week—a week entirely unproductive of poetical result. To anyone who like myself had been traveling the entire breadth of a continent, and so vast a continent as North America, it must have seemed strange that the continent had, after all, come to an end. I had seen San Francisco before, on a brief visit of two or three days in the summer of 1905, a year before the great earthquake and fire had laid the old city in ruins. Now the old city with its picturesqueness, its squalor, its harbor crammed with great sailships, its seething, sweaty, smelly Chinatown, no longer existed. Almost half of it still lay in ruins; there were vast uninhabited spaces all over the city. The other half was new, smart, and up-to-date. San Francisco was still in the process of being reborn.

I frankly did not know what to make of this phenomenon. Here the past, instead of sinking into lethargic decay as in New England or in the old South, had merely been wiped out at a stroke. A future was in the process of formation; but what kind of future? I did not know, lacking, as I did, enough knowledge of the past to pass my judgment. One could only guess that America's characteristic energy and determination, intensifying with every milestone westward, would here recreate something. But one scarcely knew whether the new city would prove to be real or merely another illusion, to be swept aside some day as the old city had been. The Panama-Pacific Exposition, built on ground facing the Golden Gate and the sun-browned, softly-molded foothills of Tamalpais beyond, seemed, in its illusory magnificence, as the colored floodlights awoke and played upon its buildings and towers, to repeat the dream architecture of my own "symphonies": its magnificence was soul-stirring, but ephemeral. I discovered, too, that the sea fog, rolling in from the Pacific night after night on the Exposition and the city itself, gave to both a still more elusive, intangible quality of remote unreality.

San Francisco evaded me completely. All that I could say of it was that here everything stood in sharpest contrast: the fierce, external energy of American effort was completely matched by the somber, fatalistic calm and inertia of wild nature; the rattling bustle of the skyscraper district was matched by the remote smolder and silence of great redwood groves and lonely shores; the braggart energy of the Anglo-Saxon stood cheek by jowl with the passionless calm of the Chinese. San Francisco presented me with a theme and a problem of which I could make nothing. Was man or nature chiefly important? The answer was given, from a standpoint more Californian than mine, ten years after my visit, in the poetry of Robinson Jeffers.

My financial resources were now at an end, so I returned from California to Chicago without making another stop, in the last weeks of September. Here I managed to subsist, largely on my own meager earnings as writer, for nearly a month, till the arrival of fresh funds enabled me to get back to Boston. Looking back on my trip—the longest I had undertaken since the summer of 1905, when I was still only a college undergraduate, and when I had first seen San Francisco and so gone north to Portland, and had been for the first time fired to write verses—looking back now on the summer of 1915, I concluded that it had been greatly worth while, although it had left me temporarily penniless. I had written the Mississippi River, the Arizona-New Mexico poems, and the "Grand Canyon Symphony." I had gone through the length and the breadth of this vast land, far more different in its backgrounds of culture and of intellectual and physical climate, than anyone who lived in it suspected, and had given my best talents to setting down what I had seen and felt of it. I had traveled from Boston to Chicago, from Chicago to northern Michigan, from northern Michigan to New Orleans, from New Orleans to western Texas, from Texas to Albuquerque, from Albuquerque to Arizona, from Arizona to San Francisco, and so back to Chicago via Salt Lake City. Recognizing in myself an ability that, so far as I knew, no American poet of that day possessed to the same extent, of being able to record the visible backgrounds of American living, rather than the life patterns of the people who lived in them, I had made a wide exploration of that background, in all its variety, as it stood there, at the middle of the second decade of the twentieth century, in the first year of the European War. I had seen, and had tried to express, both the quality and the aspects of America.

CHAPTER XVII

I arrived in Chicago about the middle of September, having already spent my last penny on the trip eastward. Somewhere along the way, at Salt Lake City or Denver, I had stopped and pawned my watch and chain, and on the money thus obtained I had kept myself from actual hunger for the last few days. I had just enough left to put my baggage in the checkroom at the station; then I walked to Miss Monroe's office downtown.

She was in the office, and she gallantly rallied to my support by agreeing to take the new group of my Arizona poems and to pay me at once for them. I inquired after cheap rooms, and was told by her to look for them about the North Side. By the afternoon of my arrival I was settled again.

I stayed there for a month. The room I had chosen in Chicago was hot, noisy, plagued with flies and the smell of the stockyards, and as barren of comfort as Ezra Pound's had been in London. About the only literary company I discovered were the editors of a new journal, the *Dial,* which had taken to appearing fortnightly. I also spent some time at the house of Mary Aldis, the wife of a wealthy Chicagoan, who lived in the outskirts. It was then or later that I made an attempt to write a one-act play. Mrs. Aldis was herself a playwright and a poet of the more realistic sort. She was connected with a little theater, but she did not like my play, which was too romantic to please her.

All the time I was in Chicago I was hoping to get back to Boston. As soon as I scraped together a little money I set out, feeling little regret at quitting a place which was even less of a home to me than New York, though it contained no less than three magazines to which I contributed; for, in addition to *Poetry* and the *Little Review,* I now began writing for the *Dial.* I wanted to go back to Boston, and settle down there and write something longer: a narrative, presumably in prose, of my adventures and impressions during my western trip that summer. In Chicago, as I had discovered, I could neither live nor write in any comfort.

When I arrived in Boston on October 20, 1915, I discovered to my horror that my old quarters at 9 Walnut Street had gone up in price, and I could not now afford them. I had already put myself under obligations to Miss Lowell, by borrowing from her the sum of twenty-five dollars necessary to bring me on to Boston, despite a resolve on my part never to ask her for money. It now took me three or four days to find a suitable room. Finally one was found, a little better than my dreadful slum lodging in Chicago. It was in a part of South Boston that had been built, as I recall, just before the Civil War, and which had long since been abandoned to the Irish and the Italians. There I lived for a month or more, enduring as I best might the upsetting condition of general poverty and discomfort, and gradually growing more disillusioned with Boston itself, till the advent of fresh funds in December enabled me to move back to my old quarters.

One reason for my state of comparative indigence was this. Early in the spring, before quitting Boston, I had made a final attempt to regulate my situation in regard to Daisy in England. I had written her finally that she need not expect me to return to her, unless she was prepared to bring a suit for divorce from her husband. Then I would return and marry her. Her husband had agreed to this, on terms entirely favorable to her. He was willing to let her keep the house, the children, and to let it appear that he was solely the guilty party. The case had been set down for the spring term in the English courts; but the courts adjourned without its being heard, and it was carried over into the fall. Since that summer I had been paying, not only for my travels in America, but for Daisy's support in England, and had also paid the fees for her lawyer in London. It is for this reason that in Chicago, and still more recently in Boston, I was frequently reduced to eating one meal a day.

America, through such poets as Frost, Masters, Robinson, Sandburg, Lindsay, was, by the end of 1915, surely showing signs of having achieved what the critic Van Wyck Brooks, writing in that very year, had called its "coming of age." A new imaginative literature was being produced, and in this process the poets had led the way. But the opposition, not only of the entrenched academic conservatives, to whom Longfellow and Tennyson spelled the last word in poetry, but still more of the nakedly commercial interests, was a terrific obstacle for anyone to surmount. The overwhelming majority of the American people were indifferent to the claims of imaginative literature. They were far more interested in the exploits of Pollyanna than in imagist poetry, which was just another stunt run by a wealthy woman from Boston, one who smoked black cigars—had anyone ever heard of such a thing? The American people were still, by and large, interested only very remotely in the War, in their own backgrounds, in the tragic and impossible situation daily faced by President Wilson. They were, one and all, interested in making as much money out of the struggle and from the neutrality of President Wilson as their pockets would hold. And most American publishers were aware of the fact, and refused to back anything unless it continued to make money.

One could only overcome the bovine indifference of the American public either by creating a public scandal, as Masters's *Spoon River* had adroitly done, or by backing one's own career with time, patience, and an independent income. Miss Lowell had tried to do both; I feared I could do neither. In respect to both money and social status, she indeed enjoyed a commanding position. She had used both skillfully to create a sensation, both with her own poems and with the imagist poets. But the credit would, naturally, accrue to her and not to those who had worked with her. Of these, I was the nearest in actual geographical position, and also, possibly, in point of literary ability. But I now was forced to admit that I could not compete in any way with her for the favor of the public, unless some unexpected stroke of good fortune came my way.

The stroke of good fortune did not materialize. My own *Irradia-*

tions, though appearing alongside of her *Imagist Poets,* had sold so badly that not half of the small edition of five hundred copies had been exhausted. I was alone and almost penniless in Boston—almost, if not quite, as helpless a figure in her hands as the young Chicago poet, Maxwell Bodenheim, whom I had recently met there, and who satisfied his restless ambition by coming to Boston to visit her, in the following spring of 1916, only to have his coat torn off his back by her sheep dogs. Meanwhile there were ominous signs that the general attitude of commercial greed on the part of publishers and public would soon be backed by something more deadly: a savage outburst of puritanic reaction against the sexual frankness of much modern literature. In England, D. H. Lawrence's *The Rainbow* had just been publicly destroyed. There was talk in America that Theodore Dreiser would be shut up by the Comstock Society. What was one to do with the sordid hypocrisy, the blatant, self-determined ignorance of great masses of mankind? Where could the poet escape? My mood reflected itself in a new poem, one of the few I wrote during the months of doubt and disillusionment that followed my return to Boston. This poem, which I do not think Miss Lowell ever saw, was called "The Piano-Organ." It was addressed to one of the various instruments of that species—I can still hear this particular one grinding out "La Marseillaise" and "La Brabançonne," in keeping with a machine with correct Allied principles—which now haunted the streets near my second-story bedroom:

In the night,
At the hour when the breezes waken,
And set to blowing down the gutters,
And off the benches of the park,
Scraps of soiled newspaper,
White butterflies aflutter in the dark;
Suddenly my soul is shaken
By a piano-organ at a near-by corner.
Its notes,
Dry, distant, shrill,
Quiver, stiff metallic motes;
Like the stars that stud the sky

In an old quadrille
Grotesquely curious;
Knowing nothing, caring less for us,
Deaf and blind to everything one feels,
Yet quivering out of their own unearthly blackness,
As out of some high stiff box here set on wheels.

And the children dance to it,
Tattered, half-fed children dancing.
They do not know the irony
Of the stars which wink and slyly
Pocket our faith, our hope and our endeavor.
The tune which sets our teeth and makes our raw nerves quiver
To them is merely gay:
The piano-organ plays away
Courage, endurance, achievements base or clever,
Bit by bit:
But the children dance to it.

A suave Italian stands turning, turning
At the little crank in the piano-organ's side;
His mustaches are black and wide,
Like Vittorio Emmanuele—
He is a dull, dishonest fellow,
He wears a mechanical grin;
But all the while he stares straight on in front of him
As if he could not hear a single thing,
But the clink of the coin as it strikes the edge of the curb,
Flung by some unseen hand from the gas-lit tenement window.

In the night
The piano-organ suddenly ceases.
Doubtless, it has been wheeled away;
But then it starts again to play.
The worn out quivering refrain
Decreases
With which the stars salute this planet's flight.
I should like to follow it, day on night,
Hearing the same tunes chink and roar,

Watching the children dance to it,
From house to house, from street to street,
Until it paused on earth's last shore,
And at the end of the world turned up to play.
And then, I wonder, would it sound
Its everlasting tune,
Or would the stars repeat to the dead, deaf moon,
The self-same notes with which they mocked this earth?

This poem, not printed till years later in England, and still now, in 1936, twenty-one years after its composition, uncollected among my works, represented an altogether new mood on my part, the mood of disabused romanticism with which post-War poetry later was to make us all so familiar. It seemed to me to be akin, with its mingling of the prosaic and the fantastic, to the poem by Pound's unknown American discovery, T. S. Eliot, entitled "The Love Song of J. Alfred Prufrock," which, months ago, I had read in Harriet Monroe's office in Chicago. I had recently read it again, as it had appeared in *Poetry* that summer, and had been moved to like it better on the second time than I had on the first. When I had first seen it, I had recommended Miss Monroe to print it, on the grounds that, though unlike anything I was doing, it was very good of its kind. Now I saw, or thought I saw, that its refusal to assume the heroic, in an age when heroism—thanks to the industrial revolution in economics and the democratic revolution in politics—had become both cheap and vulgar, was, under the pressure of adverse circumstances, my own.

I was surprised to learn from Conrad Aiken, still living next door to my old lodgings in Boston, that he knew quite well the mysterious American expatriate who had written this poem. Eliot and he had been classmates at Harvard, and "The Love Song of J. Alfred Prufrock" had been written as early as 1911. This, and the fact that Ezra Pound was now befriending Eliot, made me realize that, despite Miss Lowell's assumption that Ezra had failed in his last chance to arouse the American public, he was, in fact, still very much alive and a force to be reckoned with when it came to the discovery of new talent. The publication, the very next spring, of the oddly named *Catholic Anthology,* in which he succeeded in bringing together, between the same covers, poets as diverse as Yeats, Hueffer, Williams, Eliot, and himself, soon proved I was not mistaken. I also realized, face to face with Eliot's extreme *fin-de-siècle* romanticism, that the story of the actual flowering of the new poetry in America, if it ever came to be written, would be something entirely different from, and far more complex, than what either Miss Lowell or I had foreseen. For here, actually, were poets as various as Lindsay and Eliot, Sandburg and Stevens, all derivable from America, and all practicing their art in the same period of time.

More and more now I came to realize, in my meetings and talks with Miss Lowell, that we stood in different worlds. Her battles on behalf of the imagists, as well as the success of the first book she had written under the imagist influence, *Sword Blades and Poppy Seed,* had accustomed her to be overwhelmingly optimistic towards what she defined as the new poetry. It now frankly seemed to me that, in speaking of this new poetry, she unconsciously confused it with her own poetry. If any opposing type of new poetry ventured to show itself above the literary horizon, she only too readily brushed the intruder aside, or did her best to belittle it; as in the case of the poetry of Eliot, Aiken, and the contributors to Alfred Kreymborg's anthology, *Others.* I realized both her energy and her determination, but I was not sure that she was not mistaken. If imagism had produced her poetry, and her poetry was the new poetry, the question then naturally arose, was this new poetry so new after all?

There was nothing—we had already in our talks agreed on that point—particularly new about imagism. It was but a more lyrical, a saner and more intelligible, development of the aesthetic theories of the English Pre-Raphaelite poets, the Parnassians and the symbolists in France. To it, the chief object of a poem was to produce a certain aesthetic effect; that effect was implicit in an image or a series of images, and the business of the poet was to present his images as clearly and concisely as possible. She had been spurred by these ideas into writing a kind of poetry impossible to anyone not born to a large fortune and moving in the most intellectually advanced, cosmopolitan circles of Boston—a kind of poetry which did for American poetry what her elder contemporary, Mrs. Jack Gardiner, had already done for American art—filling a museum with brilliant examples largely derived from the past. But to do this was not to be new, particularly. It was rather to be out-of-date, old-fashioned. The new poetry, if it ever came, might well turn out to be something more brutal and realistic, on the lines of Masters and Sandburg, or something more intensely aesthetic and restrained, on the lines of Eliot and Wallace Stevens.

The battles she had already waged to get a hearing, in the face of competition from the conservatives, from the midwestern poets Miss Monroe had discovered in Chicago, from Pound and his following in England, from the extreme experimentalists which Alfred Kreymborg was now printing in his *Others* had so transformed her that, in continuing to wage her poetic war, she scarcely now realized that the imagists with whom she was associated existed at all.

Soon after my return to Boston I was asked by her to intervene in a quarrel between her and Aldington, now come to a head after smoldering since the preceding spring. As I have already pointed out, Aldington had felt, from the outbreak of the War, that it was his business as poet and man of letters not to be swayed by mob sentiment into offering himself as a futile and inglorious sacrifice. His only chance of escaping from the trenches lay in coming to America, which he might still accomplish as long as Great Britain did not adopt the conscription act, or if he could persuade the authorities to release him for some work they judged to be of importance abroad. Both possibilities were becoming more and more remote. But as early as the spring of 1915 he had met an American who had fired him with the prospect of becoming editor of a new literary magazine in the United States. He had eagerly grasped at this opportunity; however, to undertake the task successfully he needed further financial backing. Amy had at first promised him this backing, and then—faced with some losses in a theatrical venture of her own in Boston—had withdrawn her offer. Now, urged by the desperate appeals of Aldington's wife, she had seen fit to renew it, with the result that Aldington had immediately written a long and enthusiastic letter, stating that both H. D. and he were preparing to quit England, provided she could use her influence to get him released, by publicizing the fact that he was coming over to edit a magazine of strong pro-Ally sympathies. To this she now raised immediate objections; but her objections, I felt, sprang less from her own lack of sympathy with the Allies—she had, in fact, more hatred for the Germans than anyone in the whole imagist group—

than from her fear that Aldington might prove difficult to handle, and might cause her some further financial loss.

She now turned to me, and practically begged me to write to Aldington myself and to tell him that, in my opinion, the time was not favorable for launching so ambitious a venture as a new magazine in America. To say that I was astounded at this request was putting it very mildly. I knew little of Aldington, except that he was an Englishman; but I knew enough of the English to understand that they believed strongly in keeping one's word, and in the spirit of fair play. It seemed to me, frankly, that she was not playing fair with Aldington. Could I say so, being as I was, the recipient of so many favors from her? Her request to me to write and finally discourage Aldington from attempting to come over put me into a complete moral quandary. Either I must rouse all her anger, and so undo the alliance I had myself made with her, or else become the subject of Aldington's very just resentment. In the end, I capitulated, and, as I recall, wrote a letter of which I was heartily ashamed. She saw it, and approved of it before it was sent; but from then on, I never again referred to the subject—and from then on, I realized that we no longer stood together as friends, but rather as potential enemies brought together by mutual necessity in alliance, and now engaged in hostilely watching each other.

So, speedily and completely, were vanishing all the fine hopes that I had cherished on my coming to America! I had been in my own country now for a full year, and all that I had got out of it was a summer packed full with vivid travel impressions, and the prospect that, whatever I did in the future, I should have to ascribe all the credit to Amy Lowell. Small wonder that I began to feel discouraged again, as I had at the end of 1913 and 1914! For the third time now in the last three years I had attempted a fresh start, and for the third time it was leading me into a blind alley. Houghton Mifflin were now so skeptical of the success of their "New Poetry Series" that they were doubtful whether they would bring out any further volumes, except Amy's imagists (which she paid for) in the spring. So it seemed altogether likely that my "Symphonies," which were now ready, and which represented, as I felt, a development of imagism beyond Amy's powers, would not see the light.

Meanwhile, Miss Lowell herself, as the person chiefly responsible for the furore caused in academic circles by the new poetry, was busily engaged in recruiting critics who would defend it. She had already captured William Stanley Braithwaite, chief poetry critic of the *Transcript,* and she spoke enthusiastically of capturing Louis Untermeyer. Braithwaite I knew to be harmless and lacking in critical standards. His poverty and, still more, his negro blood had worked so long against him that he was prepared to be anyone's sworn defender from the moment he was invited to dinner. But the thought of Untermeyer as a potential ally made me more doubtful. I knew nothing of him except that, as a poet, he had been a staunch champion of the Whitmanian, cosmic, "social brotherhood" type of verse. He had defended the poets of this type long ago in the columns of Harold Monro's magazine in England, asserting them to be the most important poets in America. He also was a writer of clever parodies of other poets. I felt that, on all three accounts, he was a person to mistrust. And Amy's growing interest in him seemed to be an interest in literary politics, rather than in poetry.

In my growing distaste for her tactics I now turned more and more to Conrad Aiken, who still lived next door to my old lodging at 9 Walnut Street, and who had spent the summer writing the first of his tone poems, *The Jig of Forslin,* at that address. Hitherto I had known him chiefly as a shy and remote, sandy-haired figure, blinking behind his glasses, who lived next door, cherished an ambition to write poems combining the sensuous lyricism of Keats with the stark realism of Masters, disliked imagism and all its works, but confessed to a paradoxical admiration for my own poetry. Now I decided that the time had come to take him behind the scenes and reveal to him some of the inner history of imagism from the time when Pound had first taken it up to the time that Miss Lowell had begun to use it as a means to gain a growing public. I also spoke to Aiken about my own difficulties in obtaining and keeping my publishers. He was impressed, as he has since said, both with the mature originality of my own poetic attitude and with the difficulties I had encountered in getting a hearing for my work. He accordingly introduced me to a dark-haired, pale-complexioned individual named Brown, who occupied two floors of an old building near Scollay Square and the courthouse, where he was running, on next to nothing, a publishing firm by the name of the

Four Seas Company. If Houghton Mifflin failed to produce my "symphonies" in their "New Poetry Series"—in which Aiken, too, was interested—Brown might be worth falling back upon, as alternative.

Brown proved to be amusing—an equal compound of adventurous daring, Yankee resourcefulness, and complete irresponsibility. Like Aiken, he was younger than myself, and he had sprung early into the game of publicizing the new poetry. His plans for a poetry magazine and publishing house had matured so rapidly—thanks to the enthusiastic support of a fellow Bostonian, Edward J. O'Brien, one of Braithwaite's disciples—that he was ready to go to press with his *Poetry Journal* a month before Miss Monroe's *Poetry* was scheduled to make its appearance in Chicago, a fact which caused Miss Monroe to advance the date of her own publication, amid much perturbation. As I had neither seen nor heard of the *Poetry Journal* before meeting Brown in the late fall of 1915, I was interested to learn that others besides Miss Monroe and Miss Lowell had been stirred by the possibilities of a revival in American poetry at so early a date as 1912. I obtained copies of the *Poetry Journal,* agreed to contribute to it, and asked him to introduce me to Edward O'Brien, who was now living in the country, on Cape Cod. He promised to do so, and there, for the moment, the matter rested.

I was considerably more interested, at the moment, with the development of Aiken's own poetry in his *Jig of Forslin* than in Brown's publishing venture. It seemed to me that, in this sustained tone poem, with its variation from blank verse to rhymed octosyllabics, its shifts from sordid realism to wild romanticism, my next-door neighbor on Beacon Hill had achieved a new kind of American poetry, owing something certainly to Eliot and to myself, but no less modern in its implications than the poetry of either of us, and only likely to suffer because of the facility with which he produced it. He was now, as I learned, already engaged on a second long symphonic narrative, *The House of Dust,* which moved me even more strongly than did the first. It seemed to me time that Miss Lowell should recognize Aiken's talent, and should admit that a poet no less remarkable than herself inhabited Boston, despite the fact that, as she and I both knew, he had opposed the imagist poets publicly on their appearance. Accordingly, on a night early in December, I deliberately tried to defend him in a conversation we had together at her house, which resulted in an interchange of letters on our part, both of them so amusing and so revealing of our personal attitudes that I give them now to the reader:

DEAR J. G. F.:

Tonight you said a thing
Which left me much upset and wondering.

You seemed to think that rhyming was so hard,
To have the knack made any man a bard.

To turn out couplets fast as you could think
Was quite a worthy use of printer's ink.

But, pointing to your friend whom I'll not name,
I said his verse would put a child to shame.

To reach the end within a given time
And wind up sharply with a tidy rhyme,

Seemed to call forth a terrible commotion,
And make his brain whirl like a stormy ocean.

Such tricks he used to cause his words to fall
Each on its accent! And that isn't all.

Some verbs expanded with that fearful "did,"
Others condensed, and nothing neatly hid.

Was that a style of which one could be proud?
I asked you, and my horror cried out loud.

You shook your head. "He rhymes so easily,"
You sadly murmured. "It amazes me."

I vowed to you that I could do it too.
"But he does not repeat his rhymes," said you.

I told you I could rhyme for half a day,
You doubted me. And now, behold my way!

Not wishing to admit that I'm defeated,
I've done the thing, and not a rhyme repeated.

I could go on like this till you were dead,
But it is late, and I must go to bed.

I've proved my point, and if these lines don't go well,
They took me just ten minutes.

AMY LOWELL.

P. S. The postscript holds the letter's kernel,
So tell me, did you take the Poetry Journal?

To which I replied promptly, the next morning,

DEAR AMY,

Many thanks for your effusion.
I quite agree that rhyming's a delusion.

Still many a rhymester might turn out a poet,
If, with his gift, he knew how to bestow it.

As for our friend, whose name I need not speak,
I see him seldom, twice or thrice a week.

He may be fool, he may be merely knave,
Destined to fame, or to an early grave.

A year ago he said he had an offer
To edit that bad Journal; he refused the proffer.

I'd rather see him in that job than Brown;
He might have given the rag some pale renown.

His rhyme's not everything; for aught I know,
He really does his best to break their flow.

He may be honest, really! Who can tell?
Besides, I like a thief who pilfers well.

Nine tenths of all the poets in this land
Can't write as well as he: we are a band

So small (excuse this running on without a pause)
We ought to overlook his obvious flaws.

But if we cannot; urge him to do better!
We are the gainers by it; he, our debtor.

So I conclude: excuse me if I stammer.

I hope I've kept the laws of speech and grammar.

If I have not, may I be a lost wretch or
Anything but your servant

JOHN GOULD FLETCHER.

P. S. Two couplets less than yours; but yet I claim
In neither letter are the rhymes the same.

Relying on your judgment and inspection
I've left mine here with only one correction.

As for the Poetry Journal, which you miss
I haven't got it. Heaven knows where 'tis.

Amy had already skillfully maneuvered herself into a prominent position as the first president of the newly organized New England Poetry Club, thus offsetting the opposition of the Poetry Society of America in New York, which had been manifest since the meeting of the preceding spring. Now, the meetings at her home which had once been frank and full discussions of new poetical ideas between her and myself—with Mrs. Russell for sole audience—became more and more public affairs, to which I was invited because my presence might add weight to the impression she was producing on her audience. I now met at her home, not only Braithwaite, who had become an ardent admirer, but the two rival poetesses of Boston, Josephine Preston Peabody Marks and Grace Hazard Conkling.

Of the two, Mrs. Marks struck me from the outset as being the more false. She was a Victorian sentimentalist to the core, having been reigning queen of Boston poetry circles back in the days when Amy herself was a struggling novice; and her poetry, to my eyes, revealed only an arch-prettiness of phrase akin to the achievements of the well-bred ladies of the eighties who specialized in china painting. She had nonetheless jealously guarded her supremacy as America's great woman lyricist down to the days of the European War; but she was now, I could see, a waning star, so consumed by envy at the thought of Amy's growing public following as to be ready to attack her on any provocation that offered—though Amy continued to profess an admiration for her poetry, and also continued to regard her as a friend.

I, personally, found Mrs. Marks insupportable, after a few meetings. I was more intrigued, and a shade less doubtful, about Mrs. Conkling. She seemed, although not less of a sentimentalist in her own verse, genuinely interested in Amy's ideas and in mine. And she had a remarkable daughter, who at the age of twelve was already turning out excellent specimens of imagism. Whether these poems, later published with an enthusiastic preface by Amy, were actually written by Hilda Conkling, or were skillfully revised by Mrs. Conkling, I did not know. But at any rate, they seemed to me to be good examples of what Amy herself meant when she spoke of imagism.

If Mrs. Marks and Mrs. Conkling were remotely understandable as adjuncts, then the Untermeyers, in my eyes, were not. I determined to have as little to do with them as possible, and to resist to the end Amy's attempt, frankly stated within two months of my return, to include Mrs. Untermeyer in the forthcoming *Imagist Poets*. Unfortunately, I could not resist Amy's determination to have me meet them at her home. Early in February of 1916 she rang me up and informed me that she was sending her car for me on that evening, and that the car would also contain the Untermeyers. She asked me to be especially nice to them. I resented this suggestion that my behavior was something that could be turned on and off for the benefit of any new friends of hers, and I determined to be on my guard. At a little before seven, the car duly arrived at my door. I was wearing my usual sack suit and overcoat, having long ago, in Amy's presence, dispensed with the formality of evening dress; but not so the Untermeyers. A glance at the male member of the family revealed a young man resplendently handsome in swallow-tailed coat, white waistcoat, finely starched shirt front decked with a row of diamond studs, white gloves, and tie. Mrs. Untermeyer was attired to correspond. I got into the car with barely more than a gruff handshake.

I then sat silent, deciding that it was up to the Untermeyers to do the talking. He opened upon me at once, as the car sped down Beacon Hill past the snow-covered Common:

"I am glad to meet you, Fletcher, because I thought I knew something about poetry until you imagists came along and told me I was mistaken. You write in such extraordinary forms. I thought I knew all the old-fashioned forms of verse—odes, ballades, sestinas, sonnets, triolets, quatrains, and the rest. But you have now discovered new oriental forms, Chinese and Japanese forms, in which to write. Tell me something about those oriental forms."

"I suppose you mean hokkus," I said, irritated at the nature of this attack, with its clever assumption of ignorance.

"That's it, hokkus. Tell me, why do you write in hokkus? You do write them, don't you?"

As a matter of fact, I had never written a hokku in my life. My whole concern, ever since writing *Irradiations,* had been to create a new, rather than to copy any given and fixed, poetic form. I was determined to achieve the utmost freedom in pattern, rather than strive for any formal consistency, either eastern or western. The rules of Japanese versification mattered to me as little as the rules of English versification. I was about to tell Untermeyer so, when it suddenly occurred to me that this time it would be better to dissemble. As a brief example of what I had meant by imagism, I had written that winter a five-line poem, inspired by a view of skaters moving over the surface of a frozen pond, which had seemed no less interesting to me for the clear image conveyed than for the fact that this image had seemed to gain power and swiftness from an adroit combination of *a* and *o* and *oo* and long and short *i* sounds. It went as follows:

> Black swallows swooping and gliding
> In a flurry of entangled loops and curves,
> The skaters skim over the frozen river.
> And the grinding click of their skates as they impinge upon the
> surface,
> Is like the brushing together of thin wing tips of silver.

"Yes," I replied, "I have written hokkus. I wrote one only the other day, and it was all about ice hockey. Shall I repeat it to you?"

A gasp of astonishment, followed by a gleam of appreciation, came to Untermeyer's face. I had not surmised how dearly he loved a pun for its own sake. That I could combine "hockey" and "hokku" in the same sentence made me a person of some importance in his eyes. He immediately asked me to repeat the poem, and declared that it was excellent. During the dinner that followed—when I chanced also to meet Stark Young, newly come to Boston to see Miss Lowell—he did not attempt to attack either me or my poetry.

The second issue of *Some Imagist Poets,* scheduled by Houghton Mifflin to come out that spring, was already causing more trouble among the representatives of imagism concerned than had the first. Then the chief difficulty to be got over had been the fact that Pound might possibly attempt to stop the publication of an imagist anthology in which he did not figure. Now there were strong differences of opinion among the contributors themselves. In the first place, I had proposed a fighting preface, attacking openly and by name all the conservative critics, which Miss Lowell declined. In the second, she had become so completely captivated by the Untermeyers as to propose that Mrs. Untermeyer be added to the anthology. This I, in turn, refused to grant. In the third, the three English contributors—Aldington, H. D., and Flint—had all disliked one of Amy's own recently written New England dialect poems, "Off the Turnpike," and had voted against the inclusion. In the fourth, D. H. Lawrence, who had been added to the imagist ranks through Amy's own insistence, now sent in a poem so sexy in quality that she herself judged that the printers would be inclined to think it obscene. She thereupon rushed to the telephone, asked for Ferris Greenslet, the head of the firm, and read the offending poem to him in a loud voice, concluding with, "Now don't you think that is perfectly obscene?" Or so, at least, Linscott assured me, a few days later.

These differences were gradually ironed out. Since Houghton Mifflin not only now definitely agreed to bring out *Some Imagist Poets* but also relented from their earlier attitude and decided to add my "symphonies" to the list of forthcoming volumes in the "New Poetry Series," I wisely decided to let things take their course. It was altogether likely that I would be leaving again for England as soon as summer came, so I thought it best not to cause further trouble, but to let Amy go her own gait, still preserving an united front against the world. But I was frankly now becoming weary of her society; and I longed to get away into a more congenial mental climate, away from all this public lecturing and publicity-seeking in Boston, to face the problem of my own direction afresh.

The chief event of March, 1916, was my meeting with Edwin Arlington Robinson at the home of Lilla Cabot Perry. Although I had heard, long ago, from the lips of Ezra Pound, expressions of admiration concerning Robinson and his poetry, I do not recall having actually read any of it before this spring. I had known only that he was an older poet of the Masters and Frost generation—Miss Lowell, despite her years, belonged rather with the young—and that he was a conservative in manner, if not in matter. After appearing since 1896 in a series of obscure volumes, he was now about to publish *The Man Against the Sky*, which broke a silence of six years and which he himself regarded as his best effort. I had already read the title poem, and had been impressed by its attitude of stoic resignation, and of patient, questioning agnosticism—an attitude I was to discover later in Thomas Hardy. Although such an attitude had been foreign to my work, with its more obvious exploration of the primary emotions, I felt that I was now approaching it. And it was for this reason, no less than for the reason that he had slowly built up his own position as a poet through years of deprivation and neglect, that I felt drawn to Robinson.

The man himself, with his dark, ascetic face, his tightly pursed mouth, and his shy, sensitive, appealing eyes half-hidden behind glasses, impressed me deeply with an attitude of lonely integrity in defeat—an attitude, so far as I could see at that date, utterly alien to most Americans, or to the popular conception of Americans. He intrigued me, but as the occasion was a public one, I was not able to speak to him privately. I was only able to wonder whether, with his strong bent to regular verse forms, he would ever be able to see eye to eye with such a free versifier as myself. I was only able to watch, while with his eyes closed he sat listening to Amy reading aloud his poems, having first declined to do so himself. I admired his attitude, but I realized that he had come into the period when poetry again became a matter of public interest, largely through accident. Under any circumstances, he was and would always be one to pursue his chosen path alone.

Since I knew that I would shortly return to England, to resume my life there—for I had now ceased to envisage any other possibility—I devoted the remaining weeks of March and April to an examination of America's position as the most powerful neutral not yet engaged in the great European War. After the breakdown of the great Russian offensive in Galicia in the spring of 1916, the cause of the Allies seemed frankly desperate. And when the seasoned German army in the last weeks of March launched its great attack on the fortress ring of Verdun, everyone expected the Allied line to give away, despite the French boast that "they shall not pass." On the face of this situation, all signs pointed to a victory for Germany, or to a drawn contest. President Wilson had so far steered a wise but increasingly difficult course through the threatening waters of neutrality. Yet though pro-Ally and pro-German sentiment neatly balanced in most of the large cities of the eastern seaboard (they certainly balanced pretty accurately in Boston), it did not seem to me possible for the American president to retain this attitude much longer. Sooner or later another such incident as the *Lusitania* sinking would occur, which would inevitably lead to war. President Wilson's position, I thought, was growing to resemble more and more that which had faced Abraham Lincoln at the outbreak of the Civil War. Sooner or later, however unwillingly, he must come out for one side or the other. As a moderate, he, like Lincoln, had not wished war; but as president he could not rule over a divided Union. As the successful candidate of the dominant party, he was driven by extremists on both sides, no less than by the provocations already submitted to, into taking extreme measures.

It seemed to me now time that I should investigate the life and character of Abraham Lincoln. I had hitherto scarcely been interested in reading any detailed account of his career, having been brought up in the old southern belief that he was kindly but mistaken, able but ineffectual, a success largely because of Grant's superior generalship, and the victim of an assassin's bullet at the end, just at the time when the prostrate South most needed his efforts at conciliation. Now, during the last weeks in March and the first two weeks of April, I read several books on the Civil War, and rounded them off by going through Herndon's homespun, but honest, biography. I soon saw Lincoln in a new light, as the last of the heroic pioneers who had conquered this continent between the Louisiana Purchase of 1803 and the discovery of gold in California in 1849. Lincoln's virtues, the virtues of the simple, homely, unsophisticated, gangling, crude and shrewd and vigorous prairie backwoodsman he was, shone by contrast, not with the planter or mercantile aristocracy that had preceded him, but with the regime of industrial and financial corruption that had made use of him to insure their triumph, and had followed up his assassination with a complete seizure of power. Lincoln, no less than the South, had been defeated by the Civil War, even as Woodrow Wilson seemed to me, in the spring of 1916, to be facing the likelihood of a coming defeat in the situation created by the European War.

On April 19, 1916, the day of the anniversary of the battle of Lexington, I sat down to write my poem on Abraham Lincoln—the first truly patriotic poem I had written, patriotic in the same sense that Emerson's "Concord Hymn" and Whitman's "Drum-taps" and Moody's "Ode in the Time of Hesitation" had all been patriotic poems. It was also the first poem I had written in which my mind came to terms with the Anglo-Saxon strength of Biblical phraseology; the first I had written in which I said plainly that the epoch of America's pioneer strength and greatness lay in the past, not in the present; the first I had written in which the technique of imagism was complemented by stanzas expressive of nothing but plain, unabashed, didactic purpose.

Strangely enough, it was also the first important poem I had written since my coming to America in the fall of 1914, of which the first reader did not happen to be Amy Lowell. On the day after I finished it I chanced to have a caller in the shape of young Edward O'Brien, whose acquaintance I had recently made through Brown. He listened to me while I read it, and was so enthusiastic that he turned up again the next day and demanded that I give him a copy to appear in a new poetry magazine which his friend Braithwaite was preparing to bring out in Boston. I had, by this time, become so impatient of Amy and of her seeming assumption that I owed her everything, and that she was making my career no less than her own, that I let O'Brien take away the only available copy. Amy did not see it until it appeared in May. Braithwaite paid me, as I recall, exactly fifteen dollars for it—a miserable sum compared with what I knew to be its worth, but I felt glad that I had actually now begun to place poems by myself.

CHAPTER XVIII

Within a little more than a month from the writing of the Lincoln poem, I was embarked on a Dutch steamer leaving New York for England. I thus put behind me, not only Amy Lowell and her circle, not only my scarcely begun career as author, but also my own country in favor of a life which offered, as prospect, only another venture into the unknown. All that I actually knew of Daisy, whom I was now sailing to England to marry, was that she was some years—I did not know exactly how many—older than myself, that we had come together under strange and unusual circumstances, that we had been through a hard and troubled courtship to be followed by a brief interlude of a few months of happiness, followed by fresh separation and a year and a half of anxious waiting; and that in now going from my own country to hers I was plunging headlong into the dangerous proximity of the European War. The prospect was an uncertain one at best, but the thought of the love that had sprung up between Daisy and myself made me keen and eager to face it.

Had I possessed any of the canny commercial sense that had marked the actions of such an intelligent Yankee as Miss Lowell, I might indeed have hesitated before going abroad again. I might have informed Daisy that, since her divorce was about to be made absolute, I expected her to come over and join me in America; but I had scarcely envisaged such a possibility. Since a night late in April, when I had been moved to warn Amy that I would shortly be returning, I had become only the more recklessly determined to get back to England. She had asked me why I had come to this decision. I had informed her frankly that it was because I now expected to marry someone who had been still married to another at the time of my departure, whereupon she remarked that she had already suspected as much, and pressed me for further details. When I began to offer these, and to go over the events which had led to my present situation, she had abruptly cut me short with the remark that she had never previously supposed me capable of deceiving a woman's husband. I had involuntarily risen and, trembling from head to foot, started to quit her house, but in the end had checked myself sufficiently to remain. But I repeated emphatically to her that I wished my decision, as well as my personal affairs, to be respected and not discussed. Cost what it might, I would and must now go abroad to the woman who had waited for me so long.

Before I left I had come to an agreement with Houghton Mifflin to bring out the "Ghosts of an Old House" and the "symphonies" as a new volume in their poetry series, under the title of *Goblins and Pagodas*. I had also among my papers the half-written contents of a second volume, to consist entirely of my poems and polyphonic prose pieces about America, to which I had only recently added a postscript in the shape of the polyphonic prose "America, 1916." To this book I had not as yet given a title. I had recently completed a third book, consisting entirely of the love poems I had written during the whole period of my relationship with Daisy, from the fall of 1913 down to the spring of 1916, divided into five parts. This I had already, provisionally, called *Love's Tragedy*. With this much accomplished I sailed, within five months after my thirtieth birthday.

Had I not gone, I know now that my life would have been totally different—possibly more interesting than it has been, and almost certainly more outwardly successful. Apart altogether from the fact that I never succeeded in my aim of adjusting myself completely to the woman I married, nor she to me, there remains the additional fact that when I did return to America, in the summer of 1920, four full years had gone by, and another literary generation already held the stage. My opportunity was now lost because I had not seen fit to do more than half realize it. That truth must, in any case, be faced and stated. Still, I am far from regretting the past. Had I been less reckless of the consequences in 1916, I might have been less reckless in 1913 and remained an obscure scribbler of conventional verse, instead of the author of *Irradiations.* It was not for nothing that I had admired Nietzsche and his remark about destiny being the dice table of the gods.

I remember little about this voyage across the Atlantic, except that, as the ship was a slow one, it took over nine days. The ship was a neutral, and displayed that fact prominently in electric lamps on her side. There was no particular fear of submarines. A few jokes were made on this subject on the last day of the voyage, but that was all. The passengers were a mixed lot, and openly avoided clubbing with each other. Many of them—the ship was crowded full—had waved Union Jacks on leaving the docks of New York; others had as openly displayed German flags; several had stuck to the Star-Spangled Banner. The voyage was monotonous and uneventful, and no news bulletins of any sort were given out. After lunch on June 6, 1916, a perfect, sunny, cloudless day, we dropped anchor finally in Falmouth Roadstead. Those who were going to land in England were ordered into the smoking room, where we sat from one o'clock till past five, for the examination of our passports and papers.

The ordeal that awaited us was one well calculated to impress each of us with the seriousness of our situation, henceforward, in England. One by one, each of the passengers approached a table set at one end of the room. At the table were three men, one from the Home Office who sat directly facing the passenger, and two others from Scotland Yard, on either side, who looked intently at his face during the inquiry. After an examination of papers the passenger was requested to state his reasons for coming to England, what he proposed to do there, how long he intended to stay, the address to which he was traveling, and the like. I noticed, just as I approached the table, that one of the Scotland Yard men spoke to the other about the passenger who had just arisen and given place to me: "I've seen that man somewhere before." The other instantly replied, "We'll look after him ashore"—a remark which caused my own nervousness to increase. Anyway, when I arrived at the table and sat down I found I had scarcely the voice to convey above a whisper the information that I had come to England to marry.

At about six o'clock the tender was full of all those who had been granted landing cards, and at six-twenty (or rather seven-twenty by the new daylight-saving time that prevailed ashore) we disembarked at last on dry land. It was a singularly perfect day, with swallows skimming over the low green hills, densely wooded, that bordered the Fal Estuary. The charm of "England's green and pleasant land" was as potently lyrical now as ever. But the flag on the flagstaff at the pier was hanging at half-mast. A London paper, hurriedly bought, informed me that Earl Kitchener had been drowned in the North Sea in the early hours of the preceding day.

It was already past one o'clock in the morning when the train finally arrived in London, and I took lodging in a hotel near Paddington for the night. The spectacle of Falmouth Harbour, with its groups of idle, three-masted, captured German nitrate ships, its green-bowered hills, its square belfried churches, its serene peace, had lulled my soul to calm; but in the midst of it there was this strange disquieting news that Earl Kitchener was dead, at the bottom of the North Sea. And the next morning I learned from Daisy herself a still more disquieting fact: that while I had been on the Atlantic Ocean, on May 31 to June 1, a great naval battle had been fought off the peninsula of Jutland, which had shattered, once and for all, the myth of absolute naval invincibility established by Nelson, and which had led, not to the destruction of the German High Seas Fleet, but to its only too successful escape in the darkness. Perhaps, after all, I thought, as I heard the appalling losses of the British, this was a foretaste not of England's victory, but of England's coming doom.

As I sat there, listening to Daisy talk in the sunny drawing room of the suburban home which had seen so much of our love-making, looking at the books and pictures, the furniture and the rugs which I had left behind and had not seen since 1914, I wondered what my life would be like with the woman who was so soon to become my wife. She was telling me now that everyone despised President Wilson for his apparently supine neutrality, that Americans were much disliked for being "too proud to fight," that she had a hard time to say a good word for them before her friends. . . . She looked sad and subdued, I thought, as if she really had suffered. I decided to say nothing about the violently anti-Ally sentiments I had noted in Boston, which had flared up again that spring and become more vocal, ever since the Easter week uprising in Dublin. I could see no good in mentioning, even, that I was an American, and, as such, bound to strict neutrality. I had come over especially to marry her. She was glad that I had come. I would do my best now to keep any qualms to myself, and not disturb her share of happiness. My business was only to make her feel cheerful. My coming, so long delayed, had been so anxiously awaited that when I finally arrived she was less disposed to laughter than to tears. The children greeted me warmly; their mother had been worrying herself almost sick about me ever since I sailed.

I had only been a night or two in London, established in a suburban hotel within easy walking distance of the house—our marriage had to be postponed owing to an unaccountable delay over the granting of the final decree of divorce—when one night I experienced the shock of my first zeppelin air raid. Suddenly, all the lights in the hotel were shut off, including the light in my bedroom, where I sat by a table reading. People began calling out in excited voices, began feeling their way along darkened corridors. By looking out of my window I could see the sky stabbed with repeated searchlights. Soon after there came from far off, and then nearer, the sound of desultory gunfire. A woman began having hysterics in a near-by room, and a man's voice started to comfort her. I decided to go out, and then thought better of it, as all the stairways and corridors were darkened, and I might easily hurt myself trying to leave the old-fashioned rambling building. After a while there were the metallic screeches and crashes of bombs falling, more gunfire, and the clang of fire engines and ambulances in the distance. The babel of sounds went on for an hour or so, and began dying away at about one in the morning, when I attempted sleep.

The next day the newspapers informed me that England had finally won an important victory over the aerial invaders. A daring British officer had gone up, had circled above a zeppelin, and had brought it down. A second zeppelin had escaped; but with the aviator's feat as an example, England henceforth would be safe. I took a bus into London soon after, and discovered that at five or six places along the route windows were smashed over wide areas, walls toppled, and there were smoking and guttering ruins—about which the papers, busy keeping England in optimistic mood, said nothing. But from then on I realized that the remote peace of England, still uninvaded behind the bulwark of the fleet and the barrier of the narrow seas, was largely a sham.

I realized it so much that I now began to feel as I had felt nearly two years before, that my real business in life was to enlist in the British army, since I had come again to live in England. I felt this so strongly that I had a further interview with Aldington on the subject. I pointed out to him that I had now lost any belief that I might have once cherished that the Allies were altogether in the right, and that the Germans were altogether in the wrong; nor did I believe, after the Dardanelles, Jutland, and the Russian collapse, that the Allies could win. Nevertheless, here I was in London, engaged to an Englishwoman, and it seemed to me that my duty was to go. Aldington, who was now in khaki—he came up to London occasionally from an officers' training camp in Kent—bluntly told me that my duty was nothing of the sort. On the other hand, inasmuch as I had some good work which was not destructive, but creative, to do, I ought to stay out as long as possible. I was impressed by what he said. Nevertheless my conscience smote me sorely.

Since I had come over expressly to marry Daisy, and since Daisy expected me to marry her, it seemed to me that I ought, at the least, to make some attempt to leave her provided for in case I did go into the War. Inasmuch as my present income lapsed after my death, I decided to apply for a life insurance policy at a London life insurance agency. Had I seen to this before leaving America, I might have found it comparatively easy to accomplish; but the doctors who now examined me pronounced me small-chested and underweight, and the life insurance company finally quoted me a policy at a premium which was totally prohibitive in my present circumstances. I was obliged, too, to let this effort lapse. Apparently my best chance of doing anything for Daisy would be to do nothing, to follow Aldington's advice and stay well out of khaki, so long as the War lasted and America remained neutral. But I could not help feeling that I was thereby being forced to act as a coward, against my own inclinations.

On July 5, a month after my arrival, Daisy and I were quietly married at the register office in Croydon. Her final divorce had been granted about ten days after my arrival. After that the chief reason for our delay was to stifle gossip—about which she seemed abnormally sensitive—and to ascertain whether it would not be in some way possible to be married by a Church of England clergyman. Daisy was exceedingly anxious to be married in a church; I tried to humor her, but soon found that it was impossible to discover any clergyman of the Established Church who would remarry divorced persons. True, the Archbishop of Canterbury and the Bishop of London sometimes, in exceptional cases, issued special licenses permitting divorced persons to remarry. But the fee for this was fifty pounds. Since I knew nothing special about our circumstances, and since I did not have fifty pounds to throw away, I made no further effort towards a special license, and the ceremony accordingly was not performed in any church, or by any minister.

The day of our wedding we were forced to stop in London, in a packed and noisy hotel, to obtain special police permits and identity books enabling us to pursue our wedding trip as far as the Cornish coast. The following day found us in Falmouth, where I had landed a month before, and where, but for certain grim reminders of the German submarine campaign strewn up and down the coast, we were effectually shielded from the swirling currents of the War. After two weeks we returned to London, but soon after the first of August took the children to Ramsgate, where we boarded very cheaply in a house kept by an older relative of Daisy, and there stayed till the beginning of September. My chief recollection of Ramsgate, apart from the combination it afforded of middle-class trippers and boarders and magnificent Channel sunsets, was of the great hotels that stood on the chalk cliffs, now become military hospitals and crowded with the wreckage of war: the legless, armless, faceless, blinded, shattered men who had once been the flower of England. I also recall a zeppelin raid—far more violent than the one I had already gone through in London—during which guns barked unceasingly, the zeppelin itself was plainly visible from our windows, and both Daisy's relative and the children showed strong signs of panic.

When I returned to London the battle of the Somme was raging, and all England was resounding with stories of the exploits of the tank, that new instrument of war which England had secretly invented, which she had unloosed on the unprepared Germans, and which had completely taken them by surprise—or so the newspapers said. All that I actually saw of the battle of the Somme was that, every day now in London, great trains full of wounded soldiers were being discharged at Charing Cross Station for distribution to various hospitals. As the ambulances bearing these war wrecks emerged from the station, women would gather by the gates and throw roses into each ambulance as it passed slowly by. I wondered what use these flowers could be, or what they could mean, to the pitiful broken shells of humanity that lay within.

The only literary society I now had was that of H. D. and of Aldington. Aldington was not often available, being at his officers' training camp most of the time, in preparation for going overseas. H. D. was, most of the time, too distraught by the War and by the prospect of losing Aldington to provide good company. She had introduced me, however, to John Cournos, whom I have spoken of before as meeting, casually, at the imagist dinner in 1914. Somehow, after our first conversation, I discovered a bond of sympathy between Cournos and myself. This ex-Russian Jew, four years older than I, with his long, lean, melancholy face, wearing an expression equally compounded of aesthetic yearning and of Mephistophelian irony, fascinated me no less with his knowledge of Russian life and literature, which I had been recently absorbing in huge doses, than with his smoldering Hebraic mysticism, his air of perpetual exile, and his queer combination of active mentality and of fatalistic resignation. I found in Cournos a man of many careers, who had registered a splendid and unworldly failure in them all. He was just now embarking on the most ambitious of all by becoming, at thirty-four, a novelist.

I also found in him a splendid talker and listener. He soon became imbued with my two leading and favorite ideas: the idea that the great creative artist is less the possessor and shaper of his material than himself possessed and shaped by it, and the idea that the tragedy of the War lay less in its being fought than in its being fought with machines rather than with men. For my part, I took from Cournos the idea, derived through Heine, that the "gods" were still waiting in exile, ready to come back to man, together with its corollary that it was only through the great myth that the artist could fully describe human life and so state the salvation of humanity. Both these ideas presented a strange blend of animal paganism and of otherworldly Christianity; and both were characteristic of Cournos, a man in whose character lay equally blended the pagan satyr and the Hebraic messiah.

Cournos afforded a strange contrast to Amy Lowell, who had been my chief friend in Boston. He was as much the unworldly, unsuccessful Jew as Miss Lowell had been the worldly, successful Yankee; of the two, I began to feel that I preferred Cournos. I saw a great deal of him that summer and winter; but soon after Kerensky's Revolution of March, 1917, he joined a British mission to Russia and went to Petrograd. I did not see him again till a year had gone by—a year which brought the collapse of Russia and the Bolshevik Revolution, all of which he witnessed, and which he has spoken of in his autobiography. After his return he introduced me to D. H. Lawrence, who, after a long and bitter struggle with the British authorities, had been forced to quit his seaside cottage in Cornwall, and to come up, with his German wife, to London.

Lawrence interested me almost equally with his fierce, feverish intensity of spirit combined with marked physical frailty, and with his bitter and outspoken hatred of his own country. England, he felt and declared, was already doomed and hopeless. He only wanted to go away somewhere, where with a few congenial spirits he could live and work in peace—anywhere, so long as he never again saw England. I was moved by the passionate intensity with which Lawrence proclaimed these sentiments, no less than by the grain of appalling truth that lay underneath them. It was his love for England, I thought, that had finally led Lawrence to condemn her: his love for the England of Chaucer and Shakespeare and Milton and Cobbett and Blake, the England that had long ossified into Victorian hypocrisy, imperialistic greed, industrial exploitation, and economic squalor, under Queen Victoria, Gladstone, and Disraeli. England *was* probably damned and doomed, even as Lawrence had said—and though, even yet, the War might be won, it would probably be too late. That was the tragedy not only of England, but also of D. H. Lawrence, I thought, as I saw his figure, spare, gnarled, peasantlike, with its fiery beard and intense vitality, disappearing like a ghost into the night-darkened streets of London, swathed in December fog.

I also met, soon after my return to England, the mysterious T. S. Eliot of whom I had already heard through Harriet Monroe and Conrad Aiken. He struck me then, and has often seemed to me since, as a person who had cut himself off completely from all his American roots, and left them altogether behind. There was nothing in either his speech, his dress, or his demeanor that proclaimed the former middle-westerner. He seemed rather like one of those cloistered students of the Middle Ages who once roved Europe from monastery to monastery, copying old manuscripts, and belonging to no particular country. In appearance, with his pale ascetic face, his correct manners, his blend of deliberate reserve and intellectual arrogance, he resembled what the youthful Dante must have looked like—and his chief bent, I soon discovered, was to be a poet-scholar, an intelligence that was more critical than creative. Ben Jonson he seemed to think equally as great as Shakespeare; Dryden he frankly preferred to Milton; and among the moderns, he tended to rate Pound far above Yeats. The fact that Pound and I did not see each other, as well as my own feeling that Eliot had only succeeded in uprooting himself even more completely than myself, tended to make me avoid his society.

In the absence of further literary contacts my time was now spent more and more with reading. My mind had by no means arrived at the point where it was incapable of assimilating new influences in literature and in thought; on the contrary, I had, as I knew, developed more rapidly mentally in the last three years than in the seven previous ones. I had rushed headlong via English romanticism and French symbolism into modernity without weighing the alternatives or counting the steps on the way. The particular kind of aesthetic modernity that I had affected in *Irradiations* and the "symphonies" had not been without a philosophic background, but the background had been Chinese, rather than European. Behind the "symphonies" lay the quietism, the gospel of inaction and submission of Lao-tse, and also of Buddhism, with its creed hidden in nature even more effectually than the gospel Wordsworth had found there. But, after all, I was not a Chinese but a west European, on both sides of my ancestry. European culture was now facing the deadliest crisis it had ever known, and I could not help feeling that if it fell I must fall with it. Was there something in European culture I had missed? I set myself the task of finding out.

A careful reading of D. H. Lawrence, which I undertook almost immediately after my return, led me to Thomas Hardy. I had previously read only some of Hardy's prose works, and had regarded him chiefly as a contemporary and rival of Meredith, in the shift from Victorian idealism to modern realism in novel writing. Now I went through Hardy's poems, beginning with *The Dynasts,* which I read with increasing amazement and admiration just at the time when the Somme advance began to collapse, in the late fall of 1916.

I began to realize that Hardy's admirers in England had understated, rather than overstated, his genius. Tolstoy, before him, had used this theme of the Napoleonic Wars; but Tolstoy had pitted against Napoleon the Russian peasant, had made Napoleon a vain ignoramus and the Russian peasant a man of God. To Hardy's immense detachment and to Hardy's immense pity, all of mankind became equally puny and miserable. Napoleon, Nelson, the Russian peasant, the leaders of the Spanish uprising, the English people themselves, all were but victims of circumstances. Nothing remained but the spirit of irony and of pity and the awful, impersonal, inhuman immensity of God. This Wessex recluse, this last of the Victorians, had, in his neutral-toned verses, with their homespun Saxon strength of phrase, matched Sophocles, and spoken the doom not of Athens, but of western man. This, it seemed to me as I read him, was the only line of development that now lay open to the European consciousness: a disabused patience, a stoic resignation to circumstances, a pessimism that perpetually faced the alternative that "if a better may be, it demands a full look at the worst," an insight that could match the puny efforts of man's individual will with the awful, impersonal will that moved through history.

My task, I now felt, was to preserve in my poetry that freedom in form which I had already attained, together with its vividly colored background of natural and dramatic description, but gradually to infuse it with a sympathy for human life that would bring it closer to Hardy's. To describe life through nature became now my aim. The question was, How much must I sacrifice to achieve it? I saw clearly that, at any rate, I must sacrifice the personal pronoun, which had dominated the writing of *Irradiations* and of the "symphonies." No longer could I describe my own private experiences, but only experience in general. And, though I could still use natural objects as symbols to describe experience, the experience described must be something not peculiar to myself.

Some time early in October, exactly three years from the day that Daisy and I had first come together, I took the typescript of the love poems I had written her, completed before leaving the United States, and shipped them off to Houghton Mifflin, under the title, first chosen by me in opposition to Dante's *Divina Commedia,* of *Love's Tragedy.* I had been working, off and on, on this manuscript for three years. The first book, *The Aster Flower,* had been written in the October of 1913, when I was still the novice of *Irradiations* and the "Sea Symphony." The second, *Fruits of Flame,* had come during the brief interlude of our happiness together the following spring and summer: it was exactly contemporaneous with the "Green," the "Golden" and the "White Symphonies." The third, *The Empty Days,* had been written in Galveston, Texas, and in Little Rock, Arkansas, during the winter of 1914–15, on my trip south. *Dreams in the Night* had come to me in Boston the following spring; and the last, *Towards the Darkness,* during the winter of 1915–16, in Boston. I believed that this book, for all its possible abuse of the personal pronoun, all its sometimes hectic over-emotionalism, would serve as an excellent introduction and earnest of the kind of poetry to which I now proposed to devote myself. It used precisely the same technique of color, the same analogy of mood and object, the same symphonic development, the same contrast of conflicting mood and aspect, that my "symphonies" had already employed, on a subject of wider human interest and import. I saw no reason why, if the "symphonies" had been published, it could not also be published.

Meanwhile, from her summer home in Dublin, Miss Lowell had continued to write me, telling me in each letter how the movement was catching on, how the second imagist anthology was keeping up with the first, and how remarkably well she thought of my newly produced *Goblins and Pagodas.* She was also insistent that, in view of the situation, I should return to America. I had, however, decided to wait on in England, having long ago concluded that the growth of interest in the movement meant largely, in this case, the growth of interest in Amy Lowell. I did not begrudge her her fame, nor the way in which she was achieving it. But even before my departure she had been exceedingly nasty about my friendly attitude to Alfred Kreymborg, and to his *Others* group. She was so afraid that they might take sales away from the imagists, as to forbid me even the remotest show of friendliness in their direction. I thought it best to keep the ocean between us, for a time at least, and to go my own way independently.

I saw now not the least reason why Houghton Mifflin, whether I was linked with her or not, should look unfavorably on the new manuscript I was sending them. I had already one ardent admirer of my talent in the firm, in the person of Linscott; and Ferris Greenslet, the head of it, had spoken publicly in favor of my poetry, in the columns of the *Egoist.* Nor did I suppose that Miss Lowell would, under any circumstances, interfere in the course of my destiny. She was not even published by Houghton Mifflin now, I reflected, but by Macmillan. Whatever I sent them would be judged as an independent work, on its own merits.

I had sent off my manuscript and was still awaiting an answer when, at the close of October, Miss Lowell sent me a copy of her second volume, *Men, Women and Ghosts.* The book stirred me, in spite of the fact that its author and I had drifted apart, to wildest enthusiasm. Here, set out with supreme narrative and dramatic skill, were all those gorgeously decorated, psychologically keen narratives of human destiny that I had heard her read as they were written during the past two years: "Patterns," "A Roxbury Garden," "The Cross Roads," "Malmaison," "The Hammers." Here was a poetry different altogether from Masters's frontier realism, Frost's bucolic humor, Lindsay's cosmic evangelicism, Sandburg's blend of American swagger and Scandinavian mysticism. It was a poetry rich, tragic, sumptuous, aristocratic, romantic, vivid and proud. I immediately wrote an enthusiastic letter, saying that the book was a masterpiece, and promising a review for the *Egoist*—the only paper to which I then contributed in London.

On November 21 I received a cablegram requesting that the review be sent immediately to Boston. Accordingly, a day or so later, I sent it, only requesting that it should not appear in Braithwaite's paper—for

I had heard, before leaving Boston, ugly rumors to the effect that she was now financing Braithwaite; and I wished anything I wrote, either favorably or unfavorably, about her should appear in some paper independent of her influence. The review did not appear, and the next news I received was of such a startling character as to cause me to regret that it had ever been sent.

On the seventh of December I received a letter from Ada Russell, written a day before the cablegram had been sent. In it she informed me that Amy had been seriously ill with neuralgia and indigestion, followed by jaundice and insomnia. She was unable to write, but was very sorry that Greenslet had rejected the poems I had sent to Houghton Mifflin. He had been unable to make up his mind about them, and had come to her and asked her advice. She had said that though she did not like them so well as the others I had already published, she thought they would sell better. She was sorry if she had said anything to lead them to reject these poems.

The blow of this letter, coming before Houghton Mifflin had even written, or had sent back the manuscript, was decisive. Up to then I had played about with the idea of returning to America, possibly in the next spring, if the War went on. Daisy would not, I felt, object, as she was now legally an American; and the children, being under age, would naturally accompany us. I might easily settle in Boston, and resume there my literary career. But now that avenue of escape was cut off, drastically and effectually. What could I do in Boston, or anywhere else, if the only publishing house that had been favorable to my work referred privately everything I wrote to Amy Lowell? And what could I do if Amy Lowell let her annoyance that I had gone away and married sway her judgment?

I immediately sat down and wrote Amy a letter of which I give some paragraphs, without comment:

> You and I have been friends now for over three years. If you will review in your mind that period, you will perhaps find that not many of your friends have done more for you than I. I have not always seen eye to eye with you on some points; but I have never doubted your ability as a poet, and time after time I have defended you, not only in public, but in private. I have never let an opportunity slip to declare my faith in you and in your future. I say

proudly and confidently that I have done my utmost to stand by you; and, had I the power to do more, more would have been done.

Not only is this true, but it is also true that you are indebted to me for certain suggestions and criticisms of poetry which I have given you from time to time. This debt you have yourself generously acknowledged.

Now let us see what bearing all this has on the manuscript I sent to Greenslet. That manuscript was the product of three years' hard labor. I had spared no pains to make it perfect. So perfect did I consider it, that I hesitated about letting it go (it is only with my best works that I feel like this). Linscott was aware of its existence, wrote and asked me to let him see it; and through him it fell into Greenslet's hands. Greenslet, being apparently unable to make up his mind, showed it to you; and it was your opinion that turned the scale. You did not think of it in my best manner.

Even if you do not agree with me, even if you think that collection the worst I have written, I must ask you what do you mean by writing me as you did some time ago, and offering to act as my agent in America; and then publicly disparaging what I consider to be my best efforts? Is this the behavior of an agent, or a friend? Friendship is a question of give-and-take; and in my friendship with you, I have given what I have taken. If you have not enough confidence in me, as a better poet than—— or ——,—if you do not think it better worth Greenslet's while to publish me than these, then it is time we parted company. I should deeply regret having to lose a friend; but half-a-friend is worse than none. Unless you can defend my work in the same spirit with which you defended Mrs. Untermeyer's or Sandburg's or any of your friends, I have no alternative but to withdraw.

The manuscript of *Love's Tragedy* finally did arrive; having been posted on November 11, but delayed by the uncertainty of mails in those wartime days, and by the added delay of having to pass through the British censorship. I spent the month of December contemplating my first rejection at the hands of a publisher since my writing of *Irradiations* in the spring of 1913. My sole feeling was one of intense bitterness and anger at Miss Lowell, which, despite the admiration I still felt for her poetry, I could not overcome. Without asking my consent, without thinking of the damage it might do me, her hand had been the first to deal this blow and to destroy the footing I had painfully established in America. Now I no longer had a publisher there, and I must wait and wait till one came my way in England. And to make things worse, Ada Russell's letter apprising me of Amy's action, and venturing to excuse it on the grounds of illness, had come just after I received a cable begging me to send her a copy of an extremely laudatory review, which the reception of her *Men, Women and Ghosts* had already moved me to write.

There was only one thing to do, and that was to stifle my feelings and face the situation. Since Houghton Mifflin would no longer publish my work, since Miss Lowell chose to destroy my standing with the publishers whom she had been chiefly instrumental in finding, I would wait and wait indefinitely; but somehow I would get *Love's Tragedy* published in England. Whether she were right or wrong about this book's being inferior to the others, I knew I must obtain a publisher for it. But I now definitely decided, despite all promptings to return, to stick out the War in England. I could, and must, stand on my own feet henceforward, and definitely take the responsibility for my own life and writings. I knew now that Amy Lowell and I could never again be friends on the old footing. The rejection of my manuscript at her hands had been the equivalent of a stab in the back; I could never overlook that fact. Nevertheless, for the sake of our friendship in the past, I would do my best, henceforward, to forgive her and to bear with her—but I resolutely rejected the offer she soon made, after her reception of the letter I have just quoted, to bring out the book at her own expense.

While waiting for a publisher to turn up, I busied myself with war poems. The theme, however painful, was now inescapable, and I hoped to handle it in a spirit of irony and pity not unakin to that of Thomas Hardy. Meanwhile, I must wait. After all, I was only thirty, and had years before me in which I could work out my destiny. Miss Lowell had been already forty when she began, and Robinson had been forty-six before he obtained any but the smallest of audiences. If only the War would some day end, if only God would give me strength, I could work and work—and wait.

CHAPTER XIX

Nineteen-seventeen came and went, but brought no change to my situation. The winter of 1916–17 was an intensely cold and bleak one, and by the end of February, Daisy sickened with the first illness she had known since our marriage, falling victim to the prevailing influenza and remaining in bed for two weeks. Scarcely had she recovered when her daughter fell ill of the same complaint, suffering from an even worse case, with fantastically high temperatures. Inasmuch as our one servant was on the point of quitting us to go into the making of munitions, I judged it best to give my wife a brief holiday. So a little before Easter I sent her and the children off to Brighton, while I myself took a room in a London hotel, and tried to think. It was there that I had the news that America had gone into the War.

The news changed little or nothing in my situation. I had long ago decided that it was not my business to rush into uniform to be maimed or killed. I ought to stay out, write poetry, try to help culture and humanity to survive this crisis in their affairs. To this decision I had been helped by Aldington, by my own powers of reflection, even by Daisy's natural but unreasoned demand that I should stay out, and thus let my money continue to support her and the children. The fact of America's belated entry could not change my unalterable conviction that the War was senseless madness, a fever in humanity that must simply burn itself out. Although it seemed to me now that America was entering too late to do Europe or the Allies any real good, I realized that Woodrow Wilson had finally been driven into the impossible situation which I had already envisaged for him a year ago when I wrote my poem on Lincoln. I was glad now that America did not give way to sentimental hysteria, but mobilized for war in a practical matter-of-fact spirit. She was not, for example, going to rely on volunteers to help her. Conscription would exist from the moment she declared hostilities.

I put down my name at the American consulate in the list of Americans who were holding themselves ready for service at any time if called upon, stated that the only obstacle to my joining the American army was the fact that I had a wife and two stepchildren dependent on my support, and dismissed the future from my mind. If the authorities wanted me they would call upon me, in due course. I had no feelings one way or the other. From then on I fully expected to be called, as I knew the War would not end that year, though several of the English papers were still pathetically predicting Germany's collapse. Rumania was out, Serbia was out, Russia was flickering. The Allies could do nothing in the west against Hindenburg's cast-iron defenses. In England, Asquith was forced from public office; and Lloyd George, more boastful and braggart than ever, together with his coalition of Liberals and Conservatives, was put in. Nothing could happen before the late spring, now that the Somme had proved itself a failure. And for my part, I suspected that the United States would be both slow and ineffectual in getting under way, having in my mind a vivid memory of the graft, the inefficiency, the sentimental hysteria, and the corrupt administration that had marked and shamed my country during the Spanish-American War.

Alone now in London, with Cournos preparing to go to Russia, Aldington already in uniform and ready to be called upon to go overseas at any moment, Flint effectually buried in an important official position, my mind went back to the first days of the War. Thirty-two months had gone by since then, since those August days of 1914; and now America had been drawn in, probably too late. My mind went back to an early summer day of that year 1914 when, in the company of Edward Thomas, I had gone on excursion out of London to Hampton Court Palace and to Bushey Park. We had lain together in the grass, under the great horse chestnuts, while I talked of free verse and imagism, and Thomas spoke of his love of the English countryside, and of W. H. Hudson. He had reflectively chewed on a grassblade, while we sat and looked at the semitame park deer browsing in the distance, and we had both wondered what it felt like to be not a man, but an animal, and whether Walt Whitman was right in saying that the animals were more contented than man, because they did not groan or fret over their condition. Now Thomas was already dead; he had been killed at the Somme, and I would never speak to him again. History had shoveled him into a grave in France. The beautiful, sensitive poems he had written in the last months of his life were only now coming out, too late to recall him. I too probably would soon have to submit to the same fate.

The machinery of the War was relentlessly crushing out every vestige of humanity, as the British tanks had rolled over the German trenches; as the U-boats, now reaping their worst harvest, were torpedoing Allies and neutrals, soldiers and civilians alike on the high seas; as the airplanes were bombing not only the trenches, but civilians. It was useless to invoke, as the conscientious objectors were doing, Christianity against the continuance of the struggle. The churches had raised no protest, had even blessed this orgy of destruction. It was useless, too, to follow Henry Ford, and to charter a ship to try and bring peace to ravaged Europe. The dragon's teeth of battle were already too deeply sown; newer and newer crops of armed men would spring up, till western civilization went the way of ancient Rome, and the barbarian, the savage succeeded to the wreckage. The earth was entering a new dark age, and the Renaissance was at an end. What did the individual matter after all?

Soon after Easter, with the news that America had joined the Allies fresh in my mind, I went again to Hampton Court, which I had not revisited since that June day that Edward Thomas and I had been there. I was now alone. The crocuses were already out, in all their fresh bravery of gold, under the chill and leaden April sky, but no one looked much at them. The shrunken crowd of Easter holiday seekers, middle-aged men, middle-class mothers, Canadian or Australian soldiers on leave with their girls, here and there a child, were indifferent to everything except a scouting airplane that kept maneuvering up and down the Thames. I lay still and communed with my thoughts. America had come in. But Europe, the Europe I had known, was plainly dying. I would never again see it as it had been.

It seemed to me then that my only release lay in the prospect of joining such men as Edward Thomas and seeking a grave in France. The individual, whatever his philosophy, no longer counted. Nor did Christianity, that unique gift of west-European civilization to the world, count any longer. Only the machine counted, and financial greed, and nationalist hysteria coining profit out of slaughter, and wreckage and destruction. I must accept, as Thomas had accepted, my death:

> Better to die now with the golden light
> Of Europe swiftly fading
> From the summit of that mountain or this cloud;
> Better unconsciously to rest
> In the dark bosom of the earth
> Feeling each night the influence of the stars
> Wheeling through seasons their unchanging path;
> Feeling the earth heaped close and hugging me
> To deeper, denser darkness;
> While, day and night, the world
> Pursues its destiny to which war and peace
> Are as the smoke that high winds blow away.

I felt now as one already dedicated to death, and therefore prepared to meet it. If, as seemed certain, European culture could not survive the War, there was all the more reason why, in its passing, I should be taken

> Out of the ring of light that glimmers on human faces,
> Anxiously watching and praying for me.
> I set forth free from them,
> To the infinite stir and the murmur of night on the waters.

London, as I now saw, under its new lighting restrictions was at least enormously and fantastically beautiful while the spring days slowly lengthened to summer. Every street lamp had been shaded, so that it cast only a faint cone of light down on the pavement. And the night with all its magic of moonlight, starlight, river mist, sailing or floating cloud, reassumed its dominion, once threatened by electric lights, over this formidable ant heap of humanity.

Especially in the darkened City, the oldest part of London, did the night bring forth the ghosts. I recalled them later, after the War, when various British soldiers—Robert Graves among them—told me that in France, from the great Somme offensive on, they had actually seen, or thought they had, soldiers who, they knew, had been killed months before, strolling in the streets of half-ruined towns, or sitting at empty café tables. It seemed to me now that Shakespeare and Milton and Samuel Johnson, Blake and Dickens and Browning, all the great splendid company of the masters of English speech, revisited the city where they had lived, and spoke again to men living in the midst of England's crisis, with the German submarines sending a million tons of shipping to the bottom every month, and the national government straining every nerve to produce more munitions. In those eerie, uncanny, deserted streets, under the faint cones of grayish light cast on the pavement and bordered with darkness, I half expected to see figures emerging and passing, dressed in the costume of other days. Had they been seen, I do not think that I would have been astonished.

In July, before the middle of the month, came a visitation of another sort: the first great daylight air raid, when twenty of the new bomb-carrying Gothas flew over in broad sunlight and, finding London's air defenses utterly unprepared, spread havoc in a wide area from Smithfield Market to London Bridge. I saw the fighting in the distance, took train to London soon after, walked through the streets around Cheapside which lay ankle-deep in shattered glass, knew that henceforward London was not safe, and could not be made safe, from such airplane attacks launched unexpectedly.

Nor was it, as the sequel proved. The harvest moon of that year—come after Daisy and I had prolonged a holiday scheduled to last four weeks into six, because it kept us remote from London—will never be wiped from my memory entirely. Every night for a week the Gothas came over, and every night for a week there was the bang of the maroons warning London to take cover, the roar of the guns, the crash of bombs, machine guns rattling in the air between attackers and defenders, on and on for hours, until the final bugle sounded, "all clear." As my wife's mother lay at the time in a London hospital, suffering from an incurable illness, my business carried me in and out of the city a good deal, with the result that I saw the underground stations packed with weary humanity, the streets filled with scurrying people, the railway stations empty and darkened. And on one night at least, I traveled from London to my suburb on a train that progressed in total darkness. For many years, as a consequence, until long after the War, my favorite forms of nightmare were of being pursued by airplanes, and of being buried alive in a maze of underground tunnels.

As the year came to an end I realized, looking back on it, that the only period of it I had really enjoyed had been the six weeks' holiday I had spent that summer. We had chosen for our holiday, Daisy and I and the children, a spot on the Cornish coast which at that time was within easy access of much wild and unspoilt scenery of cliff and cove and sand dune, wind-swept rounded headlands of serpentine and granite reaching out into the crash and gurgle of the Atlantic breakers, long moors stretching inland ablaze with yellow gorse and purple heather, sleepy untroubled villages nestling about their granite churches in the tree-shaded hollows, with crimson fuchsias aflame at the doors of their whitewashed cottages. This land of Lyonesse, of Arthurian fable and brooding mystery, of abandoned tin mines and fishing ports and waste places, seemed not only remote from the War, but indifferent to it.

The Cornish people themselves, their smoldering Celticism aflame, cared little for England. One heard everywhere tales of their resistance to the conscription act, of lighthouse keepers who had been discovered helping the German submarines, of uninhabited islands where refueling bases for these submarines had been discovered, of secret spies and of lights seen on distant headlands. And I myself saw, in water-fashioned caves along the coast, wreckage which had been washed ashore from torpedoed ships and which inhabitants had carefully hidden and salvaged. In one lonely bay there was even a small schooner which had been driven ashore one dark night, which had been promptly looted of much of its cargo.

The spell which the wild scenery and life of Cornwall laid upon me was so powerful that under it I soon conceived of a way whereby I could write poems that had nothing more to do with the War. Here man was still pitted against the elements, sea, earth, air, fire, winning a scant sustenance from each; here the mechanical age that now openly ruled the great metropolitan areas of London and the Midlands had not yet conquered man's independence, his smoldering paganism, his integral savagery. I promptly schemed out a new book, to be called, provisionally, *Elements,* and consisting equally of descriptive and narrative pieces, somewhat on the lines of Miss Lowell's own volumes, to be divided into four parts: "Sea," "Earth," "Air," "Fire." The first would deal with man's restless, adventurous, roving explorations of the unknown, no less than with the elemental mystery of the vast ocean spaces with which he and his habitations were surrounded; the second with sowing and plowing and reaping, home building and trade, the spring and the harvest; the third with the ever-repeated and ever-unsatisfied longings and hankerings after the divine; the last with the inner fire of sex and of life, that drove him forward relentlessly. The scheme was to be the most ambitious on which I had yet embarked. It would contain, perhaps, a hundred poems, and though it might not ever be printed, it would be my swan song in case I had to go into the War. I worked on it all that summer and autumn, putting into it all that I had, all my powers of natural description, and all my loneliness and bitterness and frustration as a man.

The manuscript of *Elements* is now lost, and the poems that it once contained have been for so long vanished and scattered that I could not, even if I would, recall them to memory. One version—probably incomplete—was sent to America as early as 1917, in an attempt to win a prize contest which was undoubtedly a fraudulent one. It was only recovered with difficulty from the man who ran the contest. A second version, complete this time, after vainly traveling for years through the hands of various publishers, was given in 1929 to a friend in New York City who had done me some kindness, and he may still have it. Various of the poems that made up this book have appeared since then, in different publications. One of the earliest written, "The Black Rock," composed in Cornwall in the summer of 1917 and dedicated to Thomas Hardy, appeared later as the title poem of my book published in 1928. Two others, "Moonlight" and "Dawn," appeared in the last anthology of the imagists, in 1917, where they aroused the admiration of Amy Lowell but were ignored by the public in favor of the far more popular "Lincoln." Still another, entitled "Earth," has occasionally been reprinted since the *Yale Review* printed it in 1920; in 1936 it reappeared in another anthology. As for the rest of those hundred poems, they have all vanished; and the caves and lone shores of Cornwall, the remote coppices and uplands of the Kentish Downs that saw their birth, may, for aught I know, be recalling them still, to other wayfarers.

I am content that it should be so, just as I am content that the single faded and tattered typescript that I still possess, and which is all I have to show for the war poems on which I labored for three years, but which I made little effort to have published, should remain unread. As a poet, I realize that I have been, and must remain, for my lifetime, an anachronism. This age, though it has produced remarkable poets, cannot be said to be an age in any way favorable to poetry. The reason is that the reading and enjoyment of poetry can only be carried on by an intelligent and a leisured class. It was the intellectuals, the aristocrats of Athens—not the peasants and the fishermen—who appreciated Sophocles and Aeschylus. It was the wits, the scholars, and the courtiers of the Elizabethan age who—despite his truckling to the groundlings—valued and supported Shakespeare. It was the dandies, the bucks, and the bloods of the Regency who gave to Byron his European reputation. And if any poet is to survive our day it will be because he too appeals finally to a well-bred, well-fed, leisured minority who have the time to read and the taste to enjoy his art. In an age such as this, when the democratic standard of taste admits as literature anything from mystery thrillers to the performances of highly publicized novelists, the poet has no place. That is because the poet is a maker, a creator, a transmitter of raw fact into the different dimension of symbol and metaphor, myth and parable. Poetry has survived; but those who still read it, who know anything at all about it, who are interested in it still, are a special group, somewhat akin to the collectors of antique furniture—and, like these, their tastes are equally varied and unpredictable.

So 1917 merged into 1918, and I had nothing more to show for another year gone by than this: that towards the close of the year I had gone to a London publisher and had obtained immediate acceptance for *Love's Tragedy*, under its new title of *The Tree of Life*. So the last of the volumes which had marked the full flowering, in all its vividness, of my fresh-blown talent, duly appeared in London in the late summer of 1918, sometime after the moment when Ludendorff, gambling for a last throw, thrust his armies through Saint-Quentin to Amiens. The book was scarcely reviewed at all, and most of the reviewers treated it sneeringly. It is still in print as I write, but unread.

The final epilogue to this period was spoken by the appearance, in the same summer of 1918, of *Japanese Prints*, which Brown, in Boston, had now held for two years. For my part, I had already put behind me all of these performances of the past, and had emerged into another period of development marked by *Elements* and the war poems: a period which seemed to me to be both more heroic, more epical in outline, and more desperately serious in import. Alone and unguided except by my own instinct, I was driving fast and far towards the future.

The American authorities, though I frequently saw them, made no move in my direction. I was free to go, without wearing uniform, wherever I liked, without taking up any other work than the writing of poetry. I was striving to round out my career as I best might, for I had now no belief that the War would speedily end, and I felt that sooner or later I must be sucked into it. On the day I should be compelled to put on uniform, I decided to give up all writing. *Elements* and the war poems, taken together, had finally defined my attitude: a stoic paganism, an acceptance of nature, and a condemnation of modern mechanical progress that was harder and less sentimental than that of Wordsworth, and which was remote alike from the attitude of the organized churches and from that of nineteenth-century laissez-faire liberalism—both showing their worst fruits, just then, in the War.

The production of Miss Lowell's *Tendencies in Modern American Poetry* in the fall of 1917 had in America, at least, markedly improved my own poetic position; and had I been in my own country I might have profited by it. I was now cut off from the United States by three thousand miles of empty ocean, with no prospect for return. Indeed, the rising cost of living in England, thanks to the War, made my economic position more and more precarious. With a wife and two growing young people to support, I now found it not easy to make both ends meet. For a time, Linscott very generously and self-sacrificingly acted as my literary agent, and was instrumental in getting my work placed in various magazines. The aid he gave was frequently invaluable. But, by the beginning of 1918, I had so much manuscript on my hands that I decided not, under any circumstances, to write any more poetry. The mood I had created in *Irradiations* and the "symphonies" was not to be recaptured; so, having fairly drained myself of new emotions in the war poems and in *Elements,* and all for no result, I quitted the field.

As early as 1913 the idea had come to me that I might supplement my unsatisfactory career as poet by functioning as an art critic. My spasmodic attempts to make a painter of myself, my own eager interest in all the visual arts, had told me that I ought to try and make some further use of this faculty rather than transcribe it all into imagistic poetry. Unlike Miss Lowell, I did not feel disposed to embark on the difficult field of literary criticism; but I thought I knew enough about painters and painting to write fairly well about them. In the spring of 1913 I planned an extensive book on the impressionist and post-impressionist painters, the first comprehensive survey of the subject in existence. Manet, Monet, Pissarro, Cézanne, Gauguin, Van Gogh, Renoir, Degas, Picasso, and the cubists were to be all discussed and evaluated in its pages. The coming of my first important literary contacts, through Pound and his imagists, the development of the "symphonies," banished, temporarily, all such thoughts from my mind. Now it occurred to me that though I could not be given the time to finish so ambitious and so comprehensive a task, I might at any rate be able, before going into the War, to write a short study of at least one artist of this period.

I deliberately chose Paul Gauguin, less discussed as a painter than Cézanne, less important as a man than Van Gogh, because in him I sensed something akin to my own exile, as well as something close to my own smoldering revolt and disgust with nineteenth-century progressive civilization. Gauguin had preferred savagery, as Rousseau had and Thoreau had; and I felt now, facing the reality of tanks and submarines and poison gas and airplanes and incendiary bombs, that all three were right. So I decided, early in that year of 1918, to write a book on Gauguin—only to discover that Michael Sadleir had long entertained the same notion, and had once been on the point of fulfilling it. I proposed therefore a collaboration, but by this time Sadleir had already given up his position at his publishing office for a more important one in England's newly established Food Ministry, where he was so overworked and harried that he was utterly unable to find time to write anything. I decided to write the book on my own, hoping that Sadleir would be able to go over the manuscript later on and revise it.

All that summer of 1918, accordingly, while the supreme madness of the war fever burnt itself out among all the nations of the earth, I spent my hours in communing with Paul Gauguin amid the tropic solitudes of his distant and peaceable South Sea Eden of Tahiti—a spot of the world's surface I have never visited, though I envied Gauguin his escape at the time, and have always since then wanted to go there.

The book which resulted, published in 1921, presented at best a strongly idealized picture of a man whose life by any standard of judgment was spent in violent oscillation between the rival appeals of decadent European culture and of remote, unspoilt savagery. I was forced to admit, as I studied Gauguin more closely, that his character was neither integral nor profound. There was about the man something vulgar: the sensation seeker, the careerist, the unabashed egotist were oddly mixed in him with the mystical and fatalistic pagan. He was less an organic whole at bottom than his contemporary, Lafcadio Hearn, who also had fled from the commercial horrors of the West, to a semireal refuge in remote Japan. But at any rate, I was grateful to Gauguin for enabling me to state my own problem: either a civilization already decadent or a deliberate return to primitivism; either mankind submitting to the anonymous slavery imposed upon it by modern machine-age technique, or mankind seeking again, where it lay hidden in primitive society, for the unrealized promise of an unaccomplished golden age.

I was grateful, too, that my study of Paul Gauguin's career and development took my mind into fields remote from the War. Now, as I went about London or remained in my suburban home, writing and thinking about him, I felt less disposed to complain at my fate than previously, despite the fact that the world was entering the last desperate stage of the great conflict. I felt that it was my business to stay where I was, to regard my American career as closed, and to concentrate my remaining energies upon England and my new life there. I might make something of it, after all, despite my rebellious Americanism, my individualistic anarchism. There was a good chance that the Gauguin book could be published.

The Armistice came at last, and Sadleir, judging perhaps that my attitude towards Gauguin was an immature one, or losing whatever interest he once had in the subject, refused finally to collaborate even to the extent of revising the manuscript or suggesting ways for its revision. Nor would he, though now returning to publishing, help it as it stood to find a market. So I regretfully laid the finished book aside until the time, soon to come, when, thanks to Somerset Maugham's successful novel, the topic of Gauguin's life became a literary sensation in America.

The War was over, and I, who had not expected to survive it, now looked back on two years not rich in material rewards but crowded with many strange experiences of vicarious suffering and endurance. I had passed through the struggle without getting into uniform, without being jailed as a conscientious objector, without making any further progress in my career as one of the most discussed "new poets" in America. There the new poetry still held the stage; and people like Amy Lowell, Carl Sandburg, and Vachel Lindsay were passing from the status of freaks to that of educational subjects. Young students in colleges and universities were already studying their works, while other young students were already imitating them. Here, in England, the older and staider Georgians were gradually giving way before the uprush of young war poets, and Sassoon, Graves, Nichols, Blunden, and the tragic Wilfred Owen were having their day. Poetry was still selling, was in fact running into its second phase of interest. The anthology boom was already on its way, and Louis Untermeyer in his "Miscellany" was shortly to revive the imagist anthology notion on a broader basis.

I, however, was now out of the current, buried more effectually in England than if I had been, as I once supposed, hidden away in a trench grave in France, and completely prevented from taking part in whatever was going on. As regards my own state of mind, I cannot do better than quote from a letter I wrote to the devoted Linscott, early in 1919:

I believe that we have now more points in agreement than we ever had before. Certainly, the experience of the last three years has changed me in most ways. I am now getting middle-aged, and conservative. Most of my juvenile ardor has departed, never to return. I still believe that this wretched planet is managed and controlled by some great overwhelming Force—what most folk call "God." But neither you, nor I, nor anyone is able to understand the motives and purposes of that Force, any more than an ant could understand or appreciate a thunderstorm. Our petty minds are too feeble, too limited. We are really only the pawns, the playthings of something beyond our knowledge—and yet we like to strut about and think ourselves great, heroic and important. Truly, the irony of life is colossal.

I still suspect that there may be such a thing as human progress—though it is so slow, so painful, accomplished at such a price paid by the individual for its attainment, that I doubt whether it is worth the effort. It is all predestined to happen in any case, if at all.

I do not doubt but that the soul is immortal; but whether this implies consciousness or feeling of individuality in the future state, I think open to question. The energy we bear in us simply flows back to its Source, to be used over and over again. So far as this queer tangle of hopes and dreams and pains that is life is concerned, I fully expect Nirvana. . . . The complex of energy, of which I made a part, will go on working out its destiny.

I have written this because you asked me in your letter the question, whether I feel life to be as rich emotionally now as at 21? No, I do not. I was fortunate in keeping young longer than 21; but for about three years I have known that my youth is definitely dead. Not only have I lost a good deal of my own intensity of feeling; but, worse, I have lost much of my faith in mankind.

Especially has this been so from the day that America entered the war. Since then, I have seen with increasing clarity and bitterness, that however high our aims, however noble our intentions, something always conspires to frustrate those aims and intentions. I am quite sure that even though there is progress, the millennium will never arrive, and the last generation of mankind will have just as much evil to contend with as we have. Evil is as necessary to our existence, as good. Evil is an active principle, creating, destroying, always changing in form. Good is only a conservative principle, unchanging, inactive. Thus it happens that when we will evil, we often accomplish only good, and vice versa.

Art, then, is the only consolation. Art enables us to express what we are; it states the level to which we attain in every generation. But that art makes us any happier, any better, any more able to attain our desires, is merely an illusion. On the contrary, Art probably only increases our suffering, as you say in your letter. For that reason, artists are usually unhappy: and the greater they are, the more unhappy. I am sure that Dante and Michelangelo and Shakespeare suffered pains to which my own sufferings are slight.

In such a chastened mood, compounded equally of two years of fresh exile and of passive resistance to the great conflict, I bade farewell to the Great War.

CHAPTER XX

By the early months of 1919 I had decided to return to America; but I knew that the return, if it were made, must be made alone. Under my existing circumstances, my resources were inadequate to the task of bringing over both Daisy and her children to my own country. I had discussed the matter with her thoroughly, and had discovered that, while she admitted the force of my argument that the only prospect I had for a future literary career lay in America, she was now adamant in her refusal to leave the children behind. Although her daughter was already sixteen and her son fourteen years of age, she continued to treat them as if they were just emerging from infancy. They, in turn, continued to lavish on her the manifestations of an affection which was barely a stage removed from infantile dependence. I myself, though I had left their upbringing entirely in her hands, realized that they were now likely, under such control, to become only too docile and inhibited. So I soon saw to it that the girl, who was not clever at ordinary lessons, but who showed a strong disposition to become a painter, should be sent to a small but adequate art school in the neighborhood, while the boy, who was better at general knowledge, went to a preparatory school. As I did this at my own expense, my economic resources were now strained to the vanishing point.

Apart from my bad financial position, the only objection I now felt at returning to America was the fact that the United States had celebrated the conclusion of the War by becoming a prohibitionist nation. Not only were the United States now, by the very nature of the case, the richest and most powerful of all nations, but they had set themselves the task of remaining so permanently, by means of a piece of puritanic legislation fostered by rabidly Protestant fanatics and backed up by big business. America had, supposedly, the highest standard of living, paid the highest industrial wages of any nation on earth. The maintenance of this standard—mythical as it was—weighed more in the minds of her capitalist rulers than the continuance of moral and intellectual liberty. The theory that had made the Prohibition Amendment acceptable was that if prohibition were only put through, all workmen would inevitably save more, work more efficiently, and lead more healthy lives—a theory not only false, but cynically ruinous of human dignity and integrity. I was destined, during the next ten years, to hear this theory frequently upheld by Americans, in the intervals between their consumption of shots of bootleg whiskey and rankly poisonous gin.

It is not my purpose here to discuss in detail the effects of the Prohibition Amendment on the American people. Its effects were already noteworthy and notorious, by the summer of 1920, in a complete relaxation of the moral fiber, a growing irresponsibility, an increasing selfishness and cynicism among vast numbers of people. Some day, a serious-minded sociologist may devote a few years of his life to a detailed study of the subject, and may show how the prohibition issue, skillfully wrapped up in mass propaganda, was successfully put over, only to bring, in its train, such a variety of evils as permanently to weaken the American character. For my part, I only felt, and still feel, that if it is wrong to forbid people by law to read certain books, or to hold radical political views, it is equally wrong to forbid them by law from drinking. All the civilized nations of the world have indulged in alcoholic liquor, in one form or another, for centuries untold. Prohibition in America seemed to me a reversion to barbarism, the choice of a greater evil in preference to a lesser one. If the South, from which I had sprung, could not have been legislated out of the path that had led the southern states to secession and to civil war in 1861, neither was there, in 1919, any means by which the American people, as a whole, could ever be legislated into temperance, and persuaded to uphold the law at all costs.

Meanwhile, it was becoming clear as daylight that Woodrow Wilson was not going to have his own way in Paris. Bit by bit, Clemenceau, backed by Lloyd George, forced him to give way on every issue. Of his original fourteen points which, along with hunger and starvation and continued slaughter, had been chiefly responsible for bringing about the German collapse, nothing now remained. He was finally induced to sign a treaty which dealt with the Germans precisely as the Romans had dealt with the ancient Carthaginians. So the man who had come to Paris to be hailed as a messiah by every war-weary nation on earth, who had ridden through London's packed and awed streets on a sparkling frosty day of December sunlight, sitting side by side with the British king—so this man departed to his own country, already mistrusted by everyone, who, as I, now felt that all of the dead had died in vain. He went back only to fight the greater mistrust of his own country and to fail there also.

On a day late in April, in the midst of a capricious spring that had just brought, overnight, a sudden fall of snow on top of the already budding trees, I suddenly heard that Edward O'Brien was now in London. The news was a surprise to me, to say the least. Some years younger than myself, the spoilt and petted child of his mother, he had seemed to me when I met him in Boston, still largely a boy, a boy who, by his own account, had gone out to various waste places of the earth, such as the Magdalene Islands and Aran, in a Rimbaudlike flight from civilization, but who had kept intact thereby his Irish Celticism, his Catholicism, and his charm. With long, straight black hair, ragged and uncut about his high bullet-shaped forehead, candid blue eyes, and a sensual heavy-lipped mouth below a tiny fluff of straggly mustache, dressed commonly in frayed and threadbare garments, with a store of nervous energy animating his body and brain which had driven him through many more books than I had read, and had kept him alive and alert despite the fact that he had supported his mother by working at the most menial of literary jobs, Edward O'Brien had seemed to me then to be authentically of the material of which the Irish martyrs are made. I could easily picture him as dying in the

Dublin Easter week uprising, along with his favorite heroes, such as Padraic Pearse and Conolly. It seemed to me strange to hear, in the spring of 1919, that he was again in London, now that the Irish situation was once more flaring up into open civil war between Loyalists and Republicans. I had not suspected him of coming so coolly and so unexpectedly into the very heart of the enemy's country.

I did not, however, question O'Brien as to his motives and plans in coming to England. On the contrary, I welcomed him with delight, and accepted him as a friend. My American, or ex-American, friends in London were already reduced to one, T. S. Eliot, whom I saw very seldom. I was simply pining for some new American society, some breath of the keen, fresh, creative American energy that I had seen playing over the landscape in 1915, and which provided such a contrast to the torpor and mental inertia that had again settled over England immediately after the Armistice. O'Brien, with his boyish enthusiasm, his mental curiosity, his roguish lack of respect for the big academic pontiffs of the political and the literary world, seemed to me then an authentic example of my country's genius. Cournos, whose mind was rapidly moving away from the mystical idealism of *The Mask* into the grimly ironic Russian realism of his second novel, was—as I had discovered—too much the dispossessed Russian Jew to understand or appreciate the positive side of my country. But O'Brien, despite his medieval Catholicism, was still an authentic product of transatlantic culture. His ambition was to live half as a medieval saint, and half as an inspired playboy—an ambition which was his own undoing, for in him the strands of ascetic Christianity and of naïve, faunlike paganism never really sorted themselves out.

Within a month after his arrival we had planned to go together from London to a part of the North Wales coast said to be wild and unvisited. Cournos, who had just that spring concluded another affair with one of his numerous London sweethearts, was to accompany us. I have forgotten whether or not I agreed to be financially responsible for Cournos. At any rate, the place we picked on was not only remote but ridiculously cheap. It was at Aber, a tiny village in a wild, romantic valley fed by a celebrated waterfall, beyond Llanfairfechan, close to the celebrated Straits of Bangor and the Isle of Anglesey. Cournos and I journeyed through a late June day to find it; O'Brien was to follow in two or three days. How comfortable our lodging seemed, and how simple but satisfying our food was, there in that remote Welsh valley, removed alike from London's unrest and from the last echoes of the War! We were like three schoolboys let loose, from a nightmare which had oppressed our souls for four years—and the cost was, as I recall, barely ten dollars a week apiece.

My wife, who I had feared might oppose my going, had given less grudging consent to this scheme than to my earlier one of returning to America to live permanently. I had now plenty of work to do, having been fired by my recent reading of Henry Adams's *Education,* into a plan of writing my own life, from boyhood up to the end of the War, as a prose narrative of American education and later expatriation, disguised under fictitious names, and called *John Falconer's Fortune*—John Falconer being, of course, myself. O'Brien, too, shared with Cournos and myself our delight in the prospect of finally escaping from London, with its great and ridiculous Allied Victory March (which should have been called, rather, the Allied March of Humiliation) scheduled for July. He gleefully looked forward to living for the next month in so remote and unspoilt a region as the Aber valley then was.

So it happened that the month of July found us all safely esconced there, remote from London and enjoying to the utmost our rambles and walks about the country, excursions to Conway and Beaumaris, and minor adventures in a land already immortalized by Thomas Love Peacock and George Borrow. Early in August I removed to the near-by sea-bathing village resort of Penmaenmawr, where Daisy and the children came to live with me. O'Brien moved off to Oxford, to find a new home there where he could live with his mother, who was coming over from America that year. I had half finished the story of my own "education," and had gone from my boyhood up to the close of my college years and my first coming abroad. I had written forty thousand words of prose, and was in better mental and physical condition than I had been for the past three years.

And, miracle of miracles, there had now come to me, after all my struggles to make my poetry more stark and realistic for the past three years, a new series of short lyrics which proved, once for all, that the old symbolist leaven, the vividly pagan and pantheistic delight in nature which had marked *Irradiations* and the "symphonies," was still working strongly within me. This new set of lyrics, which came to me without premeditation and spontaneously, as I roved about the uplands and the valleys of that wild Welsh countryside, showed me not only that I had wandered less far from the path which I had marked as my own on the day I set the first "Irradiation" on paper, but also that I was still, despite the sobering effect of the War and the chastening effect of my marriage, primarily a romantic pagan, and a lyric and rhapsodic poet to boot. I called these new poems, provisionally, "Gateways," read them to O'Brien, who was enthusiastic, and dreamed again of becoming the kind of poet I had seemed to be, in my own eyes, at least, back in the spring of 1913.

These poems may still be read by anyone who cares to examine the first section of my book, *The Black Rock,* published in England and in this country, in 1928. In the meantime, I had now Edward O'Brien's warm invitation to come to Oxford and visit him there. As soon as the equinoctial gales, and the opening of the schools, had driven Daisy and myself and the two young people back to London on the twelfth of September, I availed myself gladly of his invitation. Hitherto I had entirely avoided Oxford, as I always avoided, during all the years I spent in England, that pilgrimage shrine of all American tourists, Stratford on Avon. I regarded the university city less as the idealistic "home of lost causes," in Matthew Arnold's famous phrase, than as the spot where John Ruskin had gone to pieces. Newman had retreated from the world into the chill asceticism of the cloister, and Matthew Arnold had himself become transformed from the young Hellenic idealist to the tight-lipped, dry-hearted embodiment of priggish correctitude. Frankly, I preferred to all these men the magnificent rebels, Shelley and Swinburne and William Morris—but they too had gone to Oxford! I decided, therefore, since O'Brien was so enthusiastic, to visit Oxford at last, and to see the place for myself.

Oxford achieved the effect of finally overwhelming me with the vitality of the medieval tradition. It recalled to mind, in its perfect harmoniousness of development and singleheartedness of purpose, Florence; but whereas Florence was only a remote survival of what had been, Oxford was still alive and flourishing. Despite the fact that its manufacturing suburb, Cowley, was already beginning to extend the hideousness of its bungalows about the motorworks put up by a successful British vulgarian, the city itself and its surroundings had as yet not openly succumbed to the bus traffic, Woolworth shopping, cinema palaces, and other kindred attractions of the mass-production epoch that soon succeeded my visit. Rather was Oxford still a lovely medieval shell, drained of its vitality during the War years, but now reviving for one last flare of hectic excitement before reverting to cultivated archaism.

It was filling up now with a strangely assorted, cosmopolitan group: men whose careers as students had been broken by the sternest of educations in the trenches, American Rhodes scholars planning vast projects, colonials rubbing shoulders with the sons of the British workingmen who had been successful at winning scholarships, and a considerable sprinkling of the picturesque descendants of Indian potentates, whom the farseeing British government, realizing the stern struggle in prospect over their hold on India, were now sending at their own expense through these half-deserted halls, in order to familiarize them with the mechanical magic of the West. Throughout this assemblage there were now running strange electric currents of revolt and reaction: neo-Catholicism was flourishing along with bolshevism. Oxford was turning itself into a dozen discussion clubs (since frowned on or suppressed by the authorities), where dangerous new ideas were mooted and intellectual currents ran high.

So great was its attraction that I wished I could take twelve years off my age, revert from a married to a single status, and resume here, under happier auspices, the formal education that I had abandoned long ago at Harvard. The system practiced here, as detailed to me by various Rhodes scholars, seemed infinitely superior to the mechanical course taking and credit accounting of the American universities. There the university was paramount, here the individual scholar. There the university existed only to cram the student with facts, here facts were less important than what the student did with them. There learning was divorced from experience, here an eminent don could assure me that it did not matter what the men acquired from their courses so much as what kind of other men they met. Although I had already learned to mistrust the snobbishness and organized hypocrisy of the public schools and the Established Church of

England, Oxford unquestionably seemed to me to make the most of the system and to give an unforgettable taste for fine living to those who went through the portals of its colleges.

In the midst of this motley society, seething now with all the new currents released by the War, Edward O'Brien was at home. He had established himself to the north of the city, near Headington, in a region, as I discovered, not far removed from Shotover Hill, which had still an old-fashioned, deserted stagecoach road running across its summit, and which also boasted of the authentic pond where Shelley once sailed his paper boats. I stayed there some two or three weeks, and spent an enchanted time rambling through the colleges, now decked in all their glory of Virginia creeper, or roving about the neighborhood with O'Brien himself. More poems resulted, and also new friendships: with Thomas Earp, friend of Aldous Huxley, and now an art critic of distinction, who just then was planning to bring out in London a magazine called *Coterie,* which duly printed several of my new poems of that year; with Robert Graves, who had finally taken refuge from the aftermath of the War in a remote rural cottage which he called the World's End at Islip; with several American Rhodes scholars. Imbued as I was with all the love of medieval unity and the mistrust of twentieth-century multiplicity that had disengaged itself from Henry Adams's ironic pages, hater as I was of the whole mechanical epoch of unlimited and at bottom purposeless "science," I felt that I could have been at home in Oxford, even more than O'Brien was.

Nevertheless, my literary career was making a progress that was barely one degree removed from absolute stagnation. I had given up my half-written attempt at a fictionized autobiography, and neither *Elements* nor the war poems were publishable in their entirety, as they stood. The only London magazines to which I possessed any chance of entering were Earp's *Coterie,* which did not pay, and possibly Middleton Murry's newly revived *Athenaeum.* I had recently taken out of *Elements* and the war poems those which seemed to me best worth publishing, had combined them in a single volume entitled *The Rock in the Storm,* and was offering them again around among English publishers. I finally obtained, early in 1920, an offer that an English firm would publish it if I could obtain an American publisher to market five hundred sheets. And there the matter rested. Meantime, in America,

Houghton Mifflin had already warned me that they were letting my two books go out of print, despite Miss Lowell's attempt to keep them alive for the students of her book on American poetry. Truly, my return to my own country was now overdue, to say the least.

On May 12, 1920, I departed from Southampton on the old White Star liner *Adriatic,* bound for New York. The ship was overcrowded, and as its engines were already in a bad state of repair, the voyage took eight days. Among all its passengers the only one who interested me was a young Englishman named Guy Eglinton, who had been a university student vacationing in Germany at the outbreak of the War, had not escaped in time, and had been interned with a thousand others at Ruhleben, just outside Berlin. There these prisoners, finding themselves free to do as they liked, with the world falling into chaos about them, promptly organized themselves into an informal university with courses in modern literature, music, drama, and the arts in general. Eglinton had come back to England after the Armistice, had obtained work at a London publishing house, and was now on his way to control the New York branch of this firm. He had never seen America, and was genuinely glad to find that I had not only been there, but that I was, by birth, an American. I had met other Ruhleben prisoners in London before meeting him, and I discovered in him the same kind of mentality—an enormous hyperaesthetic appetite for culture of all sorts, combined with an intense and shrinking horror of the world and of life in general. The effect of four years of Ruhleben life on its inmates had been not only to give them a singleminded devotion to all the arts which was only comparable to the devotion given to any organized religion, but to make them also feel that this devotion had nothing to do with life in the real world, which they all alike feared and detested. They were, therefore, after the Armistice, like medieval monks wandering over the world after the breakup of their monasteries, half in the world and half out of it. Or as one of them had already said to me, on the occasion of a concert we both attended in London, the world had always seemed to him so unreal that he half expected any day to be caught again, and shut up away from it. Such too was very largely Eglinton's attitude.

I made myself responsible for his safety as much as I might, ashore, during the month that I spent in New York, but was unable to see him as often as I wished, owing to the long office hours and hard work he was putting in at the reorganization of his firm. New York affected me almost as strangely as if I too had been an inmate of Ruhleben. I had come from a land and a city where everything still looked old, worn, and shabby, and where most of the inhabitants, including myself, had recently acquired the art of existing on starvation-point war rations, while momentarily expecting the last remnants of their civilization to disappear. In the year and a half that had elapsed since the Armistice, London had barely recovered. Her buildings still looked dingy, her people still wore old clothes, the throwing of millions out of employment after the Armistice had led to the first of her labor troubles, the railway strike of the winter of 1919, and other labor troubles were already now in the offing. An immense army of the unemployed were going to be paid the dole, to keep quiet. Meanwhile the War reparations, wrung from vanquished Germany, were flowing steadily as War debt into America's coffers. The Americans were now hated as viciously in London as they had been adulated during the last days of the War. Since the Senate had thrown out Wilson's peace treaty and since prohibition, America had become an outlaw nation, unfit for civilized society in English eyes. Between Europe and the American mind stood now a new Chinese wall of misunderstanding and prejudice as great and as unsurmountable in its way as the Chinese wall that was being feverishly erected between European civilization on the one hand and the new and untried experiment of Soviet Russia on the other.

New York, as I have said, affected me strangely. After a few days in an outrageously noisy hotel near the Pennsylvania Station I went to more commodious quarters in a quieter region, near Washington Square, where I remained a month. It was the longest stay that I had yet undertaken in the American metropolis; and it gave me the impression, never entirely lost, that life in New York was somehow unreal, a combination of Arabian Nights fantasy and of dime novel thriller. The city itself, and the country behind it, had been totally unaffected by the War, except that there were everywhere signs that prosperity was riding high, unprepared for such a collapse as only came ten years later. In the restaurants, the soda fountains, the quick-lunch places, everyone wore an air of being on the alert to grab his fortune tomorrow—millions were going to be spent and made, and everybody knew it. New cults, Freudian psychoanalysis, fake oriental seers and mystics, Greenwich Village orgies, were already springing up in the wake of the War. A world had collapsed overnight; America had inherited the glittering fragments and was avidly playing with them. The stage was being set for the greatest boom in her history, when everything would be valued only for its power to bring in quick and immediate returns. Wilson, sinking in nerveless collapse, was going, and Harding was coming in.

In the meantime, prohibition was already having its effect of increasing the violence of the American temperament. New York, as one of its inhabitants assured me, was becoming a "stick-up" town. Gangsters appeared in open daylight on Forty-second and Broadway. The saloons and drinking places of old had been replaced by noisy soda fountains and by jazz bands which invaded every restaurant and made night more hideous with intoxicating monotony of din. The cases of drunkenness that were to be openly seen on the streets seemed far more raucous and violent than anything I had known in London. The scramble for profit and pleasure, led by a generation only one step removed from the shadow of death, which had attacked London immediately after the Armistice, and which was already creating there a reign of sexual license unparalleled since the Restoration of 1660, was sweeping New York too, despite the revived reaction of the backwoods in favor of such things as Protestant fundamentalism and the Ku Klux Klan. To live in New York was a dizzy but, alas, a costly adventure.

During the month that I was there I besieged publishers with my poems, on my own account, only to discover that war poetry and war literature generally were no longer in demand. The revival of interest marked by such prose works as *All Quiet on the Western Front* was to come only ten years later. I had, however, unexpected success in persuading The Macmillan Company to bring out a volume containing all the American poems I had written during the earlier years of 1914–16, together with a few others I had managed to write that summer. This book I provisionally called *Breakers and Granite,* and its publication was set for early in 1921.

This done, I departed for Boston, where my younger sister, with her soldier husband and her year-old son, was now living. I was not slow in again looking up Miss Lowell. Although I had already gone publicly on record as being critical of her "externality" in my chap-book, brought out in London that May, yet the fact that I had first publicly won my spurs as her foremost defender in the years 1915 and 1916 still gave to her personality and surroundings the charm of a vivid memory. I was now to see, for the last time, the house where she lived and worked; but I was not to see the old Miss Lowell, whose work had been so long associated with my own. She had by now be-come a great public institution: Doctor of Letters of Baylor University in Texas (she traveled all the way to Waco in the extremely hot June of my arrival for the degree), the Phi Beta Kappa poet at Columbia, and the guide, mentor, and friend of all the young hopefuls at Harvard. Also she had become a sick woman, existing from operation to opera-tion, and straining alike her brain and her eyesight in her search for wider and wider historical perspectives on which to exercise her bril-liant and panoramic and, at bottom, fatalistically decorative art.

The garden at Sevenels looked lovelier than ever, with its smoke tree in full bloom and covered with large silver drops of rain on the hot afternoon of my arrival. Ada Russell was, as ever, tactful and kind, and took me out for a long walk around the neighborhood, showing me other gardens, each representing a fortune in time and in labor—gardens of millionaire families, built up during the seven-ties—shimmering under the intense July sun. They came from the period when New England, victorious industrially over the old South and the adventurous Middle West alike, had begun to expend its in-tellectual capital on the cosmopolitan luxury of country mansions, elaborate gardens, and art collections, the epoch to which Henry James had already written the epitaph in his *Ivory Tower.* The other Henry, Henry Adams, had already shown me how this epoch had been, in his eyes, only the "degradation of the democratic dogma" into its primary terms of unlimited greed and unchecked industrial exploitation. These gardens and fine estates were its chief fruits, along with the industrial squalor, the labor unrest, the overwork of the foreign-born proletariat from which their incomes sprang.

I decided now that, of the two ladies who alike inhabited Sevenels, Mrs. Russell was the more appreciative and the more sensitive. I was delighted to hear from her lips how, as the daughter of a pioneer English bookseller, she had spent her early life in remote Utah among the Mormons, and how on an early trip to the East with her father the train had been halted for hours while a great herd of buffalo walked across the railroad track. She brought back to mind the distant pattern of an earlier, more heroic, more generous, more charitable, more vividly picturesque America than now existed. Amy was at best only the final and cosmopolitan stage of that kind of existence, making enormous publicity out of her attempt to restate it in the most vivid terms for posterity.

The new poetry had become to her, through the circumstances which had made it impossible for her to marry and bear children, a substitute for living. It was now, practically speaking, a religion for itself, though she still scoffed at my attempts to equate art and the religious impulse. But it was a religion which required the continuance of the capitalistic system, in all its predatory nakedness, to sustain itself. During the last summer I visited her the emissaries of the I.W.W. were busily fomenting strikes in the two mill towns named after her family—strikes which led directly to the notorious Sacco-Vanzetti case. She expressed publicly to me her utmost fear and abhorrence of all labor agitators, and even spoke, as I remember, of hiring guards to protect her home. I had not suspected her previously of being so lacking in personal courage.

I stayed for three or four days in all at Miss Lowell's, while my sister prepared to move her household goods down to a more commodious home just outside Newport, Rhode Island, which she had rented for the summer. My stay was, therefore, barely long enough to study the new Amy Lowell in all her moods, and to arrive at the sane conclusion that whatever I had missed by failing to make of myself a public figure on her lines, what she had missed by making herself into one was in reality far greater. Our new relationship was now symbolized by this outstanding fact: that though I still listened to her reading of her poems to me as of old, I offered no poems of mine in return. I made no secret, however, of the fact that I regarded myself, compared with her enormous success, to be a failure. On the last night of my stay she read to me, in a voice full of feeling, a poem which she had just composed:

"I moved to the sound of gold and brass and heavily-clashed silver.
From the towers, the watchers see the flags of my coming:
Tall magenta flags
Stinging against a pattern of light blue.
Trumpets and tubas
Exult for me before the walls of cities;
And I pass the gates entangled in a dance of lifted tambourines.

"But you—you come only as a harebell comes.
One day there is nothing; and the next, your steepled bells are all.
The rest is background.
You are neither blue, nor violet, nor red,
But all these colors blent and faded to a charming weariness of tone;
I glare; you blossom.
Yes, alas, and when they have clanged me to my grave,
Wrapped gaudily in pale-blue and magenta,
When muted bugles and slacked drums
Have brayed a last quietus;
What then, my friend?

"Why, someone coming from the funeral
Will see you nodding underneath a hedge,
(Picking or not is nothing).
Will that person remember bones and shouting do you think?
I fancy he will listen to the music
Shaken so lightly from your whispering bells;
And think how very excellent a thing
A flower growing in a hedge most surely is.
And so, a fig for rotting carcasses!

"Waiter, bring me a bottle of Lachrima Christi,
And mind you don't break the seal;
Your health, my highly unsuccessful confrere,
Rocking your seed-bells while I drift to ashes.
The future is the future, therefore—
Damn you!"

CHAPTER XXI

At the end of August I departed from America again. During the three months of my stay I had already achieved for myself the object of getting my American poems published, and had also, during the last weeks in New York, disposed of my book on Paul Gauguin to another New York publisher. I had not succeeded in getting the two books which Houghton Mifflin had brought out, and which they had decided to let go out of print, transferred to another publisher; but I had persuaded Macmillan, who was bringing out *Breakers and Granite,* to import copies from England of *The Tree of Life.* As for the poems of the War years, I now definitely abandoned them as unsalable. I was the more pleased with this result, since it had been achieved entirely on my own account, without direct help from Miss Lowell, and in the face of handicaps, both economic and physical. The summer climate of New York, working on a constitution weakened by the nervous strain and privation of the later War years, had affected me so much that my digestive system had practically collapsed; and during the entire time I was on Manhattan Island I was in constant dread of an appendicitis operation. The month of August, spent at Newport in the company of my sisters and their families, had restored me somewhat, but I eventually departed from America in almost as poor a state of body and nerves as I had come.

I had, however, made new contacts, and had acquired new and valuable friends. One of the most valuable had been the St. Louis poet, Sara Teasdale Filsinger, about whom Miss Lowell had spoken before I left America in 1916, and whose husband had gone to the trouble of looking me up in London during the spring following the Armistice. I had been overwhelmed by the news he then brought me, that the writing of a single poem, my "Lincoln," had made me one of the most discussed poets of the day, after my departure, someone to be mentioned in the same breath with Vachel Lindsay and Amy Lowell. Since "Lincoln" had been a poem written to fit a special occasion—the occasion being America's entry in the War, which this poem anticipated by a full year—I did not suppose my work would continue to have the popularity this particular work had given it. Nevertheless I was glad to learn through Sara Teasdale's husband that my poetry, in one respect, at least, was now rousing popular acclaim. In New York I had come to know Mrs. Filsinger also and to value her as a friend.

In her I found a refreshing contrast to the enormously busy, enormously successful, dynamic, and dominating personality of Miss Lowell. Markedly fragile in appearance and shrinking from contact with humanity, she recalled H. D. in most respects, except that she had never acquired the cultivated archaism which was so marked a feature of H. D.'s talent, and which sometimes had seemed to me, in H. D.'s presence, almost an affectation. Sara Teasdale had refined her lyricism to a simplicity of statement that was very moving and very human, and that seemed to me—although it was obviously rooted in sentimental nostalgia—far removed from the elaborate and sophisticated self-exploitation that was now being practiced by such a figure as Edna St. Vincent Millay. I admired her art, equally compounded of the quietism of Christina Rossetti and the emotional intensity of Emily Dickinson, though she herself declared that she did not value it, finding, she said, her lyricism one-sided, and her own personality somewhat tiresome. Personally, I did not agree with her, for it seemed to me that her work, though limited, was singularly and scrupulously perfect. And in a world where very few American poets had this quality of craftmanship (though Elinor Wylie was to display it later), it seemed to me that Sara Teasdale deserved a niche of her own. She was two years older than I, and therefore belonged less to the modern, ultrasophisticated, post-War generation of American poets than to the older, simpler, less obviously clever, more gropingly sincere kind. As such I found her company stimulating in a quiet way, whether it was in her telling how she had grown up in St. Louis as a near neighbor to T. S. Eliot, or in anecdotes about Vachel Lindsay and his background, with which she abounded. She had warmly recommended me to try Macmillan as a publisher, and to keep on trying—advice that I concluded to take, with results as already set forth.

I had long lost any prejudice I may have felt against Lindsay's poetry. Ever since the appearance of "The Congo" and "The Chinese Nightingale" I had realized that this poet deserved the acclaim which American audiences were giving him. He had achieved a fusion of popular American subject matter and vivid rhythmic and dramatic presentation which made him the chief folk artist among the American poets. It seemed to me that he had largely fulfilled the task only half accomplished by such earlier American folk singers as James Whitcomb Riley, Irwin Russell, and Paul Laurence Dunbar. He had given to the world poetry that was sentimental and yet not false, popular and yet not cheap, democratic and yet full of heightened imagination. Through Sara Teasdale I heard that he was expected to visit London that year, and when I returned, early in September, I found that he had already arrived. His coming was well heralded. The critics of the London press had already been busy, and the foremost of the academic pontiffs, J. C. Squire, had led off his *London Mercury* of that month with the "Bryan" poem in its entirety, and had followed this up with critical remarks to the effect that Vachel Lindsay was the only American poet who mattered, inasmuch as he was the only one whose attitude and subject matter were totally and exclusively American.

I met Lindsay immediately after my return to England, and some days before his big public reading—the most elaborate public reading I have ever seen accorded to an American poet in England—at Central Hall, Westminster. What astonished me about him was his extraordinary juvenility of mind. If his poems were naïve and childlike, the cause, I soon saw, lay in Lindsay himself. He seemed to feel that they represented only one minor phase of his talent, and that his destiny had been rather to be a painter. On an afternoon visit to my home he declared that he had spent the entire morning looking at Turner's "Ulysses Deriding Polyphemus" in the Tate Gallery. To be able to paint like that was his chief ambition. He had recently, in anticipation of his arrival, sent me a copy of his *Village Magazine,* and I was enabled, by looking at its pages, to judge how far he actually could carry his pretension to be a visual artist, as well as a poet, into effect. I concluded that these naïve and at bottom monotonously similar line drawings of balloons and spiderwebs gave not only clear evidences of complete misuse of talent: they were not even a beginning towards acquiring one. Lindsay was then, as I had been at twenty-six, a talent turned back on itself, arrested, inhibited from finding ultimate expression. He had escaped, not by facing his own obstacles and overcoming them, but by becoming a mixture of backwoods evangelist and playboy; a picturesque figure certainly, but not, as Squire had said, the sole American poet, unless America was to be forever synonymous with immaturity. And Lindsay was emotionally immature still at forty.

The secret of his arrested development lay less, however, in himself than in the gaunt figure with withered face, white hair, and spectacles who stood at his side and accompanied him everywhere around London—his mother, now past seventy years of age. Her existence, I realized, revealed the secret of why Lindsay had never come to terms with himself nor with the world about him, but had escaped into a child's fairy tale world of circus calliopes, golden whales, Chinese nightingales, voodoo magic, and other bright-colored but largely unreal toys. The type was familiar: the pioneer schoolteacher, who satisfies her secret and shamefaced craving for beauty vicariously through another's destiny, while forbidding beauty to express itself outwardly in the desires and appetites of the body as well as in the inward imagination. In short, Mrs. Lindsay was the eternal and unquenchable Puritan, hating the cavalier side of the South, hating all those who, like myself, did not believe prohibition to be the greatest reform of the ages.

Listening to her as she spoke to me in my home in London, I could not help feeling that if Lindsay had been able to escape from her influence, to give himself to life bodily as well as mentally, to achieve happiness through the normal way of marriage, his mental development would not have been so pitifully onesided as to leave him, in middle age, still pathetically dreaming of how his life might have shaped itself had he become, not a poet, but a painter.

How truly Lindsay was his mother's victim only appeared twelve years after this, in the tragedy of his end. From the moment I discovered the complete hold his mother had on him I began to realize that, though he had, and could maintain, his eminent position as a popular entertainer, he could not possibly attain to final greatness as a poet because of this handicap unwittingly laid on his life by his mother's influence.

Nevertheless, here he was in London, having momentarily and successfully turned the tables on all the English lecturers—many of them obviously second-rate—who were now swarming through America. I was interested to know what my American friends would make of him. H. D. gave no opinion, being already on her way to America. Cournos, to my surprise, rather naïvely enjoyed him, as a modern version of the old troubadours. But the most illuminating comments came from T. S. Eliot and Ezra Pound. Pound, who was present at the public reading at Central Hall (I did not see him privately now, and had never done so since our break in 1916), declared before the large audience there assembled that Lindsay's poems were in reality libretti, needing the charm of Lindsay's personality and the special quality of his voice to be transmuted into art. Eliot, who had just met him, curtly replied to my eager questions with, "I am appalled at Lindsay." Neither of these verdicts seemed to me entirely correct; but of the two, I preferred Pound's.

I had returned to England, despite the definite feeling in my bones that my place as a writer lay less in England than in America, but in the full knowledge that my wife would oppose any permanent removal for herself and the children to the country for whose literature I was now putting forth my best efforts. I decided therefore to wait and to exert my best efforts to modify her position. In the next year my *Breakers and Granite* and my Gauguin book were going to be published in America, and I anticipated, not only an artistic, but a commercial success from them. Unfortunately, the success, in the latter respect at least, did not altogether meet with my expectations. The Gauguin book, printed from the manuscript I had written back in 1918, was, I knew, barely more than an introduction to its subject. I had hoped to revise it, but the poor state of my health forbade; and the fact that its American publisher, whom I had inadvertently trusted, went into bankruptcy the following year prevented me from collecting a penny from him beyond his first meager advance. *Breakers and Granite,* suffering from bad proofreading during the course of my illness, was not advertised widely by its publishers, and sold but slowly.

Nineteen-twenty now merged itself into 1921. Seven years had gone by since I had scored my first successes, and if my physical constitution had been changed by the renewal of the tissues of my body, still more had my mental outlook and my intellectual status. I was now an independent poet and critic in my own right, known to a few in England, and had recently made a fresh attempt to recommend myself to the attention of the many in America. I continued to live in England, having now firmly decided not, under any circumstances, to return to America unless I could obtain my wife's consent to accompany me. I realized, indeed, that my financial condition being what it was, it was easier to live now in England than in America. The circle of my acquaintances there was slowly widening, thanks to my contacts with Oxford and to a long-delayed friendship that was now slowly springing up between Harold Monro and myself.

Now I could, had I but chosen to make the effort, have achieved for myself a small but perhaps increasing reputation in London. But the fact that I had not succeeded in doing so during my early years, added to the fact that my interests were still almost entirely American, made me doubt whether the goal were really worth the effort. I would have preferred to make the effort in America, where a new hard-boiled generation, just emerging from the War, were busily engaged in capturing the center of the literary arena, aided by a flock of new and adventurous publishing houses. I knew that in London I would either have to accept British standards or stand aloof. Any since acceptance of British standards was, in my case, largely incompatible with the kind of literary functioning I had been most apt at achieving, my life became very largely a matter of detached and resigned contemplation.

Lindsay had come and gone from London, leaving behind nothing more important than the momentary gasp of astonishment that has followed the career of dozens of other popular entertainers there. Pound was about to quit London for Paris, declaiming bitterly at the last that England was only a corpse, kept alive by maggots. Eliot was still struggling at Lloyd's Bank. His health had seemed on the point of giving way; attempts were being made to provide him with a small fund. Though he had published in 1920 *The Sacred Wood* to the sound of general critical acclamation, his poetry still was known only to a small minority. Cournos was away at Oxford, helping O'Brien with his short-story books. H. D. was retiring, driven by ill health and unhappiness into obscurity. Looking around the English literary scene, now that Shaw, Wells, Galsworthy, and Conrad were becoming old men, and Thomas Hardy had celebrated his eightieth birthday, one had the impression of living in a land of pygmies. A generation had dropped out, during the War, and there were none left to take its place. As for the War itself, that was a dead issue, and the War poets were becoming forgotten in their turn. The present day being obviously barren, there seemed little for England to do but to foster obvious revivals of the past. Accordingly, late Elizabethan drama, Restoration comedy, and finally Victorianism itself were solemnly taken out of the vaults of the past, dusted off, and again displayed to the public. And the young heroes of that day became either uprooted and disillusioned cynics, on the lines of Aldous Huxley, or adepts in striking unusual attitudes, like the three Sitwells. London was, as Pound had said, effectually dead. One need only look across the Atlantic to find that America, by comparison, was becoming crowded with major figures.

I had decided, whether rightly or wrongly, not to return to America unless accompanied by Daisy; but I soon realized that neither she nor I was in good enough condition to make the trip, though I urged it on her with all the powers at my disposal. My own physical condition slowly improved; Daisy's did not. Her physical troubles, I soon discovered, came from the fact that she was now undergoing the change of life, a circumstance which made me reflect more and more bitterly on our disproportion of ages. Up to that time I had never attempted to find out just how much older than I she really was. She had declared that she did not recall the year of her birth, and I had accepted her statement. I had stated the difference, on the police documents and passports of the War years, to be seven years—that being my own guess—but I now discovered that it was nearer twelve. It was useless, I knew, to reproach her for being what she was. I had taken her for better or for worse; but I only felt all the more that so much ill luck and disappointment had already accompanied our marriage that the only chance of our happiness and harmony in the future lay in her acquiescence to my plan of promptly returning to my own country.

Unfortunately, Daisy's own character seemed to be now changing under the stress of her physical condition. She had been normally bright and cheerful, a practical housekeeper, devoted to her home and children, a good hostess to my friends, with an interest in the arts which, though not deep, was nevertheless genuine. She now became listless, brooding, moody, and querulous, difficult to arouse from a state of melancholy apathy. Fired by my renewed success in America, I had returned to urge on her an immediate migration; but she felt, and no doubt the feeling was normal under her present physical state, that in my asking her to abandon all of her old life, and to adapt herself to a new set of circumstances, I was accomplishing an act of final betrayal. The winter of 1920–21 was one of the most difficult I had ever lived through. I realized now how hard it was going to be for me to adjust myself henceforward to a marriage that must not only remain childless but must imply also an exile from America that might very likely remain permanent, unless I could induce my wife in some way to feel a renewed interest in living.

Early in the spring of 1921, around Easter, I succeeded in inducing her to leave the house and the young people in it to the charge of her sister, while the two of us went away for a fortnight's holiday in the Channel Islands. I would have gone further, to the South of France, but—though living conditions had cheapened since the War—I did not feel I could afford so long a trip. The change of scene and air seemed genuinely to benefit Daisy. She began to pick up and appear her normal self again, while I, for my part, did not press her to come with me to America. We decided to return to Jersey with the youngsters that summer.

On the way back, as the Channel steamer took us along through a sparkling spring day, the thought came to me that I had written next to nothing for some time—since leaving America, in fact—and that I might very well spend the next summer in writing a long poem. It had seemed to me for some time past that the real test of a poet's ability, both as artist in words and as spokesman for humanity, lay in his power to achieve a long poem of heroic or epic cast. None of the imagists had faced this test, with the sole exception of Miss Lowell, and her long panoramic poems did not seem to me to spring from any profoundly held philosophy. During my visit to America in the previous summer I had thought of taking the American Civil War as the possible subject for such a poem. I had again begun to read and ponder on the subject, but had been finally dissuaded by a conversation with Edwin Arlington Robinson, during which he pointed out, with logic which had seemed largely inescapable, that the issues which led to and precipitated that conflict had been so confused on both sides that it was next to impossible for a poet to find a logical structure that would contain and do justice to them all.

Now it seemed to me that it might yet be possible to salvage the essence of my projected Civil War poem, by transposing it out of the dimension of historic fact into the dimension of myth and fable. After all, the American Civil War had been a conflict between two opposing views, two diametrically opposite ways of living: the agrarian, feudal way of the South, and the industrial, mercantile way of the North. Did not this dualism, this divided aim in living, which had led to my country's greatest crisis, interpose itself in all human affairs? Was I not already being forced to adjust myself to just such a division in aim between the way of living practiced in England and that I had grown accustomed to in America? It seemed to me that I was. And could not such a dualism be transferred from the temporary to the universal, could it not even be upheld as the general law of the universe? It seemed to me, as the boat took me back from the Channel Islands to Southampton, that it not only could, but that in the restatement of such a dualism lay the essential theme of my projected long poem.

The house at Sydenham, which I had now decided to have repapered and refurnished—using for this purpose the money I had carefully husbanded since my American trip, in the prospect of a possible migration to America—was still in the hands of the workmen when I returned. I employed the last weeks in April in a walking excursion with Edward O'Brien through the Cotswold country, while it was being made ready. I now detailed to him my plan. I would write a long poem, dealing with the events narrated in the Bible; both Old and New Testaments would be included. It would be modeled upon William Blake's Prophetic Books, which I had studied carefully ever since the last year of the War, and also upon Milton's *Paradise Lost,* which I now concluded, despite the dislike for it expressed by Amy Lowell, Ezra Pound, and all the other imagists, to be a masterpeice. I would, however, use another style, and other supernatural machinery, than Milton's. The characters in my poem would be, first of all, man, represented by Adam, and then by his descendants; Jehovah, as creator; and Lucifer. Jehovah would be the power that creates, and strives to do good. He would be symbolized by inactive darkness, the creative darkness which brooded on the abyss at the beginning of things, the darkness in which the seeds of life take life in the womb of the earth, the darkness that eternally encompasses the light of day-born human knowledge. Lucifer, on the other hand, would be the active light-bringer, the willful, resolute, skeptical, ironic ruler of time and of history. He would be eternally thwarting, and yet unwittingly accomplishing, Jehovah's vast and formless plans. Thus man would be inevitably swayed by a dualism, alternately accepting Jehovah's and Lucifer's point of view.

The whole poem would take me, I thought, about three or four years to accomplish. And it would be in all its parts a detailed exposition of Blake's epigram, "Good is the passive that obeys reason. Evil is the active springing from energy." It would do, without the abuse of symbolism, what Blake had attempted in his Prophetic Books to do: to state the tragedy of man struggling through time to reach God, by alternate paths of inactive acceptance and of open rebellion. And its conclusion would be the Crucifixion, by which man, passively accepting death, became Jehovah on the Cross, while the entire earth was thereby Lucifer's, to work his will. Thus I would fulfill my poetic destiny and restate the creed which I had already set forth in my letter to Linscott of 1919.

This was the plan I now laid before Edward O'Brien on our walking excursion through the Cotswolds. He was enthusiastic about it, and urged me to do it. As a matter of fact, I had already begun on my writing. Groups of lines, from ten to twenty, all cast in the same semidactylic meter shifting from five to seven beats, that William Blake had first discovered and had employed in his "Vala," were forming themselves in my mind. These lines came, as much in the "symphonies" had come, spontaneously to me, whenever I reflected on any of the numberless host of characters that would people my poem. Thus my notebooks were rapidly crammed with long passages which related to Adam and Eve, to Cain and Noah, to Abraham and Jacob, to Moses, David, Solomon, Job, and Christ. All this before I had organized my poem into various sections. I now understood why Blake, who I realized must be my model here even more than Milton, had failed to achieve a coherent narrative out of any of his Prophetic Books, and also why he had claimed to write solely "according to the Spirit's dictate."

I let myself run on thus for a month or so, filling my notebook with disconnected passages, till about the middle of July, when the time came to move with my family to our holiday in Jersey, where we expected to remain till the middle of September. Then, slowly, out of all this welter of material, the first four books began to take shape. The first would deal with the creation of earth and of man. The second, with man's conquest of the earth, through the discovery of fire, symbolized in the story of Cain and Abel. The third, with the achievement of a city civilization, as opposed to a rural culture, and as expressed in the story of Cain's descendants. And the last would contain the story of Noah and the flood. These four books would serve as a beginning, as the four *Cantos* which Ezra Pound published that year were a beginning to his own long poem. I could publish them separately, as an introduction to and earnest of whatever might follow.

We—my wife and I and the young people—left London, as I have said, about the middle of July, and took train to Southampton. After a changeable and treacherous spring, a strange drought had descended on England. It had not rained since May, and the green fields already looked parched and brown, under the unvarying blue sky; even the trees and hedgerows were already scorched and withered. Nor did it rain in Jersey, while we were there, except towards the close of our stay. This long unbroken stretch of dry weather, leading to much agitation concerning a water shortage, was so strange, so uncommon, and at bottom so un-English, that it gave to my poem—on which I now worked steadily for two months, writing every day—a quality of nervous tension and of increasing excitation that was rather American than English. When I returned the first four books were already drafted. I realized that they were violent and rebellious, yet it seemed to me that this, as it stood, was the most ambitious work I had yet undertaken. I had fused together the vivid orchestral presentation of my "symphonies" with my later speculations on humanity, on life and on its destiny, on the struggle between the primitive and the cultivated, on God and man.

Already, by the time of my return, the horizon of the European situation, in which England was still inextricably involved, had darkened appreciably. The "Bolshevik menace," which the Allies had been unable to crush even by promoting civil war, had, for the moment, spent itself; the Red armies no longer threatened Warsaw, and Lenin had modified extremism and was moving towards his new economic policy. But nearer at hand were the seeds of future wars. Under the influence of the now thoroughly chauvinistic government, the French were threatening to occupy the Ruhr—and did occupy it in defiance of their Allies, in the first months of 1923. The coalition government of Lloyd George and Bonar Law could find no reply, as they had found none to the unemployed, and to the situation at home. They were now slowly crumbling in consequence, under the attacks of labor. Liberalism was passing from the English stage, as it had already passed in France, as it was about to pass in Italy. There Communists and Fascists were flaring up into open civil war. Mussolini had organized his party, and was to embark next year on his dramatic march on Rome. In Germany the weaponless, hopeless government was about to make Germany's fulfillment of the Treaty of Versailles forever impossible by passing through national bankruptcy. Truly, one hundred years after Napoleon's death, Europe was about to enter the first act of a tragedy which was infinitely greater and more poignant than the disaster which had come to it because of Napoleon. It seemed as if only some great and messianic religion, as great in its way as primitive Christianity, could free mankind.

At this juncture I heard again from O'Brien that he was leaving his home in Oxford, and also leaving his mother and Cournos behind in it. He was about to embark alone for the Continent, on an attempt to achieve what he had spoken of as his "mission" during our meeting in the spring. I had been inclined, for once, to take him seriously. The idea was staggeringly simple: to promote, not only in the Catholic Church alone, but throughout the entire Christian world, a revival—

but this time among laymen—of the spirit that had animated the early Franciscan brotherhood. O'Brien himself was to be the founder of these new Franciscans, living according to the dictates of poverty, chastity, and obedience, in the world and yet not of it, the new "holy fools," the landless and propertyless world scorners of Europe as the Treaty of Versailles had it. They would oppose bolshevism and capitalism alike with a new devotion to the Christ image, which O'Brien claimed to have seen in a vision as a child, and had recently seen again. Thousands and then millions of recruits would join them, as soon as the idea was broached; great miracles would take place, and the world would be reconverted to the faith of medieval Christianity. Now I heard from O'Brien himself that the time had come when the new creed which would remake the world would shortly be proclaimed in the market place at Florence at the spot of Savonarola's martyrdom, to mark the end of the Renaissance which had killed Savonarola, and the rebirth of the Middle Ages. He was already on his way to Paris and Italy to fulfill his destiny. He would write to me and to Cournos, his two best friends in England, as to the course of the project. He added, as conclusion to his letter, that if he failed, he hoped I would be the first to turn against him, as Judas had turned against Christ.

All this sounded sufficiently wild and even insane, but perhaps in a world where the European nations had long since gone mad only some such major insanity could save the world. Rationalistic science itself, after triumphing in every department of life from the sixteenth to the opening years of the twentieth century, had finally failed to bring about the great dream of the eighteenth century, the era in which man lived in harmony with nature, and in harmony with his own fellow men. Instead, an age of unchecked laissez-faire competition had come to a close in 1914, in the senseless slaughter of the European War, which had proven, once and for all, that man was not a rational animal, and was not governed by rational considerations. Had Christianity itself not been so unworldly throughout the Middle Ages as to believe in miracles, Europe would never have achieved any lasting culture at all. Even the Renaissance had only existed thanks to the stored-up energy of the Middle Ages, from which it turned into the barren bypaths of mechanical science. Now the Renaissance itself stood condemned, not only for the slaughter of the War, but for the shame and horror of the peace. Russia had escaped, had restored an unworldly faith, a faith no longer Christian, but combining the extremes of unworldly asceticism, and messianic belief, and fatalistic, militant, Mohammedanlike obedience to the state. Europe had no reply to Russia, unless she too could restore the faith of the Middle Ages. And if Europe was doomed, America, too, must fall.

So I half thought, as letters, exhortations, rhetorical prose poems entitled "Hard Sayings," came in a steady stream from O'Brien, first from Paris, then from Florence. Here was I, planning to conclude my long and unfinished poem with the Crucifixion of man, while my friend was already embarked on a project which touched not only literature but life itself, and which would conclude not with the Crucifixion, but with the Resurrection. I wished to heaven I could have gone with him, could have taken part in his "mission." Unfortunately, I could not do so. Although I had not once set foot on the Continent since the Armistice, although I had only once revisited America, staying in England for the sake of economy, my financial resources were far too meager for me to indulge in any evangelicism such as O'Brien was now attempting to promote. My stepson, now sixteen, was going to college that fall; my stepdaughter, now eighteen, was still at an art school, and showing strong signs of falling in love with a fellow student as penniless as herself. These, and my wife, had the first claim; therefore, as I wrote O'Brien, I must forgo participation in his project till it matured further. Then I might perhaps come in. Had he not promised me by all his gods that it would succeed, and had he not declared furthermore that I might be his Judas if it failed? I would stay where I was, and wait events.

Meantime, by every mail, further "Hard Sayings" kept pouring in from him—prose poems couched in violent Rimbaudlike rhetoric, exhorting mankind to seek a new vision of Christ. Very well; I would see what I could do in this vein. I laid aside my unfinished long poem and embarked on a series of short prose poems. These I decided to call *Parables.*

CHAPTER XXII

Parables, with additions dating from 1923, was published finally in 1925. *Branches of Adam,* the first four books, revised and shortened, of my yet unfinished long poem, appeared a year later. Both of these publications were confined to England, and though they brought about a certain amount of discussion among the reviewers there, I did not succeed in obtaining an American publisher for them. Since both are still largely unknown in the country of my birth, and both are integral to my development as a poet, I shall have to discuss them here together.

As I have already indicated, the problem of my own personal salvation, not only as poet but as man, had affected me powerfully from the very onset of my literary career. I was not one of those who found it easy to come to terms with the world, or with humanity. On the contrary, I felt that it was my destiny to scorn the world as it was, as all the important writers of the nineteenth century had scorned the world, in order that mankind might, through my example, make the world they lived in better. I had felt, as far back as 1913, that mankind was destined, not for happiness, but for perfection. And perfection was only to be achieved either through a life of physical hardship, remote obscurity, and adventurous daring such as had come to Arthur Rimbaud, or in such an abandonment of all possessions and all family ties as had been the choice of the later Tolstoy. Temporarily, I had resolved this, the first of my moral dilemmas, by accepting the religion of art in its most extreme form, and by believing that beauty, unaided, could save the world. Under the influence of this creed I had written *Irradiations* and the "symphonies," *Japanese Prints* and *The Tree of Life*. I had thereby not only achieved a literary reputation in America for myself, but had been the means of giving other poets—such as Miss Lowell and Conrad Aiken—an impetus which carried them into other fields.

The War had come, and the horror of its continuance, as well as the more than doubtfulness of its result, had made my creed of beauty henceforward untenable. My ideas now took another tack. I knew that from now on a life of adventurous physical activity would be impossible; I was no longer young enough to undertake it. A life of ascetic rejection of all property and family ties was equally impossible, so long as I had a wife and two young people dependent on me for their support. I had already won my spurs as a writer, and a writer I must remain to the end. But my first aesthetic phase, in which I expressed my gospel of salvation through nature and through personal and private feeling for nature, was now at an end. Since the coming of the War what had increasingly mattered was not nature, but humanity. As I had written Miss Lowell in 1917: "Since 1916, I have wanted with all my heart to do nothing but write about humanity—not about landscapes. But I still find I cannot say all that I have to say about life. As you say, the War has certainly brought this about in me—it has produced a tremendous clash between my imagination and the reality—and the results of that clash will change me, have already changed me tremendously. But not enough—I feel that I am still groping my way along a very dark corridor, and that the light when it does come, will glimmer upon me bit by bit."

I had begun my new attempt to deal with man and with human life, in 1916–18, by writing the two abortive books of *Elements* and of the war poems. From these I had finally turned aside, in the exultation and relief of the peace year, 1919, to the group of poems entitled "Gateways," now standing at the forefront of my book, *The Black Rock*, published in 1928. These had been largely a return, in a more heightened and religious mood, to the personal-feeling phase of my *Tree of Life*, or of my "symphonies." They had led me inevitably to the point of view expressed in *Parables* and *Branches of Adam*. What that point of view was, I must now make clear.

It had occurred to me that what was, after all, interesting about humanity was less the accidents of any individual life than the tendencies inherent in humanity as a whole. Shortly after America's entry into the War I had written Miss Lowell that "the individual counts for nothing, except as the mouthpiece or interpreter of the elemental forces of his own kind—the great simple values of life, love, death, faith, courage, endurance, suffering and the rest." She had protested that to her the individual was still paramount, that if the individual had to subordinate himself for the sake of the War, that subordination was only temporary, and was akin to combating an attack of illness. Then she had continued: "These things are likely to occur in the lives of individuals and of races, and that any philosophic system or religion for the guidance of life can be formed without taking such events into consideration, is inconceivable to me. . . . The great principles you mention—life, love, death, faith, courage, endurance, suffering—have always been the proper subjects for poetry, but I have always felt that they should be represented through images and dramas, rather than definitely spoken about. I thought we called the latter 'cosmic poetry' and all of us preferred to eschew it."

To this criticism of my new position I had replied: "To me it still seems that the individual is, after all, only the product of certain great race-tendencies that now and then surge up irresistibly or subside." And such, whether cosmic or not, remained my position at the close of the War. I still wished to write about humanity, about individuals. But the individuals I wished to write about were to be used, as the landscapes of my earlier poetry had been used, to symbolize certain eternal tendencies in man. Thereby I thought of making my art, as William Blake had said, "an allegory addressed to the intellectual understanding."

The chief tendency of humanity, throughout human history, had been, it appeared to me, man's continued and ever-renewed search for God. As St. Augustine had said, "We are lonely and dissatisfied, and our hearts are ever restless till they rest in Thee." Even Nietzsche, the severest critic of this tendency I knew, had only discovered that "God was dead" in order, immediately afterward, to proclaim a new

God, in the shape of the superman. Man's desire to become God, to fathom the secrets of the divine nature, had taken many forms, but the most dramatic, the most intensely vivid, the one which had changed the entire course of European history, was the form expressed by the figure of Jesus Christ. Although I was not officially a Christian, had never been one since the outbreak of the War and the abandonment of the spirit of Christianity by the churches, it still seemed to me, as it seemed to Dostoevski, that if "the Truth excluded the figure of Christ, I would rather abide with Christ, than with the Truth." But if the figure of Christ represented man's highest attempt towards perfection, no less valid as a part of man's nature was the figure that Dostoevski had symbolized by his "Parable of the Grand Inquisitor," the figure of Antichrist: the skeptical, ironic, practical-minded ruler of the world, who had given man "not perfection, but contentment."

My *Parables* and my long poem were both illustrations of this point of view—a point of view highly heretical, as it left man the prey of a dualism, and stated that the path to "the kingdom of heaven" lay in man himself, and not in the dogmas of the churches. It was also, though I was unaware of it at the time, a highly unpopular point of view to bring forward after the War, because at the root of it lay an uncompromising acceptance not of realism, but of idealism. The collapse of human ideals after the War was not only notoriously manifest in Church and state, but in the individual himself. In the tidal wave of universal cynicism which swept over the world in the wake of that meaningless and senseless debauch of slaughter, all that seemed left to man was the individual's private lust, his self-centered greed, his shameless and irresponsible self-seeking. By upholding man's search for God as the theme of all great poetry, in my *Parables* and my *Branches of Adam* I was committing myself to a final anachronism, greater even than the anachronism I had committed myself to by becoming primarily a poet.

It was not I, but the Irishman, James Joyce, who was the hero of this age and the idol of the post-War generation. He had carried the technique of naturalistic realism one step further than Flaubert and Zola, to the point where man's unconscious life, expressed in his dreams and his secret desires, had joined with the efforts of his conscious will. And he had shown how both sprang from the same root of greed and lust. Although still inescapably Catholic—O'Brien had assured me that he was, in fact, a spoiled priest—he had revolted against his Catholicism to the point of blaspheming all the poetic ornamentation of his faith; and had agreed with the Jewish pessimist, Sigmund Freud, in thinking that religion was merely an illusion. I could, and did, admire his courage, his honesty, his refusal to compromise, his denial of every ideal, his acceptance of mankind as a race of Yahoos. To him even his hero, himself, Stephen Dedalus, the last impulse of nineteenth-century idealism in him grown self-centered and solipsistic, was nothing but a tragic failure. The triumphant force of life was no longer in him, but in the horrible Leopold Bloom. Neither heroism, nor faith, nor courage, nor any of the values I had mentioned in my letter to Miss Lowell, mattered now at all. Mankind was henceforth merely animal, groveling in a sty. Or as another ultramodern poet had said:

> "After such knowledge, what forgiveness? Think now
> History has many cunning passages, contrived corridors
> And issues, deceives with whispering ambitions,
> Guides us by vanities. Think now
> She gives when our attention is distracted
> And what she gives, gives with such supple confusions
> That the giving famishes the craving. Gives too late
> What's not believed in, or if still believed,
> In memory only, reconsidered passion. Gives too soon
> Into weak hands, what's thought can be dispensed with
> Till the refusal propagates a fear. Think
> Neither fear nor courage saves us. Unnatural vices
> Are fathered by our heroism. Virtues
> Are forced upon us by our impudent crimes."

Soon after Edward O'Brien's vast and messianic mission to redeem humanity had collapsed, in the spring of 1922, before the more immediate and insistent claims of a female novelist of the "emancipated" sort, I took again the road to Paris, which I had not seen since the spring of 1913. I decided to go where James Joyce—from his obscure retreat in the Latin Quarter—now lorded it over the vast hordes of uprooted Americans, Japanese, English, East Europeans, Scandinavians, and Jews, over the seething chaos of homosexuals, Lesbians, neo-Royalists, Communists, dadaists, and hangers-on of every new movement under the sun. I had not seen Joyce except for one casual encounter in London, when I sat studying his dark and somberly flushed face, with its eyes peering half blind behind their thick lenses, in a restaurant for an hour. But by 1923 I had read his *Ulysses*, and this was sufficient. I had written my own *Parables* and *Branches of Adam* largely as a counterblast. They still awaited a publisher. I was content to wait till I could find one. In the meantime I would go to Paris and there see what had become of the city where my first major creative outburst had come, in 1913.

The experience was disheartening. Paris was no longer a city, if by a city one means a social and cultural unity, governed by unwritten but accepted standards, and revealing a single set of dominating characteristics. Rather was it megalopolis, a seething chaos where a dozen to twenty nationalities fought like dogs over the fragments of that culture which had still been in French hands down to 1914, and which was in French hands no longer. The French themselves were interested now in nothing but politics—and as masters in their own eyes of the European political game, as the dominating military and economic power of Europe, they had left culture to the foreigner to carry on. What the foreigner made of it was a queer mixture of drinking den and brothel, if one could dignify the nightly spectacle of Montparnasse by applying to it such names. One need actually learn no more French to take part in it than was necessary to order one's drinks and obtain one's rooms. Even that meager knowledge was not necessary, for the French, having now devalued their currency, were rapidly learning American-English in order to cope with the mob of barbarians who, in increasing swarms, were invading their capital. The spectacle of the great cafés, the Dôme, the Rotonde, with their glittering electric signs resembling Coney Island or Broadway, the drunken fights within, and the feverish and utterly uprooted mobs sitting at the tables absorbing all they wanted of French culture by the quart, was so fascinating to the remaining Parisians that they gathered every evening on the pavements outside to see what was going on within. Under the pressure of this all-pervading invasion, even the traditional French politeness was breaking down. Americans were becoming not only disliked, but despised, by the few Frenchmen who still believed in the cultural traditions of their country.

Such was Paris under the influence of what the other great literary figure of the period, the American expatriate Gertrude Stein, had called the "lost generation": no longer the great center of literature and of art, but the greatest market and rag fair of culture and of international license in the world. I was destined to see it three times during the post-War years: first, ten years after my *Irradiations,* in the summer of 1923; then in the spring of 1925; and the last time in the summer of 1930. Each time, the city which I had once preferred to London, and where I had learned and felt so much about my own art of poetry in my early years, left on me the same impression: an organism still functioning, but with the heart gone out of it. Where now were the French virtues of clarity, of logic, of reason, of intellectual *esprit* that had formed and maintained this heart? No one seemed to know; or if any people did, it was only a few radical and advanced Socialists, like the editors of the magazine *Europe* whom I met through Léon Bazalgette, the French translator of Whitman, on my second visit, and for whom I promised to do occasional papers on the literary and intellectual life of England.

The sole result of the War had been that each nation engaged in it had changed its virtues and its vices with another, as the Irish mystic, AE, long ago prophesied. The French were now like the pre-War Germans; the Germans were like the pre-War English; the English were certainly trying to become as French as possible. The Russians had become Americans, and the Americans become Russians.

Before my first post-War visit to Paris, in the spring of 1923, I decided again to visit America, and finally persuaded my wife to accompany me. Accordingly, we left together on the sixth of April, arriving in New York on the twelfth, and we sailed again for Europe on the nineteenth of May. Except for a brief visit to my younger sister's home in Washington, the entire time was now spent in New York itself, and gave me the effect of having seen only a cruder edition of the French capital. New York had by now grown hard-boiled and completely sophisticated, a spectacular cosmopolitan city of borrowed culture, able, thanks to its financial predominance, to attract all the celebrities and semi-celebrities of Europe into its orbit, and much more inclined to make something of them than of the native American product. It was an island of transplanted Europeans, anchored off the Atlantic coast, and ignoring the backwoods as completely as if that vast hinterland were occupied by none other than Red Indians. One could flourish in it, if one had unlimited impudence or had acquired a European reputation; but I had not taken sufficient care of my European reputation to be the kind of public figure New York then enjoyed. Indeed, the fact that I had lived in London and had not come to visit Paris since the Armistice worked as a handicap, as I soon discovered when a bright young intellectual working in the office of the ultracosmopolitan *Dial* accosted me with the remark, "So you live in London? I could never understand how anyone could prefer living in London to living in Paris. It's just as if someone said they preferred to live in Philadelphia to living in New York."

Personally, I felt, after my brief visit to Washington—it was the first time I had ever seen the American capital—that I would have preferred to live in Washington rather than in New York, if I could have discovered the remotest signs of any intellectual life there. Apparently, however, New York had drained from the provinces—for in those days all the states were only provinces of New York—their intellectual life to such an extent that the only alternatives open to the creative artist in America were either to move to Manhattan Island and endure the process of "sophistication," or to face intellectual starvation in the backwoods. It was during this visit that I again encountered Edgar Lee Masters, who had come from Chicago finally to live in the midst of the more spectacular attractions of Manhattan Island. I ran across him at The Players, in Gramercy Park, and we had, I recall, a long talk together, during which I detailed to him my hopes of someday returning permanently to the United States. I have not forgotten his reply. He said: "Well, you have a choice of evils. You can either live here, where it is very expensive to live, and have some intellectual society, or you can bury yourself in the backwoods, where it is cheap, but where you will have no one to talk to above the intellectual level of the garage mechanic." Such, as frankly expressed by Masters, was the creed of the New Yorker of those days.

In New York I made certain new contacts, and renewed a few old ones, during the brief five weeks of my stay. I had already become interested in a new literary weekly called the *Freeman* which had unexpectedly printed, in September, 1922, a flattering as well as an intelligent review of my life of Paul Gauguin. I discovered that I knew one of the editors, Van Wyck Brooks, a contemporary of mine at Harvard (where I did not know him), whom I vaguely recalled meeting in the summer of 1913 in a restaurant in London. I had been stirred by his two early ventures in social and intellectual criticism, *America's Coming of Age* and *Letters and Leadership,* which, appearing as they did in the War years, had seemed to me to state better and more honestly than any books I knew the actual hopes for maturity, as well as the moral dilemmas now facing America. I now sought him out, finding in him a finely balanced, generous, and sensitive son of New England, equally interested in literature from the aesthetic as from the moral point of view, with a background of reading and study that proclaimed the scholar. I laid before him the proposition that I should become the English correspondent of the *Freeman,* only to find that though his fellow editors were interested in England, both socially and intellectually, the idea of having any foreign correspondents—for anything else but wars, finance, and politics—had not yet penetrated to their minds. Nevertheless, Brooks took to me and I to him. He promised, since no one in the office of the paper knew much about poetry, and since poetry was still a matter for discussion, to let me review all the poetry books which came in; and he was as good as his word.

My connection with the *Freeman* lasted only for a year; in the spring of 1924 the subsidy which had sustained the paper was withdrawn, and the *Freeman* vanished. But during that time I steadily wrote for the paper, not only on poetry, but occasionally also on other topics. And I was grateful to Brooks for the fact that the sums these articles brought enabled me better to make both ends meet, and also gave me a vent for my own critical opinions. The only other vent open to me at that time, or later, was in London, where T. S. Eliot founded his *Criterion* in this same year of 1923. In Eliot's case, I never felt so free to express my own opinions as in the case of the *Freeman.* Although I had consistently admired Eliot's poetry, I could see no direct connection between it and his critical opinions. As a poet he was a disabused romantic, a sophisticated ultramodern. As a critic he was an upholder of classicism and of tradition. It seemed to me that Brooks's theory of literature (which Professor Babbitt of Harvard, Eliot's acknowledged master, would have dubbed sneeringly "romantic humanitarianism") agreed better with his practice as a writer than did Eliot's, which was altogether too dependent on the accidents of his own purely personal and individual taste. I frankly failed to see the connection between Eliot's classicism and respect for tradition and the fact that his poetry was neither classical nor traditional, but the last word in modern experimentalism.

While I was in New York I also renewed my acquaintance with Louis Untermeyer, now busily editing his *American Poetry, A Miscellany,* which had become the successor to our early imagist anthologies. I had a last glimpse as well of Miss Lowell, who came to New York to look up material in the Morgan Library for her Keats book. At the time I did not realize that a last glimpse it was; in any case, I knew that Miss Lowell and I had traveled so far apart that it was useless for either of us to make any moves towards a renewal of friendship. She had published, in September of the preceding year, her great literary hoax, *A Critical Fable.* Conrad Aiken, who had by now come to live in England, had shown to me a copy and had spoken of it indignantly, and I was fully disposed to share his indignation. Miss Lowell was now forty-eight years old, the author of five solid books of poetry, each of which had been immediately successful, a successful translator of Chinese poetry, and a person in great demand as reader and lecturer. She was the maker of several great poetic reputations and of a host of smaller ones. She dominated her epoch, and there were few—either editors or publishers, poets or the mere public—who had the temerity to gainsay her.

I had written, on receipt of her *Critical Fable,* saying that I thought she ought not to have published it, that it was poor sport for her to commit this kind of hoax; and I had also gone to the trouble of defending Eliot against her aspersions. *A Critical Fable* had seemed to me totally lacking in either critical or in literary value. Its appearance, and still more the deliberate mystification of the public which had accompanied its bringing out, had shown it up once and for all for what it was—a mere advertising device, unworthy of its author's, or of any author's, name and reputation. Compared to the success of notoriety which my former friend and coworker in American poetry was achieving, Eliot's rise in name and reputation in England, achieved at heavy mental and physical cost, was a thing to admire and respect, however much I differed from him. With the publication of *A Critical Fable* all friendship was buried between us. Henceforward, I felt indifferent. Though seeing her in New York, absorbed in her book on Keats, so little changed in appearance or in style of dress from what she was when I first saw her in London, so much still the active eager student, still learning, still experimenting, so much and forever the practical woman of the world, I felt that Amy Lowell was to be pitied, not blamed, for having made her life what it was. I felt, as we sat together at the dinner table in the Hotel Belmont, that the intensive labor she was undertaking to finish her book on Keats would end by killing her; and so, two years later, it did, under dramatic circumstances.

By the end of May I had again returned to London, glad that I had been able to make renewed contacts with my own country in the company of my wife, and still more glad that the long and exhausting trip had been made without serious damage to her health. When I returned, literary London was already ringing with the praises of Eliot, who in that spring had brought out his *Waste Land,* that monumental landmark of post-War and personal disillusionment, which, to a degree greater than even the critics of that day surmised, brought to an effective close the ten years' furore that had been made concerning the new poetry in America, and paved the way directly to a still newer poetry, which is still being written, discussed, and debated today, emerging this time from both sides of the Atlantic.

I recall that Alfred Kreymborg, newly come to London that spring from Rome, after the daring and valuable experiment of his editorship on the magazine *Broom*—one of the first and probably the most important of the English-language journals that flourished on the Continent during those prohibition years—I recall that Kreymborg and I, in the presence of a London admirer of Eliot's talent, sat down and read aloud together *The Waste Land,* taking alternate sections. Its blend of bitter realism and symbolic myth, of fierce Augustinian puritanism and magnificent, sumptuous versifying on the Caroline or

Jacobean model, made of it, I realized, not only another example of the new poetry such as had appeared in profusion during the past ten years, but, even more, a mark that other poets might shoot at and strive to emulate. The only objection I could make to it was one later voiced in my hearing by Havelock Ellis, to the effect that it was altogether too much of a pastiche from other poets. Eliot's vivid keenness of poetic scholarship, his exact memory of what hundreds of other poets had written before him, seemed always on the point of stifling his own ability to originate, to create afresh, to advance into new poetic territory. *The Waste Land,* besides being much else, was also a battlefield between the claims of tradition and of Eliot's individual talent, in which neither side decisively won, though possibly tradition was given an unconclusive and doubtful victory.

Meditating on this poem, so completely akin in feeling to the disillusionment suffered by thousands who, like myself, had believed that European civilization might find a rebirth, as a consequence of the War, and who were now already facing the manifest and dreadful possibility that European civilization would inevitably perish, I felt more and more akin to Eliot—though I shared little of the squeamish horror of sex which seemed to be manifest in his poem, or the desire to support my own poetry by references and quotations to dead-and-gone poets. I too, as he, had been through the War, had exiled myself, had been attracted alike to the Christian myth, though repelled by organized Christianity, had eventually come not to a land of promise and of fertile achievement, but to a barren waste land of disappointment and futility.

Accordingly, early in 1924, ten years after the outbreak of the War, I sat down and composed my own *Waste Land* in the shape of a poem, conceived as my "symphonies" had been conceived, in four sections, and entitled "Autobiography." Into it I poured all my contempt and hatred for the age of speed, jazz, vulgarity, and high-pressure salesmanship which had followed upon the War in Europe, no less than in America; my long-sustained and abiding memory of the yet epic and unspoilt magnificence of the Mississippi Valley, as I had seen it, in 1915; my desperate waverings back and forth between Europe and my own country; my feelings that love, in my own case, had slowly and inevitably become transformed to frustration; my loneliness, following upon my final abandonment by O'Brien and Cournos, who had been the two chief friends of the years immediately succeeding the Armistice; and my final protesting regret at the general course which life for me had taken. Thus this poem marked the end of my third, or religious, phase, as *The Tree of Life* had marked the end of the second, or aesthetic. (In the first phase, the phase of the publication of my early volumes, I had been simply groping.) The conclusion I reached at the close of this poem was unlike Eliot. Where he and his *Waste Land* had ended in a mass of disconnected fragments, "shored against my ruins," an agony that could finish only in whimpering hysteria and in the confession of complete defeat, my "Autobiography" strove to strike the note of a harder and starker, more stoic and more resolved, Anglo-Saxon paganism.

Man did the gods make,
Nature's sole master;
Broad-browed and lordly,
King of earth's harvests.
Many the gifts they gave to him,
Much joy he won therefrom.
He whom they abandon,
Exile from their glory.

Weak, puling, foolish,
He strives to remember
His kingdoms forgotten.
Pitiful, lonely
Last remnant of man!
With him shall the gods not reckon;
Neither length of days,
Nor lasting renown,
Nor love requited
Shall be his. . . .

Strive then no longer;
Waken or slumber,
Labor or suffer,

With your small day be content.
Yet be at peace within your inner mind;
And you will find
Far, far, beyond your loneliness and pain,
Grey memories ripening under heavy rain.

CHAPTER XXIII

I was now beginning to feel, increasingly, the difficulties and obstacles that had come into my path as an American now permanently expatriated in London. Yet I was not without many friends in England. Indeed, the years between 1923 and 1927 were a period rich in such contacts. During that time I had so many friends there that I felt at home in England rather than anywhere else, and was more frequently in danger of losing all connection with America than at any earlier or later time.

Foremost among my English friends I must set the figure of Eliot. Although he had not then taken the final step of becoming a British subject, had not flung down the challenge to his own age and country of proclaiming himself a "Royalist, an Anglo-Catholic, and a Conservative," he was already English in appearance, English in the bent of his tastes, and English too largely in his mind. He had turned away from his own early background and upbringing, which—though it happened to occur at St. Louis—was entirely New England-minded, and had recovered, in England itself, a native East Anglianism of thought which I, as a southerner, did not altogether share or appreciate. Nevertheless I was sufficiently familiar with the English background to find its roots in seventeenth-century metaphysical poetry, and sufficiently dogmatic and uncompromising as well to realize that it would shake the tolerant English out of their post-War lethargy. Tall, pale, and distinguished-looking, Eliot's slightly stooped figure attracted everyone—myself included—with its blend of conservative caution and of calculated daring. I decided that he had the most brilliant mind of anyone I knew; but it was a mind that in respect to the larger issues of life gave mainly negative results. My own tendency and direction had been far more pragmatic and provisional than his, and I could not, as he had done, "erect my personal impressions into universal laws." His critical intelligence was more suited to an age of crisis than mine, since I was less the critic, and hoped to be more the creator.

He now began to believe, as I did not, that a stern self-discipline of the mind, through adherence to some rigidly fixed tradition, was a primary necessity for creator as well as for critic. To employ a phrase made later by G. K. Chesterton, he held that "the primary object of opening the mind, as of opening the mouth, was to close it again on something solid." I, on the contrary, held that, in the chaos of modernity, all that the mind could do was to rely on itself, and gradually establish a largely personal and individual tradition. He now began to react against the American humanist group, under whose direction he had spent the years of his education, and to feel that the moral discipline they upheld as the goal of secular education could not be upheld by education—in short, he began to weaken in the direction of dogmatic religion. Thereby he not only set himself apart from Irving Babbitt and all his disciples, under whom he had grown to maturity, but also from the still commanding figure of Matthew Arnold, whose mind, in so many other respects, so much resembled the Gallic clarity of his own.

I doubted whether Eliot was altogether right; at least I did not feel that it was necessary, in my own case, to give a complete adherence to any established church, in order to continue to feel religious and even mystical. Dostoevski, to cite but one instance, had been not only highly religious, but highly heretical as regards all established religion. Vincent Van Gogh, in whose mind I now became more and more interested, had lived a magnificently religious life, and had remained a complete skeptic, for reasons entirely unconnected with his occasional lapses into insanity. And men like William Blake and Friedrich Nietzsche had followed a similar course. Like these, I preferred to remain a heretic, an outlaw from the churches, feeling that it was necessary for the churches first to revise their dogmas, rather than for me to accept what I could not believe literally. As for Eliot's remark that in respect to acceptance of dogma, it was a case of "the spirit killeth, but the letter giveth life," I rejected it altogether.

Apart from this widely divergent method of approach to the chief problem of religious belief, I found Eliot's mind both interesting and stimulating. He displayed an extraordinary acuteness, not, indeed, in his analysis of the general relation of literature to life, or of culture to religion, or of emotion to its resultant in art, but in his discussion of individual writers, individual styles, and individual phases of artistic creation. Thus, he had been practically first among the expatriate Americans of his generation to see and to stress the significance of Donne, that self-tormented and overwhelmingly cerebral genius in whom the medieval urge to otherworldliness, and the pride of the Renaissance secular learning, had fought their long duel to the death. He had been the first to see the connection between the post-War age of abstract mathematical and logical speculation on the one hand, and of revived racial and national hatreds on the other, with just such a period as the seventeenth century of religious wars and of Spinoza, Descartes, Newton, Milton, and the metaphysical poets. He had tried to rebuild an abstract classicism out of the ruins of nineteenth-century romanticism. I did not see how it could be done, believing that romanticism had already, whether for good or ill, too deeply marked mankind—as well as Eliot himself—with its restless longings for the impossible and the infinite, for its work to be undone; but I honored and admired his attempt.

He was extremely kind to me, permitting me even to uphold Spengler's entirely mystical and probably thoroughly unscientific thesis of race consciousness—which finally landed Spengler in the Nazi fold—against his own friend Wyndham Lewis, and also to take a fling at I. A. Richards's too dryly scientific concepts of the functions of language, in the columns of his periodical. As an editor, I found him to be practically ideal, willing for opinions to be mooted that ran contrary to his own avowed toryism, so long as those opinions were not merely emotional prejudices, but were backed up by something resembling intellectual judgment. In a way, this refusal on his part to insist on any general agreement among his contributors led to his undoing: it made the contributors themselves less a coherent body of doctrine, than a number of assembled but divergent minds, each approaching a problem from a limited angle motivated by some intense intellectual attraction or antipathy. Critically speaking, every one of his contributors was brilliant, but, like Eliot himself, they indulged only too frequently in the "criticism of criticism." This soon made their weekly luncheon discussions which they at first attended, and their own occasional monthly dinner reunions which followed, sufficiently tiresome affairs; all were so eager to disprove each other that few dared say anything at all to the purpose.

High among Eliot's contributors stood the Yorkshireman, Herbert Read, whose dryly exact cast of mind, pawky sense of humor, and taciturn habits of speech made his opinions much sought after. He had emerged from the War with a high British decoration, and with the instinctive semipagan, semimystical fatalism of the born soldier. Read was, in consequence perhaps of his War experiences, ever careful in those years to conceal the romantic side of his own disposition and talent; it had been carefully excised from his poetry, and only occasionally appeared in his prose. But I saw enough of him to realize that he remained an unbeliever, despite his association with Eliot, in the official dogmas of Christianity, and that he had leanings towards political and economic radicalism. Having discovered further that he considered beauty of equal, if not superior, value to mankind, as either goodness or truth, I was convinced that he was, in fact, a disguised romantic, and in this I was not mistaken.

There were also to be seen at the *Criterion* lunches and dinners, Harold Monro, now graying and aging, as taciturn in his own way as Read, writing poems in which a pathetic sincerity of spirit often scored effects as good as the most elaborate technique; F. S. Flint, getting even vaguer and more ineffectual with the falling years; the eager, lyrical, likable Richard Church, who was my special friend; the tolerant, witty, and friendly Bonamy Dobrée, whose special subject was the eighteenth century; and several others. They were all interesting in their own way; and yet I, hearing them talk, doubted whether some of my earliest friends in London had not talked with more verve and originality. For across them all lay the renewed tensions and rifts of the post-War world—Europe, rent to pieces by revivified nationalistic hatreds, and slowly perishing, while the alien lights of America and of Russia, on either side, seemingly rose higher and higher.

The "*Criterion* gang" was not the sole group with whom I had links in London. Through them I became acquainted with two daring young spirits of the War years at Cambridge University, I. A. Richards and C. K. Ogden, who had caused considerable stir by publishing, despite the activities of the censorship, their *Cambridge Review,* which was as critical of the Allies' aims as it had been of the Germans' during the years 1914–18, and who had gone thence into the question of aesthetics, the relationship of the human imagination to scientific reality, to linguistics, and the "meaning of meaning." These two men provided an instructive contrast. Richards, lean, dark, saturnine, and reserved, had buried himself in scholarly research, was engaged in the task of proving, by means of strict logical analysis, the validity of great literature and imaginative creation. Ogden, rotund, bespectacled, smiling with the benevolence of a Mr. Pickwick, was swimming happily and pragmatically along the stream of the world, his fingers deep in the pie of a large London publishing house, and was now absorbed in passing out contracts right and left for his popular and amusing series of small booklets, "Today and Tomorrow." It was through Ogden that my *Parables* were published, and I shall never forget the day when he appeared before me, in the office of a London literary weekly for which I then occasionally wrote, and with his overcoat pockets bulging deep with books and manuscripts smilingly passed out to me a contract, after an examination of my manuscript that must have been extremely perfunctory. I had never had a book accepted before on such terms, and for a moment I did not know whether Ogden was merely joking. This happy disciple of Jeremy Bentham and the Utilitarians was, I concluded, a real philanthropist; and his later invention of "Basic English" has shown to the world that Ogden will always run true to form.

My artist acquaintances were now not less important than my literary ones. They comprised the ex-American, McKnight Kauffer, who had come from Chicago to London and become the most discussed and best paid poster artist in London; another ex-American, Jacob Epstein, whom I had met in the days before the War, long before he became a sculptor of sensational notoriety, and whom I saw only infrequently; and Leon Underwood, who had emerged from the War to establish an informal but brilliantly creative art school which functioned for a few years at his own studio near Hammersmith, and where everything was practiced in turn from modern white-line woodcuts to sculpture and painting. The only American among my artist friends who was not permanently a resident of London was another artist woodcutter, John J. A. Murphy, who deserves a few paragraphs to himself, as providing me, during those years, with one of the chief links that enabled me to keep up my connections with my own country.

During my visit to New York in the summer of 1920, I had been invited by an enterprising bookseller-publisher of Greenwich Village to an evening party in the rooms above his establishment. When I arrived a numerous collection of people had already gathered. I was introduced by my host to a few of them, and we all sat down and consumed iced drinks and talked, while the heat of the evening drifted in and out of the open windows. I had just begun a conversation with Gaston Lachaise, a sculptor of whom I had only recently heard, when a man, whom Lachaise introduced to me as Rockwell Kent, came over and somewhat brusquely interrupted our conversation. Our talk, which had previously hinged about the relation of realism to abstract form in sculpture, was now diverted by Kent into a narrative of his own exploits as explorer and illustrator. Feeling frankly bored, I excused myself and went over to the other side of the room, where a man was sitting alone who, in appearance, I judged, was the handsomest specimen of Homo sapiens present. With a well-rounded oval head, bright blue eyes, and a challenging and yet open expression on his face, he was apparently waiting for someone to approach him. In a moment I had introduced myself to him, and had learned his name in turn; and so I came to know John J. A. Murphy.

Murphy had grown up among the same Catholic Irish in Boston who had produced O'Brien. He had insisted, despite the opposition of his puritanically-minded parents, on going to art classes in that city, and during the years when I myself was making my first steps towards establishing myself as a poet, had come to London, where he worked from 1913 to 1916 in Frank Brangwyn's studio at Hammersmith, acting there as general assistant to the most popular and successful artist-decorator of the day. He had thus undergone the selfsame apprenticeship to a master that had been the lot of all the great artists of the Italian Renaissance; and it had left him with a fund of amusing anecdotes about Brangwyn, his methods of work, his dependence on his pupils, his refusal to think beyond the immediate tasks of his day, and his fringe of hangers-on, apprentices, and frank imitators, which was inexhaustible. In Murphy's hands Brangwyn became a figure out of one of Vasari's *Lives*—a strange blend of artist-prince, hermit, and shrewd, moneygrubbing peasant. Murphy had escaped from under Brangwyn's wing in the end, taking with him an exact and detailed knowledge of woodcutting, etching, and all printing processes, and had gone to Paris, where he had been caught up by the War and by matrimony. He had there begun to emerge as a brilliant white-line woodcutter. He had come back to America after the Armistice and had established himself in New York. But two years after our first meeting there, he returned to London and lived throughout 1922–23 in a studio off St. John's Wood, holding a highly successful one-man show of his woodcuts—the first of its kind—at the Leicester Galleries early in 1923.

He now introduced me to no less a person than Campbell Dodgson, keeper of the Print Room at the British Museum, and editor of the *Print-collector's Quarterly*. Thus it came about that, through Murphy, I resumed my work, interrupted since the appearance of my book on Gauguin, as a writer on art topics, leading off with an article about his own woodcuts. I became again, through this contact, an art critic in the special field of the modern white-line woodcut; but unlike so many critics of that day and hour, I did not concern myself with the abstract development of modern art that had come through cubism, but preferred to confine my discussions of both woodcutters and woodcuts to those who had remained fundamentally representational. Indeed, all these cubists, futurists, dadaists, and surrealists of the post-War years seemed to me—and still seem—to regard art even more illogically than the confirmed academicians. Pictorial art, which they professed not only to practice, but still more to advance, is not and cannot be made either a direct and photographic imitation of reality, or a mathematical dissection and rearrangement of reality. It is in fact reality selected, heightened, restated in its salient characteristics, adapted to a given material, and made thereby into a new and independent creation. The work of art, by its very nature, partakes of both abstraction and of direct emotional sympathy; and the artist, in creating it, both makes and contemplates his creation, as the Bible tells us God is able to do.

Such an artist as Picasso, for example, with his immense technical resources, his vast intellectual capacity, has never yet faced the complex of intellectual and emotional processes which results in a personal style. He has literally never learned how to create anything. He has but shifted from manner to manner, from phase to phase, without acquiring a single thing that may be called permanently rooted in common experience, and yet, undoubtedly, his own. Therefore Picasso is, and has remained—unlike his precursor Cézanne—an artist without style; for the secret of any style lies in the creative grasp of any given subject matter and material, and not in its visible rearrangement into new aspects. Picasso's work, literally, is an attempt at creation from the void. It is remarkable from the point of view of its observational knowledge, but from the point of view of its degree of feeling and meaning, its ability to induce that *participation mystique,* which, according to anthropologists, is the basis of all primitive art and religion, it has nothing to offer. In this it is akin to the literary art of one of Picasso's earliest discoverers, the ex-American Gertrude Stein. I had met Miss Stein in Paris as early as 1913, had read some of her work in a magazine then published by Alfred Stieglitz, and I was not ready—nor am I ready now—to accord to her the epithet of "genius."

Murphy, in his life and work, made an amusing and instructive contrast to Leon Underwood. The one was entirely the calm, self-contained craftsman, catholic only in the sense that all men are catholic, planning each step in life and art well in advance, and constructing his work according to well-laid-out logical formulas; the other, nervous, dynamic, irritable, contemptuous of all fixed dogmas, forever jumping from one experiment to another, a mine of ideas, good, bad, and ridiculous. It was through two such divergent temperaments as these, both working the restricted field of the modern white-line woodcut—though I later came to know of other instances of divergence, such as the artists Paul Nash and Eric Gill—that I came to be aware of the fearful chaos and disorder of the twentieth century, just as apparent now in the art world as in the field of literature, economics, politics, and religion. It was at this time that I first heard of Spengler, and obtained the original German text, struggling through most of its two volumes before the English translation appeared.

Spengler was ready with an explanation of the disorder and failings of modernity that was even more all-inclusive and devastating than Henry Adams's. According to his creed, there had been exactly nine great culture periods in the world: Egyptian, Mesopotamian, East Indian, Chinese, Hellenistic, Roman, Magian, Faustian, and Aztec-Mayan, each being distinct from the other, and each representing different varieties of race consciousness. Each—excepting the Aztec-Mayan, which was cut off just as it stood at the point of its highest possible achievement—passed through the successive stages of tribalism, feudalism, nationalism, and fusion of state and religious cult into a single Caesaristic, imperialistic scheme, which gradually petrified into the end term of all culture, which was what we called modern civilization. Then came the breakup and the return to chaos through a revival of otherworldly religion, leading on to a new cycle of culture in areas where the primary urge for race consciousness had not yet been exhausted or fully developed.

Europe, in Spengler's view, had already reached the final point where only the Caesaristic state and the petrification of forms could avert collapse. Any new culture could no longer come from the European area, dominated by Faustian man. It must come from such inchoate and as yet "unripened" regions of culture as Russia and the United States of America. As a late European, born three centuries too late to see the highwater point of European culture, Spengler was forced to throw in his lot with the Caesaristic state of the future. But it might be still open to Americans and to Russians to make another choice. My reading of Spengler, together with my own feeling that it was only in America that I could find full freedom for my own creative energy, caused me to regret more and more deeply the circumstances that still kept me tied to England.

In the last weeks of January, 1925, my wife and I left London for a holiday abroad, this time turning our steps towards Italy. Under a new treatment which she was now taking, Daisy's health was considerably improving; but she had been so ill every winter of the last four years that I dreaded to keep her in London during the coldest months. Moreover, I was now intensely curious to see for myself how Italy was faring under Benito Mussolini, the first of the Caesars whose advent on the European stage Spengler had accurately predicted. I must admit that I not only went to Italy in a spirit disposed to be critical of Mussolini and of all the achievements of fascism, but that I came away favorably impressed.

The first four weeks of our stay, till nearly the close of February, were spent between Portofino and Rapallo, on that lovely Ligurian Riviera lying south of Genoa, which I had never before seen, and which had so inspired Friedrich Nietzsche. Whether it was the association with Nietzsche's memory or the welcome release from London's dismal fogs, frosts, and damps that requickened me, I do not know; but the halcyon calm of that enchanted coast, guarded by great snow peaks, with its profusion of ilexes, myrtles, olives, and mimosas crowding down to the blue waters of the lazy Mediterranean, softened the grim features of Mussolini's Caesarism and made the combined triumphs of the machine age and supernationalism quite bearable. Even Daisy, who had never before been on the Continent, forgot her hypochondria and enjoyed the cosmopolitan crowd at our hotel, spending her days sketching outdoors with the avidity of a child.

At the end of February we went on to Florence, spending two weeks there in the still chilly and bleak upland of Tuscany, and from thence descended to Rome, a place full of happy memories for me, for in it, long ago, in the winter of 1908–09, I had first grown intimately familiar with Keats, Shelley, Byron, and the English romantics, had spent hours pensively musing on the relics of Rome's vanished greatness, and had been alternately absorbed and repelled by the pomp and ceremonial, the dogmatic formalism, and the reactionary excesses of Catholicism. Unfortunately, these happy memories were not to be recovered, for on the first day of our arrival a telegram announcing that both of the young people we had left behind in London were ill recalled us.

As an earnest of my trip, I returned with my "Cycle of Liguria" (later incorporated in *The Black Rock*) completed, five poems, two of them in symphonic form, dedicated to Columbus and to Nietzsche, and three others, in which salient features of the Riviera landscape were used as symbols to describe phases of existence and dominating characteristics of the Mediterranean mind. This series, I thought, served as a sublimation of my own maturer ideas concerning life and death, human ambition and pioneering, in action and in thought, as well as the earlier and longer series of the "symphonies" had served to express more aesthetic and less reflective reactions. The poems it contained displayed my fears and hopes for mankind as clearly as the series called "Autobiography," written the previous year, had shown my inner conflicts and disillusionments.

Shortly after my return to London, in May, 1925, I learned that Miss Lowell was dead. The news came as a startling surprise, for up to the last moment I had expected to see her in London, and to resume, perhaps, on a new and better footing, our old association. When I had last seen her in New York, in the spring of 1923, I had feared that her work on Keats would end by killing her; but now the Keats book was triumphantly completed, she had sent me the two handsome volumes for a Christmas present, had informed me and all my friends in London that she was expecting to come to London to lecture on behalf of the Keats Memorial and to read her own poetry in April, and then had canceled—at the last moment—her sailing. I had heard that she was again ill, but had not suspected that the nature of her illness was critical, and would rapidly prove to be fatal, as it worked on an organism that had literally and completely exhausted itself in its efforts. The dramatic suddenness of her dying, as well as the fact that I felt sure she had by no means attained the final height of her own talent, made her departure seem like a break of the threads of my own life. I found myself equally at a loss to explain to the world the special relationship in which we had once stood towards each other, and reasons for our later divergencies in feeling. When called upon to write something in commemoration I could only set down my feelings in this wholly inadequate tribute—inadequate because it described the woman I knew originally, rather than the public figure she had made of herself:

> Whenever I think of you, I seem to hear bell-notes calling
> From the fretted tracery of a great proud Gothic tower:
> Music jangled, frozen and brazen, falling

Downwards through a busy city, hour on hour:
Air-borne lacework of sound: strange that this image should be rising
Whenever in casual talk anyone mentions your name.
But you were a challenge, startling and surprising,
In an age of banal achievement and pettier fame.

The asters and the goldenrod on your hillslopes will still be blooming
Autumn on brilliant autumn against the hemlocks' dark screen;
And the oaks and the maples flare scarlet and gold, but you will not be knowing
Them, or the lilacs, purple puffs of smoke on the green.
There stand the bushes still, but only I can remember
Globed drops of silver rain on the heart-shaped leaves,
Or the cry of the crows over sifting leaves in September,
But not for that, the worn heart worries and grieves:—

It is for lack of your vitally fighting spirit
That gave and took blows but never broke till the last:
A man's in a woman's body—let them portion out blame or merit,
I only know this one thing, and that it has passed.
Bravely you fought and died; and no other world you wanted,
When you left this world behind.
Not all of you has gone yet. By bell-notes I am haunted:
Music of challenge, how you ring on in my mind!

The dramatic suddenness of her departure left me with the realization that, despite her worldly side, she had perhaps understood me better, had stood closer to me in spirit, than any of my friends in America. And it left me also with the regret that I had not seen her at the height of her mental powers, dealing with the literary world of London, as she had learned to deal with and dominate the literary world in America. Lindsay had come, in 1920, and had been a brief wonder, soon forgotten. Robinson had noiselessly slipped into England, in the summer of 1923, to slip out, as much the self-contained, hermitlike figure of stoic aloofness as he had come. Eliot had won acceptance only by a process of deracination, and Pound had doubly expatriated himself by migrating permanently to Italy. But none of these enabled me to get a perspective on myself, to see clearly just what function I myself was fulfilling by remaining in England. Miss Lowell, I felt, might have done so, had she come. But now that opportunity was lost, and I was left to wonder what kind of impression she would have made on the stolid and phlegmatic English, had her good fortune vouchsafed her one more opportunity to triumph.

The summer of 1925, following on our trip to Italy, was spent in an effort to write a play dealing with the life of Paul Gauguin—a subject to which I had been drawn afresh through my interest in the letters, newly translated into German, of Vincent Van Gogh to his brother Theodore. Of the two, it was now Van Gogh who appeared to me the greater artist, a verdict that I am sure the public shares. Cézanne had spent his life in an heroic struggle to formalize and stylize impressionism. Gauguin had used the formal discoveries of Cézanne to describe a life half compounded of exotic Bohemianism and half of pagan self-glorification. Van Gogh had found in stylized impressionism a means to describe life in terms of his own spiritual adventure, as a Christian without dogmas, but not without the Cross. He had neither attempted escape nor found it, but had lived through his own gospel of artistry, in the spirit of his own Jesus, "who was the greatest artist who ever lived, because his fingers molded living men and women." It seemed to me that the subject of the encounter of these two men, the sophisticated Parisian turned nature worshiper and the Dutch evangelist turned painter, and struggling with the corruptions of the age, offered magnificent dramatic material. It also touched on my own life at several points, since both Van Gogh and Gauguin were exiles. In the end, I had to own myself defeated; but someday I yet hope to make a play out of all this material.

The writing of this play, and the growing multifariousness of my own intellectual interests, ranging through the fields of the visual arts, had kept me busily engaged in London or on the Continent now for three years. I had not again attempted to visit America since my going there in the spring of 1923 with Daisy, though I had kept in mind the possibility that at some future time, when her health became definitely better and her children's future disposed of, I might attempt a permanent removal. Now my activities were suddenly brought to a sharp halt. In the early months of 1926, perhaps as a result of mental overstimulation, certainly as a result of the British diet to which I never became entirely reconciled or accustomed, I had warning in the shape of an almost complete nervous and physical breakdown. After over a month of sleeplessness, a month of loss of appetite, a month of restless desire to get away from London and to go somewhere else where the air would be cleaner, the sunlight purer, and the pressure of the mob less continuous, I utterly collapsed. A wise doctor, experienced in human conflicts, with a background of considerable culture and knowledge not only of the body but of the soul, put me into a London nursing home, kept me there two weeks, gave my wife a sane and sensible talk, and sent me away to the country with her for two weeks longer about the first of April. By the fifteenth, I was cured. It was fortunate that my breakdown came when it did, for on the first of May the general strike spread its pall over the whole of England. The outcome of that disaster, the last in a series that had come to the country I had now lived in for nearly sixteen years, made me resolved, as soon as my strength had returned, to quit England permanently.

The summer of 1926 was the first summer since my marriage, ten years before, that my wife and I had spent alone together. My stepdaughter, now aged twenty-three, had finished her art course and was hoping to launch out independently as a painter and poster designer in London. She went away that summer on a sketching trip with friends in the south of England. My stepson, who had a year before given up a college career in favor of newspaper work, was already earning a salary, and snatched two weeks' holiday on the Belgian coast while we were away. Meantime, my wife and I spent eight happy weeks rambling about and sketching in the open air on the Pembrokeshire coast, close to, but fortunately out of sight of, the worst distressed areas in England—a land where two hundred and fifty thousand miners were now permanently out of work, and where they and their dependents, numbering up to a million, had no further alternative but acceptance of the dole, or starvation. To such a pass had England's vast and top-heavy industrial structure, the glory of Victorianism, with its eighty per cent of population taken off the land and driven into the factories, now come!

It was now agreed between us that in the fall the stepson should be left behind in England, while I, with Daisy and my stepdaughter, should definitely remove to America, to try out our fortunes together.

I was now past forty, but a new life and a fresh success in the literary field did not seem to me altogether beyond the bounds of possibility. I could see for myself that America, outwardly at least, was becoming every day more and more materially powerful and prosperous, while England, where I had chosen to live, had only crowned the fatal blunder of backing France at the Versailles peace by still another, and more fatal, blunder of failing to take account of a desperate internal social and economic situation. The European crisis dragged on from year to year, from conference to conference, with no chances of betterment so long as France and Germany continued to hate each other, with Austria helpless in the hands of her former enemies, and Italy, under Mussolini, continually threatening to break the peace afresh. England could now do nothing except to pin a desperate and futile faith on the League of Nations.

Now, in addition to all these growing international complications, England's domestic situation was even more hopeless. Since those fantastic first two weeks in May when all the machinery of her civilization had been halted, with not an engine wheel or bus wheel turning, with all factories closed, with no newspapers published, with the electric light and water supply only kept going by the grace of the laboring class, there was no further hope for Great Britain. I myself had seen London take on the aspect of a besieged city, with busses staffed by amateurs and stoned by the mob, with taxis at a premium, with street-corner intersections packed ten deep with weary walkers and struggling cyclists, with convoys of army trucks, guarded by steel-helmeted troops, coming up from the docks to provision the city. No; there was no further hope for England.

Mr. Baldwin and his Conservatives, together with the determination of the middle class to carry on somehow, had managed to scramble out of this impasse. Here was the result. Not far from where we were staying, in the midst of wild moorland and wooded hill scenery, were whole towns where not one wheel was turning, nor would ever turn again; where the chimneys loomed smokeless against the sky, the long drab rows of stone houses stood stark and lethargic, and men stood about with their hands in their pockets saying nothing, with semistarvation and defeat written on their faces. They, or their sons, had fought through a war waged, it was said, on behalf of civilization. Now they were facing the outcome; not a heroic death, not a self-sacrifice for some higher end, but a long process of slow starvation, like rats caught in a trap. What could I, American that I was, do under such circumstances but feel that I must go, and go soon? The statesmanship of England had failed; European Christianity had failed; there was only one alternative, to accept America as my destiny.

On the fifteenth of September, 1926, the house at Sydenham was carefully locked and bolted. My stepson moved into bachelor lodgings near London, while I, my wife, and stepdaughter bade farewell to the home that had been ours for ten years, and took ship to America. We left behind my books and all our furniture; but it was agreed that we should stay together in America, all that winter if we could manage it, and that I would return and dispose of the house and furniture in the spring.

CHAPTER XXIV

The trip that I took to America in the fall of 1926 was, as it happened, the turning point of my entire life. The seven months that I then spent in the United States, from the last weeks of September to the close of April, revealed to me once and for all that my future as a writer lay entirely on the American continent. Had I not been possessed by an incurable quixotry of spirit I would, then and there, have refused to quit my country again, and so not only have changed completely my status as a writer, but my position as a man.

We arrived in New York after an uneventful voyage, chiefly remarkable for passing through the tail end of the great Florida hurricane, on the twenty-second of September. My stepdaughter had proved herself to be a bad sailor all the way across, and my wife had spent most of the time looking after her.

Before I had sailed I had already arranged to give a series of lectures in the South during the winter. During the summer of 1925 I had met in London the man who was now engaged in obtaining for me these lectures—Professor Armstrong, of Baylor College, at Waco, Texas. I had heard of him before, when I visited Amy Lowell for the last time at her home in the summer of 1920. She had just come up to Boston after receiving an honorary degree at Baylor, and she was enthusiastic about what Professor Armstrong had done for the college, and about his unique Browning collection. I too had heard about the Browning collection, later on, in London. When I met Professor

Armstrong he was a red-faced, white-haired Texan busily shepherding a horde of some sixty tourists through London. He seemed to me to be a man with the boundless energy of a prairie mustang, a great generosity and patience of spirit, and an enthusiasm for literature which was backed up by little taste or discrimination—a combination, by the way, only possible in the Middle West, or the Southwest. He declared that he had presented a lecturer in the shape of one poet every year at Baylor for the past twenty-five years, since the beginning of the century; and he invited me cordially to be the twenty-sixth poet to come and lecture on his campus. I had hesitated about accepting his invitation, since I had never publicly lectured in my life. Now, in the fall of 1926, I at last decided to accept.

The lectures, however, were not to take place till January, 1927. Professor Armstrong had written around to various colleges and preparatory schools in Texas with which he was familiar, and had arranged a tour, which would consist of about twelve lectures in all. For these I had asked, and had readily obtained, a fee of a hundred dollars apiece. Thus I was actually to obtain, after deducting Professor Armstrong's twenty-five-percent commission, a sum of nearly a thousand dollars as the price of two weeks' touring in Texas; for all my lectures were to take place in that short period. The only drawbacks were two: in the first place, I knew no more about lecturing than the man in the moon; in the second, Texas was a long way off from New York, and I could not, in any case, set out on my way there before December.

Meanwhile, here I was with my wife and twenty-three-year-old stepdaughter, newly come to New York, faced with the problem of getting two people settled somehow for the winter, before I undertook, alone, my lecture trip—for I knew that my wife would not and could not undertake the long trip to Texas, even if I could afford it for her. The problem of obtaining a flat was therefore our first problem, and a difficult one it proved. Anyone who has lived in New York during the boom years, or indeed in the depression ones, knows that in this respect living in New York is much like living in bolshevik Moscow, except that it costs rather more. New York is permanently overcrowded. I had not taken the trouble to write to the few friends I had there and warn them that I was bringing over my wife and stepdaughter, and ask them to obtain for me a convenient flat; so I had left myself with the desperate task of trying to find one. Worse, I had arrived within a week of the fatal first of October, when leases are renewed and the whole nomad population of the metropolis shifts into its new quarters. Murphy, who had met us at the boat, was genuinely shocked and surprised that I had brought over my wife and stepdaughter without saying anything about it. He was helpful and solicitous, tried to find us a reasonably cheap hotel, mentioned various locations we might look into, and was in every way generous. But, for all that, the first few days ashore were a nightmare which I would gladly forget.

At last, after scouring the city by taxi and afoot, in all directions, we managed to find a place somewhere near West Twenty-third Street in the Chelsea section, in an old brownstone house, at a rental which I could just afford to pay. There were two bedrooms, one for my wife and myself, and one for my stepdaughter, a small but adequate sitting room, a bathroom, and a tiny kitchenette. The rooms faced south and were comparatively quiet; the furniture looked old, dark, heavy, and rather shabby; and the landlady was a greasy, somewhat slatternly-looking woman, who spoke English with a strong Teutonic accent. I decided that the place would do, since it was the only place we had found, after three days' intensive search, that did not demand a year's lease, or insist on a fantastically high rental. We moved in, unpacked our trunks, and settled down.

We had been there only about a week when my stepdaughter discovered that the bed she was occupying was harboring some specimens of a familiar insect—an insect so familiar indeed, in southern Europe, that its presence in most Mediterranean towns is said to date back to the days of the mighty Romans. The greasy landlady with the German accent was summoned, and professed an immense surprise that there were such things as what she called "bucks" on her premises. She promised to disinfect the offending bed at once, which was done. Ten more days passed in comparative quiet. Then there was a fresh outbreak of the plague. I began to think, now, that America was no land of promise, and that Murphy had been right in making it clear to me from the moment I landed that I had done foolishly in bringing with me my wife and stepdaughter. Almost a month had gone by. My stepdaughter had gone, unavailingly, to several firms of commercial poster designers, to which she had already been given letters of introduction by McKnight Kauffer in London. She had shown at each one specimens of her work, had been given vague encouragement, had been told to call again, or had been informed flatly that her work was not commercial enough to sell, and she was already losing heart in consequence. I had obtained a few scattered reviewing jobs, had been promised consideration for my poems by one or two editors, if I would send in specimens, and had definitely failed to obtain an American publisher for my *Branches of Adam,* which had appeared in London the preceding spring. And now the furnished apartment we had just taken was untenable! The situation was obviously desperate. Fortunately, there was another way out.

From the moment of our arrival my younger sister, who had only that spring induced her husband to quit the army and had gone with her two children to an old estate in Maryland which she was now engaged in farming, had been insistent that we should come down and visit her. Accordingly, as soon as our month's lease of the Chelsea apartment was terminated, about the twenty-fifth of October, we piled ourselves aboard the train and set out for Baltimore. We were welcomed thus to Verdant Valley and to the beautiful estate of some six hundred acres my sister had bought there, just at the moment when the scarlet leaves of the oaks, the vivid chromes of the tulip trees and hickories, were giving place to the somber slates and blacks of the winter—and in this fact lay the underlying cause of another failure to find a harborage for the winter for my wife and stepdaughter.

The old but picturesque farmhouse my sister had taken for a home, lying at the bottom of a grassy, well-watered valley, surrounded by long rolling ridges, that made the scene resemble, on a larger and vaster scale, the Downs country of Wiltshire or Leicestershire in England, was in a bad state of repair. Though heated by a furnace, this furnace was so thoroughly out of order as to be totally useless; and on the nights of killing frost that had already set in, the house resembled the interior of an iceberg. My wife broke out in renewed complaints of American discomforts. My stepdaughter found nothing to do but to ride the saddle horses with which the place was well stocked. And I soon saw that we would find ourselves as unadjustable to the conditions of living in the country as we had been in New York City. Within a few days of our arrival we excused ourselves on some pretext from staying longer, and returned to New York.

It was now the beginning of November; my supply of actual cash was running low; and we were faced with the necessity of obtaining another, and if possible a cheaper, apartment. By a final stroke of good luck we managed to hit upon one that was reasonably priced, within a few days of our return. It was in the East Twenties, close at hand to Madison Square and to the Metropolitan Life Tower, in a neighborhood that was far more noisy than that where we had spent our first month, but it was spotlessly clean and neat, with new furniture. The rooms were very small, but the kitchenette was far superior, and Daisy decided to economize by preparing to cook most of our meals. There we spent the month of November, with expenses cut to the minimum, and with no further trouble except from the street noises and from occasional mice that visited us. And there the events occurred which changed my second American venture since the War from failure to success, and which finally decided Daisy to return to England.

I had discovered that Murphy, since I had seen him in England three years previously, had become increasingly prosperous. He had always been a slow and painstakingly deliberate worker in his woodcutting; but by now the woodcutting was practically abandoned. He was now earning a salary of no less than fifteen thousand dollars a year—about three times as much as I had ever had at any period of my life—on a popular magazine of the commercial type. He was the layout man on this magazine, his job being simply to take the material (the stories, articles, and illustrations) as it came in, and arrange it so as to present readable and attractive numbers to the buyers of the magazine—and, incidentally, so as to set off the advertisements, from which the magazine derived its chief revenue, in as vivid a way as possible. The job was an easy one, and demanded no special talent. Anyone with a pair of scissors and a fairly good sense of balanced design could do it easily. Yet for this he was being paid the fantastic sum of fifteen thousand dollars annually, and was now disporting himself in an elaborate studio apartment, decorated and furnished in the most advanced modern style, uptown, while at the same time he maintained another and smaller, but more convenient and less showy, combined studio and office downtown, in the Chelsea section, where most of his work was accomplished. I could not help but compare our respective positions. I had striven to add works of permanence to American literature for more than a dozen years, and was barely a step from bankruptcy. Murphy, who had known how to sell himself to the highest bidder, was a wealthy man. Truly, this America was a land of supreme waste, and the values of New York were all false values.

To do him justice, Murphy had no illusions about the worth of the work he was doing. He knew, and showed that he knew, that everything in connection with the periodical he was helping to sell was fraudulent, and that, were not the Americans the most gullible pack of fools in the world, such things would never be permitted one instant to exist. But he was prepared to be tolerant towards the corruption of life and thought that the very existence of the magazine implied. The standards of the American market place which such periodicals upheld were not his standards; nevertheless, one must play the game according to the rules already set up, and he was prepared to go halfway with his editors and with the proprietors, and to see whether things could not be changed by boring steadily from within. I, who had already seen the weakness of the tolerant position in my own experience with Amy Lowell, had now come to America prepared, if need be, to starve rather than sacrifice a single one of my principles. But Murphy's persuasiveness, his frank openness, his real courage, and his charitable patience slowly prevailed. I could not leave my family to starve out the winter in New York, where my position was growing more and more difficult and impossible to sustain. He assured me that I too could find a way to make money easily on his paper. Although I felt as if I were conniving at a criminal act, I gradually yielded while he unfolded his plan.

He had already informed me that the editor was little better than an irresponsible drunkard—a small-town American who had married young, acquired a numerous family, had slaved from the start at newspaper work, and had been just lucky enough to make the right contacts at the right time with the right people, so that he had found himself, at much the same age as Murphy or myself, an editor of an immensely popular periodical with a salary of twenty-five thousand a year and unlimited opportunity to make more on the side by means of the fact that this business, like every other American business of the time, was run in a wasteful and disorderly fashion, with no one really responsible or ready to take full responsibility. The result was what might have been expected. Burlington—for so I shall call the editor in question—had promptly packed his wife and children off to the country, had acquired an expensive apartment in New York, where he held orgiastic parties on bootleg liquor, had picked up the usual chatter of Greenwich Village and Montparnasse, and had tried to pose as an advanced intellectual. He was now trying to make the magazine highbrow, with pages devoted to literature and current events. Why, said Murphy, to me, should I not join these pages, and write on "personalities"? For five hundred words, two or three short paragraphs at the most, monthly, I would receive no less than three hundred dollars! Murphy would see Burlington about it, and see that the contract was duly signed and delivered.

The prospect fairly took my breath away. My income would be more than doubled, and I need scarcely do any work at all, in order to achieve this result. Yet I felt that I owed it to myself, and to all my principles, not to yield to Murphy's blandishments so easily. I had always striven to give full value for whatever my writings had brought in; and though they had never brought in enough to enable me to live on my earnings solely, and though I was still dependent on my annuity from my father's estate, I was ready to go on in this course. Still, my situation with respect to my present venture in America was slowly worsening. I was forcing my wife and stepdaughter to live in considerable discomfort, for the sake of maintaining my integrity as a writer; and I did not see how they could be asked to go on, under such circumstances. An opportunity much better was close at hand, could I but swallow my puritanic conscience and accept the prospect that Murphy now put before me. True, I could say nothing in the five hundred words I would write every month that would be to any purpose, or be worth one-tenth the sum of three hundred dollars that I was going to be paid for them. But, after all, so many others were doing as badly as I! The "artist" who drew the girl on the cover for that magazine was being paid a thousand dollars every month for his design.

I yielded; and Murphy agreed to put my name before Burlington, to talk me up as an outstanding intellectual, and to arrange for a meeting. But Burlington, as it proved, had now suddenly grown suspicious. Although he wished above all things to pose as an advanced intellectual and to surround himself with intelligent people, as well as make his magazine, as far as possible, the vehicle of all sophisticated ideas, he was not sure how his proprietors and advertisers would take it; and so he began to dodge the issue. Thus matters stood when a new factor entered into the situation.

Daisy had readily agreed to share expenses for this American trip on an equal footing with me. Up to that time I had given her regularly two-thirds of my income, for the upkeep of the house and for food and clothing for herself and the children. Now, faced with the actual cost of American living during the greatest and most fantastic boom in American history, she began to object strenuously at the amounts she was called upon to disburse. She had come over, not only for my sake, but for her daughter's; but it was now only too apparent that the girl would never succeed in earning money in New York. Personally, I doubted whether the girl had really tried hard enough, or had sufficiently studied the conditions under which success was possible. She could not put herself forward, could not sell herself, but hung back out of shyness. But I could not change her from a shy Englishwoman to a go-getting American. In addition to all this, Daisy herself had grown more and more dissatisfied with America from the moment we landed. Our first apartment had been both dirty and verminous; my sister's country home had been cold and unlivable; the place where we were now installed was too small for comfort, and she felt she should not be asked to endure it for the entire winter.

And now, to make matters worse, she had just received a letter from her son, informing her that he had recently visited the house at Sydenham to get some clothes he left behind, only to discover that burglars had entered. Several locked doors and cupboards had been forced open, but nothing of value was missing. Though the house and its contents were completely insured against burglars, we now had clear warning that since it had once been entered it might be easily entered again—particularly as the back of the house fronted on a semipublic park, and burglars might easily scale the fence and enter by the long French windows on that side. My wife felt that we had made a great mistake in not putting all our valuables into storage, and she now began to write to her son, urging him to quit London and go back to the house to live.

December was at hand, and in one month at the utmost I must go south. I might, or I might not, get the post on the magazine which Murphy was now practically promising. Perhaps, although I did not doubt Murphy's willingness, his resourcefulness, or his loyalty, it would be wisest—considering Burlington's known shiftiness—to discount the promise in advance. My annuity was due again, and, divided into two portions, it just provided sufficient funds to keep Daisy and her daughter where they were for about three or four months longer, and to send me down to Texas, where I could begin earning money. I put the situation frankly to my wife. Which would she rather do now: go or stay? She replied that she would far rather return to England and spend Christmas there at home with her son and her friends and relatives than stay on. And so a few days later I saw her off from the pier, and was, after all, rather relieved that she had chosen, for herself and her daughter, the easiest way out.

Two days after her departure, while I still lived on in the apartment we had taken together (the lease had not yet run out), there came a sudden telephone call from Murphy. He had run Burlington down at last, and we were meeting at lunch that very day at the Commodore Hotel. I must wear my best clothes, must be fulsome in my compliments to Burlington on his editorial skill, must praise his taste in every way, and all would be well. The time was twelve-thirty—and I simply must not fail to be on hand. I promised, marveling at this change in my circumstances, as sudden and dramatic as if Murphy had waved an enchanter's wand and summoned some spirit of the air to come to my rescue.

Burlington kept the pair of us waiting about half an hour in the Commodore lobby. When he appeared, correctly and faultlessly attired, carefully pretending that important business had kept him detained at the office, I decided to feel rather sorry for him—an attitude quite unnecessary under the circumstances, as events proved. For one could easily see, by strong indications of nervousness under the surface of a countenance kept steadily impassive, that he was "running a bluff," and that he knew it. He was obviously no intellectual, and I could not help wondering why he wanted to appear one.

As Murphy had advised me, I duly flattered him on his achievements as editor, praising his taste and discrimination in the selection of his contributors, and especially praising the new feature pages of reviews he was inaugurating. His expression, as I uttered all these compliments, was so vague and so fatuous that I seriously began to wonder whether, after all, he or Murphy had been chiefly responsible for these new features in the paper. I then said that the idea had come to me to write on "the personality of the month." I then mentioned some with whom I was familiar, and whom I considered worthy of being nominated into this class.

He seemed vaguely interested. "Why didn't you mention H. L. Mencken among your personalities of the month?" he suddenly asked.

I was utterly nonplused. Though I was aware of the fact that Mencken's *American Mercury* was an outstanding journalistic success, it did not seem to me that, as a personality, Mencken stood in the same class as Unamuno, Spengler, Havelock Ellis, Santayana, or others I had proposed to discuss. But apparently it would not do to say so. Apparently Mencken's habit of laughing at all Americans as being nothing but small-town morons, his attitude of an adolescent who, just because he has read a few "naughty" books and said a few spicily unconventional things, thinks himself immensely superior to every other adolescent, had caught on. What, after all, was the mental age of America? I wondered.

I lamely indicated that Mencken, for the moment, did not seem to be of sufficient importance to be worth my discussion. But Burlington persisted.

"I'd be very interested to see what you have to say about this fellow Mencken," he went on.

What could I say except that Mencken was the typical smalltown atheist, who, because he happened to have read Darwin and Huxley, thought himself thereby competent to destroy the beliefs of others without giving them something better in which to believe? The prospect of having to pay any attention at all to so small a phenomenon as H. L. Mencken literally appalled me. It was with difficulty that I restrained my temper. But Murphy covered up my embarrassment by remarking:

"I suppose, then, Burlington, you are interested in Fletcher sufficiently to give him a contract?"

"You may have your contract for two years, provided you will write your first article about Mencken," said Burlington firmly.

I murmured agreement, and said that I hoped the articles would be satisfactory. We shook hands and parted. My contract was to begin on the first of January.

A few days later I left for the South, having spent my last hours in New York reading Mencken's latest work on democracy and trying to determine, since Mencken did not believe in democracy, just what it was that he did believe in. An article was slowly forming itself in my head. But when I sat down to write it I soon discovered that to say anything at all to the purpose in the space of five hundred words was twice as difficult as to say it in a thousand.

Meantime, at the last moment, my sister in Little Rock telegraphed me that she had arranged for me to lecture there on the night of my arrival, a few nights before Christmas. Thus my lectures would begin in my home town, in less than three weeks' time. Also, one day before quitting New York, Burlington duly sent in his contract. This, though it only read "for one year" instead of the two years he had conversationally offered, would result in more than doubling my income for the next twelve months. Truly, I was becoming "successful" far beyond my hopes.

As I have said, I knew no more about public lecturing than the man in the moon, and I did not realize that all the American public, tired of its small-town standards, demanded of its lecturers was not something in the nature of substantial thought, but rather a display of personal temperament on the platform—such temperament as Amy Lowell and Vachel Lindsay and Carl Sandburg possessed, and were expert at turning loose upon their audiences. I was still so naïve as to think that the American people might take their own desire for culture seriously enough to be interested in the notion that art was something more than an expensive and useless luxury. Accordingly, I had prepared a long learned paper on poetry in general, showing how epic, lyric, dramatic, and philosophic poetry had historically played their parts, as representing different cultural stages, among the ancient Greeks and the English, and predicting a future for American poetry in the direction either of the epic or of the drama. This I now proposed to read through and inflict on every audience I had to face. I did not have, and was not sure I could ever acquire, the facility of an impromptu speaker. Equipped with my dissertation, I now quitted New York for the hinterland. The afternoon of the second day after my departure found my train approaching Memphis, and the Mississippi River, in the central interior of America.

The interior of America! Thanks to the early and rapid development of railroad communications it had ceased to be, since the days of my childhood, the strange wilderness out of which Washington and Jefferson and Andrew Jackson, and indeed all American leaders and presidents down to Lincoln, had emerged. It had not been, since the Civil War, the raw frontier which had inspired Francis Parkman, where Emerson had gone lecturing in his declining years, and which Whitman had thought of as providing the final explanation of his poetry. Yet though the last frontier had already been spanned by the opening of the Cherokee strip in Oklahoma, three years after my birth, educated Americans were still, for the most part, as unaware of their own country as travelers in the African jungle are unaware of what exists beyond the trail they follow. The only way of seeing America was still by Pullman car and railroad train—and so Americans consented to be caged up for days in traveling caravans of steel and glass, moving from town to town through sunlight and darkness, with nothing between but the vast monotony of a continental landscape of lonely woods and fields, galvanized into attention by the wail of the locomotive whistle, that loneliest and most characteristically wild of all American sounds.

I was now crossing the Mississippi at the precise historic moment when this mode of railroad travel was giving way, even in the remote interior, to travel by automobile; when Americans were really learning to go through the country, and not forever over it. I was seeing America by train—I who had met and talked with those who recalled buffalo herds crossing the tracks in the early days of western railroading! I was already forty, and had not yet experienced my country except from a train window; but in a few years that country would be everywhere open for me to see by a now more familiar mode of travel. And I was now re-entering Arkansas, my own native state, which I had not visited since 1914, in the early days of the European War. Twelve years had passed since then. And I who was then an obscure scribbler in the imagist ranks was now a public figure, able to demand a hundred dollars apiece for my lectures. Little Rock had, in fact, already offered me a hundred and fifty.

The afternoon was growing dark with lashing rain as the train rattled and crawled across the steel bridge over the muddy Mississippi. It was already hours late, having been due to leave Memphis that morning. My brain was lulled to a complete trance by two days and nights of steady traveling. Beyond the Mississippi stood still the vast swamps, the endless woods of oak and hickory and cypress that I had known ever since my boyhood, that I had not seen for twelve years. Amid them, here and there, were the same clearings: stumps half grubbed up, land drained at last, raw, unpainted shacks standing amid dead cotton plants; everywhere mud and the desolation of a featureless flat landscape under perpetual rain; the aching loneliness, the somber darkness of the lowland South at the onset of winter. What was culture, what was civilization, to this country? It was only a thin veneer laid over a vast wilderness that still lay sprawling and savage beyond the railroad track! Was not my lecturing, my bringing of culture to these backwoods, merely another bluff, a fraud as gross in its way as the fraud whereby I had already imposed myself on Burlington and was intending to impose myself on the readers of his magazine? Was thought, or poetry, or art of any sort, anything more than the most needless of luxuries, here in this vast featureless land where man stood still naked and defenseless before the fury of the elements, still pouring endlessly as the rain was from an overcharged sky? I had already laughed and sneered at the way in which lecturers from Europe were swarming in hordes through America; now I was prepared to sympathize with them and to half admire them in their efforts. The train creaked, groaned, and slithered along the badly ballasted track in response to my meditation.

It was half-past six before the train arrived at the Little Rock station. I was due to stand on the platform at the new High School auditorium at nine. The rain had grown into a deluge, and the automobile which bore me to my sister's house roared through streets inches deep under water. The house, though it was the same, outwardly, in which my childhood had been spent, inwardly was totally transformed. My sister had completely altered the arrangement and appearance of every room. I found myself so deprived of all familiar features that I was practically lost, as soon as I got upstairs, and scarcely knew my way down to the dining room. The place was far handsomer, brighter, and yet somehow less humanly interesting than the home I had last seen, much as my mother had left it, in the last months of 1914. And here I was, newly come from England, bringing with me a London accent and a smattering of European culture back to Arkansas, to retail my wares upon a lecture platform.

I scarcely knew whether to laugh or to cry at the prospect, but the time was too brief in any case to do either. Fate and fortune had singled me out to appear in two hours before my own people—some of them being those I had known in my boyhood, now grown gray, with growing children, to listen and to puzzle over me. In half an hour I was dressed and ready. By half-past eight I had eaten and was ready to set out. The rain was still pouring down ceaselessly. Indeed, twenty miles off to the west the roads were now under water to such an extent that cars were marooned and country homes cut off. I faced at last a small group of perhaps fifty to seventy-five people, who had braved the deluge, and to them I read through my paper. The rain was roaring on the roof at such a rate that I doubt if any heard beyond the third row. The next day the downpour stopped as abruptly as it had come, and fair, open weather followed on through Christmas. All that I had learned from my experience was that I was not in the least a sufferer from stage fright, and that I now regretted not having forced myself to memorize every word of my speech so that I might at least learn how to address an audience without continually referring to a paper held in my hands. For the rest, I decided to return the guarantee of a hundred and fifty dollars I had demanded, to the organization of university women who had raised it, to be applied by them to the development of a much-needed institution, a junior college for my home city.

My subsequent lecturing in Texas, during the month that followed Christmas, merely added to my grudging respect for backwoods

American audiences. What did all these people, with their often pathetic eagerness to learn something, their indomitable patience, their strange, shy refusal to comment—few, if any, ever asked me a single question, though I invited them to do so—what did all these people expect to gain by paying down their dollars to hear me talk? Was I actually giving them anything, I wondered? Did it at all matter what I said, and whether they understood me or not? I began to realize how vast and unpredictable the life in the interior of this continent actually is, and how little I or anyone else could do anything about it.

Someone, an intelligent Englishman, had said that American life represented the utmost of outer standardization covering up and concealing the utmost extreme of inner diversity. That was true; and it was also true that the moment anyone broke away from the mass, he became as much a pioneer in a new daring as the first settlers who had gone into Kentucky with Daniel Boone. The only standards that applied to the mass were purely economic standards. Art and culture would be accepted if people thought they could afford them; otherwise not. Texas, for example, could afford art and culture better than Arkansas, because it was a wealthier state. But Texas culture was, for the most part, imitation New York culture. Mencken's *American Mercury* (the article I did on him, by the way, was never allowed to see the light of print) sold in vast quantities all through Texas, all through the Bible belt, the fundamentalist, antievolutionist South! Yet what kinship was there between a Texan prairie and Manhattan Island—or between New England granite hill slopes and Arkansas lowland cotton plantations—or between Johns Hopkins at Mencken's own Baltimore and my own state university at Fayetteville?

In Europe, as everyone knew, since Napoleon's day, nationalism had become an epidemic disease, a cancer eating slowly into the vitals of the medieval, universally held European tradition. In America nationalism in this sense had never even existed. People did not want it, would not achieve it, feared that if it was fostered, with its distinctive notes of a folk tradition, a welding together of city and country, a new development of culture with distinctive regional backgrounds and a pervasive American flavor, it would only reveal to most of them their own emptiness and lack of intelligent purpose in life. Therefore, they had swallowed the most easily acceptable substitute: a big city culture equally compounded of sensation and thrill and glamour and the vulgarest kind of commercialism, the showmanship of Barnum and of Burlington.

Where culture in Europe had begun with the unity of the Middle Ages, to become more and more divided and nationalistic since the Renaissance, in America—after tentative beginnings in New England, in the old South, even in the Middle and Far West—culture had begun to be captured and canalized towards New York as early as the close of the Civil War. Thus the metropolis that had stood on the edge of the country, at the border of the Atlantic, and had been, at the best, but a moneyed imitation of expensive European taste, ignoring everything local and peculiar or prepared to make fun of it, now dictated what clothes people should wear, what books they should like, what plays they should see, what brains they should have, from one end of the country to the other. Not only were local traditions merely something to be forgotten; they were totally unessential and useless. The answer to such local pieties, such regional peculiarities, had already been made in the skyscrapers of Texas cities, as well as in the new business district and the new state capitol at Little Rock.

America had become a continent overdeveloped in physical, and undeveloped in mental, dimensions. In resources, in machinery, in the sheer weight of numbers, in the irresponsible control of man by economic forces, it surpassed the world; but culturally and intellectually it slumbered on, unwilling to find its direction, unready to achieve its destiny.

CHAPTER XXV

At the close of February I quitted Arkansas again, having in my brain confused memories of vast, monotonously rolling, dead-brown Texas landscapes under bleak northers and wintry sunlight, sudden ice storms that weighed down branches of leafless forests on the Ozark border, and the rugged, beautiful hill country, like the Cotswolds on an enormous scale, that lay around Nashville, Tennessee. I had lectured in rain storms, in sleet storms, to halls crowded with giggling schoolgirls, and to other halls half empty and deserted. I had visited no less than four states, and I might now call myself a veteran public performer. Yet I was still undecided about the future, still restless and more unsettled than ever after two months of hard and perpetual travel.

The solution of my problem lay, it seemed to me, in New York City. New York, I saw, controlled all the avenues of communication, all the machinery of publicity. Anyone who was being talked about in New York could be talked about in the rest of the country. No one counted as a writer who did not have, and could not sustain, a New York reputation. If I had decided then and there to stay on in Arkansas, to settle back in my own home town, and to attempt nothing further, I would have rapidly grown as insignificant as anyone there—and I could find no painters, no musicians, and only one possible writer of any importance in the entire length and breadth of my state. It was not because of the accident of my birth in Arkansas that I had achieved a reputation, but despite of it; and I felt I owed thanks to nobody that this reputation had been achieved. I had emigrated early, had attained a position independently of all local influence, and so I must remain.

So, after writing a few poems, expressive of the feelings of one who knew himself to be, henceforward, an exiled Arkansan, I departed, and again took the road to New York. Maybe I could make there, as an independent writer, some niche for myself. Maybe I could even enlarge on the position I had already acquired through Murphy's machination. I was ready to make the attempt in any case, and to see what would come of it.

There was, however, another alternative which I weighed, but soon saw I could not accept. In the last weeks of my stay in the South I was invited by the Centennial Club of Nashville to come and lecture before them. I was the more eager to go, for I had already heard of a new group of poets at Nashville who called themselves the "Fugitives," and who were associated with Vanderbilt University. This group, of whom the leading figures were John Crowe Ransom, Donald Davidson, and Allen Tate, had been busy during the post-War years in bringing out a magazine, followed later by successful and much-discussed volumes of poetry; and in 1928 they finally appeared in a comprehensive anthology of their productions. I had heard of them as early as the spring of 1922, when I had been asked to come to Oxford to address a literary club there on the subject of modern American poetry, only to find that one of the active members of the club was an American Rhodes scholar who was also a Fugitive, and so much of a friend to Ransom as to be shocked by the fact that this poet, whose name I had never heard of before, had been omitted from my survey of the most distinguished American verse. I had repaired the omission not only by reading Ransom, but by becoming a subscriber and a contributor to the original Fugitive magazine. And now I was about to meet some of the members of this group, who had appeared on the American horizon when the first fuss and fume over the new poetry was largely dying down, and who had certainly written a kind of poetry decidedly different from the poetry of Robinson, Frost, Lindsay, Sandburg, Miss Lowell, or myself.

Personally, I was as eager to make this new contact as it was possible for me to be. These Fugitives had already interested me not only because they were poets, but because they were also southerners. I had long since been wondering just what relation my own poetry, with its complex basis of cadenced rhythm, its vivid, direct presentation of natural scenery, its symbolic alliance of mood and object, had to do with any southern tradition in verse writing. Poe I knew well, and I had also heard of Chivers; but who else was there except Lanier, who seemed to me largely a vague sentimentalist, a Swinburne gone religious? And what was I doing in the ranks of southern poets with my avowed admiration for Whitman?—even though he had glorified the live oaks of Louisiana, and had written a poem about the "magnet South"? Would not Tennyson, idol as he still was of all the schoolteachers and the women's clubs, been more to the purpose? Whitman not only believed in democracy, but in the laboring class; he was no better than a Socialist. And no one doubted on which side his heart had been engaged before and during the Civil War.

During the years when, as an imagist, I had stood side by side with Miss Lowell, fighting the battles of the new poetry, I had vainly scanned the horizon for any other southern poet to bear me company. The only one I could disover was Conrad Aiken, who had been born in Savannah, Georgia, though his people were New Englanders and he had been brought up in New England. I did indeed discover in Aiken a flow of melody that undoubtedly derived from Keats and Poe; so far, at least, he was southern. Also his art was fundamentally unrealistic. But he had used it as the vehicle of a long and profound psychologic probing of mood and thought that was neither southern nor northern, but ultracosmopolitan. Aiken could give me no help as to what any future southern poetry might be like. But perhaps these Fugitives, as the single close-connected, articulated literary group of the South, could. They had refused to state their definite program; yet no one reading their poetry could fail to find resemblances between them, even more marked than had existed between the original members of the imagist group.

The chief difficulty with their poetry, from my point of view, was that it proceeded from a process of intellectual ratiocination, rather than from any emotional identification with the subjects which they handled. Faced with the waning of public interest in the new poetry, as well as with the general wave of ironic disillusionment that had swept over the world in the wake of the World War, they had set themselves the task of beating the young sophisticates at their own game and of producing a kind of poetry that expressed, at best, an elaborate intellectual irony. In the case of John Crowe Ransom, who, from his seniority, might be called their leader, this irony was so frequently employed that it was difficult to say, in the case of many of his poems, whether they were written because of a distaste for life and humanity, or emerged from some source of secret and carefully concealed sympathy. Eliot had—before Ransom—specialized in poetry of this type; but Eliot was a modern cosmopolitan, a *poète maudit,* a follower of Baudelaire, struggling to escape from his own sophisticated background by way of Anglo-Catholicism. All the Fugitives seemed to me to be echoing Eliot in a less personal fashion: where he was an uprooted expatriate, seeking for eternal and absolute values in a world that had gone back to chaos, they still kept a local point of reference for their art, in the shape of their feeling for the old South and its tradition. I did not see how they could reconcile their love for this tradition, nor indeed for any tradition, with their habits of intellectual analysis. Traditions, after all, were held because men wanted them; one could not reason a man into believing in tradition.

Faced with the prospect of lecturing before the Centennial Club, with an audience that, I knew, would probably contain several of the Fugitives, I decided not to modify my lecture in any important respect. I would still point out, as I had to all my other American audiences, that American poetry was inevitably likely to remain directly epic and dramatic, rather than reflective and analytically philosophical. I would leave it to my audience to challenge me on any of these assumptions.

The lecture was duly delivered, and I was not challenged at all. On the contrary, I remained at Nashville two or three days, and had not only the pleasure of meeting Ransom, but of meeting Donald Davidson, and of finding both far less intellectually formidable than I had previously supposed. Both of these poets had, I saw, been extremely fortunate in finding teaching posts which sustained them economically in a city where there was a certain amount of intellectual give-and-take and some feeling still for art and culture. They were university teachers as well as poets; and perhaps it was just as well that

American poetry should now retreat from the vulgar scramble for place and pelf in the American literary market, and retire for a time into the quiet of classic halls of learning. I, however, knew that I could not follow Ransom's or Davidson's example. I had arrived at a point where I would have frankly preferred to do so, knowing that an academic job, at regular rates of pay, would mean a greater feeling of security and steadier employment, in my case, than the perpetual uncertainty of free-lancing. But I had not even a college degree, not even a humble A.B. to add to my name; and college jobs went, as I knew, to college graduates. I could only envy the good fortune of Ransom and Davidson, from a distance.

Of these two leaders in the Fugitive ranks, I decided that Ransom had the better mind, but that Davidson was the more lovable as a human being. The academic discipline had, indeed, rested lightly on Ransom's shoulders, from the days when, after a brilliant pre-War career as Rhodes scholar at Oxford, he had returned to Nashville. He might have become a teacher of philosophy as well as, if not better than, a teacher of literature, having a mind extremely logical, of unemotional toughness, and an ability to defend intellectually positions where his heart was nowise engaged. He lacked the enthusiasm for literary bypaths, the breadth of understanding, the outlandish crotchets and prejudices of such a lifelong student of literature as Ezra Pound, for instance. He was not a refashioner, but a steady follower of tradition. But I found it difficult to determine why, under the circumstances, he had launched forth as a poet, his prevailing mental temperature being impassive, phlegmatic, and nonpoetical. I decided that his irony and his emotional reserve would leave him, so far as I was concerned, no more sympathetic as a poet than Eliot had been. It was next to impossible for me to penetrate through the protective shell of academic scholarship to the man underneath. Though I continued to admire his poetry after our first encounter, I felt that we had little, if anything, in common.

Davidson, as I have already said, was more lovable. He was both more conscientious as a teacher, and more ill at ease in such a position, since his mental vista was not primarily that of a logician, but that of a creator. He was more interested in the South on the emotional side than on the intellectual, I discovered; and for this reason, my heart warmed to him. He was capable of an unstudied frankness in regard to his ideals and beliefs, on many occasions, where Ransom would have employed all his resources of mental reserve; and for just this reason, Davidson was, like myself, far more discontented and unhappy at bottom than Ransom. He was, indeed, more or less lost amid the confused sophistications of modernity, and had set himself directly against the popular current, feeling that in so far as he cared for the South at all, it was only for the premechanical, agrarian, plantation South which had gone to defeat at Appomattox that he cared. I could understand and even share this point of view, for all its pessimism; for it was indeed largely my own.

I had been given by both men the address of Allen Tate, the youngest—and, it was said, the most brilliant—recruit to their group, who had recently gone to New York City in an effort to achieve a living by free-lance writing. Accordingly, as soon as I arrived in New York again, I looked up Tate, wishing to complete my knowledge of the entire Fugitive group by firsthand acquaintance. I found, however, that if I had been somewhat dubious and critical of the Fugitives in the cases of Ransom and Davidson, the doubtfulness of my standing as a presumptive ally must be tenfold greater in the case of Allen Tate, though, even more than these others, Tate too was indubitably southern in his temperament and in the cast of his mind.

My difficulty with Tate was that he seemingly belonged altogether to a different generation from the one I had known and cherished. Ransom had been born only two years after myself, and Davidson five years after Ransom. But both belonged, I felt sure, in spirit, to the pre-War period, the last stage of the horse-and-buggy epoch, the years that had come to maturity or to some degree of mental judgment before the World War, the airplane, the motion picture, and the radio were let loose on a helplessly enslaved world. Tate was of the generation that had felt the shadow of the War falling across their very childhood. He had been born in the last year of the century, six years after Davidson, and in those six years there apparently lay a world of differences.

The sophistication that had seemed at the utmost speculative and external to Ransom and to Davidson (though less in Ransom's case than in Davidson's) had, in Tate, sunk so deep within the very fiber of his being as to be ineradicable. Not even acceptance by the public (his poetry was as much admired among the intellectuals as his biographies, on which he was now working, found their audience among the majority), not even a happy marriage with a sensitive, intelligent, artistic woman of his own people, could apparently save him. For Tate was, as Poe and Coleridge and Baudelaire had been before him, a perfectionist. Some terrible remnant of a world-blasting, medieval Catholicism was at work within him, reducing to ashes not only everything in his own day and time, but all human existence itself. The world lay under the shadow of damnation. The last historic hope for America had faded in 1860. Since then one could only contrast the fruitless activity of a degraded democracy with the ultimate eternal quietude of complete death.

In Tate, it seemed to me, the attitude of complete spiritual defeat, of which Eliot had already been the spokesman in England, became for the first time manifest and indubitably universal in American poetry. And to this had come all the fierce hopes, the daring adventurous enterprises, the vivid imaginative insights of all those poets who, scarcely more than a dozen years before, had set themselves to fulfill Whitman's predictions and make a new poetry fit for a new world! To Tate and to his kind the world had been made safe for democracy, but not for poetry. Democracy had triumphed at the Armistice, only to leave man under the greater—and final—damnation of no longer being able to find anything in life worth believing. A fierce and inveterate Calvinism of the spirit must now combine with a search for an aesthetic perfection no less absolute, if anything at all was to be saved. And the violent criticism, the complete negation of what others had done, however badly, to advance the course of American poetry, was matched, in Tate's case, by a reasoning faculty that fed upon and was destructive of its own creative impulses. With a fine forehead and a sensibility not inferior to any poet, Tate was at the same time endowed with a critical faculty so acute that it made him at the worst a poet *manqué*, at the very best a poet who moved cumbrously in self-devised chains.

I might have discovered the same quality of spirit in Hart Crane, whose work was just then making a stir among the younger set, and with whom Tate had already struck up a friendship, but I did not meet Crane in the flesh. From what I heard about him, as well as from his poetry, I judged that his vast ambitions to re-create an American myth, his gusty rhetoric, his combination of *enfant terrible* of Bohemianism and disciple of Whitman, made of Crane far more of a poet, though less sure of his own ideas, than Tate.

I had returned to New York after my inspection of the hinterland feeling that Spengler might be, after all, mistaken. America could not create a new vital local culture on her own account, but could only absorb and transmit all that late European and decadent cosmopolitan culture could offer her. The lost generation, whom I had seen at first hand in Montparnasse, and the new movement in poetry towards a hard and arid intellectualization of sensibility—a movement of which Eliot and the Fugitives were symptoms—drove me inescapably towards this conclusion. I would see, then, whether I could not outsophisticate the sophisticated.

I was aware that during the last thirty years of the nineteenth century and the first quarter of the twentieth, a number of works had appeared in various European languages which were of first-rate literary importance, but of which scarcely anyone in America had so much as heard. Who, for example, in all the seething millions that lived in New York's avenues and prided themselves on their up-to-dateness, knew of Miguel de Unamuno, Carl Spitteler, Nicholas Berdyaev, C. F. Ramuz, or Paul Claudel—to name only five? The volumes of the "Modern Library" which an enterprising New York publishing house was bringing out on the market, and which represented the popular opinion of what had been important in the nineteenth and twentieth centuries, were selling already in vast numbers. Why should I not add to them by becoming the editor of a "Modern European Library," a series of translations of as yet unknown European masterpieces? I had my list ready, and could choose my own translators. If I could obtain the direction of so ambitious an enterprise, after my successes at lecturing and as writer on the———*Magazine,* I felt I should at last rest content.

Unfortunately, the notion of bringing out ten or fifteen books all translated from various European languages, *en bloc,* did not strike the New York publishers as being in any way feasible. European books were being translated and put out on the New York market every year. But no one wanted more than one such book at a time; more than this was unheard of. And that an American, albeit an expatriated American, should walk into a Manhattan publishing office, slap down a list of untranslated European books on the desk, and announce himself as being prepared to get the lot translated, was also unheard of. The New York publishers were prepared to spend large sums in going abroad each year to buy in London, Vienna, or Paris translation rights to such works from enterprising agents; but no one had ever thought of saving that expense by hiring an American like myself to do the job.

In the two months of March and April which I spent in New York City, contacting there every publishing firm of importance, I made an important discovery: that the publishers, for the most part, were quite as naïve, quite as uncertain of what would be successful, quite as unsure how that cat, the public, was about to jump, as most Americans were during those years of prohibition, license, and the wildest boom in American history. And the main difference between a publisher and an author like myself was that the publisher had more money to gamble with, liked to think of himself as having more judgment, liked to make a bigger fuss over whatever it was he was doing. I visited practically every publishing house in Manhattan Island with my project for a "Modern European Library" during that spring of 1927, and at each one I was told that the idea was interesting, but must be declined.

Two months spent in a dark and airless room off a noisy street in Greenwich Village had only led to fresh disappointment and exasperation of my nerves. What was the way to make an impression on this city of half-Americanized aliens, to whom their own semicosmopolitanism, mingled with shrewd commercial judgment, was all of America that counted, and equal as such to my own real cosmopolitanism, gained at the price of a long stay abroad? How could I compete with their wild parties, their alleged literary teas, their publicity stunts, their refusal to consider anything from any standpoint beyond that of the last five minutes of their existences? Soon their annual invasion of Europe would begin; they would all go off to the Continent, scatter their largesse, and return supposing that they had acquired European culture. My idea of a series of translations to show them what European culture really was, had been no idea at all. What else could I do?

I might resume the notion that I had entertained, as far back as 1920, of writing a long epic poem dealing with the Civil War. This meant, however, that I must first find some place to live for the summer. New York was an impossible place for me to live and work in. The South would be, in the heat of summer, even less livable. And all my friends, except Linscott, had gone away from Boston. I had not even considered the possibility of entering the MacDowell Colony. Moreover, all the documentary material on the subject of the Civil War which I would want to use was still at Sydenham, in the care of my wife. I could write my Civil War poem just as well in England as in America—if not better—if I wanted to do so. But did I want this? My feeling was now that the interest in American poetry was distinctly waning, and that neither Civil War epics nor anything else would be popular with the public. I did not foresee then that the idea of a Civil War epic would triumphantly be taken up and carried to success by Stephen Vincent Benét, two years later.

There was still something else I could do, however, besides writing poetry. My three months' stay in New York made me feel that what my country chiefly needed was a little healthy criticism. We had become a nation of lawbreakers, the richest and yet the most purposeless of nations, hard-boiled, ruthless, and utterly without respect for anything that did not smell of big business. All this the Harding-Coolidge regime had done, but it was time now to ask, for what purpose? There had been a time when I hoped that Van Wyck Brooks would continue to ask this question, and to supply this criticism. But Brooks's health had broken down, and Lewis Mumford had already taken his place as chief of the younger liberal critics.

Mumford was more glib, more vague, more artfully persuasive than Brooks; but as I read his *Golden Day,* which had recently been received with loud acclaim, I felt that its thesis was false and its optimism hollow. The thesis was that New England had been chiefly responsible for the only renaissance of letters that the American continent had ever known; that this golden day of New England had somehow, since the Civil War, transformed itself into the gilded age of vulgarity and greed, for which Wall Street and the Middle West were chiefly responsible; and that now the gilded age was approaching its end, and there could only be a new renaissance of American culture based on radical socialism. But the answer to that theory was: New England had been responsible for the Middle West; the Middle West had taken its tone, its thought, its very life from New England; therefore New England's thought and philosophy had very radical defects, failed in themselves to supply the good life for Americans. As for the buoyant optimism of Mumford's conclusion, his faith that echoed Whitman's conclusion, "Allons! The road is still before us!"—that seemed to me neither justified by the critical situation now facing American letters, with New York irresponsibly controlling the entire enormous gamble of American book production, literary log rolling, puffing, and praising by the reviewers, nor necessary, indeed to Mumford's thesis. He might as well have ended his book on a sour as a sweet note. He might have said, instead of what he did say, "Such a result, so soon, and from such a beginning!"

I concluded, once more, that Spengler had been utterly wrong, or at least lacking in perspective, when he exempted America and Russia from the sentence of condemnation he had already passed on western European civilization. Both America and Russia had from the beginning been offshoots of European life to an entirely different set of circumstances. In Russia European enlightenment had been grafted upon a centralized oriental tyranny. In America it had been loosely disseminated throughout a decentralized, expanding federation of states, pushing further and further away from their remote backgrounds into the wilderness. In Russia unity was imposed from within; in America it had been compelled from without. In Russia every practical activity of man had to be in accordance with a predetermined theory of conduct. In America every theory of conduct had been made to pass the test of whether it was practical under given circumstances. In Russia the minds of men wavered continually between Scandinavian and east European national aggressiveness and sheer oriental passivity and fatalism; the Russian mind was balanced between East and West. In America men's minds wavered between the prosperity of the active, pushing industrialist and the poverty of the tradition-loving conservative farmer; the American mind was balanced between North and South. And, if European civilization was submerged, neither American nor Russian could survive for an instant. So much for Spengler's thesis and for Mumford's optimism.

I saw that I had the subject of a prose book in my hands: a book that would delve into the psychology of nations, as other men had delved into the psychology of individuals; that would utilize the two great frontier nations bordering on Europe, Russia and the United States of America, as parallel and yet contrasting developments of European ways of living applied to conditions or populations that were non-European, and therefore destined to fail even more spectacularly than Europe was at present failing. But to write this book I needed a larger knowledge of Russia, particularly, than I possessed, and more perspective. At least, I might attempt it. If I returned to England I could, I thought, obtain a new perspective on the American problem; it would be better than to remain in America, where frequently it was difficult to see the wood for the trees. And I thought that a year's reading and study would bring me enough insight to deal adequately with Russia—though, as a matter of fact, I had not a first-hand contact with that country, and, like most people after the Russian Revolution, hesitated now before acquiring one. A year of preparation and six months of writing my book would suffice, I thought. By the beginning of 1929 I might consider it finished. But first I must go back to Europe, where I might live and write in some degree of security and comfort.

Accordingly, in the last week of April I set sail, and the first of May found me passing between grassy banks lined with vivid primroses, rolling over moors aflame with gorse, admiring the lush green meadows, the tender leaves of the willows and oaks, the slow, placid streams mirroring the soft blue of the cloudflecked sky, as I sat aboard a Great Western railway train bound from Paddington to London.

It was, I admit, the wrong decision. I should have stayed, should have striven by all means in my power to adjust myself to America, should have sacrificed my books, my income, my work as an author, rather than go back to a marriage which had never achieved any reasonable and harmonious adjustment between two people of different ages and different nationalities, and which had just broken up afresh over the question where we were to live. I was returning to England in order to embark on a weighty and important prose book for which I needed long study, hard concentration, and complete peace of mind, if I was to achieve any success in a field which I had not even attempted previously. Although in England I had a house to work in and books to write with, my domestic situation was not such that I could achieve the study, the concentration, or the peace of mind necessary.

My wife did not meet me at the station in London. The reason was, I discovered later, that she had got rid of another cook and general helper, and was again servantless. The house at Sydenham with its eleven ill-lit rooms arranged on three floors and basement, its absurd Gothic red-brick façades and windows, its lack even of a garden, its general air of gentility gone shabby, was more uncomfortable now to live in than ever. Daisy and I together had to struggle with the kitchen stove, with dishes, with housecleaning. The two young people, both now hoping desperately to marry, kept away from the house as much as possible. May, June, and July brought me no nearer my book. I did not write a line. Finally, in August I decided to take my wife away for a tour of the Italian lakes. Italy, after all, in the spring of 1925 had given us two months of comparative well-being. Perhaps it would help us again.

Unfortunately, it did not. While the 1925 trip had been made with my wife in better health than had been hers for some time past, it was with a querulous and exhausted woman worn out by housework that I now started for Italy. The trip was uncomfortable, expensive, hot, and an utter waste of time and money. On it I threw away all that I had ever earned as writer for the———*Magazine,* and to no result. By the middle of September we were back again where we were, with this one difference: that by offering double wages we at last found a servant who would come and relieve us of some of the burden of housework, so that life again became endurable, and I was able to concentrate on my task.

It was not until winter had settled down on London—the extremely hard winter of 1927–28, with its strange and unexpected three-day snowstorm sweeping through South England after Christmas, to cut off whole communities in Kent and Sussex from communication by road—that I began my book. All through the bleak days of January and February and on into the spring I wrestled with it, and on into the summer and the fall. After the New Year my money from the magazine lapsed, and my income was again cut in two. But nothing mattered now, except finishing *The Two Frontiers.* So I worked on and on.

CHAPTER XXVI

By January, 1929, my task on *The Two Frontiers* was finished. I had worked on the manuscript for a year, and I felt it was as good as I could make it. Whatever its value as a thesis concerning two semi-European, seminomadic powers that had risen on the stage of the world only during the eighteenth century, had grown more and more threatening and powerful during the nineteenth, and now bade fair to divide the entire European heritage between them in the twentieth, I felt that my book was of a sort that would lead inevitably to much argument and discussion. I had, at any rate, displayed both the American and the Russian problem in a new light, and had shown how difficult it would be for historians to predict the future of these two great land areas with any degree of certainty.

My book was submitted to the London publishing house that had brought out in the preceding spring my book of poetry, *The Black Rock,* which had been unexpectedly well received in both the English and the American press. To my great surprise, *The Two Frontiers* was declined, on the plea that historical surveys of this nature were no longer selling, and that the firm in question felt it must practice certain economies. I did not feel that I was sufficiently acquainted with the London publishing world to try elsewhere, and I thought my reputation sufficiently established not to court another rebuff.

Accordingly, in the early spring of 1929 I again took ship for New York City. This time I came over with no intention of remaining. My one object was to sell my prose book to a New York publisher, so that the year's work I had done would not be done in vain. I succeeded in my task, and returned to England in about six weeks.

Unlike London, which had slowly and grumblingly adapted itself to modernity since the War, and which was still—despite cheap motor cars, gramophones, radios, suburban strip building, the disappearance of old landmarks like Regent Street, the threatened disappearance of the Foundling Hospital—unlike London, New York was now almost completely transformed, and was still violently rushing skyward under the influence of a boom which had lasted nine years. Prohibition still nominally ruled, but any passer-by could direct the visitor to the nearest speak-easy, provided the visitor was willing to gamble an even chance on the prospect of finding himself poisoned when he came out. New buildings were going up so fast that no one any longer could name or count them; and all were skyscrapers. On Fifth Avenue, above Forty-second Street, the last specimens of the millionaire palaces that had been the marvel of my young manhood were disappearing, their place being taken by immense apartment buildings and by the most exclusive shops, now moving steadily uptown. Nearly all the landmarks of my childhood were gone: the old Park Avenue and the Belmont Hotels, the Church of the Heavenly Rest, the Vanderbilt houses on Fifth Avenue. Worst of all, the old Waldorf-Astoria was closing down, would be demolished, and on its site would rise a skyscraper that would out-top everything yet built, including the daring and violently modern Chrysler Building, already started skyward to the east of the Grand Central Station. New York had become a violently futuristic city of steel and stone; and this city had now but one thought, the Stock Exchange.

All over the city, alongside the crowded speak-easies, the equally crowded bucket shops had sprung up, with their throngs sitting fascinated before the blackboards on which the daily fluctuations of stocks were chalked up, and with their ticker tapes clicking faster than ever beside them. Every day the volume of transactions on the Stock Exchange broke new records. Men coming out of their offices late in the afternoon after a tiring day would scramble for the newspapers announcing Wall Street's closing prices. On the faces of those riding home by the crowded subway or the elevated could be seen ravages of fear, or momentary gleams of triumph, as the stocks they had favored that day registered losses or gains. Herbert Hoover had been elected to succeed Calvin Coolidge. The boom, which had swept on and on unchecked throughout Coolidge's administration, now touched fantastic heights. Everyone was drunk with the prospect of unlimited prosperity, boundless spending and squandering. The entire city had become an enormous Monte Carlo in which everyone "had a tip" and was about to win his fortune.

I was surprised to learn that Murphy too was gambling with all the rest. He had laid his other work aside, and was anxiously hanging on to the telephone receiver, his face brightening or darkening as he asked the price of "American Can." I wondered at the reason why he should be so swept away, and was told that playing the stock market was the new, American, and up-to-date version of the adventurous daring of the Elizabethan Englishmen of the past. Personally, I knew that there was nothing to be said in reply to an attitude so completely based on unreasoning emotion, so little aware of tangible reality. After all, the Elizabethans had sought for and had found a world which existed not alone in fantasy, but which had its roots also in solid actuality. What actuality lay behind this world of paper profits in which Murphy and millions of others were becoming daily engulfed? It was equally as fantastic and even more false than the mass utopia towards which Russia was now proceeding; and I felt certain that time would soon, in any case, sweep it all away. It was swept away sooner even than I expected, six months after my visit, just at the time when my book came out with the New York firm that published it.

The Two Frontiers did not sell, and was not discussed as I had hoped it would be. No one was interested in anything beyond the resounding crash of Wall Street. A year later everyone, facing the inevitable and complete collapse of the spectacular boom, began feverishly buying books on Russia, lauding to the skies Russia's foresight in carrying out, under her state socialism, a five-year plan, while in America capitalism had failed, under conditions of free competition, to plan in any way for the future.

But these books, though published in great numbers, and eagerly discussed and read, failed to attract attention to mine, which had been critical both of Russia's centralized state socialism and of free American individualism, but which had appeared before the great economic crisis was set free to sweep around the world. I recall but one criticism, in a prominent New York literary supplement, which seemed typical of all. The disillusioned young radical who wrote it, himself a product of Harvard and of Montparnasse, said that in my text I sometimes contradicted myself, sometimes spoke of the human will as being free, and at other times spoke of everything, including the will, as being conditioned by material and economic factors. Therefore my book, he declared, contained no well-grounded or consistent philosophy.

I disagreed at the time, and beg leave to disagree still. The human will is undoubtedly free, and to argue that there is only one course open for that will, working through history, to follow, is to repeat the fatal flaw, the warped defect, of Marx's own, as of all, social revolutionary determinism. At the same time, the will is only free to operate on a given set of circumstances already provided for it by the past. Nor is there, in these two apparently contradictory statements, the slightest disagreement. To take but a single instance, derived from my own experience: in my own poetry, and in its development and achievement, I have been free to write about the subjects I have been interested in, free to develop the forms in which I choose to write. But I have not been free to choose any or every subject. My subjects, as well as the interest I have taken in them, have been dictated to me by the given circumstances of my life. Thus in every case I have been governed not by free will, nor by necessity, but by a sort of necessitous free will, a free will always acting within the confines of some given set of conditions. And what is true of me is also true of all mankind.

The failure of *The Two Frontiers* to reach even a small and select audience, an audience of the "happy few," in Stendhal's phrase, was the most damaging blow I had as yet received during my career as an author. Throughout 1930 I kept hoping that the book would be taken up and talked about. Possibly it is harder for a book which attempts to present an entirely new and unexpected angle of insight, but which is passed over in silence by the professional reviewers, to make its way nowadays, in this age of mass production and mass propaganda, than it was in Stendhal's day, or at any time in the past. I do not contend that this venture of mine into the field of the historical survey, and of historical criticism, produced a masterpiece, though my effort was undoubtedly an interesting and a significant one. I have, as yet, not even reread the book *The Two Frontiers* since its appearance. The fact that it did not sell, and did not take, was too great a shock for me to bear.

Throughout 1930 and 1931 my literary career was practically at a standstill. I was still in England, with no expectation of leaving, as it seemed, on the whole, easier for me to live there than anywhere else. I had shot my bolt and made my effort, and if the times did not favor me that was none of my fault. But my mind was still as active as ever, and, as so frequently before in my case, needing new fields to exercise itself, it went off in two different directions simultaneously. I became not only interested in the future of America and of Russia, but in the future of Europe as their background; and this led directly to a new set of contacts, which did me no good.

My *Two Frontiers* had concluded on a note of absolute pessimism concerning the destiny of America and of Russia, a pessimism that, as I see it now, was not justified by later events. I pictured in my last chapter a presumptive clash between the two great powers of America and the U.S.S.R.—a clash that would, in fact, be inevitable, provided one assumed that Russia in any case must stand or fall by communism, while America is always to be taken as the greatest and most openly powerful upholder of capitalism in the world. But fresh thought along lines of my own study has now convinced me how greatly I was mistaken in my first diagnosis. America only accepts capitalism pragmatically, because it either works now or has worked in the past; just as Russia only accepts communism theoretically, with infinite modifications—which at present rather tend to produce a system of competitive mass production for rewards regulated by the state—in actual practice. Russia still is, therefore, under all its present applications, a centralized autocratic state working towards the goal of theoretical equality under communism, just as America is still, as it was at the time of the Revolution and the Civil War, a decentralized group of semi-independent states working towards the goal of practical co-operation for the common good. In Russia, whatever real communism does exist is imposed from above, not from below. Sentimentally the Russian is still a Nihilist; but the state makes war on his nihilism. In America, capitalism is actually only an obvious surface veneer to the native Americanism which lies underneath, the spirit of common instinctive action in the cause of mutual aid and mutual benefit, which found so many brilliant examples on the frontier, in the Indian and the Revolutionary wars, in the Civil War, and so down to today. There is no reason therefore to suppose that in either Russia's case or in America's case their cultures, being composed in each case of a virtue carefully balanced by its opposite defect, may not persist, and even possibly outlast Europe.

I had, however, in my book, reached a diametrically opposite and pessimistic conclusion, and now my mind began to react against its own pessimism.

In writing my book, and in concluding that neither America nor Russia could surpass or outlive the older European cultures from which both had borrowed certain leading traits, I had only too often forgotten that in neither country had a settled adjustment between the individual and the state been achieved. I had forgotten to note, in every case, that in America the state acts as the negative, the conservative factor; the action of the individual, whether for good or evil, often outruns it. In Russia, on the contrary, the state is the dynamic, the revolutionary factor, since the time of Peter the Great at least; and the actions of the individual are forced to conform, to measure up to it. In passing sentence on America and on Russia equally, I had forgotten too that, after all was said and done, I was an American.

It now seemed to me that the only factor which would save America either culturally or spiritually, and so overcome the monotonous mass drift into the big cities, with their "atmosphere of boom and collapse" such as Georges Duhamel's *Scènes de la Vie Future*—a book I discovered everyone in Paris reading in the summer of 1930—spoke about, was to stress the fact that all American culture was primarily local and regional, not metropolitan at all. I felt that the future of American culture—and a healthy culture was the first sign of a healthy prosperity in America's case—could be secured only by a development of regional culture on an enormous scale, as a deliberate antidote to the pseudo culture, equally compounded of sophistication and commercialism, of such a city as New York.

In the spring of 1929, while I was in New York City, Allen Tate had approached me and had stated that the Fugitive group was now preparing for a symposium of essays, to which he invited me to become a contributor. Although I had been somewhat doubtful of his group's attempts to reduce all American poetry to an abstract exercise in intellectualization, I felt I was completely in sympathy with them when it came to the question of a social, political, and moral program upholding the ideals of southern agrarianism at the expense of northern industrialism. Nay, more: I felt, and still feel, that the fact that these southerners were now banding together and producing a critique of northern industrial civilization, and a defense of the culture of the old South, was in a way an answer to the prayer I had cherished since my going abroad in 1908, that some part of America might in some way be delivered from the incubus of the machine, from a false "prosperity" emerging through applied science and industrial exploitation, and revolt in favor of a premechanical, preindustrial, handicraft state of proprietorship. I was so thoroughly in agreement with the ideas to be mooted in the symposium in question that I instantly agreed with Tate to take part in it. In subsequent correspondence with Davidson I agreed to do an essay on education. I worked on this essay all during the late spring of 1929; by June of that year it was in Davidson's hands.

By upholding the cause not only of American regionalism, but also of political sectionalism, in so far as such sectionalism had served to maintain the rich variety, the color, and the charm of American life, I had affirmed for the last time my faith in my own country, not indeed the country of New York and Chicago post-War, postprohibition sophisticates, but the genuine rural America of the beloved community, the America that had produced Concord, Richmond, Charleston, the older San Francisco, New Orleans, the bygone community of New Harmony. And it was for the sake of my regional faith that, four years after I wrote in the southern symposium, *I'll Take My Stand,* my essay on "Education—Past and Present," I returned not only to America, but to a specific spot in America, my own native town in Arkansas. But though this part of my brain functioned correctly, and came to the right decision as regards the future promise of a rural as opposed to an industrial America, the other part of my brain was still overmuch concerned with the future of Europe, still doubtful whether America could survive if Europe collapsed. So I came to a wrong decision in my life by attempting to find some means of saving, not America only, but Europe as well.

I had been mildly interested since 1917 in a group of people, among whom were several associated with the handicrafts, either as actual handicraftsmen or as engaged in marketing handicraft work, who had organized in London a society devoted to the study of psychology, known, from the name of its nominal founder, as the Adler Society. I had been, for years before this, familiar with some of the great theorists of modern psychology, having read Freud and disagreed completely with his theory both of the Oedipus complex and of the primacy of sex. I had also tackled Jung and found him to be both more complex and more rewarding, as one having better insight into the obscure creative processes which govern the artist. I had not, so far as I know, even heard of Adler before 1927. Now I discovered that Adler had both popularized and vulgarized Nietzsche's "will to power," and had also rediscovered the familial instinct, which nineteenth century individualism had largely lost sight of. It seemed to me, however, that Adler had oversimplified the problem in ascribing all psychic troubles to his famous "inferiority complex" and to an urge for overcompensation. Freud was profound, and probably wrong; Jung was also profound, and probably right; but Adler was neither. Nevertheless, I became mildly interested in the Adler Society, which contained a good many of my friends, the craftsmen, and I attended many of their lectures in 1928 and 1929.

In 1930 I suddenly heard that the Society was being reformed on a new basis. It was now coming out with avowed political and economic as well as psychological aims. Adler was, in politics, an advanced Socialist, and this new society had his tacit approval, being organized to promote greater economic equality, political liberalism and cultural opportunity among the people of England. England was now menaced by the same economic crisis that had already engulfed America. In Germany Hitler and the Nazi party were growing, and the crisis was daily getting worse. In Austria, things were completely desperate; and the disease might easily spread to France and to Scandinavia. The aim of the reformed Adler Society was nothing less than the creation of a "New Europe." Psychological study would be henceforth secondary. What would take its place would be a basic study of the entire European background, economic, political, and cultural, together with a consideration of means for meeting recurrent crises in European destiny and ways for promoting European survival.

It is interesting to note that all this ambitious program, with its obvious appeal to those who, for some reason or other, wished to canalize their neuroticism into the easy and obvious direction of "saving the world," was, as I learned later, brought out to cover up a significant fact; that early in the year 1930 a quarrel had arisen about the way the Society was being conducted, between a group of medical men who had helped to found it and a strange adventurer turned charlatan, an Anglo-Serb who had been chiefly instrumental in its inception, and who had taken the liberty of insulting one of the doctors in question with his own verbose arrogance. The doctors had all seceded and started a new Adler Society of their own, with the result that the Anglo-Serb was left to hold the bag, consisting mainly of certain rented premises and a library of philosophical and psychological works. In order to save the situation which threatened ruin, the "New Europe" was thereupon founded, and I was now requested to join it.

Unfortunately, without making sufficient inquiry as to the actual situation within the Society, I agreed to do so. My mind, as I have already pointed out, had begun to develop along a new line of thinking: the question of the local and regional cultures of my country, and of what could be done to save them, was now becoming my chief problem. It seemed to me that in order to preserve American local culture in full richness and variety something else was demanded: the final integration of Europe into a single economic and political entity, the creation of a United States of Europe, with the consequent ending of all nationalistic wars and revivified hatreds between the nations. The New Europe claimed to be working towards that end; I decided to join it. The fact that there was no logical connection whatever between my promotion of the cause of American regionalism and the achievement of European integration which was the New Europe's aim, was entirely ignored by me for the moment. My mind was again off working in two directions at once, after the momentary attempt to synthesize all my interests in the thesis of *The Two Frontiers*. I did not at all realize that in that way lay madness.

During the last months of 1930 I lectured once or twice at the premises of the New Europe, using as my text the ideas presented in *The Two Frontiers,* which had finally come out in England in the summer of 1930, under the title of *Europe's Two Frontiers.* I would have done yet more lecturing for this organization, but I was not paid. I undertook to do it, not out of any special friendliness, but because I felt that my book—generally ignored by the English, as by the American reviewers—deserved what advertisement I could give it. I did not feel that it was worth while to go on giving lectures for nothing, and so I did not offer to give more. At the same time I felt more and more restless and dissatisfied, and again the overwhelming desire came over me to return to my own country. A short time before Christmas, 1930, I actually purchased a steamer ticket and began making preparations for departure, though without any clear idea of what I either could or would do once I arrived in the United States. The ticket was in the end unused, because an attack of bronchitis laid me low, and my Christmas that year was spent in bed.

Early in 1931 I received a communication from the University of Virginia to the effect that they were holding a round table conference on the subject of regionalism, in July. Allen Tate had been asked to attend this, and to debate the subject along with Stuart Chase, Lewis Mumford, Benton Mackaye, Professor Howard Odum of the University of North Carolina, the late Henry Wright, Clarence Stein, and other speakers. Tate had at first accepted, and then had decided at the last moment not to go. He had suggested me as a substitute. The fact that the authorities at the University of Virginia obviously wanted someone to represent the agrarian group made me feel that it was my clear duty to attend, and to make what impression I could by arguing an anti-industrialist, antimechanical thesis before this audience. I was aware that the symposium *I'll Take My Stand,* in which I had taken part, had been brought out along with my book *The Two Frontiers* just at the outset of the great stock market crash, and at the beginning of the great depression. Now one heard fantastic tales from America, how the big eastern cities were filling up with unemployment and bread lines, how factory after factory was closing down, how the farmers of the wheat belt were burning their crops in their household furnaces, how the cotton belt, hard-hit by the great flood I had barely missed seeing in 1927, and by the searing drought of 1930, was utterly ruined.

The most powerful and the most highly industrialized of all modern western capitalistic states, the country that had been least hard-hit by the War, that had known, since, ten years of seeming prosperity, was being engulfed slowly but steadily in an everdarkening, economic maelstrom of collapse. And now England, which had begun to improve slightly since the general strike of 1926, was again in straits, as the doctrines of economic nationalism and of prohibitive tariffs rose anew and spread over the world.

I decided to go, in any case, to see for myself just what was happening in America, and what changes were taking place under the surface of my country, which had become so completely and fantastically changed overnight as to be suddenly concerned with nothing but unemployment and the relief problem. Unemployment in America! That seemed fantastic to me, who had seen in New York in 1923 and 1926, and in the spring of 1929, how the employment agencies there were offering three jobs to every man who would fill them, who had watched all the stages of the great transformation from the horse-and-buggy epoch down to the age of the skyscraper and the cheap automobile, who had read of Herbert Hoover's intention to put "a chicken in every pot and a car in every garage," who had seen how the hatred and mistrust of Americans in Europe had grown because of tales of fabulous prosperity, who had read that in New York bricklayers were being paid sixteen dollars a day!

It seemed to me now time to restate my old thesis against the age of competitive industrialism, which I had first learned from the study of John Ruskin and William Morris after I had gone abroad from Harvard, in the summer of 1908, and which had grown into an absolute matter of conviction since the War. What better opportunity offered than this of the Virginia round table conference on regionalism? The future of regionalism in America seemed to me to be bound up with something else—some unknown and incalculable moral factor of conscious agrarianism, which would set its face alike against further centralization of industry and against the big-city culture of sophistication which had followed upon that centralization, from the days of the eighteen seventies down to the great boom of the nineteen twenties. What factor was there in the American intellectual landscape which had set itself the task of consciously upholding the cause of agrarianism, except that small group of twelve southerners, who with myself as a member had brought out the symposium *I'll Take My Stand?* I could find none. Moreover, perhaps now the time was ripe for America to take moral stock, to see that behind all this talk of economic planning which had followed the coming of the great depression lay another question, not of economics, but of ethics—a question of what were the best elements upon which man *could* plan, and which would be the most conducive to the good and the full life.

I left London at the close of June to take part in the University of Virginia round table. I arrived in New York on the afternoon of the thirtieth of that month, as I remember; it was a day of such windless calm and clarity of atmosphere that the top of the newly built Empire State Building, standing on its midtown site where the old Waldorf-Astoria had been, was visible fully twenty miles out to sea. Yet this calm was the calm of relaxation, of creeping economic paralysis, of exhaustion, of approaching death. I who had seen the Woolworth Tower shooting skyward in the fall of 1914, now in the summer of 1931 descended again the gangplank, walked past that great cliff of new stone and chromium steel gone a thousand feet skyward above my head, and said: "All this has been. This is the symbol of an America that has already passed. Henceforth there must be no more buildings like this; but rather broad acres, clean skies, the beauty of rural centers and of human dwelling places." Or, as I expressed it shortly afterwards, in my "Elegy on an Empty Skyscraper":

> There is wide space between
> Man's topmast and his keel, and in it death
> Comes without stir or noise or sound of breath.
>
> No one shall find his room, or take his place
> In it, as stowaway, or come-aboard:
> Nor shall the meagre window-blind be lowered,
> Nor shall the dark be leveled by a face.

After a few days of New York's gasping heat, I turned southward to Charlottesville, where the round table was being held. The University of Virginia lived up to the expectations I had formed of it. The classical simplicity of its buildings, the Jeffersonian dignity of its setting, quite overwhelmed me, and made me feel that, however dark the prospect might be that now overshadowed the America of the great boom, a nobler, wiser, saner, and finer American had once dreamed of a different destiny. Monticello, poised on its hilltop, commanding vast views to the Shenandoah on one side, and over tidewater Virginia on the other, only confirmed the impression. Could America, which had once produced so high, so varied, so splendid a life as Jefferson's, be said to have failed? Perhaps the last ten years of the Harding-Coolidge-Hoover regime had only been an unhappy nightmare. Perhaps by that grave in the Monticello grounds which bore the inscription, "Thomas Jefferson, author of the Declaration of Independence, the Statute for Religious Freedom, and Founder of the University of Virginia," there yet brooded a spirit which would arouse Americans to a task more humane than the blind worship of success, the piling up of fresh symbols of the almighty power of organized greed.

The conference was a resounding success. Despite the terrific heat, I sustained my position of a lone hand battling against the tide of modernity for four days, and managed at least to keep most of my ground and cause one or two to revise their extremely urban-centered views. I discovered that I could speak from notes, and even extempore, once my intense interest in the subject carried me away. My only steadfast supporter was H. C. Nixon, who had come all the way from New Orleans, and who was not scheduled as one of the leading speakers. I had read his essay in *I'll Take My Stand,* and knew that he was an agrarian; now I realized that he was an agrarian with a social purpose, and with a desire for deeds no less than for phrases. I left Charlottesville in the company of a young Virginian studying civil government at Columbia University. He drove me in his car down to Richmond, where I spent one day looking at the old city, and at the Confederate Battle Abbey, with its murals, just outside. Here I took train for Hampton Roads, where I was to catch the night boat for Baltimore.

Whether it was the excitement of that conference, or the intense July heat in which it was held, I do not know; but in Richmond and on the boat up to Baltimore I began to suffer from insomnia, which in fact pursued me for the next two weeks, and was a foretaste of that nervous collapse that followed after my return to England. I had previously known what a prolonged bout of insomnia would be like, at the time of my breakdown in the spring of 1926, and I knew what it would lead to; so I strove to guard against it by resting as much as possible, by attempting naps during the afternoon, by conserving all my physical resources. Those who have never known this sort of trouble can have little conception of how it feels. After a night of restless tossing to and fro, of confused dreams that do not provide normal sleep, one wakens feeling stale, with little expectation or hope of accomplishing anything during the day. The sun, as it gets higher and brighter, seems to be more and more pitiless, burning its way through the skull to the brain in an endless and changeless exasperation which transforms time itself to a meaningless eternity. The morning is got through somehow, and in the afternoon one lies down, to snatch a little exhausted sleep. As night comes on, one's exasperation and dread return: another day has gone, has reduced one's resistance a little more, has peeled off from one's skin another layer of strength; and now the soul, more naked and helpless, has to wrestle with the powers of darkness once again. This goes on till hallucination takes the place of reality—a point I now managed to avoid, but which duly arrived in the next fall.

The two weeks that followed the Virginia round table, spent at my sister's beautiful farm in Maryland, were occupied in fighting off insomnia, and in striving to get the upper hand of my own frayed nerves. My sister, whose economic and financial situation, prosperous when she first took up farming in 1926, had now become doubtful under the depression, was sympathetic, but scarcely understood what was the matter with me. And I felt too exhausted to explain. The fact of the matter was, I was subjecting my body and blood, already become less resilient after forty-five years of living, and probably thickened by the English climate and diet, to the severe trial of an American July for the first time since 1920; and I was now paying the penalty by feeling a constant giddiness when I went out for a walk in the sun, a sense of suffocation when I lay down, ringing in my ears, and other unpleasant symptoms. I stayed at my sister's place till the twenty-sixth of July. Then I fled northwards to New York, where my elder sister had promised to come up from Little Rock and visit me for a week.

When she arrived I was already a little better; but I needed this improvement in my condition, in order to be able to face her. I had not seen her since the spring of 1927, and my last visit to Arkansas. I was shocked and surprised at the change that had now taken place. She had been ill since early that spring with a condition of the blood which the doctors had at first diagnosed as anemia, but which later proved to be due to an overwhelming predominance of red, not white, corpuscles. She was obviously now a very sick woman. I had intended to confide in her some of my own doubts and hesitations concerning the advisability of my continuing to live in England, and to take her advice; but she was obviously in no condition to receive my confidences. We stayed in New York for a day, and then went up together to Boston, where we remained a week with some friends. She then left for Arkansas. As we parted, I had a moment of dread at the thought I might never see her again.

New York was impossible to me in my weakened and exhausted condition. It was now about the sixth or seventh of August, and the heat continued unabated. Fortunately, I had received an invitation to come and stay as long as I liked at the home of Lloyd Goodrich, a young art-critic friend whom I had seen a good deal of in New York in the spring of 1929, and again in London during the following fall and winter. He had a cottage of his own on the seacoast of Rhode Island, north of Newport, where he was now living with his wife and young baby. I decided to go, and spent there the next two weeks, successfully escaping New York's torrid climate, sea bathing and walking in the open air, writing verses, and gradually improving in my health and nerves. Goodrich was working on his life of Thomas Eakins, the great American portraitist, and we discussed the book together. His wife was both hospitable and kind, and their baby, born a little under a year ago, was a darling. The New England coast charmed me with its combination of ultramodern up-to-dateness and remote loneliness. I frankly envied Goodrich his good fortune and his happiness. It was the last interlude of comparative peace I was to obtain for nearly two years.

At the end of August, with my resources rapidly diminishing, I again quitted America. The utmost I had been able to obtain from the now depressed and sweltering publishing firms and their allies on Manhattan Island was a definite promise from a clean, efficient-looking young publisher's agent who had read my *Two Frontiers* that if I could follow it up by writing a lighter and more popular book drawing the contrast between English and American economic, political, and cultural life, he could practically promise to find me a publisher. The depression was now settled deeper than ever, and no one knew precisely when it would end. I suspect that this agent was whistling to keep up his own as well as my courage. I had already seen bread lines forming in Baltimore and New York, and was glad enough to get away from America for the coming winter.

I arrived in London early in September, in the midst of a new crisis caused by England's going off the gold standard, the devaluation of the pound, the abandonment of free trade, and the advent of the Nationalist government to power. My acquaintances of the New Europe were very active now. Within a week of my arrival they held an elaborate three-day conference at the home of one of their members in the village of Ditchling, in Sussex—a conference attended by no less a person than the now aging and somewhat wearisomely verbose Sir Patrick Geddes, whom I had heard a great deal about beforehand through Lewis Mumford. I was suffering from sleeplessness again, and I should have been away in the country resting, instead of taking part in so many talks and discussions. So much mental activity without an object was dangerous, but the atmosphere was hectic with excitement. In Germany, the Nazis were already victoriously coming to power, and a new and darker shadow was being spread over Europe. Every European nation except Finland was now defaulting on its War debts to America, and yet the seeds of a new war were already being sown, in defiance of pacifist sentiment and the League of Nations. England herself had barely escaped national bankruptcy, and was utterly bankrupt of new ideas and energy. I stopped thinking, in my condition of nervous exhaustion, of just how ridiculous, how damaging my alliance with those connected with the New Europe might be, and plunged into the midst of their society. I did not realize that thereby I was only exchanging a chaos sufficiently great for one still greater.

October and November passed, with frequent lectures at the New Europe, while at the same time I began to write my new prose book on the cultural relationships between England and America. The agent in New York to whom I had mooted my plan had urged me to get my book ready by the first of the year, in order to meet a date for spring publication. I was vainly trying to crowd a book which should have taken a full year to write into three months, was lecturing every week, and was becoming more and more worried about my own mental condition. The people at the New Europe were freakish, to say the least, but they seemed to be exercising a queer hold on me. They were all full of windy talk—that collection of neurotic women, sentimental vegetarians, charlatans, and self-deceivers—about the "crisis," "the eleventh hour," "the principle of self-realization through self-identification," and other recondite matters. All this was none of my business. Had I been in any normal state of body or mind, I would have known as much, but I was not. I was being drawn deeper, at every moment, into the atmosphere of a mad cult.

It was early in December that I finally became embroiled with a woman of this group—a heavy-set, middle-aged, gray-haired creature of loose morals who, as I failed to realize until it was too late, was on the brink of the menopause and taking her last fling, and in every way closer to actual insanity than I myself. I was by this time in such a state of mental irresponsibility that there is very little that I remember of the affair, except that the woman in question belonged to yet another sect in London which believed not only in clairvoyance, astrology, spiritualism, vegetarianism, but also in the invisible presence of angels, which she assured me, had sent her to save me from my unhappy marriage. And I was blind fool enough to give credence to this notion, for the moment, until it was too late.

January and February passed with ample time to regret my conduct. I had abandoned my home at Sydenham, had committed myself to complete irresponsibility, without thought of the damage I was doing to my wife and stepchildren or in the eyes of my friends in London. The people who were running the New Europe alone seemed in no wise shocked or surprised at what I had done. Indeed, they were mostly aware of my new liaison, and had urged it on me. They did not seem to realize, as I now realized in brief moments of returning lucidity, how I had but leapt from the frying pan into the fire. It was I who now looked longingly back to the peace and ease of mind that had often been mine during my marriage. I had spent weeks dodging missiles thrown at me, enduring outbreaks of savage rage on the part of one whose slatternliness was only equaled by her vulgarity. I had taken up modern "emancipated" living with a vengeance, by living with one who shared neither my ideas nor my friends, who was as incapable of comprehending the former as she was hostile and contemptuous of the latter. And I had worsened my physical and mental condition immeasurably by a relationship which was not only unworthy, but abnormal.

In February, 1932, in a state of nerves that beggared all description, I returned to my wife, who was still hoping and expecting that some day I would come back to her. I had caused her hideous suffering! I returned home feeling that I could never hold up my head again; for I knew now, not only how unworthily I had acted, but to what kind of person I had entrusted myself for the past three months. As I feared, it was now impossible for Daisy and myself to come to a readjustment of the situation. Her pride and her confidence in me had been too deeply and lastingly hurt, and my own nerves were still in such a permanently shaky state that recovery on my part seemed almost out of the question. The five months that passed from February to July were spent in a last fruitless effort to come to some kind of understanding. Early in July I had an accident, suffering a severe fall, in which I was knocked unconscious and broke a shoulder blade. I awakened to find myself in a hospital. I was glad enough to take the enforced rest and peace which my stay in the ward granted. But though my body improved, my nerves were shattered. Acting on medical advice, I went to a sanitarium at last, in September, 1932. There I spent five months, slowly recovering my mental poise, until I emerged completely cured in the last weeks of February, 1933. Had I but consulted the doctor who had originally cured me in 1926, as early as the beginning of September, 1931, or had I gone either voluntarily or at my wife's wish to a sanitarium as early as the close of that summer, I could have avoided all that happened to me during this period.

February now gave way to March; and Herbert Hoover, in America, was giving way to Franklin Roosevelt and the New Deal. Over the radio in London I heard clearly the inaugural address of America's new president, at the very apex of the deepest and most deadly crisis in America's economic, social, and moral history since that crisis, faintly recalled from my boyhood, which Cleveland, another Democrat, had striven to break. I thrilled to the new President's courage, his vitality, his vision. Four days later, and I was on the high seas, quitting England for the last time, on my way safe home at last to America. I had left my wife with quite sufficient to live on; but I knew, as we parted, that I would never see her again.

CHAPTER XXVII

On the sixteenth of March, 1933, after passing through a sudden snowstorm that swarmed out of the Narrows to greet us, the *Aquitania* berthed, about half-past two in the afternoon, at her pier in New York. It was not until nearly five o'clock that I quitted the customs shed. Being wearied from the voyage, I stopped overnight, went to bed early, and did not start for the South till the following day. After two days spent at my sister's farm in Maryland, I again took train for Little Rock, arriving there early in the morning of the first day of official spring.

I had come back to an America again transformed by those vast forces, emerging from our own control or lack of control of our national resources and environment, and gradually affecting all our social, economic, moral, and political structures. These forces seemingly govern human life on this continent. The Marxians are so far right, that their famous "economic interpretation" of history seems to have been devised especially to explain, first, the shifts, in Colonial and in Revolutionary times, between the seaboard and the backwoods; second, the expansion of the population westward and the rise of the frontier democracy; third, the great clash between the industrial mode of living practiced by the North and the agrarian mode practiced by the South; fourth, the final expansion of the West; fifth, the rise of heavy industry on an enormous scale, and the contemporaneous mushroom growth of finance; which have been, altogether, chiefly responsible for the entire development of the United States and for our present position as a nation.

The only trouble with the Marxians is that they are not intelligent enough to ascribe these economic, political, and cultural changes to their correct natural causes. They think of history, even American history, as being a clash purely between bourgeois and proletariat, whereas in America there has never been but one class, the bourgeois or the potential bourgeois. Those who are not bourgeois are individual anarchists, whatever they may call themselves. In the United States all fundamental historical changes have taken place because of different sets of conditions, natural and economic, that middle-class man has met with in the course of his restless exploration, settlement, development, and exploitation of this vast area for his habitation. And there is no reason why these conditions could not be controlled by man by some means short of "proletarian" revolution.

A new shift was now obviously at hand, but no one knew in what direction it would lead. (Do many know today?) The entire North American continent had just reached the bottom of the trough of another economic hurricane, and was trying to take stock of itself before setting forth on another course. People no longer depended for their prosperity and happiness on what had been called "the noble experiment" of prohibition. No longer did they believe that by blindly following Wall Street they could reach another land of promise. No longer did they altogether rely on the world of glamorous possibilities offered by the great industrialists, and by their faithful allies, the bankers. No longer did they hope for some short cut to economic salvation. It was now time to work hard, to save whatever could be saved, to turn over the soil, to do some serious thinking. Millions during the past two years had migrated from the cities to the country; other millions were patiently awaiting relief in the cities. Every great community in the land was on the verge of bankruptcy, and every bank in the United States was closed.

The individual, after all, could do little; but I realized that a considerable amount of pioneer resistance to hard conditions must be still persisting in the American people, to see how untroubled and apparently cheerful all were, as they emerged into spring from the fourth winter of their great depression. For now a cycle of scarcity had set in for the first time, with no new lands for the great majority to go to and settle, and with machine industry carried to such a pitch that it no longer created, but rather destroyed, the possibility of further employment. Unemployment stood at the vast total of from twelve to sixteen millions, none knew how many, nor what should be done with the unemployed. "Rugged individualism" had completely broken down. The balance between urban and country living had long ago been totally destroyed, and none knew how it could be restored. And to this we had been brought by our industrial and financial wizards of the past, by the Morgans and the Mellons, the Insulls and the Van Sweringens. Yet the people remained cheerful, even confident!

I no longer felt pessimistic concerning my country's cultural future, no longer doubted that it would achieve its own great cultural forms and expressions, similar possibly to those of Europe, but distinctively American in substance and in spirit. For if the temper of the common people remained unsoured and unspoilt after the boundless orgy of greed and display that had marked the twenties, after the great disillusionment that had set in with the thirties; if the temper of the common people still could sustain a faith in this country, then it was presumably immortal, and there was an undying hope for democracy. I knew that, apart from all political and economic changes, the future of culture in America depended on the achievement of a cultural elite, which American education had signally failed to accomplish. But I now felt myself disposed to believe that even this might be possible, inasmuch as the American people, misled and confused, were only beginning to realize for the first time since Bryan's campaign for the presidency in 1896 that a political issue could be a real issue, could have its bearings on their culture no less than on their pocketbooks.

American culture, then, must be primarily regional, not metropolitan. The Southwest and the South were the more likely to achieve it, being regions where the oversuccessful propaganda of "prosperity" had not drugged the people too far into acquiescence. Nor had the resulting down-drag of the depression in the South and the Southwest given rise to such an attitude of defeatism as had already come about in the North and East. Southern culture was now already producing the most active literary movement, the most discussed and debated group of writers, in the entire United States. The Southwest, too, was being slowly but steadily heard from. The obvious sicknesses of America's economic and political structure were perhaps at last leading the way to the goal that the new poets back in 1913 had envisioned, but not realized: a true American renaissance in all cultural fields.

The thrill of first setting foot again on the American continent was now less than the thrill of my returning to Arkansas—this time, so far as I could tell, to live there permanently. I saw no reason, in that spring of 1933, why Arkansas should not achieve a genuine culture of its own, as significant in the pattern of American living as the culture of New England or of New York had been. My hope, however, of the achievement of any very vital and original culture for my native state has now largely waned; but I still see no reason why Arkansas could not some day do it, if there were only enough people to try and continue trying, and if their communities could but grant them active and enthusiastic support. The lack of support, moral and financial, for genuine expressions of local and indigenous culture is one of the most flagrantly vicious facts in American life today. How many American authors, artists, intellectuals have made reputations, only by getting away from their own native backgrounds, and by successfully ignoring the small-town disposition to criticize, to derogate, to think of all imaginative literature and art as scandalous folly, which we all share, as our own fatal inheritance from our Puritan or pioneer forefathers? H. L. Mencken had long since singled me out as having achieved a reputation only because I quitted my native state with rejoicings, at the age of twenty-one. I had come back to try to prove him mistaken; but I now found that those people of my native state were generally less interested in the fact that I had come back as an Arkansan, than in the other fact that I had lived for so long in England.

Nevertheless, here I was; though the sight of Main Street, with half its shops standing vacant and the other half struggling to keep open, despite the fact that all the banks remained obstinately closed, did not encourage any very ambitious hopes for the future. Long ago Georg Brandes had predicted, for America, an artistic and cultural renaissance as great as anything ever achieved by Florence or Venice—both, from the start, purely mercantile states—as soon as the mercantile interests themselves became aware that in the beautification of their communities, by means of works of art of all sorts, lay the maintenance of their further glory and prosperity. Brandes had been mistaken: the mercantile interests had continued to dominate America throughout the twenties, and the land had not been culturally enriched, except perhaps by the purchase of more "old masters" by the millionaire class, from Europe. Now the federal government itself stepped in, and by creating the Public Works of Art Project acknowledged that American painting, American sculpture, American architecture, had a right to exist—a step that could have been taken, should have been taken, twenty years ago, and which in itself raised my hopes to boundless heights concerning the activities of the New Deal and the Roosevelt administration.

My sole feeling of disillusionment concerning the position of the new administration, during the first year of Mr. Roosevelt's presidency, arose from the fact that quite a number of the most brilliant intellectuals of the radical left wing refused entirely to support it; while the American people generally, who were certainly not intellectual and who had done very little political thinking, supported it only sentimentally, without realizing definitely that it inevitably brought up, in sharpened form, the fundamental question of all politics, the question of the real relation between the executive, the legislative, and the judicial branches of government, as well as the question of how far the capitalist system, in its centralized, heavy-industrial form, could or should be either checked or saved. The young intellectuals of the left wing had, apparently, long since left off thinking on those points. To them, imbued as they had all been, for five years past, with the idea that nothing could save America except a state-controlled five-year plan, unaware as they all were of the fact that the American temper was pragmatic, not absolutist, ignorant as they had all shown themselves to be concerning the real characteristics of their country, nothing now sufficed but a dictatorship. To them Stalin was still a saint, and Lenin a god. During the first year of the New Deal the burden of criticism came from the left. Roosevelt had not gone far enough to please the American Muscovites.

Then, rapidly, the tune changed. It was seen that every element of reaction in the country, the so-called Liberty League in the van, was vocally opposing the man who, during the first weeks of his presidency, if he had been the monster they painted him to be, could have utterly overridden not only the flimsy bulwark of a paper constitution, unintended to be final by the very men who wrote it, but could also have broken down the power of the financial interests by completely transforming the American banking system, if he had but chosen to do so. It was, unfortunately, by that time too late for the radicals in question to sneak back to the ways of a sane and intelligent liberalism. "Liberal" like "bourgeois" had only too long become a term of contempt in their mouths.

It is not, however, my intention to write here a history of my times, nor of my political opinions. Men will differ on politics as on everything else, and in a democracy he is indeed either a wise or a lucky man who can accurately predict the future. It was primarily as a cultural agent that I had come back, and as a cultural agent that I chose to remain.

The culture that I envisaged for America was to be American, rather than internationally "proletarian." Whether it sprang from proletarian roots or not, it depended in the long run on local and regional aptitudes and conditions, which were not the same in the South or the Southwest as in New York City. In short, culturally speaking, I would have done with that vast abstraction known to political oratory and to predatory capitalism alike as "America" and as "one-hundred-per-cent Americanism." In its place there would be for me henceforward the "United States": united by the fact that they could communicate with each other and think freely; states of the soul, as much as, if not more than, the body politic. Economically, I favored for these states the most far-reaching control possible by the federal government; since the history of America, from the time of the building of the first railroads, had shown that competitive capital grabbed whatever it could grab, with complete indifference to local needs, to regional aptitudes, to local cultures, and had only thereby encompassed the waste and destruction of both natural and human resources. Politically, I believed in an advanced liberalism, since I held with complete freedom of speech and freedom of expression. Culturally, I knew myself to be a conservative, bent on restoring the classic American traditions of the first fifty years following upon the Revolution. The only "state rights" of importance then, were cultural rights; and these I would have preserved.

The spring passed pleasantly in Arkansas, with extended automobile trips to Natchez, where the Garden Week Festival revealed to me the splendor of the old South in decay, and to Fayetteville and Eureka Springs, where for the first time I obtained more than a fleeting glimpse of the Ozark region, awaking to the wild beauty of another mountain spring. I felt a great kinship of spirit stirring in me at the sight of these long wooded ridges, these dense forests, and these lonely mountain settlements with their unspoilt people.

Although I regretted the ugliness and the squalor, the hideous filling stations, the unattractive lunchstands, the rusting junk heaps, and the blatant roadside signs which the automobile had brought in its train, yet I could not help but rejoice that it was now possible to see America by some other means than that universally used in my boyhood, the railroad. How little of our own country we actually knew, we who were of the railroad generation! We had never even used our senses sufficiently to discover what the country actually looked and felt and smelt like, beyond the boundaries of the railroad tracks and the streets of the cities. And our souls had been starved in consequence. A new physical transformation of America had now taken place, by the penetration of the backwoods everywhere with good roads. What this would lead to, no one could say; but at least, after three centuries of effort, the entire vast and mysterious continent, so huge in scale compared to all European countries, so monotonous and yet so strangely beautiful, so wild and so incalculable, lay open to our eyes and to our imaginations, for the price of a cheap car. We had conquered at last our background, had come face to face with our physical heritage.

I did not wish to stay on in Arkansas over the long, enervating months of the summer, but I had hesitated before committing myself to any decision where I was to go. The decision was taken largely from my hands by my elder sister, now fortunately restored to health, who recalled with what pleasure she herself had spent recently a full year in Arizona and New Mexico. I had not lived in that part of the world since, as a young man fresh from Harvard, I had spent the summer of

1907 in this region west of the Rockies. I had kept the memory of that country, and of its savage and lonely magnificence, so complete in my mind that it had reawakened in almost full detail during the course of my train journey westward in 1915. But I had not seen Santa Fe itself, where my sister suggested that I should go, since 1907. I hesitated to go now, as I feared that the automobile might have had the effect of spoiling altogether a land always associated in my heart with the western mustang. Nevertheless, I went, and in the end was more glad than I could easily say, that I had gone.

We who are in the interior of the United States all share one outstanding characteristic. We are, for the most part, "progressive." But in New Mexico we have a land—one of our own United States—which is not progressive, where life still moves to the rhythm set by remote Indian paganism, where it is ordered according to the simple medieval pattern set by Spanish Christianity, where everything human and divine is governed alike by the scarcity of water, so that the population scarcely varies, and booms and depressions are alike unknown, where modern up-to-dateness jostles the most remote primitivism. I had seen this land once remotely, as in a dream, on my emergence from Harvard, and it had alike tantalized and appalled me. Now I was to see it again after many artists and at least one great woman writer, Mary Austin, had discovered its extraordinary beauty. A quarter of a century had passed between those two dates; yet fundamentally this land had not changed underneath, though the phenomena of its surface life had become more complicated.

New Mexico is neither culturally, politically, nor economically North American. It is still, and I suspect always will be, Spanish-American—almost as much so as old Mexico. It was conquered by the North Americans and made part of the United States, but as long as the Rockies keep their place, and the Rio Grande and its tributaries continue to vary the magnificent monotony of tawny, boundless deserts with tracts of irrigated fertility, it will not change. And this, as well as the pellucid air, the remoteness of the Pueblo past, the proud indigence of the Spanish-speaking population, have given it a quality that other parts of America do not possess. Time does not matter in New Mexico. Today does not matter. All is *mañana*—tomorrow.

I sometimes think that when we—the Anglos, as the New Mexicans call us—have finished playing about with and exploiting and wrecking our entire continent, that which is fundamentally New Mexican in our culture will then at last be found; not, indeed, as the exotic plaything that the modern artists, writers, and tourists have made it, but as a quality of our life itself, of life reduced again to the lowest dimensions of primeval necessity, and again arranged according to the ordered fitness of a handicraft culture. Here, indeed, was a place where regionalism might be considered safe for many generations to come—because it was no cult, no conscious attempt to restore the past, but the most inevitable response of the human organism to its existing conditions of environment.

I stayed in Santa Fe from the middle of June until early in September, making new contacts there, notably with Mary Austin, who had already reached and passed her years of fertility as a writer, but whose indomitably brave spirit persisted a little longer to inhabit the frail shell of a body already consumed by its own inner flame. I also became acquainted with another cultural pioneer of this New Mexican region, the beautiful, otherworldly Celtic idealist and painter, Gerald Cassidy—a name as yet as good as unknown in the annals of American art, but twice as worth knowing as others who have many time his renown. These were of the America that was already passing away; what of the America that must come? I left Santa Fe for Chicago, where the Century of Progress Exposition, which was America in her most progressive and possessive mood, had already been displaying its wares to hundreds of thousands that summer. I soon saw what it was—a riot of overpublicized "science" successfully mixed up with a strong dash of sheer vulgarity, and served up to the American public as the neatest and slickest way of making money. After a pair of visits, I turned my back on it and confined my investigations to the great art exhibit held at the same time, but not at the same location, by Chicago's own Art Institute. Here, side by side, were two Americas: one exploited by mass publicity tricked out in the latest scientific dress, and eventuating in the antics of a fan dancer; the other, where hundreds of American painters, most of whom I had never seen before, wove their patterns of color and form to set beside the stately names of the great masters. I knew which America I, at least, would choose.

Later on in that fall I went for a first lecture trip to Oklahoma—an experience repeated the following year. This state provided as complete a contrast to New Mexico or to Arkansas as could be wished. Where, in New Mexico, a persistent folk tradition had lasted undisturbed from the seventeenth to the first decade of the twentieth century, and had then not been destroyed but had rather been taken up and elaborated upon by groups of intellectuals from other parts of the country; where, in Arkansas, a folk tradition, partly frontier and partly southern, had been well established before the Civil War, and then had slowly been strangled by the insurgent growth of middle-western industrialism and by Wall Street's financial notions; where these two things had happened, Oklahoma had come into being quite ignorant of possessing any traditions whatsoever. Like Topsy, Oklahoma had "just growed." From the time that the Cherokee strip was opened in 1889, three years after I was born, from the time the first oil well had been successfully pierced at Bartlesville in 1896, Oklahoma had sped from the background of the primeval frontier to the most sophisticated modernism, with no stops by the way. I could discover no one there whose grandfather had even so much as seen the country, scarcely one among the generation over forty who had been born there. The entire cultural and economic development of the whole United States had been run through in the course of a single generation: from Osage or Kiowa tribalism to the drunken antics of the descendants of middle-western oil magnates, from the outlaw traditions of the nineties to such degenerate descendants as "Pretty Boy" Floyd. Yet even here the university was striving to uphold the standard of an intelligent regionalism. All one could do was to educate, to have faith in the people, and to wait on events.

The multifarious variety of American life and the small degree to which most people were conscious of their opportunities under it became the two leading impressions in my mind, in my first year in the United States. Most people, despite the cataclysm of the depression, despite the attempts of the New Deal to shock and galvanize them into facing the immense problems of the world's greatest experiment in democracy, were still seeking a rough-and-ready, purely temporary and pragmatic solution of the issues they were facing—with the inevitable result that most were taking the easiest way out. The American spirit, as so many times in the past, would probably not be equal, not quite measure up, to the American opportunity—with the result that after a little more than two years of the New Deal everybody would want to be let alone to get back to where they were in the twenties! That spirit, I fear, still rules over most of this land today, though I do not believe we can ever go back to the twenties, even though we should wish to do so, again and again.

Nor would it help us to go back to them. The period of the twenties immensely multiplied our literary and artistic talent, without providing for that talent any clear basis on which to live and operate. It wavered between the cosmopolitan, deracinated, sophisticated outlook of the city and a direct, local, rooted, and indigenous folk expression of the hinterland without being able to settle its mind on either. It culminated in a furious critical battle between humanist and expressionist, which was largely fought out over false and unreal issues. For my part, I was glad to see it go, gladder still if no one should ever wish to revive it—because it immensely enriched, without deepening in any respect, American culture. And, as Goethe had said, everything that enriches man's mind but does not give him command over himself is evil.

By the winter of 1933–34 it appeared to me more than ever doubtful if the tide of eighteenth-century idealism which had given to the founders of this republic their intellectual and ethical postulates and assumptions could make any further headway—unless reinforced by local pieties, folkways, a restoration of handicraft training—against the technological and abstractly "scientific" drift which had governed the advance of modern machinery. The battle was on now between mathematical logic on the one hand and the tradition of sentimental romanticism on the other—and a pragmatic Yankee-bred naturalism, however shrewd and farseeing, was no solution. The only hope lay rather in a purposeful and purified romanticism: a romanticism without those excesses of hysterical self-pity that Irving Babbitt and his disciples had condemned so vigorously in Shelley and Rousseau.

I spent that winter and early spring going over the entire romantic period in English, and, by implication, on the European Continent also, for the benefit of a handful of pupils gathered to hear me at Little Rock's Junior College. My conclusion was as anyone who had either known me or romanticism itself might have predicted, that romanticism, like everything else, must be judged by its fruits. It was useless to dodge it, in shrinking dislike, as Eliot and some of the more reactionary agrarians had seemingly done. It was equally useless to take refuge in a skeptical and detached cynicism in relation to it. It had at least intensified human sensibility beyond anything previously known in literature or in life, if only because it had rooted all things—the relation of form to feeling, of politics to life, even the relation of human nature to the supernatural itself—in human sensibility. And its fruits were therefore better, after all, for man's spiritual and intellectual consumption than the fruits of those who had believed that, by increasing the number of mechanical inventions, man's spirit could be made to progress of itself. The problem, I saw, once again, of the entire future of human culture in the United States might be summed up in a few words. It was a question of whether man could or would master the machines, or whether the machines would end by mastering man.

CHAPTER XXVIII

In the month of May, 1933, I had read, in *Scribner's Magazine*, an article signed "Charlie May Simon" about a woman who had gone, with her artist husband, to the wildest part of the Arkansas Ozarks, and had homesteaded there. The article moved me with its deep and unmistakable evidences of sympathy for the mountain people, and with its direct knowledge, through experience, of their simple ways of life. I recall that I read it aloud to my elder sister, in whose house I was living, and expressed myself as wishing to meet its author, whom I regarded as an exceptional woman. The opportunity soon came, in the early months of 1934.

In February of that year I heard that Charlie May Simon and her husband were in Little Rock. A few days later they called at the house, the "old house" of my childhood. The mysterious author of the article that had aroused my interest turned out to be a young woman with lovely bronze-gold hair, clear gray eyes, a delicately shaped figure, a soft, beautiful speaking voice, and a shy remoteness of bearing that seemed akin to the quality I had already sensed dimly during my own brief and superficial journeys in the Ozark region. She was, altogether, extremely attractive, I thought, and considerably younger than I; probably not more than thirty. Her husband, I could see at a glance, was nervous and ill-at-ease in Arkansas. He was incurably foreign to the environment he now lived in, and was likely to remain so. His attitude towards the backwoods was still largely that of New York City.

I did not know whether my own attitude was, in fact, any better than his. I knew only that, in my father's day, men must have faced exactly the same conditions, and that my blood had come down from just such a source, from a life exactly parallel to that which was still being lived today in the western half of my state. I had completely outgrown it and had steadily ignored it, as if it had never existed. True, I had written, during my last years in London, a poem called "Lost Corner" and one or two others which had attempted to deal with this phase of Arkansas life I never knew or shared. But what did all the rest of my talent—what did Mallarmé or Debussy or Amy Lowell or T. S. Eliot or anything else—amount to, set against the gray limestones and the white quartz, the breath-taking remoteness of hazy valleys running between high, flat-topped ridges buried under seething masses of hickory, oak, and pine, such as they had been ever since the dawn of creation? What had I to do with the remote unpainted cabins, the silent gaunt figures who walked about among them, the rhythms of a life that had gone on unchanged for so many years? All this was less familiar to me than the life of the Pueblo Indians.

A month or so later, just when I was completing my course on the romantic period in the Junior College, Charlie May Simon came to live with her husband in Little Rock. This time they stayed until the close of May. There was a competition afoot, sponsored by the Federal Art Project, to have the interior of the Arkansas state capitol decorated with mural paintings—a project that came to nothing in the end. Howard Simon was among those taking part in the contest, and I did what I could for him. During the months of April and May, notably, I saw a great deal of his wife, and was more and more impressed with her fine instinct for aesthetics, her profound knowledge of the backwoods people and their ways of living, her general modesty and sweetness of character.

Sometime, early in May, I set out with my sister to explore the remote fastnesses of the Ouachita Forest, where Charlie May and Howard Simon had built their mountain retreat three years ago. I fear that on that day I was as thoroughly crotchety—Charlie May has since reminded me that when she first heard of me I was described to her as being "a crotchety southern gentleman"—as I have ever been in my life. A glimpse or two into a mountain cabin by the way sufficed to show me that these people lived in conditions of almost unbelievable primitiveness—and if the sordidness of the slums of England had always horrified me in the past, how much more did these cabins, with their walls papered with old newspapers, their unscreened doors and windows, their utter lack of any of the amenities to which I had been accustomed since my childhood? The car in which we were riding finally became stuck at the bottom of an unbridged creek, and refused to budge for several minutes, in the very midst of an interminable forest. I thoroughly lost my temper, and did not recover it fully until Charlie May and I went gathering wild flowers along the roadside, while the car was scrambling out of the stream.

Charlie May's home, aptly named by her "Possum Trot," proved to be a neatly built, well-kept log cabin, standing by itself amid solemn and lonely pine trees. It had books and pictures, a sense of culture and refinement, a brave, indomitable quality of its own, remote alike from the preciously "arty" and from the stark barrenness of the dwellings I had just seen. But Charlie May had studied art in Paris, had been a capable sculptress before her marriage and her coming here to live. She had come back because this was her background, because the folk of her own blood had once walked in these hills, because her father had lived out his early life among them, and had made a notable book from his own early experiences. To live here was, for her, to return to her own sources of living: it was natural. She had written, in addition to the magazine article I had already read, a book for children dealing with the mountain people. It would be published that summer. Meanwhile, as I had noted for some time past, her husband kept on speaking of New York, and of how he felt the necessity of going back there.

In the first weeks of June, soon after I had arranged to go out to Santa Fe that summer, I learned that my two new acquaintances had suddenly decided to travel on by car to New York. I did not suppose that I would see either of them again; or if I did, the only one that I either hoped or cared to see was Charlie May. Her knowledge of the upland Ozark background and of my own native region was far deeper, fuller, and more sympathetic than mine; and she had equally charmed me with her appearance, her manners, her attitude towards life. Both my sister and I had decided that she was an exceptional woman, and I frankly envied her husband. Now that she was gone, it was in no good mood that I set out for the West again.

The summer at Santa Fe passed without further incident, except that during the last weeks of July a parcel came my way. I opened it and saw that it contained *Robin on the Mountain* by Charlie May Simon. So I spent some days there reading about Robin Lamb and Johnny Shelby, America and Hebert, and the difficulties attending homesteading in the Ozarks—difficulties that, I am sure, my friend the author must have known in even larger measure from her own experience. For a child's book, this seemed to me remarkably stark, honest, and realistic throughout, though, as I had already said to its author, I knew but little about juvenile literature.

I had already spent the months of April and May, before leaving Arkansas, in writing the first two books of an epic poem which was to deal with the entire history of my state, from De Soto's discovery of the Mississippi in 1541, down to the present day. This poem had been commissioned by the editor of the *Arkansas Gazette,* the leading newspaper of Little Rock, for a special supplement to come out on the state centenary, June 15, 1936. I did not attempt to write more of it while away in New Mexico, but on my return to Little Rock, early in September, I resumed it again.

By the first weeks of October I was forced to stop work. I had now carried the history of Arkansas down to the Civil War. But who in Arkansas cared now about the Civil War or about what, culturally no less than politically, socially no less than economically, men had fought over desperately seventy years gone by, in a contest that had lasted four full years and had been the major disaster befalling American civilization? Another heritage, not better but at least more up-to-date, and thoroughly acceptable as a substitute, had at any rate taken the place of whatever the South was achieving at the time of the Civil War. One could not destroy that new and untried heritage and restore the old by the force of mere indignation. It would be better to do what my friend, the author of *Robin,* had done—go off and live quietly in the Ozarks with the mountain folk, who had never lived any differently since long before the Civil War, and who regarded, I had once been told, the Great War of 1917–18 as merely "another brush with the Yankees." But my friend had already gone to New York.

About the twelfth of October I managed to obtain money from my younger sister, and set off for New York. I hated New York now, with every fiber of my being. If I could have had my way I would have bombed every skyscraper of them all. I was coming to New York merely in order to find a literary agent who would undertake to handle my work, so that I would not have to spend so much time and effort contacting editors and publishers in a city I knew well to be a Gehenna of greed, and the most un-American of all American cities. No; that was not the only reason. I was coming in order to see Charlie May again.

I found the Simons installed in a tiny studio off a Greenwich Village street, in a living space so small that obviously only one person of the household had been able to accomplish any work in it—and that person was Howard Simon. I realized what a hard struggle my hostess was having, and, hoping to help in some way, induced Murphy to quit his hermitlike isolation uptown and come down to see them. Perhaps he might be able to throw some work in their direction as he had once helped me, long ago. I wished I could see my hostess alone, and tell her how I had missed her since she had left Arkansas, and how I had felt sure that Arkansas was still her place. Whatever I had wished to do for my state, I wished for her also—but on the sole occasion when we were alone together, no words would come. After all, she was a married woman, and had said to me last spring that her chief desire and ambition had been to be a good wife to her husband.

So I left, after five days of New York, without obtaining the literary agent I had hoped to find for my type of work, and without obtaining any assurance of seeing Charlie May in Arkansas again. I had again met Henry Seidel Canby and William Rose Benét, whom I had known far back in the days when they were editing together the New York *Evening Post Book Supplement;* when I was still just getting over the War, striving to adjust myself to possibly permanent expatriation, and becoming a bit cool and doubtful of my own reputation of having entered American literature arm-in-arm with Amy Lowell. They were now running the *Saturday Review,* which they had patiently and gradually built up to be the best weekly critical organ of its kind in America.

But I had not been in their office since the spring of 1929, so deeply had I become prejudiced against New York and all things Manhattanese. Now, in 1934, so strong did this prejudice persist, that I fear our first meeting for five years was scarcely friendly on my part—which was my fault altogether, as I know.

I also met again Mark Van Doren, whom I had known ever since Allen Tate introduced me to him during my stay in New York in the spring of 1929. Although he is much younger than I, being in fact of Tate's own generation, he has always seemed to me to possess certain qualities which one could find only in the older poets, and which might be summed up by saying that at the bottom of them lay a tough-rooted Americanism of mind that was strong alike for its independence in thinking and for its scorn of fashionable theory, a quality conspicuously lacking in the post-War generation. He was also deeply imbued with the specific American myth: that dream of a country of proud industrious free men, pioneers in both living and thinking, who tamed the wilderness with their broad-axes, transformed it to fertile farms and busy, beautiful towns, gave to both God and man their due rights, and died in the consciousness that here was indeed a new land, a land "fit for orators and bards" and heroes to live in—a land that has been nullified forever by the greed and self-seeking that followed the Civil War. As a piece of authentic midwestern Illinois timber transported to New York City, and still keeping some of the prairie about his roots, I valued Mark Van Doren. Something of the same quality is also apparent in his brother Carl, as his recent autobiography can testify.

I remained in New York only five days, as I had work that called me back to Arkansas. The fourth book of my "Epic of Arkansas" remained to be written, and I knew it would be hardest of all to write, as it must deal with the reconstruction period and the transition down to the present day. Concerning reconstruction, none of my father's or mother's generation had ever been able to speak without feeling, and without letting anger appear in their voices; and I knew that whatever one might think of their version of the Civil War, their opinion concerning reconstruction was essentially sound. I decided to make this book of my poem more detailed, more realistic, and to draw the clear lesson, apparent in all American history for the past seventy years, that all gangs of politicians in power—whether Democrat or Republican, it matters not—can, under democracy, not only despoil the people but go on corrupting and despoiling them forever, while mouthing the shibboleths of democracy meanwhile, unless the people themselves, through threat of revolution, take the issue into their own hands. This was the opinion of Thomas Jefferson, and it is also mine; but it was difficult to embody all this in poetry.

I struggled on through November and December writing my fourth book; by January 3, 1935, my forty-ninth birthday, it was finished. But in the end I was obliged to abandon it, and to be satisfied with a far briefer, more generalized, and less accurately pointed account. The editor of the paper in which it was to appear feared that various people, descendants of the once dominant carpetbag aristocracy still living on in Arkansas, might take offense at this fresh stirring up of old quarrels and controversies, now best forgotten; and so he succeeded at last in curbing my own unreconstructed southernism.

With the completion of my Arkansas poem, I felt that the work I could do for my native state was as good as done. I had lectured about the state, had attempted teaching, had written a poem which had entailed a year of study and research, and had tried to foster the arts in every way possible. I had made contacts with whatever cultural and artistic forces there were in the landscape: with the one able musical composer, Laurence Powell, himself a permanent exile from England, who was making a brave uphill struggle to live and to create a local symphony orchestra; with Adrian Brewer, a middle-western painter who had an equally hard struggle to survive in Arkansas, and who had been only able to do so through capitalizing on his ability to paint acceptable portraits; with the Austrian-born pianist, Josef Rosenberg, whose status had been complicated by personal tragedy; with the archaeologist S. C. Dellinger, still dreaming on, at my miserably endowed state university, of revealing the wealth of Indian culture that lay buried in our soil; with Charles Davis, a delicate poet turned newspaperman; with Eleanor Risley of Mena, and with Charles J. Finger of Fayetteville. I felt that I had now come into contact with every cultural agency in the state; and taken all together, they were scarcely enough. I had now lived for two years in Arkansas and had cut myself totally off, thereby, from the theater—one of my strongest intellectual passions—from good music and painting, and from the give-and-take of ideas. Perhaps Edgar Lee Masters, with his sardonic remark about burying myself in the backwoods and talking to no one above the intellectual level of the garage mechanic, had been right, after all.

Meantime, Charlie May was still in New York with her husband, again writing a book for children. Since Christmas I had hoped to see her again in Arkansas; and I knew that if I could not, sooner or later I must come to New York to see her. I could not forget her, nor the charm of her personality as I had seen it displayed in her mountain retreat at Possum Trot and in Little Rock. It seemed to me that her real place lay not in New York, but in Arkansas; but she had chosen otherwise, for the sake of her husband.

As early as the end of April, after a short trip to Baton Rouge to take part in a literary conference at Louisiana State University—a trip during which I had the interesting experience of seeing, face to face, that singular and disturbing figure in American politics, Huey Long—I decided that since Charlie May was not likely to return to Little Rock, I must go to New York to be at least near to her. . . . I had still friends there, and connections with the literary world, which might enable me to find enough work reviewing or teaching, so that I could live there and meet her. I was unaware at the time that Charlie May, for her part, had decided to come down to Arkansas for the same purpose. I had arranged, by the middle of May, to come north and spend the month of August in a well-known literary and artistic colony in New York State; this would at least bring me into her proximity. But as the time grew nearer I began to worry lest, after all, she might come down that summer, just as I was departing, and we thereby miss each other.

On the fifteenth of July, with my trunks packed and my departure arranged for, I sent her a telegram asking whether she were likely to come down, and stating that I was leaving in ten days' time. I had missed her companionship for so long that I feared I might do so again. The telegram was sent off in the morning. Early that afternoon I received a telephone call, and heard her voice speaking. She was in Little Rock, having driven down with her husband and his younger brother; they had just arrived. They were on their way to Possum Trot, Charlie May's homestead, now, but a day later, they would return. The day came, and on an afternoon of humid southern heat and glowing sunlight, broken by scowling thunderclouds rattling their sharp bullets of hail over the leaves, I learned that we had cherished, since January, the selfsame plan of being near each other. And I discovered not only that I was in love with Charlie May—I had been in love with her for months past, and had tried vainly to forget her—but that my love was fully returned.

By now it was too late to change my definite arrangements to go north, though I knew now that I would not want to stay there, or anywhere where Charlie May was not living. Also, it was too late for either of us to do anything about the fact that we were still legally married people. I had been completely separated from my wife ever since my coming to America, but Charlie May still had her husband with her in Arkansas. I thought it best to let her make full arrangements concerning the future. I felt that I must neither advise nor interfere.

My stay at the literary colony came to a close at the end of August; on the second of September I moved down the Hudson to New York City. While I was at the colony, there had come to me Charlie May's second book, the beautifully written and tenderly fresh *Lost Corner,* composed during the long winter and spring she had spent in New York City. The adventures of Jeb and Melissa, and their adoption by Mr. Boggs, delighted me even more than had the incidents set forth in *Robin on the Mountain.* And the book had been dedicated to me, because it used a title taken from one of my poems. I felt overwhelmed by the honor, and somehow brought into still closer kinship with Charlie May.

For the first week in September, I was invited to come as a guest to the home of Van Wyck Brooks. I had not seen him for twelve years, since the days when he had let me act as poetry critic of the *Freeman.* Then he was known as the keen, candid controversialist who had written *America's Coming of Age* and *Letters and Leadership* and a much-discussed and debated life of Mark Twain. Now he was older, grayer, more solid of body, richer within and more conservative without, busily engaged on completing his monumental *Flowering of New En-*

gland, a book which may be remembered when this book of mine is forgotten. I sat under his apple tree and talked with him about life and letters till the sun quit the sky.

Within a few days of my return to Arkansas, about the middle of September, some friends of mine in Little Rock decided to drive out to Possum Trot. I had already asked whether I could accompany them, in case they were going; and I was now eager for the opportunity. So I saw again, for the second time, Charlie May's homestead. The day was windless and hot; summer had not yet burnt itself out amid the great pinewoods of Perry County. We three males present amused ourselves by shooting with a rifle at pine chips thrown in the air—I as usual being the poorest shot. Some neighbors passed by along the lonely dirt road, sitting upright, mountain-fashion, in the bed of a wagon drawn by skinny mules, and Charlie May stopped them at the corner of the stake-and-rider fence to chat with them. I can see her still, as she took the baby from the arms of one gingham-clad, sunbonneted mother, and petted it—and I thought of how lovely she looked. Later, we sat and ate sandwiches at the long table in the cool, log-walled living room, with its two stone fireplaces, one at each end.

As we talked and ate, all the while I was wishing I could get rid of the others and be with Charlie May alone. I knew that my arms would soon be stealing around her, that I wanted her to be mine utterly, that there was no one in the world whom I wanted but her. I was not ashamed of my love; but we were not allowed a moment together. After lunch, we did indeed steal out of the house together, to sit for an instant side by side close to the honeysuckle-wreathed well at the back of the house; but we were soon interrupted by Howard Simon, who came out and looked at me sourly and suspiciously. My heart felt no qualm of conscience at the prospect of betraying another husband. Nothing in the least mattered to me but Charlie May.

A few days later I learned the news that Howard Simon was going back to New York alone. Charlie May was staying in my native state. She was going to the White River, to live there on a houseboat and gather material for a third book, this time about the river people.

It was time to declare myself. By the end of September we were engaged—two married people waiting for the painful preliminaries that would grant us both our freedom, still to go through. No, say rather, two lovers learning for the first time the real meaning of love, the perfect comradeship and unity of interests that can build up a life that goes through and beyond them. At forty-nine, but now feeling twenty years younger, I knew at last that the gods had relented and had given me their greatest gift—a mate. In my love for Charlie May now lay life's highest possible achievement. In winning and keeping her love in return lay all that I had ever dreamed of, on coming back to America, and to my former state.

We were married on January 18, 1936, in the presence of only three witnesses and a minister, an enlightened modernist who had long gone his own gait in the Presbyterian Church, and who was pleased at performing a ceremony which the Episcopalian minister of the church with which I had been associated since boyhood could not perform. I was so moved by the simple rite that I could scarcely speak the responses, and my hands trembled as they put the ring on Charlie May's hand. I had bought a new ring for the occasion—a dainty thin hoop of platinum, its band engraved with tiny orange-blossom decoration. It was actually the first wedding ring I had ever presented to any woman. My former wife in England had let me use the old one, from her previous marriage, for the ceremony of twenty years ago.

In this ring, and in its tiny circumference, I saw enclosed all my hopes and aspirations in life.

> Laughter and gipsying and a living place
> In memory; a path I would retrace,
> And shall, perhaps, in life-blood of a son.
> All this is in my ring, which makes us one.

We were one, and I knew it, in the only abiding sense which a man could be one with any woman in his life. Twenty years before, I had married another woman, who had also been married when we came together, and who was divorced before we could marry. But there the parallel stopped. What had brought me and Daisy together had been an overpowering physical urge on my part, which I had fought hard to suppress. Perhaps on her part a sort of vague, maternal, protective instinct towards me, combining with a feeling that her own marriage was proving a failure, had urged her to take this step. There was neither community of interests, nor the give-and-take of companionship, nor kinship springing from the possession of the same background of country and experience, nor ability to share creative expression between us. Once the physical aspect of sex had been known and tasted, our marriage must inevitably break down of itself. It had only persisted so long as it had, largely because of my obstinacy. But in the case of Charlie May, marriage would prove to be an adventure of two spirits similarly endowed, attracted to each other not only on a physical basis, but on the basis of work and play in common which could be shared—of friendship and companionship and ability to comprehend each other, in living and in thinking. Love, I now saw, held more than just a physical attraction. The physical attraction was but the symbol of the deeper union for life and for eternity.

We stayed on in Little Rock, with brief visits to Memphis, where I had the pleasure of meeting Charlie May's parents, and to Natchez at the close of March, where I renewed acquaintance with the Garden Week Festival, and the splendors of the old South in decay. Charlie May, busy as she was with her third book, *Teeny Gay,* yet had plenty of time to entertain my friends, to act as a capable and efficient housewife, and to take part with me in the exceptionally fine season of musical entertainments that came to Little Rock in the spring months of our centennial year. Thus we saw and heard together Nelson Eddy and the Russian ballet, the Philadelphia Symphony and the pianist Josef Hofmann. And in the meanwhile I busied myself trying to organize an Arkansas Folk Society, in the hope of putting on a folk festival of mountaineer ballads and square dances, negro spirituals, and folk plays, later on in the summer.

On the first of May, with the dogwood finished, the iris already blooming, and the roses coming on fast, we got into our car—a wedding present from my sister—and started north. Stops at Memphis, to bid farewell to Charlie May's parents, a dip into the Great Smokies, now a riot of spring bloom, a week in Washington, where we took a side trip to Wakefield and Stratford and down the peninsula to Williamsburg—that marvel of remade eighteenth-century splendor—and then finally a week in New York, brought me again to Boston just before Decoration Day. This day we spent at Lexington and at Concord, exploring Sleepy Hollow Cemetery and searching for Thoreau's grave amid the boom of barbaric cannon and the marching of beflagged paraders. Then we got into our car again and came on up to Peterboro, arriving at the MacDowell Colony just as spring was giving way to summer. The tall blue iris, we noticed, had accompanied us north, every step of the way.

At the MacDowell Colony and in Peterboro itself this book has been written: begun when the pink moccasin flower was still in bloom in Peterboro's woods, and finished as the last goldenrod and asters are slowly finished. And all that time, life has kept the two of us together in a perpetual honeymoon of work shared, and of perfect love and companionship, till the autumn now rides high in the sky:

As slantingly we saw the autumn sun
Break through the boughs; before it there was carried
A sudden golden shower—leaves in strong tumult
Whirling and falling, tumbled to the ground;
So I knew here that autumn had come north,
Into this land of granite, fern, and pine;
While in my heart I kept for you alone
Love like a torch uplifted, night and day.

Two years have passed since I wished I were yours,
More than a year since I hoped you were mine.
Now through the slackening sunlight runs the hour
With wild grape crowned, with fiery sumach leaves
Twined in its cloud-dark hair, to bring the news
Already guessed, that stirs my heart like wine:—
How that, of every being in my world,
None, save but you, has known my inmost soul.

We walk together, and all life is changed;
We work together and our work is blest;
We sit together in a simple room,
And now that room is Paradise, a world.
Then sunset, and sweet good-night, and our kiss:
The spiritual bread that feeds us in our prayers.
Iseult and Helen were but fools to this;
Angels in heaven envy us this way.

As slantingly there falls the autumn sun
Through the dark boughs, the wind shakes down the leaves.
O, my beloved, years like leaves were scattered
Long ago, ere you came into my life!
This is the tale of withered, worn-out years;
How many may remain, as each one falls,
I'll mark its death with acts more great than words,
To show to men how nobly passed our day.

Proudly I claim you mine, and no one else;
Proudly I breathe beside you, night and noon;
Proudly I seek with you my human lot,
To live, to keep, to honor all that's yours,
To love you, to protect you, and to share
Whatever joys or griefs may fill our years;
And, after that, let come close-folded earth
About us, and for men another dawn.
Let gods go on: I need not envy them.
Here is enough for me and for my day!

This is the story of my life. Now that it is finished I ask myself what it has all meant to me to have lived it. In asking this question, I am inquiring on behalf of those who may have read thus far, no less than on behalf of myself. For it is surely obvious that my life has been, from the point of view of most practical folk, a supremely useless and unproductive one. I have not grown one grain more of the world's wheat, or cultivated one acre more of the world's land. I have not helped the factory wheels to turn faster, nor aided and abetted the invention of new machinery. (Indeed, I have so little mechanical talent, to this day, that I can scarce operate a typewriter, and cannot drive a car.) I have not indulged in business, nor made a business of the work that lay nearest my heart. Despite the boom and the depression, I still do not own one share of stock; and the only land I now possess is a half share in Charlie May's Ozark homestead, and a cemetery lot in Little Rock.

Yet, perhaps, if figured by more than material gains, my life has been well worth the living. Personally, if I had to, I would gladly live it all over again. I have made mistakes, no doubt, and suffered reverses, but it has still been worth while, even if I made the supremely fatal mistake of supposing, at twenty-one, that I must be a poet. Even if I was mistaken in this, even if I have not written one line of verse that can survive, it has been worth my while to have tried and to have failed at my task. Perhaps it is better to have tried and have failed than to have tried and have succeeded. Edwin Arlington Robinson seems to have thought so—and I feel I can agree with him, now that he has passed on and left us.

In an age so imbued with the importance of documentary information, so ridden with the vain pretensions of science to solve all our problems, material as well as spiritual, so chained to the machinery of mass publicity, so realistic, in short, he must indeed be a brave man who dares to pretend to write poetry at all. For to the poet there are no facts unless they are infused throughout with the transforming light of the human imagination. "The gods as we have them were made by the poets; and Homer was the first myth-maker." The rhythmic sequence of words, colored by strong emotion, "recollected in tranquillity," and infused with figurative, symbolic meaning: that is poetry. Words, substances, experiences themselves are but signposts to something else, and to something greater, that goes on through their agency—an interchange of understanding between the voice and the reader, the writer and his invisible audience. Perhaps Shelley was not far wrong in saying that "poets are the unacknowledged legislators of mankind."

Yet life is in many ways unamenable to our efforts to find a reason for it, to make it into a pattern of abiding significance. Facts are stubborn things. Much that has befallen me may have befallen me, not through reasons, but only by chance. It may have been chance that directed me towards poetry in the first instance, though I do not think so. It may have been chance that I happened to come along at a time when many other poets of high merit appeared on the American scene, though I do not think that either. It almost certainly was pure chance that associated me in the public mind, in the first instance, with the imagists and with Miss Lowell. It is surely largely chance whether anything I now write or have written can survive. Only the other day I learned of the death of Harriet Monroe, for instance; another strong link gone with that period of 1912–29 which was so decisive for my own development, and for all, except the very youngest, "proletarian" generation! Was it mere chance that made Miss Monroe, in Chicago, start her magazine just at the time when modern poetry was about to take a new step forward—or is there some purpose behind all the changes in literary fashion, the dominance of poetry in some periods and of prose in others? I do not know.

At all events, I have chosen my path. It has taken me already a long way. The way still leads on. Life—this life of mine—is merely a song by the way. I am content to travel on, wherever life may lead me.

"I have not so far lived my life, that I need ever fear for my death."

INDEX